THE ECUMENICAL LEGACY OF
JOHANNES CARDINAL WILLEBRANDS (1909-2006)

BIBLIOTHECA
EPHEMERIDUM THEOLOGICARUM LOVANIENSIUM

UNIVERSITÉ CATHOLIQUE DE LOUVAIN
LOUVAIN-LA-NEUVE

KATHOLIEKE UNIVERSITEIT LEUVEN
LEUVEN

BIBLIOTHECA EPHEMERIDUM THEOLOGICARUM LOVANIENSIUM

CCLIII

THE ECUMENICAL LEGACY OF JOHANNES CARDINAL WILLEBRANDS (1909-2006)

EDITED BY

ADELBERT DENAUX – PETER DE MEY

IN COLLABORATION WITH

MARIA TER STEEG AND LORELEI FUCHS

PEETERS

LEUVEN – PARIS – WALPOLE, MA

2012

A catalogue record for this book is available from the Library of Congress.

ISBN 978-90-429-2735-3
D/2012/0602/148

© 2012 – Peeters, Bondgenotenlaan 153, B-3000 Leuven (Belgium)

PREFACE

Johannes Cardinal Willebrands (1909-2006) certainly was among the significant contributors to the Roman Catholic Church's embrace of ecumenism. Through his stimulating role as secretary of the Catholic Conference for Ecumenical Questions (1952-1962) he prepared the ecumenical openness of the bishops of the Second Vatican Council. As secretary of the Secretariat for Promoting Christian Unity (SPCU, 1960-1968), and as president of the SPCU (currently Pontifical Council for Promoting Christian Unity, PCPCU, 1968-1989), he played a central role in establishing ecumenical structures within the Roman Catholic Church and in initiating bilateral dialogues with the churches and ecclesial communities that are not in communion with the Catholic Church. On the occasion of the centenary of his birthday (4 September 1909), two symposia were organised in memory of Cardinal Willebrands, one in Utrecht and the other in Rome.

In Utrecht, an international ecumenical conference about the legacy of Willebrands was held from 2-5 September 2009. It was a joint initiative of the Cardinal Willebrands Archive, located in Utrecht, the Tilburg School of Catholic Theology (TST) and its Cardinal Willebrands Research Centre (CWRC), and the Centre for Ecumenical Research of the Faculty of Theology of the Catholic University of Leuven. In a closing celebration at the Cathedral of Utrecht, Walter Cardinal Kasper, President of the PCPCU, gave an address on the heritage of Willebrands and the future of ecumenism.

On 29 November 2009, the PCPCU also organised a symposium at the Pontifical Gregorian University. In a number of papers Willebrands' various contributions to the ecumenical movement were explored. The Rome conference was honoured by the presence of Cardinal Kasper and of the Archbishop of Canterbury, Dr. Rowan Williams. The majority of the papers presented at both conferences are now made available in this volume.

Adelbert Denaux, the dean of the Tilburg School of Catholic Theology, contributes a biographical introduction in which special attention is paid to Willebrands' plans for the creation of an ecumenical community modeled on Newman's oratory in Birmingham. Four contributions focus on Willebrands' formation and his early commitment to ecumenism. Anton Houtepen(†), former professor of Ecumenism at the University of

Utrecht, describes the formative years of Willebrands prior to his nomination as secretary of the Secretariat for Christian unity. Willebrands' move from professor in philosophy to full-time ecumenist is best understood against the background of certain developments in the Netherlands – e.g. the adoption of a new name for the *Apologetic Association Petrus Canisius* – and in the Catholic Church worldwide. Terrence Merrigan, systematic theologian of the Catholic University of Leuven and a specialist of John Henry Newman, studies the enduring significance of Newman for Willebrands' ecumenical views. He is particularly fascinated by the similarities between Newman's reflections on the development of Christian truth and Willebrands' description of the confessional traditions within the church as *typoi* or 'types'. Peter De Mey, Merrigan's colleague and chair of the Leuven Centre for Ecumenical Research, focuses on Willebrands' leadership within the Catholic Conference for Ecumenical Questions (1952-1963). He gives special attention to an important position paper on the current state of ecumenism which the board in 1959 had sent to a substantial portion of the world episcopate in preparation for the Second Vatican Council, as well as to the growth in ecumenical understanding which can be derived from Willebrands' opening speeches at the subsequent meetings of the Catholic Conference for Ecumenical Questions. Theo Salemink, Church historian at the Tilburg School of Catholic Theology, introduces two recent editions of previously unpublished sources by Johannes Willebrands, his own edition of the diaries of Willebrands from the years 1958-1961 and the edition of Willebrands' agendas during the Council (1963-1965) by Leo Declerck.

The second part focuses on 'Willebrands and the development of the Catholic view on ecumenism during the Second Vatican Council'. The Italian Church historian Mauro Velati first sketches Willebrands' role during the Council, with particular attention to his contacts with the non-Catholic observers and to the impact of the SPCU on the conciliar documents. At the end of Willebrands' long career as president of the PCPCU, the Johann-Adam-Möhler Institute for Ecumenics gathered his most important writings and speeches in a book entitled *Mandatum Unitatis*. Wolfgang Thönissen, the director of this institute, offers the reader a reconstruction of Willebrands' ecumenical theology on the basis of his writings. It is a theology which strongly focuses on the event and the ecclesiological teaching of the Second Vatican Council. Willebrands' views on the ecclesiology of communion and on the notion of *subsistit* should not be forgotten in the current debate on the hermeneutics of the council. The same points, as well as the remaining significance of Willebrands' view on the complementary unity of diverse *typoi* of Church life, are highlighted in the contribution of Jesuit theologian Jared Wicks on Willebrands as an exponent of Catholic ecumenical theology.

Four contributions focus on 'Willebrands and ecumenism'. Willebrands' relations with the Eastern Christian churches are treated in a lengthy contribution by Michel Van Parys of the Benedictine monastery of Chevetogne. The reader is informed about the early history of Willebrands' interest in Eastern Christianity, about the many visits and contacts which he had as secretary of the SPCU before and during the Council, and about post-conciliar Catholic relations with the Byzantine Orthodox Churches, the Eastern Orthodox Churches and the Eastern Catholic Churches. In the final part of his contribution Van Parys reconstructs the ecumenical views of Willebrands in a more systematic way. This article is followed by three different assessments of Willebrands' ecumenical work as it related to the churches of the West and to the World Council of Churches. John Radano, who was the head of the Western section of the PCPCU from 1985-2008, focuses on some of Willebrands' contacts and activities with the WCC, with the Lutheran World Federation and with the World Alliance of Reformed Churches. William Henn, professor of ecumenism at the Gregorian university, also discusses Willebrands' contacts with the WCC, but he is rather more interested in the image Willebrands gives of the WCC in his writings. Günther Gassmann writes about the Joint Working Group between the Catholic Church and the WCC in which he and Willebrands had been co-members. His article also contains a fine description of Willebrands' significance for Protestantism.

Willebrands also played an important role in the dialogue between the Catholic Church and the Jewish people. This aspect of his work is highlighted in Part IV. In the opening article of this section Mathijs Lamberigts and Leo Declerck, of the Leuven Centre for the Study of the Second Vatican Council concentrate on Willebrands' role in the negotiations with the patriarchs of the Middle East during the final stage of the approval of *Nostra Aetate*. The heart of the contribution of systematic theologian Marcel Poorthuis of the Tilburg School of Catholic Theology consists in a portrayal of Willebrands as a theologian of Jewish-Christian dialogue. Poorthuis asks three questions: "Is Judaism the / a people of God, and is the Church the / a people of God?"; "In what way does the relationship with Judaism affect the Christian reading of the Bible?"; and "Can there be a Christian mission to the Jews?". Pier Francesco Fumagalli, of the Pontifical Commission for Religious Relations with the Jews, summarises Willebrands' thought and action regarding Jewish-Christian relations with a few particularly fruitful and apt Hebrew terms used to express his fundamental contribution in this field. This part ends with a testimony from a Jewish perspective, by Judith Hershcopf Banki, who under the leadership of Rabbi Marc H. Tanenbaum was involved in the American Jewish Committee.

The volume closes with Cardinal Kasper's address on the legacy of Willebrands and the future of ecumenism, with two testimonies of close friends and collaborators, and with a bibliography of Willebrands, by Maria ter Steeg, the co-founder of the Willebrands Archives and co-organiser of the Utrecht conference.

We hope that this publication is the starting point of further scholarly research on the role and the significance of this great pioneer of ecumenism in the Roman Catholic Church. One initiative should already be mentioned. The Cardinal Willebrands Research Centre has recently approached Dr. Karim Schelkens, postdoctoral fellow of the Fund for Scientific Research Flanders, and a member of the Centre for the Study of the Second Vatican Council of the Faculty of Theology and Religious Studies (KU Leuven) to write a scientific biography of Willebrands.

We thank Mrs. Sandra Arenas for her help in preparing the manuscript. We want to acknowledge the patient and valuable technical assistance of Mrs. Rita Corstjens and to thank the board of the BETL for including this volume in its prestigious series, as well as the staff of Peeters Publishers for producing this beautiful volume.

Adelbert DENAUX
Peter DE MEY
Maria TER STEEG
Lorelei F. FUCHS

TABLE OF CONTENTS

JOHANNES CARDINAL WILLEBRANDS (1909-2006)
HIS LIFE AND HIS SPIRITUALITY

OPENING LECTURE

The late Cardinal Johannes Willebrands certainly was a leading figure in the second half of the 20th century, not only in the Catholic Church of the Netherlands, but also throughout the entire Roman Catholic Church. This is because of the pioneering role he played in the field of ecumenism and the high responsibilities he received and successfully fulfilled in this regard. Hence, the hundredth anniversary of his birth in 2009 provided an appropriate occasion to celebrate his life and work. Moreover, the unexpected discovery of his pre-conciliar diary, written in Dutch between 1958 and 1961 and of his council agenda, written in Dutch between 1963 and 1965, and the wish to put them at the disposal of historians and ecumenists throughout the world was another incentive to organise this conference.

With this conference, the organisers wanted to arouse scholarly interest and to invite colleagues to collect the sources and the data needed to write a comprehensive, scientifically well-founded biography of Willebrands. He has been too important a player in the life of the Christian churches not to wish to know more about his life, his actions, his convictions and his influence. Moreover, the group of *intimi*, who knew the cardinal personally or collaborated with him, is growing smaller. They constitute a unique source of information, which within two decades will be no more. Therefore, the Willebrands Archive has started a programme of interviewing some of these people.

In my opening lecture, I would first like to offer a brief biography. In this brief survey, we will pay more attention to the first period of his life (from 1909 till 1960), which we might call the 'Dutch period'. The second phase of his life, the 'Roman period' lasted from 1960 until 1996, and is much better known. During this period, he fulfilled an official role on an international level; so, we will deal only shortly with this period. Secondly, I would like to point to one aspect of his early years, namely, his desire to establish what he calls an "ecumenical community". This desire took several years to become a concrete project, but was never realised. I have chosen to focus on this aspect, because it clearly shows the close link in Willebrands' life between ecumenism and spirituality.

I. A BRIEF BIOGRAPHY[1]

Johannes Gerardus Maria Willebrands was born on September 4, 1909, in Bovenkarspel (in the North of Holland). He was the eldest son of a family of 9 children. At the age of 12, he wanted to become a Redemptorist priest, but he changed his mind. At that time, he decided that it suited him better to become a diocesan priest. He studied philosophy and theology at the major seminary of Warmond (1928-1934). On May 26, 1934, he was ordained a priest. He was then sent to Rome to do graduate studies in philosophy at the Angelicum. His research was not focused on Thomas Aquinas, as one would expect, but on John Henry Newman, the famous English convert. In 1937, he obtained his doctorate in philosophy cum laude, with a thesis entitled: "John Henry Cardinal Newman. Zijn denkleer en haar toepassing op de kennis van God door het geweten" (English translation: *John Henry Cardinal Newman: His Epistemology and Its Application on the Knowledge of God through Conscience*). Back in the Netherlands, he was appointed assistant priest ("kapelaan") in the beguinage church of Amsterdam. In 1940, he became professor of philosophy at Warmond, where future priests received two years training in philosophy, before starting their theological studies. His main subject was the history of philosophy. In 1947, he became director of this institute, the "Philosophicum", and continued in this function until 1958, the year the Dutch Bishops Conference appointed him as "Episcopal Delegate for the Ecumenical Questions".

At this juncture, it is worth noting that Willebrands spent 18 years of his life teaching philosophy. I think this must have influenced his subsequent life and thinking. Unfortunately, no research has yet been done about these formative years. All kinds of questions could be asked here: how did Willebrands deal with Neo-Thomism, the then predominant philosophical approach in Roman Catholic institutes? Did his doctoral research on Newman and his teaching the history of philosophy allow him to put Neo-Thomism into historical perspective? How did the philosopher he was help him to become such a sagacious theologian? For eighteen years, he taught philosophy. For more than forty years, he gave conferences, delivered addresses, wrote papers, as a real theological teacher. How should we understand these differences in his life? He

---

1. See PCPCU *Information Service* 101 (1999/II-III) 57-192: "A Tribute to Johannes Cardinal Willebrands on the Occasion of his Ninetieth Birthday". See also K. SCHELKENS, *Willebrands, Johannes Maria Gerardus (1909-2006)*, in T. BAUTZ (ed.), *Biobibliographisches Kirchenlexikon*, Bd 32, Nordhausen, Bautz Verlag, 2011, cc. 1530-1548.

certainly felt that it was a personal deficit to not have completed an academic study of theology, and we know he compensated for this deficiency by the *privatissima* given to him by his friend Yves Congar.

Whatever the case, on August 1, 1958, having the mature age of 49, he was appointed by the Dutch Bishops Conference to be their "Episcopal Delegate for Ecumenical Questions" throughout the Netherlands[2]. Through this appointment, Willebrands was finally appointed to an official position, in which he could completely devote himself to the work for which his heart had been longing for years: "the ecumenical work" ("het oecumenisch werk"). This was an unprecedented event, being the first such appointment anywhere in the Roman Catholic Church: and "first made it possible to give some institutional expression to ecumenical activity within the Catholic Church"[3]. This appointment did not come as a surprise. It was the result of an ecumenical "calling" which, according to his own memory, started as early as 1946[4] and which he never betrayed in spite of many hindrances. At this point, let us recall the main aspects of Willebrands' interest in ecumenism before his official position at a national level. Already during the Second World War, he joined an ecumenical group called "de Larense kring" or Laren Circle (founded in 1943). On June 1, 1948, the year of the foundation of the WCC in Amsterdam, he became the chair of the Saint Willibrord Association. This Association was the successor to "the Apologetic Association Petrus Canisius", founded in 1904. While the Petrus Canisius Association had been directed against Protestants in a spirit of apologetic self defence, the Willibrord Association tried to establish a dialogue, in an open ecumenical spirit. Johannes Willebrands played a key role in this change of attitude[5]. In 1951, together with his life long friend, a priest from the diocese of Utrecht, Frans Thijssen, he travelled throughout Europe and met with several western European bishops and theologians about the possibility to set up an organisation for ecumenical specialists. Although

---

2. His Diary opens with the remark: "In consultation with Msgr. J.P. Huibers and on behalf of the Venerable Episcopacy (writings Msgr. Alfrink N° 1129/58 d.d. 26.7.'58), appointed as episcopal delegate for ecumenical affairs by Msgr. Dr. B. Alfrink". The fact that he starts writing a diary at this date shows he was aware of the historic importance of this appointment. See T. SALEMINK (ed.), *"You will be called Repairer of the Breach"*: *The Diary of J.G.M. Willebrands 1958-1961*, Leuven, Peeters, 2009, p. 37.

3. Cf. J. GROOTAERS, *Jan Cardinal Willebrands: The Recognition of Ecumenism in the Roman Catholic Church*, in *One in Christ* 6 (1970) 23-44, p. 25.

4. See in this volume, A. HOUTEPEN, *The Formative Years of Cardinal Willebrands: Ecumenical Developments in the Netherlands 1940-1960*, pp. 15-29.

5. See on this J. JACOBS, *Nieuwe visies op een oud visioen: Een portret van de Sint Willibrord Vereniging 1948-1998*, Tilburg, Valkhof Pers, 1998, pp. 31-91.

this was an informal enterprise, Willebrands was wise enough to inform the Dutch Bishops and some influential people in Rome, such as S. Tromp, SJ, C. Boyer, SJ and Augustin Bea, SJ. This effort resulted in the establishment of the Conférence Catholique pour les questions oecuméniques (Catholic Conference for Ecumenical Questions), of which he became the active and inspiring secretary[6]. The first meeting took place in 1952, at Fribourg in Switzerland and the last in 1963, at Gazada near Milan. "The primary purpose of the Catholic Conference ... was to promote harmony, collaboration and a common spirit among Catholic ecumenists, and to keep them widely informed on the progress of the ecumenical movement"[7]. Significantly, the Conference also developed unofficial contacts with the World Council of Churches. I will not elaborate on Willebrands' involvement in the Catholic Conference for Ecumenical Questions. This has been achieved by more competent people than me[8]; however, certain aspects have not yet been thoroughly examined. I am, therefore, delighted that my colleague from Leuven, Prof. Peter De Mey, has written a paper on the development of Willebrands' theological thinking within the framework and as a secretary of the Catholic Conference.

In addition, it must be said that Willebrands' appointment in 1958 as "Episcopal Delegate" was also the result of his constant insistence to his bishop, Msgr. J.P. Huibers of Haarlem, that a combination of being director of the Philosophicum at Warmond, his growing ecumenical engagement as chair of the Saint Willibrord Association and as secretary of the Catholic Conference for Ecumenical Questions was no longer bearable. To our knowledge, he first expresses this complaint in a letter dated

---

6. From his *Diary* (see n. 2), pp. 151-152, we are sure now that Willebrands was the initiator. To Prof. Janez Vodopivec's remark that the existence of the Conférence Catholique was something providential and to his question how he did get this idea, Willebrands answers on 18 May 1960: "I vividly remember the moment when the thought entered my head. In 1950, in Hotel Noord-Brabant in Utrecht, during the break of meeting of the SWV. I always had the feeling that Divine Providence had given me the idea, yet, I had always felt powerless and worthless to be given such a responsibility. The cooperation of all the members has been fantastic – and the growing importance of the Conférence [Catholique] has not reduced my sense of unworthiness and powerlessness. On the contrary. Although I have grown, through the support and help of so many, the real discrepancies between my own abilities, my preparedness and the task at hand, is only resolved in the Lord Jesus. Therein lies the problem of my trust in Him. Therein lies the core task of everything".

7. *Information Service* 101, 64.

8. See GROOTAERS, *Jan Cardinal Willebrands* (n. 3); T. STRANSKY, *The Foundation of the Secretariat for Promoting Christian Unity*, in A. STACPOOLE (ed.), *Vatican II by Those Who Were There*, London, Geoffrey Chapman, 1986, 62-87; *Information Service* 101, 62-69 (The Editor).

11 February 1953[9]. This complaint is then repeated again and again until his bishop, in consultation with his colleagues, among whom Bernard Cardinal Alfrink, creates – so to speak – a new function in which Willebrands' ecumenical vocation can be given a free rein. By the way, even if one may agree that his was a "vocation from above", one observes at the same time his strong will and insisting tenacity to obtain his goal: to get rid of his secure job at Warmond and to be set completely free for the more vague and risky work in ecumenical affairs. To do this, he contacted several Dutch bishops, he tried to implicate international figures, he referred to the Instruction "De motione oecumenica" of the Holy Office of 20-12-1949 (Letter 31-01-1958 to J.P. Huibers), and he himself even proposed the name for the new office (Letter to Huibers 31-01-1958)[10]. Nevertheless, it still took at least five years before Willebrands received a positive answer to his request to be totally free for ecumenical work. One can understand why his bishop was not eager to yield immediately: to set a priest free for doing "ecumenical work" was just not done in those years.

9. Willebrands Archive, Letter Willebrands to Mgr. J.P. Huibers, 11 February 1953, pp. 2-3: "Ik spreek echter in dit schrijven over mijn persoonlijke situatie omdat ik persoonlijk daardoor in moeilijkheden kom. Immers ik behoef U hoegenaamd niet uit te leggen, dat de taak van directeur van het Philosophicum en professor, en om de ernstige verantwoordelijkheid en om de vele tijd, die deze functie eist, een man vrijwel geheel opvragen. Daarom schrijf ik U, na lange tijd te hebben geaarzeld en gewacht, deze brief. Ik meen nml. te moeten vaststellen, dat ik de twee functies – directeur van het Philosophicum en voorzitter van de St Willibrord Vereniging – niet langer meer tesamen kan vervullen. Ik kan dit op een dubbele wijze constateren: zowel objectief, omdat het werk van beide niet tegelijk goed kan vervuld worden, het een schaadt het ander, en mèèr dan het belang van beide functies gedoogt; en ook subjectief, want ofschoon ik een goede gezondheid bezit, voel ik toch, dat dit op de duur niet vol te houden is. Ik acht mij in geweten verplicht U van deze situatie op de hoogte te stellen. Ik heb deze in het voorafgaande meer uitvoerig geschetst, omdat U een inzicht daarin zoudt hebben, opdat U deze zoudt kunnen beoordelen. Ik heb geen ander verlangen dan mij aan Uw oordeel te onderwerpen".

10. Willebrands Archive, Letter Willebrands to Mgr. J.P. Huibers, 31 January 1958, where he points to an earlier letter of the Bishop which says that a title has to be found for the new function the Bishops want to give him, and which is not at the service of the St. Willibrord Vereniging, but directly of the Episcopate. Then he makes the following suggestion: "Zou de titel niet kunnen luiden: 'Bisschoppelijk gedelegeerde voor het oecumenisch werk'? Deze titel geeft een volmacht aan, omdat ik dan namens de Bisschoppen optreed. De naam President veronderstelt misschien meer een bepaald lichaam waarvan men president is, en men zou hier en daar kunnen vrezen dat ik iets wil accapareren. Het woord 'nationaal' zou ik liever willen vermijden. Er is ook een 'oecumenische raad van kerken in Nederland' aan protestantse zijde en men zou kunnen vragen wie de 'natie' vertegenwoordigt. Eerst als een bepaald instituut ontstaat zou men kunnen zien of de titel president geschikt is".

His role as a national public figure came to an end when on June 24, 1960, Pope John XXIII appointed him secretary of the newly created Secretariat for Promoting Christian Unity (SPCU)[11]. From then on, Willebrands became an international public figure, not only in his church, but in the Christian world at large. Indeed, after Pope John XXIII made his unexpected announcement of calling together a universal council (January 1959), the Archbishop of Paderborn, Dr. Lorenz Jaeger, through the mediation of Cardinal Bea, forwarded a petition to Pope John (on March 11, 1960) to create a pontifical commission to promote Christian unity. The Pope agreed and asked Bea to organise such a commission and appointed him to head it, with Willebrands as his secretary. For eight years, until 1968, the tandem Bea-Willebrands set up a new type of "curial" organisation that managed to give shape to what we may call the "ecumenical conversion" of the Roman Catholic Church. It should be noted that many members and consultors of the initial phase of the SPCU were former members of the Catholic Conference of Ecumenical Questions.

In his position as secretary, "Msgr. Willebrands was largely responsible for the organization of the Secretariat and established official contacts with representatives of many Churches and ecclesial communities, and ecumenical organizations such as the WCC. He took a major role in the SPCU's work during the Second Vatican Council which included assisting the non-Catholic observers to the Council, and work in drafting of the Council's *Decree on Ecumenism, Declaration on Religious Liberty, Declaration on the Relation of the Church to Non-Christian Religions*, and a substantial part of the *Constitution on Divine Revelation*"[12].

When during the Vatican council on June 28 1964, Pope Paul VI consecrated him titular bishop of Mauritania, the prudent progressive expert, able to combine openness and continuity, became a leader. He was one of the few people, who determined the policy to be followed to reach the desired end in drafting some of the most important texts of Vatican II[13].

---

11. By the Motu proprio *Superno Dei Nutu* (June 5, 1960). Willebrands heard about his appointment some days later, on 28 June 1960, via the Catholic Dutch Press Office (KNP), as he writes in his *Diary* (n. 2), p. 172: "In Warmond (...) In the afternoon, the KNP calls me: Radio Vaticana has announced my appointment as Secretary of the Secretariat for Christian Unity. I don't know anything about this. It's more likely that this announcement is true: it fits with the talk that Dr. Thijssen and I recently had with Cardinal Bea and, moreover, Radio Vaticana is usually trustworthy with this type of information". His first talk as secretary with Cardinal Bea took place on 8 July 1960 (*ibid.*, p. 175).
12. *Information Service* 101, 60.
13. Cf. GROOTAERS, *Jan Cardinal Willebrands* (n. 3), *passim*.

Significantly, as episcopal motto he choose: *Veritatem in caritate* (Eph 4,15). All his life, he remained faithful to the great Catholic tradition, but at the same time, he knew that its "truth" could neither be communicated by Catholics, nor be understood by other Christian brothers and sisters, unless it was brought in mutual respect, in readiness to listen to the real questions asked by other Christians and by entering into the risky "dialogue of love". In the course of the years, he met all kind of difficulties, within and outside his own church. But his strong and quiet conviction, and his "exceptional gifts in the field of diplomatic ecumenism, in which patience and preparedness, perseverance and discretion all play an important part, found a way to overcome the difficult circumstances"[14].

When the SPCU's first president, Augustin Cardinal Bea, died on November 16 1968, his secretary, Bishop Willebrands, was the obvious candidate to succeed him. On April 12 1969, Pope Paul VI appointed him the second President of the SPCU, and a few days later, during the Consistory of April 28 1969, created him cardinal. For twenty years, Willebrands held the office with great competence and great authority. Together with his staff, he set up the necessary structures to implement, *ad intra* and *ad extra*, the irreversible ecumenical option of Vatican II. The Ecumenical Directory (first edition) set up a framework for ecumenical commitment within the local churches. A whole series of bilateral dialogues tried to clarify the relationship with the different churches or confessional families. Forms of collaboration with the WCC were established, even though the Roman Catholic Church did not become a member of it. In 1974, a Commission for Religious Relations with the Jews was created, and Willebrands became its first president.

This long period of presidency was interrupted for eight years, when on December 6 1975, he was named Archbishop of Utrecht, with the delicate task of helping to reconcile the divided church in the Netherlands. However, this intermezzo was but partial. Although no longer living in Rome, he was asked to continue as president of the SPCU. On 8 December 1983, he resigned as Archbishop of Utrecht, aware that his mission had not achieved the desired results. He returned to Rome and resumed his fulltime position as president of the Secretariat (from 1988, Pontifical Council) for Promoting Christian Unity. At the end of 1989, he resigned as president of the PCPCU, but continued to live in Rome until 1997. In that year, he returned to his native country and found a warm hospitable home with the Franciscan Sisters at Denekamp, where he was gently cared for until his death on August 2, 2006.

14. *Ibid.*, p. 29.

II. LIVING THE CHURCH AS *OIKOUMENÈ* IN AN ECUMENICAL COMMUNITY

There are so many more things to be said about Cardinal Willebrands. A lot of questions about his life, his character, his relations, his friendships, his collaboration with women, his desire to keep a diary in spite of his hectic life and his ecclesiastical 'career' remain unanswered. There is still much research to be done in order to understand his role and significance. We need an inventory of all archives that contain materials about him. We need an exhaustive list of his publications. Many materials in Rome and the Netherlands are not yet open to the public, but what is available, e.g. in the Willebrands Archive, offers a wealth of material, in which we hope students will be interested. As an example, I would like to point to just one aspect that struck me when preparing my lecture. When reading his personal writings, it is clear that for Willebrands, the "ecumenical work" – as he called it – was not just a question of theology, diplomacy or institutional temperament, important though these things may be. In his opinion, it was ultimately a question of spirituality, of living the Church as *oikoumenè*.

As early as 1955, Willebrands' request to be set free for ecumenical work was linked to another wish, namely, to set up a community of ecumenically minded priests and lay people. In the Willebrands Archive, we find at least three attempts to describe what he meant by it, because his bishop, Msgr. Huibers, wanted to help his priest to clarify this initially rather vague longing. We also find a number of letters to different bishops, in which Willebrands explains his desire. The first letter, to his own bishop, is dated March 4, 1955[15]. Shortly before, a third version of a "Concept for an ecumenical community" was drafted. Let me just read to you a part of a handwritten text which is kept in the Willebrands Archive (probably dated at the beginning of 1955), where he tries to formulate his intuition. I quote some paragraphs (my translation):

---

15. Willebrands Archive, Letter Willebrands to Mgr. J.P. Huibers, 4 March 1955: "In overleg met Dr. F. Thijssen uit Utrecht, die mij in al deze zaken terzijde staat, is in mij het verlangen ontstaan om in Nederland te komen tot de Stichting van een Oratorium van St. Philippus Neri. Dit plan zouden wij aan de Bisschoppen willen voorleggen, met de bede, dat zij hieraan hun goedkeuring willen verlenen. Deze gemeenschap van een Oratorium heb ik verlangd vooreerst om de concrete doelstelling van het oecumenische werk, waartoe ook in het bizonder behoort de taak van geestelijke en pastorale vorming van deze afgescheiden Christenen en predikanten, die tot de Kerk terugkeren. Het oecumenische werk, zoals dit bij ons is gegroeid zal bestendig moeten worden voortgezet. Vervolgens omwille van de speciale spiritualiteit, die toch zuiver katholiek moet zijn, en die zich juist binnen deze gemeenschap veilig kan ontwikkelen, – vervolgens omdat het Oratorium niets anders is dan een gemeenschap van saeculiere priesters, die geen exemptie kent, maar onder de directe jurisdictie van de Bisschop blijft".

When the Bishop allows me to leave Warmond, to commit myself totally to the ecumenical work, then, my desire would be to establish a Centre, a middle point and a point of support ("een midden- en steunpunt") for the spirituality of priests and lay people. This spirituality would be characterised by the ecumenical aspect.

The ecumenical aspect is proper to the Catholic Church, her members and her doctrine. 'Ecumenical' means 'all-embracing'/'comprehensive' ("alomvattend"). It encompasses the whole human being, his whole life in all its forms and expressions, his whole person, his thought, will and action. Only the essence, the principle is all-embracing.

What is all-embracing is universal, catholic. It does not fall into particularities, which so to speak are detached from the core, do not live from the "principle" ("beginsel"), are not carried by the essence. We should not choose one particular aspect, or even put it forward. What our time, our priests and lay people are asking, is exactly that the meaning of all particular aspects or matters might become manifest in relation to the salvation brought by Christ. This meaning can only be given through and from the principle. E.g. the meaning of Mary and the meaning of all what is called 'Marian'.

The all-embracing is one. One is the principle that encompasses the whole creation; one is the principle of the Holy Trinity. Alpha and Omega. Principium et finis. One is the communion of the Church, the Holy Church. *Credo in unam, sanctam catholicam Ecclesiam.* In this oneness we want to live. We want it in its fullness, to possess it in its comprehensiveness. We do not want to be deprived from its life-giving fullness through particularization of some aspects. One in Christ, and through Him in the Father.

The ecumenical aspect which is proper to Christian life asks for total commitment, because it is all all-embracing. It asks for reflection on and awareness of the essential mysteries of salvation, in order to give sense and meaning to the whole of life. It asks for a strong and unbreakable understanding of the unity of all in Christ, who fulfils all in all. It is living from the mystery of the Church. It brings us in the expectation of that fullness in which all that is already present in germ today, but hindered and assailed by sin, will be perfect and in glory, the kingdom of God.

If we ourselves live from the fullness of Truth, then Truth, not only considered in Itself but also in the way it gets shape and becomes manifest in us in concrete terms, will be able to encompass all humans and let them share in the fullness of Christ, to unite all in the unity of Christ. It will witness to Christ. We will be witnesses, by what we proclaim about Him, by what we are in Him.

This is an impressive text, a personal meditation in which Willebrands tries to express his deepest conviction. Every human being has an exterior and interior life: on the one hand, he is a *persona*, a public figure; on the other hand, he is *anima*. He contains an interior space where he is relating to the inner self and to God. We know that Willebrands was a very discrete person, who did not allow others to enter into the inner space of his *anima*. But occasionally, he wrote down for himself what inspired him. The text I just read is an example of this. It would be worth while to analyze this text and better understand the kind of language he is using. For example, on which spiritual traditions he is relying? It seems to me there is a Newmannian flavour in this meditative text.

In April 1959, together with Frans Thijssen, Willebrands visited the Oratory of Munich. Both found it very inspiring for their own project[16]. The last letter I found, which deals with the Oratory, is addressed to the Archbishop of Utrecht, Bernard Cardinal Alfrink, dated March 7, 1960. This letter contains some information about the plans to create such a community, possibly in the form of an Oratory set up by Philippus Neri and adapted by Cardinal John Henry Newman[17]. Willebrands had some doubts whether the bishops understood his plan. On May 18, 1960, he wrote in his Diary:

> When we return from Höfer's, Hein ten Kortenaar is waiting for us at home. We talk about the situation with the Oratorium, the last details. Something needs to happen and fast.
> I point out that Msgr. Alfrink as well as the Bishop of Haarlem have objections to the traditional form of an Oratorium. Do they understand what we want? We don't want a scientific institute, or a university one. We want a spiritual community, where Christ is worshiped and adored, with a special emphasis on the unity of Christians in His Church. Of course, we will need to study for that and do scientific research. But the work itself is no academic exercise; it is a supernatural, holy task. This community demands a more complete surrender than scientific research. We also have a personal

---

16. *Diary* (n. 2), pp. 90-92.
17. Willebrands Archive, Letter Willebrands to Bernard Cardinal Alfrink, 7 March 1960: "Mijn tweede punt betreft de gemeenschap die enkele werkers op oecumenisch terrein gaarne zouden stichten. … Wij voelen echter steeds sterker de aandrang hiertoe en de noodzaak voor ons werk. We zijn overtuigd dat het niet alleen een instituut zal moeten zijn, maar een geestelijke gemeenschap. Onze gedachten gaan uit naar het Oratorium van Philippus Neri, zoals dit is voortgezet door Kardinaal Newman en tegenwoordig in Duitsland. Wij hebben de behoefte aan een orgaan tot studie en voorlichting op oecumenisch gebied en het lijkt niet onmogelijk tot dit doel het Schild te verkrijgen. Eerst als wij samen zijn en een bescheiden bureau hebben zullen wij dit aankunnen. Voor een bibliotheek heb ik reeds een behoorlijke collectie boeken en tijdschriften verzameld. Wij zouden ook een kerk of kapel willen hebben, wij hebben ons eigenlijk het geheel rond een kerk gedacht. Het werk en onze veelvuldige activiteiten vragen een centrum. Kardinaal Ottaviani zei mij eens [op 23 juni 1959] dat de wetenschappelijke vorming van een bekeerde dominee in zijn voorbereiding tot het priesterschap wel te regelen was, maar dat de vorming tot een priesterlijk leven nog niet bevredigend was opgelost. Toen ik hem sprak over ons plan om een Oratorium te stichten, zei hij: Ecco la Provvidenza! Uit dit punt blijkt dat het hier niet alleen gaat om een wetenschappelijk instituut. Ik hoop deze zaak in dit jaar een stuk verder te mogen brengen. Ik heb er over gesproken met Mgr Huibers en Mgr van Dodewaard, in verband met mogelijkheden in Amsterdam en ik zou de gehele kwestie gaarne met Uwe Eminentie eens doorspreken". Willebrands and Alfrink met each other on 3 May 1960.

need for a community. The work, the trips and journeys, the exertion of energy, the insecurities, demand a home. Otherwise, we will be pulled around and pushed to extremes. I don't have a home in Warmond anymore: as good as it is, inexpensive and friendly. But I am living outside of the house and the house has its life outside of mine. It no longer acts as a magnet that attracts me and orients my life. The same is true for Frans and Hans Weterman. Will the Lord give this to us? How great is my trust in Him, my faith? Am I prepared to accept His Gifts, as He offers them, where He offers them and when? In this case, I am also pivotal. When my movement isn't pure and authentic, as the Lord directs and moves me, everything will unravel. Or, the Lord, who without a doubt doesn't need me, will accomplish it without me. But that would be horrible for me and incomprehensible for the others. The Lord help me ut fidelis inveniar! We chose the Oratorium, not as a historical form, not to copy it from Rome, or Birmingham, or Munich, but because we believe that it offers a starting point and sufficient space to develop an own form. The form will be determined by the goal, that is, ecumenical work. We think that it will be possible for it to become a hub, even when we are not all living in the same house. Lay people could be invited into our community, who offer their lives for ecumenical work, remain unmarried, have completed theological studies or other studies. De Cittadella in Assisi is inspirational. It would be more correct when the Oratorium did not fall under the Congregation of Religious, but under the Council – to allow its uniqueness to come to the fore juridically[18].

Shortly before his appointment as secretary of the Secretariat in Rome, while he and his friends became aware that he was a possible candidate for this job, he discussed the possible consequences for the intended Oratorium with Hein ten Kortenaar (on June 3, 1960):

We talk about the question of the Oratorium and the new situation. Certainly, there is a threatening situation – but does this mean that the whole plan will not go through? Or should we try to solve the difficulties? Can I remain in the Netherlands? Should we begin something that we can't finish? To what extent is my presence, given the small number, necessary? Should we still wait? My personal opinion is that an ecumenical centre in the Netherlands is more necessary now than ever before and, therefore, urgent. Also that we need to establish this centre. The objections that threaten my cooperation are serious; they are in the line of our work. If I have to do ecumenical work in Rome, or so much that I am often away, then, the mandate is important in ecumenical terms. It can give a stimulus and support to our Oratorium. And it is still totally unclear whether and to what extent I will be pulled to Rome. In any case, I would personally prefer to not live in Rome – and it would benefit the work when I wouldn't get stuck in Rome, with the danger to suffocate and to be suffocated[19].

18. *Diary* (n. 2), pp. 152-153.
19. *Ibid.*, p. 166.

After having settled in Rome, and knowing that he was a central figure in the planning of an Oratorium in the Netherlands, Willebrands becomes aware that maybe it was not God's will. He summarizes his conversation with Hein ten Kortenaar on 19 July 1960 as follows:

> The talk with Hein is of course about the foundation of an Ecumenical Community in the Netherlands and the difficulties that have arisen since my departure. Amongst the participants, I was the binding factor. Also, the initiative came from me. Will someone else take this role over; is it enough that I gave them the idea? Hans Weterman will have to do it then. He is still obligated by his responsibility as a student moderator. Hein will write him. He had really hoped that this would go through and that this plan would be an answer to the questions that concern him. Now the Lord is giving a clear response to our prayers, and perhaps it is against our plans to establish an Ecumenical Community in the Netherlands[20].

Willebrands even considered the possibility of establishing an ecumenical house or Oratorium in Rome itself:

> Even for the short time that I have been in Rome, I increasingly have the longing for a home in Rome, where there is an ecumenical centre, where priests (and perhaps also laymen) can live and work together; a small church, where the liturgy is celebrated according to our understanding, where the liturgy is the expression of the Church, as it is and as it wants to be. Where the separated brethren in Rome can be received, where they find hospitality. Maybe a Taizé. Can St. Lioba in Egmond help us with this?[21].

But his office at the Secretariat for Promoting Christian Unity and the intensive work for all the ecumenical aspects in the preparation and the completion of the council of Vatican II, including much traveling all over the world, made it impossible for Willebrands to pursue his dream. From then on, instead of a local Oratorium, the *oikoumenè* of all Christian churches became his living space.

Tilburg School of Catholic Theology   Adelbert DENAUX
Tilburg University
Heidelberglaan 2
NL 3508 TC Utrecht
The Netherlands

---

20. *Ibid.*, p. 181.
21. *Ibid.*

I. WILLEBRANDS' FORMATION AND EARLY COMMITMENT TO ECUMENISM

THE FORMATIVE YEARS OF CARDINAL WILLEBRANDS

ECUMENICAL DEVELOPMENTS IN THE NETHERLANDS 1940-1960

To find the way to your destiny, you must know from where you start
(from an instruction for navigation-systems)

INTRODUCTION

Often we are called to a task we have not foreseen, for which we are not prepared. In 1946, I received a call which later proved to be a vocation from above, to abandon studies and teaching of philosophy and to engage myself in activities for the restoration of unity among Christians[1].

This humble confession of one of the greatest pioneers of the ecumenical movement of the 20th century may astonish us, later readers. Though somewhat exaggerated, in many respects it was true. Neither his personal theological training at the Haarlem diocesan seminary in Warmond, the Netherlands (1928-1934) nor his advanced studies at the Angelicum in Rome (1934-1937) had prepared him for the great work of his life, the restoration of Christian unity[2].

---

1. Johannes Cardinal Willebrands, Lecture dd 5 Mai 1987 at a Conference of the National Association of Diocesan Ecumenical Officers in Atlanta, GA: J. WILLEBRANDS, *The Passion for Unity*, in *One in Christ* 23 (1987) 285-297, p. 285.

2. After his ordination to the priesthood as a member of the presbyterium of the Diocese of Haarlem, the Netherlands, in 1934, Johannes Willebrands was sent by his bishop to Rome for advanced studies in philosophy at the Dominican University Angelicum, where he wrote his dissertation on Cardinal Newman, defended and accepted *cum laude* in 1937. Upon his return to the Netherlands in the same year, he served for a while as a chaplain at the Beguinage in the Centre of Amsterdam and was appointed in 1940 to teach the history of philosophy at the Haarlem Diocesan Seminary in Warmond. He became the director of its Philosophical Department in 1945. In 1946 Cardinal De Jong appointed him the president of the *Apolegetic Association Petrus Canisius* with a mandate to coordinate and to improve apostolic activities among non-Roman Catholics. Within this mandate he organized in 1948 a palace-revolution by renaming and restructuring this apologetic association into the *Ecumenical Association St. Willbrord*. From here he started his European ecumenical network of Roman catholic ecumenical experts, theologians and bishops, the *Catholic Conference for Ecumenical Questions,* of which he became the secretary. According to an intensive correspondence with the bishop of Haarlem in the Archives (Cardinal Willebrands' Archive (KWA) file 54), he had to combine this function with his ecumenical activities almost to his exhaustion and great frustration for more than twelve years until 1958. In that year Cardinal Alfrink appointed

As all of us know, the Roman Catholic Church itself was not ready for ecumenism before the second half of the twentieth century. Like the Churches themselves, and especially the Roman Catholic Church, Johannes Willebrands, therefore, had to go through *an ecumenical learning process*, which he described a few years later (1948) in an ecumenical policy statement as a process in three phases: starting with a dialogue of love and listening with respect and tolerance to the "separated brethren", then to understand and to describe their confessional beliefs, doctrinal positions and spirituality correctly with reliable phenomenological methods – *non polemice* – (UR 9). Finally to engage with them in a dialogue of truth, communicating with them *"par cum pari"* (UR 9) and learning *from* them in order to better grasp the truth of the gospel and to correct one's own always partial, time-bound and still imperfect interpretations and applications of divine eschatological truth (UR 11 and 12)[3]. Influenced strongly by John Henry Newman, he thus fulfilled the Pauline admonition of Phil 2,3-5: "There must be no competition among you, no conceit; but everybody is to be self-effacing. Always consider the other person to be better than yourself. In your minds you must be the same as Christ Jesus". Or that other one: "to live by the truth and in love", the Jerusalem Bible's translation of Eph 4,15, Johannes Willebrands' later episcopal maxim: *facientes veritatem in caritate*[4].

In this lecture I want to sketch briefly[5] the ecclesiastical and especially the theological landscape wherein Johannes Willebrands in the period before Vatican II had to navigate towards the goal of visible unity of all Christian Churches, the great passion of his life and the most important, though not yet completed learning process of Christianity in the 20th century.

him as the official delegate of the Dutch episcopate for ecumenical questions and contacts.

3. Cf., *Unitatis Redintegratio* §7 (UR), where a similar programme is phrased in terms of a confession of guilt, of conversion and reformation of the Roman Catholic Church itself.

4. The full chapter 4 from Ephesians may be read as Willebrands' ecumenical guideline for all his activities. It was, together with John 17 one of the biblical cornerstones of the conciliar decree *Unitatis Redintegratio* (2, 7).

5. For an overview of the immense literature on the history of Dutch Catholicism in the 19th and 20th centuries, see L. WINKELER, *Geschiedschrijving sedert 1945 over het katholiek leven in Nederland in de negentiende en twintigste eeuw*, in *Trajecta* 5 (1996) 111-133.

I. ECUMENISM: SUSPECTED AND FORBIDDEN FOR
ROMAN CATHOLICS (1928-1948)

In the first half of the 20th century, consecutive popes and the Holy Office, bishops and most theologians suspected the upcoming ecumenical movement of "religious indifferentism" or of an "unfriendly competition" with the Roman Catholic self-understanding to be the only true Church of Christ, the *Una Sancta*, to which all non-Roman Catholic Christians and their communities had to return (so the Encyclical *Mortalium Animos* 1928). Following a strict line of interpretation of canon 1325 of the 1917 *Code of Canon Law*, the participation of Roman Catholics in local ecumenical initiatives was forbidden, let alone their commitment to international ecumenical conferences like those of Life and Work or Faith and Order. In spite of this Roman Catholic suspicion and rejection of the ecumenical movement, there had been some laudable interconfessional initiatives involving Roman Catholics in the Interbellum and during the Second World War[6]. A few Roman Catholic theologians had written systematic theological or historical studies on the ecumenical movement[7]. Local ecumenical initiatives like the *Malines Conversations* between Anglican and Roman Catholic theologians in Belgium 1921-1926, the *Una Sancta Movement* in Germany and the work of Lambert Beauduin and his *Monks of Unity* in Amay-sur Meuse, continued in Chevetogne (1929), Belgium, all ended up with verdicts on their

---

6. In spite of the prohibitions of canon 1325 §3 of CIC 1917, Roman Catholics in England had participated in the preparation of ecumenical conferences on social issues during and after the First World War, but the English bishops had to cancel their cooperation on the command of the Roman Curia. Individual Roman Catholics, however, did participate in the preparations for the Faith and Order Conferences of Lausanne 1927 and Edinburgh 1937. On the latter there were even four Roman Catholic "unofficial observers": see O. TOMKINS, *The Roman Catholic Church and the Ecumenical Movement 1910-1948*, in R. ROUSE – S. NEILL (eds.), *A History of the Ecumenical Movement 1517-1948*, London, SPCK, ²1967, 677-696, pp. 681, 685.

7. E.g. M. PRIBILLA, *Um kirchliche Einheit*, Freiburg, Herder, 1929; Y. CONGAR, *Chrétiens désunis: Principes d'un œcuménisme catholique*, Paris, Cerf, 1937; R. GROSCHE, *Pilgernde Kirche*, Freiburg, Herder, 1938; G. SÖHNGEN, *Symbol und Wirklichkeit im Kultmysterium*, Bonn, Hanstein, 1937; M.D. KOSTER, *Ekklesiologie im Werden*, Paderborn, Bonifacius, 1940. It is interesting that many of these theologians were active in pastoral care for students or in adult education projects. The book *Chrétiens désunis* by Y. Congar was in fact a collection of lectures he held at various places in France. Roman catholic ecumenism in this period, generally speaking, was not so much developed at theological faculties or seminaries but by inspiring lectures of prophets of ecumenism at the grassroots level. Ecumenism, in most churches, started from below, inspired by students' movements, religious orders and organisations of mixed couples.

leaders[8]. A polemical and apologetic style characterized theological journals and popular catechetical literature, dealing with controversial issues
relating to church and sacraments, grace and salvation, scripture and tradition[9]. No wonder, therefore, that the first Roman Catholic ecumenical
pioneers in the Netherlands and in Europe up to the 1950s had to do their
work, when not as underground dissidents, in any case as volunteers, so
to say in their free time. Their conversations and contacts were scarcely
welcomed by their bishops, the Roman Curia or the pope[10].

In spite of all these negative attitudes, the Roman Catholic Church was
preparing itself in the period under review by a serious theological self-
reflection on the Church-idea, the shape of the liturgy and a more creative
and open approach to the Bible, all of these being fostered by patristic
studies, a *relecture* of pre-Reformation scholastic positions, fighting
Thomism by Thomas himself, and, especially in Germany, a fresh interpretation of the true intentions of the Reformers[11].

The three most influential encyclicals of Pope Pius XII – *Mystici
Corporis Christi* (1943), *Divino Afflante Spiritu* (1943) and *Mediator Dei*
(1947) – implicitly opened the doors for a better mutual understanding

8. On Lambert Beauduin: R. LOONBEEK – J. MORTIAU, *Un pionnier: Dom Lambert
Beauduin 1873-1960: Liturgie et unité des chrétiens*, Louvain-la-Neuve, Collège Erasme
etc., 2001; J.J. VON ALLMEN (ed.), *Veilleur avant l'aurore: Colloque Lambert Beauduin*,
Chevetogne, Éditions de Chevetogne, 1978. Most Eastern-Orthodox Churches followed a
similar policy until the end of the fifties; see N. ZERNOV, *The Eastern Churches and the
Ecumenical Movement in the Twentieth Century*, in ROUSE – NEILL (eds.), *A History of the
Ecumenical Movement 1517-1948* (n. 5), 645-674, p. 670.

9. Exemplary for the Netherlands were the popular pamphlets of the *Geert Groote
Society*, various apologetic works meant as catechetical instructions for newcomers into
the Roman Catholic Church and apologetic periodicals like *Het Schild* or *Nederlandse
Katholieke Stemmen*. Even more academic theological journals like *Studia Catholica* or
Bijdragen van de Nederlandse Jezuieten were full of polemical articles, criticical chroni-
cles about developments in protestant churches and mostly pejorative reviews of protestant
theological publications.

10. At the first Conference of the newly founded Secretariat for Promoting Christian
Unity in Gazzada, 1961, Johannes Willebrands noted in his diary his feelings of gratitude
and surprise, that all of a sudden, ecumenism was blessed and ecumenists praised by the
highest authority of the Roman Catholic Church: "How many people are here, who have
given their life to work for unity, to work for the separated brothers, without ever receiving
any encouragement or gratitude from the hierarchical institutions? Now there is a special
blessing from the Holy Father for their work" (*Diary* 1961).

11. On Luther, see J. LORTZ, *Die Reformation in Deutschland*, Freiburg, Herder, 1939;
E. ISERLOH, *Der Kampf um die Messe in den ersten Jahren der Auseinandersetzungen mit
Luther*, Münster, Aschendorff, 1952; On the Tridentine Council and the Reformators, see
H. JEDIN, *Der Abschluss des Trienter Konzils 1562/63: Ein Rückblick nach vier Jahrhun-
derten*, Münster, Aschendorff, 1963; on Calvin, see A. GANOCZY, *Calvin, théologien de
l'Église et du ministère* (Unam Sanctam, 48), Paris, Cerf, 1964; on Zwingli, see J. POLLET,
Huldrych Zwingli d'après les recherches récentes, Paris, P.U.F., 1963.

between theologians of the separated churches and their Roman Catholic counterparts, be it yet without giving up the full identification of the Roman Catholic Church, its liturgy, sacraments and ministry, and its interpretation of the Bible with the truth inherited from Christ and the apostles, guaranteed by the faith of Peter and his successors, the bishops of Rome throughout the centuries.

The encyclical *Humani Generis* (1950) may be read as a last warning signal against a too easy theological alliance with the post-war "new theology", its new hermeneutical approach of Scripture and Tradition and its positive exchange of views with non-Roman Catholic values and spirituality. Then, in the same year, Pius XII issued the decree *Ecclesia catholica*, which brought the official blessing of the pope for careful ecumenical dialogues between experts from different churches. Johannes Willebrands' ecumenical activities from then on could be carried through with the legitimation of both various local bishops and with the *venia Sanctae Sedis*[12].

II. NON-THEOLOGICAL AND THEOLOGICAL FACTORS PROMOTING THE ECUMENICAL LEARNING PROCESS OF ROMAN CATHOLICS IN THE NETHERLANDS 1940-1960

In his own country, Johannes Willebrands had to work on barren fields, even up to the fifties. In the pillarized society of the Netherlands before and at least a decade after the Second World War, Protestants, Catholics, liberals and socialists each had their own program of emancipation for their constituencies through confessional schools, identity-bound press and broadcasting companies, social organisations, political parties and welfare agencies. Prejudice and triumphalism reigned on both sides of the confessional spectrum. Roman Catholics suffered from a minority complex over against Protestants, many of whom still considered the Netherlands a Protestant nation. Mixed marriages were exceptional, while heavily discouraged and even deterred by the churches. As the Dutch historian Jan Roes stated in 1975 in his article on the prehistory of Roman Catholic ecumenism in the Netherlands before Vatican II: "Dutch Catholics became only slowly and by bits and pieces familiar

---

12. Be it not always without tensions with the Holy Office, especially with his compatriot Sebastian Tromp S.J., most probably the ghost writer of *Mystici Corporis*, who has visited the Netherlands' seminaries and study-houses in 1956, censuring some of the most creative Dutch systematic theologians, like K. Steur at the Warmond diocesan seminary and F. Duynstee at the Catholic University of Nijmegen.

with the ecumenical movement, which originated and grew nearly fully
outside their ranks"[13].

1. *Non-theological Factors*

Ecumenism indeed came in from the outside, first of all through non-
theological factors. Perhaps the most important of such factors were the
reflections on international cooperation, promoted since the First World
War.

President Woodrow Wilson's "League of Nations" had inspired people like the Greek Orthodox metropolitan Germanos, the Lutheran bishop
Nathan Söderblom and the Anglican archbishop William Temple to
organize a "League of Churches" as a counterforce against international
communism and soon after against fascist ideologies coming up in
Europe. The Life and Work Movement with its Stockholm 1925 and
Oxford 1937 conferences was the first result of such common ecclesiastical reflection on international peace and solidarity and on the role of the
State in democracy.

During and after the Second World War plans were worked out for a
post-war peace and human rights organisation, resulting in the institution
of the United Nations Organisation in 1948 and the beginning of an European Community structure in 1950[14]. Though both of these initiatives
were blamed for being "secularist" projects, in fact it were mainly Christian statesmen and theologians who had taken such initiatives. When they
were realized, they fostered transconfessional and ecumenical programs
for justice and peace, tolerance and freedom of religion in the world.

In the Netherlands, a most important non-theological but certainly a
strong spiritual factor were the common war-time experiences 1940-
1945. Peril, suffering and imprisonment in concentration camps brought
many Reformed and Catholic clergy and opinion leaders into close spiritual exchange and friendship. Protestant church leaders and Roman
Catholic bishops had protested in public pastoral letters condemning the
ethnic cleansing and massive removal of Jewish compatriots, and the

13. J. ROES, *Een hele beweging...*, in A. HOUTEPEN, *Heel de kerk: Een oekumenisch
werkboek*, Hilversum, Gooi en Sticht, 1977, p. 35.
14. Cf. J. ZEILSTRA, *European Unity in Ecumenical Thinking 1937-1948*, Zoetermeer,
Boekencentrum, 1995. Conversations on European Unity already begun in the interbellum
and continued during the War under the aegis of the Geneva Secretariat of the World
Council of Churches in Process of Formation, led by Dr. W.A. Visser 't Hooft. Main sup-
porters of such European Union were British bishop Bell, American lawyer and later
Foreign Minister Foster Dulles together with a couple of German, Dutch and French
political philosophers and strategists.

Nazi measures against public church life. This war-time solidarity and spiritual sharing of resources and the post-war shocking discovery of the immense crimes and cruelties of the Holocaust, followed by immediate relief-activities on behalf of refugees, returning prisoners of war and so many other homeless and hungry people all over Europe, created a fully new climate of Christian collaboration and conversation, like those of CIMADE (Comité inter-mouvement auprès des évacués) in France, of Roger Schütz and his Community of Taizé.

The national catastrophe of the flood in 1953 when many Protestant families received housing and hospitality with Roman Catholic families had a special impact on ecumenism in the Netherlands, leading to an inter-church ecumenical commission, the so called Delta Council. After the 1956 revolt in Hungary, many Hungarian refugees joined Dutch families of another confession. Industrial labour migration broke up the existing confessional divide of villages and cities in the Netherlands, fostered mixed marriages, led to growing unchurchliness and secularisation of public life and so caused much *"unrest in pastoral care"*[15]. It led to renewal movements in catechesis, proclamation, liturgy and theological education, which took advantage of consultations with similar movements in other Christian churches. In his extended contribution on ecumenism and pastoral care, Johannes Willebrands' companion Frans Thijssen pleaded for a more self-critical, less triumphalist attitude of the Roman Catholic clergy in their pastoral approach, contacts and conversations with the "separated brethren", especially those of the churches of the Reformation. He wanted them to recognize the "gold" which they have inherited through their traditions of faith in Christ and through the

---

15. So the title of a collective work *Onrust in de zielzorg*, Utrecht – Brussel, Het Spectrum, 1950, edited by a team of Roman Catholic lay leaders and theologians, among whom friends of Johannes Willebrands A.C. Ramselaar and F. Thijssen. The book, inspired very much by the famous Lenten-Letters of Cardinal Suhard (Paris 1947 and 1948), is a kind of self-reflection on the quality and (in)adequacy of Roman Catholic liturgical life, pastoral care, catechesis, theological education and proclamation in view of cultural, scientific, technical and political developments and a serious appeal to a greater lay-participation and to the abandonment of clerical complacency, formalism and traditionalism in church life and ecclesiastical policy. In one of the contributions to this collective work by G. de Gier, M.S.C., we find a fine exposition on the meaning of the sacraments, being living signs and symbols of the hidden divine mystery, mediating to us the mysteries of redemption in Christ: his life, his passion and his glory: a participation in divine life itself. Such vision corrects popular ideas about the sacraments as means of auxiliary grace or moral help, and of mechanical interpretations of their working, leading to quantitative measurements of the number of holy communions instead of qualitative spiritual preparation and a consequent Christian community life, both in church and society, says the author.

work of the Holy Spirit in them, from which Roman Catholics should
learn a lot.

These common experiences and new international cooperation gener-
ated great hopes for confessional cooperation and national community
building after the war. Unfortunately conservative forces among the
church leaders and within confessional organisations won the overhand
and preferred the restoration of the pre-war isolationism and pillarization
of society[16]. From his archives it becomes clear, that Johannes Willebrands and a few Roman Catholic and Reformed allies were not in favour
of this restorative policy, but wanted a new beginning and a more
ecumenical attitude of Roman Catholic lay and clergy towards the
rebuilding of the destroyed country so that it may become a more open
society.

2. *Theological Factors*

Theological factors, however, have been as influential to the formation
of the ecumenical movement and its gradual acceptance by the Roman
Catholic magisterium. Not only the inspiring positive results of the Faith
and Order Movement and its conferences of Lausanne 1927 and Edinburgh 1937, but some decisive changes in the Protestant and Roman
Catholic theological landscapes as such were basic to the idea of ecumenism as a common cause of all Christian churches. On the Protestant side
dialectical theology brought creative new insights from the fields of systematic and biblical theology, leading to a less organisational and more
Christ-centred ecclesiology, to a more dynamic view on the sacraments,
to a less liberal and this-worldy understanding of the Kingdom of God
and eschatology and, most of all to a *relecture* of the christological
definitions of the ecumenical councils and creeds. Roman Catholic theologians took up these Protestant challenges and revised the neo-Thomis-
tic system through a *relecture* of the Latin and Greek patristic heritage.
On that basis they developed a fresh view on grace and justification from
a deeper soteriological perspective which transcended the Roman Catholic concentration on human cooperation with divine grace and the merits

---

16. See e.g. *the Pastoral Letters* of the Dutch bishops 1945, 1946 etc., *Katholiek
Archief* 1 (1946-47) 49-52 and the repeated pleas of archbishop De Jong to maintain a
catholic broadcasting organisation, *Katholiek Archief* 1 (1946-1947) 32, 48. On the
Protestant side the 1950 *Pastoral Letter on the Roman Catholic Church* was a warning
against all too radical ecumenical and catholicizing tendencies within the Reformed
Church, accusing the Roman Catholic church of a stubborn triumphalism and power
policy.

of virtues and good works. They thus offered a serious alternative for the strong forensic overtones of Protestant soteriology, and the accompanying dualism in the doctrine of God's providence and gracious care as revealed in Jesus Christ. Finally, from there, a more ecumenical ecclesiology and the acceptance of the work of the Holy Spirit outside the borders of the Church and of Christianity became possible.

In the Netherlands several of Johannes Willebrands' colleagues at the Warmond seminary and others from religious houses of study, together with some theologians of the Nijmegen Catholic University, took up Protestant theological challenges in a sometimes critical but mainly friendly and respectful academic discourse[17]. From 1935 onwards they did it in the form of critical reviews of the work of their protestant university colleagues. So we find various studies about Karl Barth's ideas on justification already in 1945[18], a dissertation on Karl Barth's idea of revelation and its consequences for anthropology and theological epistemology in 1946, on the idea of the Church in the works of the 19th century Dutch Reformed opinion leader Abraham Kuyper in 1947, on the Liturgical Movement in the Netherlands Reformed Church and on the 19th century confessional divisions within Dutch Protestantism[19]. Roman Catholic theologians wrote creative biblical theological studies on the mystery of the incarnation upon which the Christian faith and the Church are founded[20]. Others reflected on aspects of christology, soteriology and eschatology from the perspective of spirituality and biblical piety[21]. When one reads through the volumes of theological journals from the period 1935-1960, the contributions of those theologians are still like pearls that one must find amidst an impenetrable wilderness of scholastic and apologetic school-discussions and casuistics about typical Roman Catholic theological questions of the time.

17. See their multiple contributions in *Studia Catholica* from 1935 onwards.

18. K. STEUR, *Notities over de Rechtvaardigmaking, zoals Katholieken haar zien*, Bussum, Paul Brand, 1945, with similar views like those of H. KÜNG, *Rechtfertigung*, Einsiedeln, Johannes Verlag, 1957, twelve years later!

19. J.C. GROOT, *Karl Barth en het theologische kenprobleem*, Heiloo, Kinheim, 1946; B. VAN LEEUWEN, *Het kerkbegrip in de theologie van Abraham Kuyper*, Franeker, Wever, 1946; H.A.M. FIOLET, *Een kerk in onrust om haar belijdenis: Een phaenomenologische studie over het ontstaan van de richtingenstrijd in de Nederlandse hervormde Kerk*, Nijkerk, Callenbach, 1953; J. LESCRAUWAET, *De liturgische beweging onder de Nederlandse Hervormden in oecumenisch perspectief*, Bussum, Paul Brand, 1957.

20. G.P. KRELING, *Collected Works*, in F. DE GRIJS, et al., *Het goddelijk geheim – theologisch werk van G.P. Kreling*, Kampen, Kok, 1979.

21. See *Studia Catholica* Volumes 1935-1960, articles by Steur, Groot, Greitemann (all from Warmond seminary), Hulsbosch, Grossouw, Kreling (from Catholic University Nijmegen), Fortmann (Rijsenburg seminary).

When Johannes Willebrands became the president of the *Apologetic Association Petrus Canisius* in 1946, he also became the editor in chief of its official journal, *Het Schild* (*The Shield*). This meant a gradual change in style which resulted in many articles about the ecumenical movement and about theological developments within the member churches of the WCC. Many of these were written by former Protestants, who had come over to the Roman Catholic Church and with whom Johannes Willebrands formed networks of friendship. Perhaps the most important theological shift behind this fundamental turnover was of a pneumatological nature, expressed by Willebrands in a lecture in Zwolle in 1954. I quote: "Outside the Church, the Holy Spirit is at work as well. It is a Catholic dogma, to confess, that all baptized Christians – whether truly baptized or only *in voto* – are united with Christ through sanctifying grace and thus related to his Mystical Body. The only thing which would remove a baptized person from the Lord and separate him from sanctifying grace is sin. But do we have the right to say: he lives in sin? May we minimize the grace given to him? If he enjoys grace, he enjoys the gifts of the Holy Spirit. If he has learned the truth through this or that religious community, then the Holy Spirit has been willing to use such community to learn him the truth"[22].

III. ECUMENICAL DEVELOPMENTS WITHIN THE NETHERLANDS
PROTESTANT CHURCHES 1939-1960

As we said: Roman Catholic ecumenism in the Netherlands grew slowly and, indeed, mainly from the outside, propagated by the Reformed and Old-Catholic churches. In the Netherlands initiatives of the World

---

22. *KWA* nr 23 (speeches 1951-1959). In the rest of this lecture, however, like in many other lectures, Johannes Willebrands stated, that this outspoken conviction with regard to individual believers from other churches, does not yet imply the recognition of their churches as members of the Mystical Body of Christ. He propagates thus the theory of "elementa ecclesiae", which says that baptism, the proclamation of the Word of God or prayer life, being practiced in the other churches, are used by the Holy Spirit for the salvation of the faithful, without the recognition of their faith communities as true churches of Christ or "sister-churches". With the terms "churches and ecclesial communties" *Unitatis Redintegratio* did not completely solve the question of the ecclesial status of churches not in communion with Rome, but made it the object of a serious ecumenical dialogue, meanwhile taking exception for the Orthodox Churches of the East and for the Old-Catholic Churches of the Union of Utrecht on the basis of their faithful and true (c.q. "valid") sacramental life and apostolic succession of the episcopate. This half-way solution is still a serious stumbling-block in ecumenical dialogues with the Churches of the West, not being yet in full communion with the bishop of Rome.

Alliance for Promoting International Friendship through the Churches and of the representatives to the Life and Work and Faith and Order movements, organized in the Dutch Stockholm and Lausanne committees, had led in 1935 to the constitution of an Ecumenical Council, of which several Protestant and the Old Catholic Church of the Netherlands were members. During the war years 1940-1945 its partly underground substitute was an *Inter-Church Consultation on Press and Broadcasting*. After the war, in 1946, it continued as *The Ecumenical Council of Churches in the Netherlands*[23]. From all these ecumenical initiatives and consultations the Roman Catholic Church together with the Synodal Reformed Churches in the Netherlands held aloof until the sixties. Various split-off Christian Reformed Churches and Evangelical or Pentecostal communities rejected the ecumenical movement for its leftist political statements and/or its alleged theological liberalism until recently.

Perhaps more influential to the growth of a better mutual understanding between the Christian churches in the Netherlands were some important theological and liturgical movements and developments in the Netherlands Reformed Church which led to a complete new church order of this largest Protestant church in the Netherlands in 1951.

The *Liturgical Movement* aimed at the restoration of the worship traditions of the Early Church, partly influenced by Anglo-Catholic liturgical practice and theology and by Roman Catholic *ressourcement* in German monastic centres like those of Maria Laach, but profiting as well from comparative study of religious symbols and rituals by both Protestant (Van der Leeuw) and Roman Catholic (Steur, Fortmann) scholars.

Second the *Movement for Community Building* (Gemeenteopbouw), which worked hard at the grassroots-level, helped by national educational centres, to overcome the infertile internal dogmatic divisions of the Netherlands Reformed Church. All of its "prophets" (Banning, Eykman and Kraemer) pleaded strongly for better relations with the Roman Catholic Church[24].

Next to these church-wide renewal movements, a group of Reformed ministers, organized in the movement *Reformatie en Catholiciteit* (Reformation and Catholicity) started to question the structures of ministry in the Reformed tradition and its breach with apostolic succession, its abandonment of the episcopate and its changes in the threefold pattern

23. For the history of these Dutch ecumenical councils, see H.J. TER HAAR ROMENY, *De geschiedenis van de eerste Oecumenische Raad in Nederland, ook in zijn internationale context – 10 mei 1935-10 mei 1946*, 's-Gravenhage, Boekencentrum, 1989.

24. See the book of H. KRAEMER, *De roeping der kerk, ten aanzien van de wereld en van het Nederlandsche volk,* 's Gravenhage, D.A. Daamen, 1945, pp. 119-121.

of the ministry, developed in the Early Church, and still shared by the majority of the Christian Churches. Some of these ministers pleaded for an additional ordination by a bishop supposed to be in apostolic succession, e.g. from the Anglican Communion[25].

Finally, its *New Church Order* of 1951 made the Netherlands Reformed Church free from state influence and harvested important results from internal and external ecumenical insights on authentic confession, biblical and liturgical renewal and on the nature and mission of the church in the modern world. It offered a less clerical top-down governance, making the General Synod a truly representative instrument of church policy and *episkopé* in matters of doctrine and church discipline. This internal church reform had a definite emittance towards the other Protestant churches and also captured the interest of Dutch Roman Catholics, longing for a breakthrough of the isolated confessional position of the Roman Catholic Church[26].

A very important role has been played by circles of Protestant ministers, Roman Catholic clergy and some active lay people, directly related to the international ecumenical movement, e.g. the Laren circle, founded in 1943, of which Johannes Willebrands became a member, together with his colleague, J.C. Groot (1908-1994) and his life-long friend, Frans Thijssen (1904-1990). Among the Protestant members were the New Testament scholar S.F. Berkelbach van der Sprenkel (1882-1967) from Utrecht University, one of the leading theologians of Faith and Order since Lausanne 1927 and the president of the Continuation Committee of the Edinburgh Faith and Order Conference. Further influential participants were Reformed minister, Nico van den Akker (1917-2000), the founder of various other ecumenical circles in the Netherlands after the

25. Their points of view were summarized in the collective manifesto *Hervorming en Catholiciteit* (1952), with contributions from Gerretsen, Van den Brink, Loos, Van der Linde and others, many of whom became Roman Catholics after the rejection of their appeal by the Netherlands Reformed Synod that same year.

26. Hopes for a more ecumenical attitude regarding the Roman Catholic Church was rather soon extinguished by a pastoral instruction of the Netherlands Reformed Church's General Synod in 1951 (*Herderlijk Schrijven betreffende de Rooms-Katholieke Kerk*). It reacted against the catholicizing tendencies in the liturgy, the theology of the sacraments and ministry of some groups within Dutch Protestantism as we just mentioned. The document got a firm and honest reaction from the part of six Roman Catholic academic theologians from the Catholic University of Nijmegen, who tried to correct what they considered to be false images and prejudices about Roman Catholic dogma and discipline (*Antwoord op het Herderlijk Schrijven 1952*). Further reflections followed in the collective work, edited by H. VAN DER LINDE – F. THIJSSEN, *Geloofsinhoud en geloofsbeleving: Een peiling binnen Reformatie en Katholieke Kerk in Nederland*, Utrecht – Antwerpen, Het Spectrum, 1951, one of the first forms of a bilateral conversation between Roman Catholic and Reformed theologians in the Netherlands.

war, Reformed minister Henk van der Linde (1915-2008) and Willem Hendrik van de Pol (1897-1988), who both came over to the Roman Catholic Church after the war, becoming ordained priests and professors of ecumenical theology and phenomenology of Protestantism respectively at the Catholic University of Nijmegen.

All of his life Willebrands remained faithful to his experience within these ecumenical circles, sharing in their spiritual ecumenism and prayer life, and learning to live a deeper and wider catholicity through free and respectful conversations – for a while without much publicity – with Protestant, Old Catholic and Eastern Orthodox theologians. More in the open, Johannes Willebrands became one of the pioneers of Roman Catholic ecumenism in the Netherlands, when in 1946 he was appointed the new president of the *Apologetic Association Saint Petrus Canisius,* and managed in 1948 to change its name and goal into the *Ecumenical Association Saint Willibrord.* Supported by this ecumenical association, in 1950 he established, together with Frans Thijssen, the *Catholic Conference for Ecumenical Questions,* a network of international theologians and bishops, consulting together on ecumenical themes of Roman Catholic concern[27]. This network was the first systematic contribution within the Roman Catholic Church to widen its horizon to what the Spirit was saying through the other Christian traditions, to listen to their complaints and desires for reform and to plead for these reforms in the Roman Catholic Church itself: a more dynamic understanding of the Bible and Tradition, of Grace and Justification, the Sacraments and Ministry, the Kingdom of God and the Church, all of these based on a fresh reflection on the relation of Christology, Eschatology and the Church, thus preparing many themes of the Second Vatican Council.

CONCLUSION

On the eve of Vatican II, Johannes Willebrands published two articles in the Dutch theological journal *Nederlandse Katholieke Stemmen* – he became a member of its board in 1956 – about the coming Ecumenical Council and about the New Testament notion of *diaspora.* The latter article reveals, perhaps, his deepest theological and spiritual motivation for his journey as a humble ecumenical pilgrim throughout the world.

---

27. See J. JACOBS, *"Naar één oecumenische beweging"* : *De Katholieke Conferentie voor Oecumenische Vragen: een leerschool en gids, 1951-1965,* Tilburg, Tilburg University Press, 1991 and the article by P. DE MEY in this volume, pp. 49-77.

With a quotation from this article I want to conclude this paper on some formative influences on the later Cardinal Willebrands' ecumenical vocation and career, which he considered to be "a vocation from above".

After a thorough analysis of the Old Testament, New Testament and Patristic use and meaning of the word *diaspora* and modern theological and sociological applications of the term by Lutheran and Roman Catholic scholars – still a rather rare comprehensive approach of a theological subject within Roman Catholic theological literature of the time – Johannes Willebrands reflects on the ecclesiological consequences of his findings:

> The meaning of the word "paroikia" in the Scriptures and in the works of the Church-Fathers is an adequate reflection of the *diaspora*-situation of the Church worldwide. The Church, as a sign in this world that refers to another world, works most convincingly in such regions, where she lives in *diaspora* in the sociological sense of the world. In such sociological situations of *diaspora*. the Church will be less exposed to the temptations of worldly glory or the use of power (...) This local church in *diaspora* does not possess the splendour of Rome's Saint Peter – "where the kings of the earth arrive to adore Him and all nations to serve Him" – but she manifests the coming of the Son of God as a *kenosis*. (...) She realizes Christian communion in the celebration of the Eucharist, where God is honoured by the sacrifice of the Lord, where the Church meets the God of grace and life in the sacraments and knows herself one with Him: as the *ekklésia kyriaké,* the communion in the Lord, united in the Eucharist around the preaching of the Word and the breaking of the Bread. (...). There we meet the divine initiative, from where the Church is permanently born and perfected (...). There the unity of the faithful with Christ and with one another becomes visible and real in a most personal way at the eucharistic meal. The celebration refers at the same time to the Wedding Feast of the Lamb: Word and Sacrament testify to and create communion with Him who has redeemed us through Cross and Resurrection. (...). *Church-in-Diaspora* is *Ecclesia* and *as such* she is communion in the Lord. She is *Ecclesia peregrinans* and as such she is aware of her being a community of foreigners and strangers in the world who expect the Return of the Lord. She is also the *Church of the Gospel* and as such she is *witness*: (...). In the *diaspora* the Church, as a communion and in all her members, will be a witness to this Gospel or she shall not be at all[28].

The last sentence expresses Johannes Willebrands' prophetic ecumenical awareness, which was the leading thread of his epochal spiritual ecumenism. At the centre of all ecumenical endeavours stands the local eucharistic community, to be served, strengthened and held together,

---

28. J. WILLEBRANDS, *Kerk-in-Diaspora als gestalte en opgave*, in *Nederlandse Katholieke Stemmen* 55 (1959) 207-221 (pp. 218-220, *passim*).

however, by a universal *communion of communions*, a conciliar communion of the Christian traditions from East and West, North and South,
united with the bishop of Rome, who carries the Petrine ministry of being
the Servant of Unity. If this prophetic vision should ever be fulfilled, the
fruits of the seeds sown by Johannes Willebrands during more than forty
years of his ecumenical ministry should be harvested[29] and received in
the acceptable time of the Lord by the leaders of the Christian World
Communions and by the people of God as a whole.

Anton HOUTEPEN †

---

29. See W. KASPER, *Harvesting the Fruits: Aspects of Christian Faith in Ecumenical Dialogue*, London – New York, Continuum, 2009.

THE ENDURING INFLUENCE OF NEWMAN ON
WILLEBRANDS' ECUMENICAL VIEWS

I. INTRODUCTION: THE SHOULDERS OF A GIANT

Many of us have been privileged to spend months or even years absorbing the ideas and the influence – and often even the literary style – of a great thinker. We have wrestled with our author; we have loved and perhaps even hated him. And then one day, we are compelled to move on. But we never really leave a great author behind. He has moulded us, and planted deep within our hearts and minds certain indelible impressions, certain guiding ideas of which we are sometimes even hardly aware but which will forever shape our worldview. If we are fortunate in our choice, we will have climbed onto the shoulders of a giant and we will see further and more clearly than we ever could have seen without him. Perhaps one day – when our own unexamined first principles are challenged – we will become aware of the extent of our debt to our mentor. But that is not so important. What matters is that we have been formed by a great mind and perhaps even contributed to the dissemination of his thought.

This, I think, is true of Johannes Willebrands who spent some of the most formative years of his life in the company of John Henry Newman. It is well known that Willebrands wrote his doctoral dissertation on Newman's religious epistemology, and his first academic publications were the fruits of that study. It would, therefore, not be at all difficult to make a case for Newman's influence on Willebrands' understanding of the formation of the Christian mind. Nor would it be difficult to trace the influence of Newman on his personal piety.

It is also well known that Willebrands envisioned the establishment of an Oratory, modelled on Newman's Oratory in Birmingham, and that he took very concrete steps towards its creation. From the outset, Willebrands saw the promotion of ecumenism as one of the major goals of this new foundation. And here, too, he invoked Newman's example[1].

---

1. See Theo SALEMINK (ed.), *"You Will Be Called Repairer of the Breach" : The Diary of J.G.M. Willebrands*, Leuven, Peeters, 2009, p. 169, 358. Writing in 1960, Willebrands observed that "Cardinal Newman gave his Oratory an ecumenical spirit".

In this paper, however, I would like to examine another possible line of influence, one that has attracted less attention. It seems to me that a case can be made for saying that Willebrands understood the development of the ecumenical movement in the light of Newman's analysis of the way in which the Christian truth comes to expression in history. More precisely, I think that Willebrands saw the ecumenical movement as contributing to the full manifestation of Christian truth. I deliberately do not use the word 'recovery' of Christian truth, because neither Newman, nor I think, Willebrands, held that Christian truth could ever be lost to the Church. That being said, however, both authors recognized that the course of history could seriously impede the progress of Christian truth in the world. In what follows, I shall attempt to demonstrate this claim by reading Willebrands in the light of Newman. I shall do this in three steps. First, I shall reflect on Newman's analysis of the development of Christian truth. Then, secondly, I shall examine Willebrands' reflections on Newman's analysis. And, finally, I shall turn back to Willebrands' thoughts on ecumenical theology to highlight certain parallels with Newman's thought.

II. Newman on the Development of Christian Truth

Newman's most important work on revelation and its manifestation in the world is undoubtedly his 1845 study, *An Essay on the Development of Christian Doctrine*, the book that marked Newman's transition from the Anglican to the Roman Catholic communion[2]. However, while he was still an active member of the Anglican Church, indeed an ardent apologist for the Anglican tradition, Newman wrote what might be called a precursor to the *Essay on Development*. This work, first published in 1837, is best known under an abbreviated title, *The Via Media*[3]. As this

---

2. John Henry NEWMAN, *An Essay on the Development of Christian Doctrine*, Notre Dame, IN, University of Notre Dame Press, 1989. Newman revised the original *Essay* somewhat when it was republished in 1876. The 1876 edition is the one most often used by scholars. The text of the original 1845 edition was published in 1973. See John Henry NEWMAN, *An Essay on the Development of Christian Doctrine: The Edition of 1845*, ed. J.M. CAMERON, Harmondsworth, Penguin, 1973. For the purposes of this paper, we shall refer to the 1876 edition.

3. John Henry NEWMAN, *The Via Media of the Anglican Church*, 2 vols., Westminster, MD, Christian Classics, 1978. The first volume of this work contains a somewhat amended version of Newman's defense of Anglicanism that appeared in 1837 under the title *Lectures on the Prophetical Office of the Church Viewed Relatively to Romanism and Popular Protestantism*. When Newman republished the original work in 1877, he not only edited the text somewhat but also added an extended "Preface" in which he sets out his

title suggests, the work was intended as a defence of Anglican ecclesiology. In this study, Newman distinguishes two forms of tradition, the episcopal and the prophetical.

The *episcopal tradition* comes to clearest expression in the Creed, and is the fruit of a complex process of transmission, being "rehearsed and confessed at baptism, committed and received from Bishop to Bishop, [and] forced upon the attention of each Christian" who receives it, in turn, according to the "capacity of [his or her] individual mind". This core, creedal tradition is already discernible in Scripture itself where, Newman says, it is called the *hypotyposis*, or "outline of sound words" spoken of in 2 Tim 1,13. It inevitably – and necessarily – becomes the object of, and gives rise to, extensive commentary and explanation[4].

The *prophetical tradition*, on the other hand, is 'expounded' by 'prophets or doctors', who serve as the "interpreters of the revelation; they unfold and define its mysteries, they illuminate its documents, they harmonize its contents, they apply its promises"[5]. The complex system of teaching and practice expounded by the 'prophets and doctors' must not simply be equated with the prophetical tradition though it is the main vehicle for its dissemination and preservation. Newman clearly struggled with the precise nature of the relationship between the prophetical tradition as such, and its expression in the life and teaching of the Church or, more accurately, those 'prophets and doctors' whose task it was to expound revelation. So, for example, he describes the prophetical tradition as

> a vast system, not to be comprised in a few sentences, not to be embodied in one code or treatise, but consisting of a certain body of Truth, pervading the Church like an atmosphere, irregular in its shape from its very profusion and exuberance; at times separable only in idea from Episcopal Tradition, yet at times melting away into legend and fable; partly written, partly

defense of Roman Catholicism. Volume 1 of the work now known as *The Via Media* therefore contains Newman's 'apology' for both Anglicanism and Roman Catholicism. Volume 2 of the *The Via Media* contains articles written by Newman between 1830 and his "Retraction of Anti-Catholic Statements" in 1845. For a detailed discussion of the origins and significance of the original work, see H.D. WEIDNER, *Editor's Introduction*, in John Henry NEWMAN, *The Via Media of the Anglican Church*, ed. H.D. WEIDNER, Oxford, Clarendon, 1990, xiii-lxxix. Newman's Preface to the 1877 (or 'third' edition, since a second edition of the *Lectures on the Prophetical Office* was published in 1838) can be found in Weidner's critical edition on pp. 10-57. For a reflection on Newman's analysis of the Church, see Avery DULLES, *The Threefold Office in Newman's Ecclesiology*, in I. KER – A.G. HILL (eds.), *Newman after a Hundred Years*, Oxford, Clarendon, 1990, 375-399; see also Avery DULLES, *John Henry Newman*, New York, Continuum, 2002, pp. 66-67.

4. NEWMAN, *The Via Media of the Anglican Church* (n. 3), vol. 1, p. 249.

5. *Ibid.*, p. 250.

unwritten, partly the interpretation, partly the supplement of Scripture, partly preserved in intellectual expressions, partly latent in the spirit and temper of Christians; poured to and fro in closets and upon the housetops, in liturgies, in controversial works, in obscure fragments, in sermons, in popular prejudices, in local customs[6].

While this tradition has come to expression in "the writings of eminent men", Newman insists that it 'exists' "primarily in the bosom of the Church itself". Hence, it bears a greater resemblance to "what St. Paul calls 'the mind of the Spirit' [Rom 8,6], the thought and principle which breathed in the Church, her accustomed and *unconscious* [our emphasis] mode of viewing things, and the body of her received notions, [than to] any definite and systematic collection of dogmas elaborated by the intellect"[7].

The fluidity, indeed the near intangibility, of the prophetical tradition is manifest in Newman's acknowledgement that it has sometimes shaded into 'legends and fables', that it is obscured by 'popular prejudices', and that it is sometimes found in 'local customs'. Indeed, despite his determination to associate it with the work of the Spirit, Newman is obliged to acknowledge that while a portion of the prophetical tradition "was fixed and perpetuated in the shape of formal articles or doctrines" in response to disputes within the Church, and "preserved to a considerable extent in the writings of the Fathers", the fragmentation of the Christian Church meant that the tradition had been dissipated or absorbed into local practices. The Church, in "her various branches, [had] developed portions of it for themselves, out of the existing mass, and, according to the accidental influences which prevailed at the time". Moreover, they did this with varying degrees of success, "well or ill, rudely or accurately", such that the value of particular expressions of the prophetical tradition varied (and varies) greatly. Consequently, those portions of it which came to expression in "developed and fixed doctrines are entitled to very different degrees of credit". According to Newman, those expressions of the prophetical tradition "which are recognized by the Church at an early date, are of more authority than such as are determined at a later; those which have the joint assent of many independent Churches, than those which are the result of some preponderating influence; those that are sanctioned dispassionately, than those which are settled in fear, anger, or jealousy"[8].

6. *Ibid.*
7. *Ibid.*, p. 251.
8. *Ibid.*, p. 252.

The upshot of all this is that while, for a time, "the whole Church agreed together in giving one and the same account of this [prophetical] Tradition", this consensus has been lost. What remains then, after the passage of centuries and the hardening of views that inevitably accompanied the divisions within Christianity, is not the pure 'breath' of the apostolic community, but the tainted and partial gaspings of a fragmented Church[9]. Newman's Anglo-Catholic apologetic hinged on the view that this fragmentation made the branch-theory of the Church a necessity. If there were any hope whatsoever of accessing or appropriating the fullness of Christian truth, then this could only be achieved by the struggle for consensus among those churches which took apostolic tradition seriously. In the meantime, what was needed was cooperation founded on the recognition that, since the "prophetical tradition has been corrupted in its details, in spite of its general accuracy and its agreement with Episcopal", there will inevitably be "lesser points of doctrine as well as greater points, whatever be their number and limit, from which a person may possibly dissent, as doubting their Apostolical origin, without incurring any anathema or public censure"[10].

In his *Essay on the Development of Christian Doctrine,* which was published in 1845 and during the composition of which Newman decided to join the Roman Catholic Church, he abandoned the distinction between the episcopal and the prophetical office. He did, however, retain the view that the content of Christian revelation, what he calls the 'idea' of Christianity, is the possession of the Church as a whole[11]. As Newman expresses it:

> ... [Christ] is found, through His preachers, to have imprinted the Image or idea of Himself in the minds of His subjects individually; and that Image, apprehended and worshipped in individual minds, becomes a principle of association, and a real bond of those subjects one with another, who are thus united to the body by being united to that Image; and moreover that Image,

9. See *ibid.*, p. 251 where Newman says that the "Anglo-Catholic theory" of the Church acknowledges that, "though the Prophetical Tradition comes from God, and ought to have been religiously preserved, and was so in great measure and for a long time, yet that no such especial means were taken for its preservation as those which have secured to us the Creed, – that it was rather what St. Paul calls 'the mind of the Spirit', the thought and principle which breathed in the Church, her accustomed and unconscious mode of viewing things, and the body of her received notions, than any definite and systematic collection of dogmas elaborated by the intellect".

10. *Ibid.*, p. 25.

11. For an extensive analysis of Newman's understanding of revelation and the 'idea' of Christianity, see Terrence MERRIGAN, *Revelation*, in I. KER – T. MERRIGAN (eds.), *The Cambridge Companion to John Henry Newman*, Cambridge, Cambridge University Press, 2009, 47-72.

which is their moral life, when they have been already converted, is also the original instrument of their conversion. It is the Image of Him who fulfils the one great need of human nature, the Healer of its wounds, the Physician of the soul, this Image it is which both creates faith, and then rewards it[12].

The Christian "idea" of Christ exists in the "mind of the Church", as the correlate to the "fact of revelation". The "idea" in the mind of believers is not, properly speaking, the object of faith. It is, however, the means by which the object of faith is apprehended. In the words of John Coulson, "an 'idea' is not reality at its most real but an image of what acts upon us in the manner of objects of sense–perception"[13].

Christianity is at once possessed of, and possessed by, the "idea" of the Incarnate Christ[14]. This "idea" was communicated to the apostles *"per modum unius"* in and through Jesus' life, death and resurrection (though their knowledge of it was to a great extent implicit). It is preserved in the Church by the operation of the Holy Spirit. Newman uses a variety of terms to describe the idea as it exists in the mind of the Church. These include the following: "impression" or "image" (1843)[15]; a "deep internal sense" (1847)[16]; a "real apprehension" (1870)[17]. All of

12. John Henry NEWMAN, *An Essay in Aid of a Grammar of Assent*, London, Longmans, Green & Co., 1903, p. 464.

13. John COULSON, *Newman and the Common Tradition*, Oxford, Clarendon, 1970, p. 64.

14. See Nicholas LASH, *Newman on Development: The Search for an Explanation in History*, London, Sheed and Ward, 1975, pp. 140-141: "Although, in 1845, Newman insisted that the task of ascertaining the 'leading idea', as it has been called, of Christianity ... is beyond us..., in 1878 he admitted the propriety, 'for the convenience of arrangement', of considering 'the Incarnation the central truth of the gospel, and the source whence we are to draw out its principles' (*Dev.*, 324)". Lash observes that "in making explicit that centrality of the fact and doctrine of the incarnation which most deeply characterises his conception of Christianity, Newman was not, in 1878 reversing the judgement made, in 1845, concerning the impossibility of ascertaining the 'leading idea' of Christianity". Lash sees the later emphasis as, in part, the consequence of "apologetic considerations", (i.e., the refusal of Liberalism) and as, in any case, consistent with Newman's constant "theological conviction". He notes that Newman speaks of the doctrine of the incarnation as the "central", not the "leading" idea.

15. NEWMAN, *Essay on Development* (n. 2), pp. 316, 320, 321, 323, 327, 329, 330.

16. John Henry NEWMAN, *Roman Catholic Writings on Doctrinal Development*, translation and commentary by James GAFFNEY, London, Sheed & Ward, 1997, p. 19: "Initially the word of God enters the mind of the Catholic world through the ears of faith. It penetrates that mind, recedes inside it, and remains hidden there, becoming a kind of deep internal sense. It is brought into play by the ministering and teaching Church".

17. *Grammar of Assent* (n. 12), pp. 22-30. For a discussion of the role of "real apprehension" in the assent of faith, see Terrence MERRIGAN, *Newman on Faith in the Trinity*, in Ian KER – Terrence MERRIGAN (eds.), *Newman and Faith* (Louvain Theological and Pastoral Monographs, 31), Leuven, Peeters; Grand Rapids, MI, Eerdmans, 2004, 93-116, especially pp. 96-99.

these terms suggest that what is at stake here is a profound awareness or grasp of the reality that the idea represents.

However, a "great" idea, such as the "idea" of Christianity, does not unfold itself in the mind alone. As Newman says, "In proportion to its native vigour and subtlety", it will "introduce itself into the framework and details of social life", and give rise to a whole range of social forms. These include codes of ethical conduct, structures of government and organization, philosophical and theological systems, rituals and doctrines, and so on[18]. In this way, the Christian 'idea' becomes a religion. Christianity, Newman wrote, had first appeared "as worship, springing up and spreading in the lower ranks of society … Then it seized upon the intellectual and cultivated class, and created a theology and schools of learning. Lastly it seated itself, as an ecclesiastical polity, among princes, and chose Rome for its centre"[19].

Christianity is, therefore, a complex, comprehensive fact of history, and the manifestation of its invigorating "idea" is determined by history's permutations and convolutions[20]. This is indeed the case with any "philosophy [idea] or polity which takes possession of the intellect and heart, and has any wide or extended dominion"[21]. In the case of Christianity, however, the question of the impact of history on the "idea" is particularly acute. This is because the churches allege – and justify their existence by an appeal to – a real and unbroken continuity between "the religion taught by Christ and His apostles" and their own. The public manifestations of an idea inevitably influence the way in which the "idea" is received and understood, for better or worse as the case may be[22].

Newman struggled with the inescapable ambiguity of Christian revelation – namely, that while it is very much a matter of human words and human history, it is ultimately the history of the Word and therefore a divine history. After all, as Nicholas Lash has pointed out, in the final analysis, the dynamism and organizing power of the Christian idea is born of its foundation in the risen Christ, God's living Word in history. It is this rootedness in Christ which accounts for Newman's tendency "to express the transcendence of the 'idea' by hypostatizing, or personalizing

18. NEWMAN, *Essay on Development* (n. 2), p. 37.
19. NEWMAN, *The Via Media of the Anglican Church* (n. 3), vol. 1, p. 41; see also *Essay on Development* (n. 2), pp. 77-78.
20. *Essay on Development* (n. 2), p. 39.
21. *Ibid..*, p. 29.
22. *Ibid.*, pp. 38-39, 92. MERRIGAN, *Revelation* (n. 11).

it"[23]. The true "object" of the Christian "idea", then, is Christ Himself, the living Word of God who "exists underneath and before all of the expressions which Christians have invented to expound it"[24]. That being said, however, Christ's fate in the world is still, in some very real sense, in the hands of men and women.

Newman was not prepared "to abandon the tension between immutability and change, between the transcendent and the historical", which this entailed[25]. He was, therefore, obliged to provide an account of how revelation could be preserved in a changing world that was scarred by human sinfulness. Only by doing so could he justify the claim, made in the *Essay on Development*, that the whole "superstructure" of Christian tradition is "the proper representative of one idea, *being in substance what that idea meant from the first*, its complete image as seen in a combination of diversified aspects, with the suggestions and corrections of many minds, and the illustration of many experiences"[26]. Newman poses the problem quite directly:

> If Christianity be a social religion, as it certainly is, and if it be based on certain ideas acknowledged as divine, or a creed, (which shall here be assumed,) and if these ideas have various aspects, and make distinct impressions on different minds, and issue in consequence in a multiplicity of developments, true, or false, or mixed …, what power will suffice to meet and to do justice to these conflicting conditions …?[27].

Newman's Catholic answer to his own question was the church, understood as a community invested with infallible authority. There was, he claimed, need for "a supreme authority ruling and reconciling individual judgments by a divine right and a recognised wisdom"[28], "an infallible

23. Nicholas LASH, *Change in Focus*, London, Sheed & Ward, 1973, p. 92; *Newman on Development* (n. 14), pp. 74-75, 48.

24. H. Francis DAVIS, *Newman and the Theology of the Living Word*, in *Newman Studien* 6 (1964) 167-177, pp. 171, 173.

25. LASH, *Newman on Development* (n. 14), p. 53.

26. See NEWMAN, *Essay on Development* (n. 2), pp. 36, 38 (emphasis added). In *ibid.*, p. 36 Newman equates a 'living idea' with an 'active principle'. Elsewhere in his writings (for example, *Grammar of Assent* [n. 12], pp. 465-466), he refers to the presence of Christ and His Spirit as the 'principle' of Christianity. See LASH, *Newman on Development* (n. 14), pp. 106-109. There are at least some grounds for thinking that 'complete' here (*Essay on Development*, p. 38) means not so much 'definitive' as 'adequate'. Seen in this light, the life of the contemporary Church can be regarded as an adequate 'representative' of the 'idea', just as the patristic Church was (and Newman clearly thought it was). In other words, it would seem that there is, in Newman, a tendency to see the Church, as 'realization' of the idea, in terms of a sort of 'continuum', that is to say, as 'sufficient' at any given moment.

27. *Essay on Development* (n. 2), p. 89.

28. *Ibid.*

expounder" of Christian truth[29]. As he puts it, "A revelation is not given, if there be no authority to decide what it is that is given"[30], and to act in order to preserve that revelation from "perversion and corruption"[31]. As he explained, in the *Essay on Development*:

> If Christianity is both social and dogmatic, and intended for all ages, it must humanly speaking have an infallible expounder. Else you will secure unity of form at the loss of unity of doctrine, or unity of doctrine at the loss of unity of form; you will have to choose between a comprehension of opinions and a resolution into parties, between latitudinarian and sectarian error. You may be tolerant or intolerant of contrarieties of thought, but contrarieties you will have. By the Church of England a hollow uniformity is preferred to an infallible chair; and by the sects of England, an interminable division. Germany and Geneva began with persecution, and have ended in skepticism. The doctrine of infallibility is a less violent hypothesis than this sacrifice either of faith or of charity. It secures the object, while it gives definiteness and force to the matter, of the Revelation[32].

By 1845, then, Newman had abandoned the notion that revealed truth had somehow been lost to the Church or at least obscured by the passage of time. He had no more need of the prophetical tradition, understood as an ambiguous quantity that could be invoked both to explain disunity and to inspire a quest for deeper unity. What did remain, however, was a profound sensitivity to the notion that Christian truth was, in a very real sense, historically determined, that is to say, that every concrete expression of the Christian 'idea', whether it concerns the Church's structure, or its discipline or even its doctrine, is in some sense contextual. It is not an end in itself. There is, then, a need for constant vigilance, a vigilance that comes to expression in the willingness to ask of particular traditions and practices whether they still serve the "idea" or, more accurately, the living Christ who is the origin of the "idea", or whether they need radical rethinking and reconfiguration. This Newmanian spirit, it might be argued, was very much alive in the mind and heart of Cardinal Willebrands. That is the subject of the following reflection.

29. *Ibid.*, p. 90.
30. *Ibid.*, p. 89.
31. *Ibid.*, p. 92.
32. *Ibid.*, pp. 31, 86, 87-88, 92.

III. WILLEBRANDS' APPROPRIATION OF NEWMAN'S
UNDERSTANDING OF TRUTH AND HISTORY

Willebrands was thoroughly familiar with Newman's thought on the historical development of Christianity. In 1946, he published an article in the Dutch theological journal, *Bijdragen*[33], in which he compared Newman's and Hegel's views on the relationship between truth and history. His comments on Hegel need not concern us here. Indeed, it is clear from the article that Willebrands is most interested in Newman.

Willebrands draws on both the *Lectures on the Prophetical Office* and the *Essay on Development* to examine Newman's views. Indeed, Willebrands provides a very nearly literal translation of Newman's description of the prophetical tradition which we referred to above. He then goes on to comment on that text. Newman's original text reads as follows:

> I say, then, that the Creed is a collection of definite articles set apart from the first, passing from hand to hand, rehearsed and confessed at Baptism, committed and received from Bishop to Bishop, forced upon the attention of each Christian, and thus demanding and securing due explanation of its meaning. It is received on what may fitly be called, if it must have a distinctive name, Episcopal Tradition. Besides, it is delineated and recognized in Scripture itself, where it is called the Hypotyposis, or 'outline of sound words'; and again, in the writings of the Fathers, as in some of the passages cited in the last Lecture. But independently of this written evidence in its favour, we may observe that a Tradition, thus formally and statedly enunciated and delivered from hand to hand, is of the nature of a written document, and has an evidence of its Apostolical origin the same in kind with that adducible for the Scriptures. For the same reason, though it is not pertinent here to insist on it, rites and ceremonies too are something more than mere oral Traditions, and, as being so, carry with them a considerable presumption in behalf of the things signified by them. And all this, let it be observed, is independent of the question of the Catholicity or Universality of the rites or doctrines which are thus formally sealed and handed down; a property which in this case attaches to both of them, and becomes an additional argument for their Apostolical origin. *§11*: Such then is Episcopal Tradition, – to be received according to the capacity of each individual mind. But besides this, there is what may be called Prophetical Tradition. Almighty God placed in His Church first Apostles, or Bishops, secondarily Prophets. Apostles rule and preach, Prophets expound. Prophets or Doctors are the interpreters of the revelation; they unfold and define its mysteries, they illuminate its documents, they harmonize its contents, they

---

33. This article was the fruit of a lecture given to the 'Association for Thomistic Philosophy' ('Vereeniging [sic] voor Thomistische wijsbegeerte') at Witten in October 1945. See J.G.M. WILLEBRANDS, *De ontwikkeling der idee volgens Newman vergeleken met Hegel*, in *Bijdragen* 7 (1946) 60-79.

apply its promises. Their teaching is a vast system, not to be comprised in a few sentences, not to be embodied in one code or treatise, but consisting of a certain body of Truth, pervading the Church like an atmosphere, irregular in its shape from its very profusion and exuberance; at times separable only in idea from Episcopal Tradition, yet at times melting away into legend and fable]; partly written, partly unwritten, partly the interpretation, partly the supplement of Scripture, partly preserved in intellectual expressions, partly latent in the spirit and temper of Christians; poured to and fro in closets and upon the housetops, in liturgies, in controversial works, in obscure fragments, in sermons, in popular prejudices, in local customs. This I call Prophetical Tradition, existing primarily in the bosom of the Church itself, and recorded in such measure as Providence has determined in the writings of eminent men. This is obviously of a very different kind from the Episcopal Tradition, yet in its first origin it is equally Apostolical, and, viewed as a whole, equally claims our zealous maintenance. 'Keep that which is committed to thy charge', is St. Paul's injunction to Timothy, and for this reason, because from its vastness indefiniteness it is especially exposed to corruption, if the Church fails in vigilance. This is that body of teaching which is offered to all Christians even at the present day, though in various forms and measures of truth, in different parts of Christendom, partly being a comment, partly an addition upon the articles of the Creed. §12: Now what has been said has sufficed to show, how it may easily happen that this Prophetical Tradition has been corrupted in its details, in spite of its general accuracy and its agreement with Episcopal; and if so, there will be lesser points of doctrine as well as greater points, whatever be their number and limit, from which a person may possibly dissent, as doubting their Apostolical origin, without incurring any anathema or public censure. And this is supposed on the Anglo-Catholic theory actually to be the case; that, though the Prophetical Tradition comes from God, and ought to have been religiously preserved, and was so in great measure and for a long time, yet that no such especial means were taken for its preservation as those which have secured to us the Creed, – that it was rather what St. Paul calls 'the mind of the Spirit', the thought and principle which breathed in the Church, her accustomed and unconscious mode of viewing things, and the body of her received notions, than any definite and systematic collection of dogmas elaborated by the intellect. Partially, indeed, it was fixed and perpetuated in the shape of formal articles or doctrines, as the rise of errors or other causes gave occasion; and it is preserved to a considerable extent in the writings of the Fathers. For a time the whole Church agreed together in giving one and the same account of this Tradition; but in course of years, love waxing cold and schisms abounding, her various branches developed portions of it for themselves, out of the existing mass, and, according to the accidental influences which prevailed at the time, did the work well or ill, rudely or accurately. It follows, that these developed and fixed doctrines are entitled to very different degrees of credit, though always to attention. Those which are recognized by the Church at an early date, are of more authority than such as are determined at a later; those which have the joint assent of many independent Churches, than those which are the result of some preponderating influence; those that are sanctioned dispassionately, than those which are settled in fear, anger, or jealousy. Accordingly, some Councils speak far more authoritatively than others, though all which appeal to Tradition may be presumed to have some element of truth in them. And this view, I would take even of the decrees of Trent. They claim indeed to be Apostolic; and I would grant so much, that they are the ruins and perversions of Primitive Tradition[34].

34. NEWMAN, *The Via Media of the Anglican Church* (n. 3), vol. 1, pp. 249-250: §10. This is the Dutch translation as found in WILLEBRANDS, *De ontwikkeling der idee volgens Hegel vergeleken met Newman* (see n. 33), pp. 65-66: "Newman onderscheidt Episcopal Tradition en Prophetical Tradition. De traditie der bisschoppen wordt samengevat in het Credo, een verzameling van geloofsartikelen, vastgesteld van den beginne, overgeleverd van hand tot hand, herhaald en beleden in het Doopsel, overgeleverd en aanvaard van bisschop tot bisschop, opgelegd aan iedereen christen. St. Paulus spreekt hierover als over de *hypotyposis*, "het richtsnoer van gezonde leerling" (2 Tim 1,13). Hiertoe behooren ook de riten en ceremoniën, die van Apostolischen oorsprong zijn, meer dan louter mondelinge overleveringen, een sterke presumptie bevattend voor de leer waarvan zij getuigenis afleggen. Daarnaast bestaat de Prophetische Traditie of het werk der theologie. Deze naam is door Newman gekozen, omdat St. Paulus spreekt van profeten en leeraren als verklaarders der openbaring. Zij ontvouwen en definiëren de geloofsgeheimen, zij verklaren de documenten der openbaring, zij toonen haar innerlijke harmonie aan, zij laten uitkomen haar beantwoording aan de menschelijke verwachtingen. Hun leer is een uitgebreid systeem, dat men niet in enkele zinnen kan samenvatten, niet kan vastleggen in een handboekje of tractaat, zij bestaat in een organisch geheel van waarheid, dat als een atmosfeer de Kerk doordringt, zonder regelmaat van vormen, juist door haar uitbreiding en rijken inhoud; in bepaalde tijden valt deze profetische traditie met die der bisschoppen samen, in andere tijden echter vervalt zij tot fabels en legenden, zij is ten deele geschreven ten deele ongeschreven, ten deele interpretatie, ten deele aanvulling der H. Schrift, ten deele vastgelegd in wetenschappelijke vormen, ten deele verborgen levend in den geest en het karakter der christenen. Zij leeft in de binnenkamers en worden verkondigd van de daken, zij leeft in liturgieën, in controversen, in duistere uitspraken, in preken, in populaire vooroordelen, in plaatselijke gewoonten. Zij bestaat primair in den schoot der Kerk zelf en is vastgelegd in beperkte mate, naargelang de Voorzienigheid bepaald heeft, in de werken van eminente mannen. Deze traditie is datgene, wat St. Paulus noemt τὸ φρόνημα τοῦ πνεύματος (Rom 8,6), het denken, het beginsel dat ademt in de Kerk, haar dagelijksche en onbewuste wijze om de dingen te zien en te beleven.

Wat Newman hier beschrijft als de prophetische traditie, is niet exclusief aan de Kerk eigen. Haar aequivalent is in alle gemeenschappen aanwezig, in groote gemeenschappen als in staten en volkeren, in kleine als in een universiteit of in een religieuse orde. Ze is de geest, het leven, ontastbaar toch werkelijk, niet te definieeren toch goed te erkennen. Vroeger zou Newman juist dezen geest, deze werkelijkheid hebben bepaald als een engel of een *daimon*. Nu bestaat ze niet meer als een persoonlijke geest, zij bestaat eenerzijds buiten den menschelijken geest als een werkelijkheid, hetzij bepaald door factoren, die vrij gewild zijn, als b.v. een religieuse gemeenschap. Anderzijds bestaat ze in den geest als Idea. En gelijk de gemeenschap meer is dan de loutere optelsom der leden, zoo is ook de geest der gemeenschap onderscheiden van den individueelen geest der leden. De Idea der gemeenschap is een concrete, samengestelde Idea; wie niet meer kent dan zichzelf en zijn eigen Idea, bezit niet meer dan één aspect, kent niet de geheele idea. Men kan zich dezen geest alleen eigen maken, men kan zich dus alleen een Idea ervan vormen, door televen in het milieu, waarin hij ademt. Het gaat om iets concreets, een abstracte bepaling kan nooit de volheid hiervan uitdrukken".

In his commentary, Willebrands explains that the notion of the prophetical tradition can be applied to all sorts of corporate bodies, ranging from nations and peoples to universities and religious orders. In the case of all of these groups, their tradition exists in the mind of the community in the fashion of an 'idea'. Willebrands describes the tradition as the "the spirit, [or] the life" of these bodies. He describes it as "intangible but real, resisting definition but easily recognizable". This tradition is affected by factors external to, and independent of, the body that possesses it. It is never simply reducible to the sum total of the ideas possessed by the members of the body. Individual members of the community know only particular aspects of the 'idea'. No single individual can claim to know it in its entirety. The only way to acquire knowledge of the idea is to immerse oneself in the community that possesses it, the place where it "breathes", as Willebrands puts it. The idea is something 'concrete', something real. It can never be captured in an abstraction. However, where it takes possession of the minds and hearts of individuals and communities, it is a force to be reckoned with and its manifestations will be as many and as varied as time and circumstance allow[35].

With Newman, Willebrands acknowledges that the progress of the idea is never predictable and that it may never be completely realized in history. Indeed, the idea is always under threat from decay and corruption and, without special divine assistance, it is almost certainly doomed to perish[36].

---

35. WILLEBRANDS, *De ontwikkeling der idee volgens Newman vergeleken met Hegel* (n. 33), p. 66.

36. *Ibid.*, p. 71. See especially p. 75. On p. 71, Willebrands refers to Newman's *Essay on Development* (n. 2), pp. 37-39. Two passages, in particular, are cited at length (in Dutch). Newman's original English text (i.e., those passages cited literally by Willebrands) reads as follows: "Moreover, an idea not only modifies, but is modified, or at least influenced, by the state of things in which it is carried out, and is dependent in various ways on the circumstances which surround it" (*Essay on Development*, p. 39). "The development then of an idea is not like an investigation worked out on paper, in which each successive advance is a pure evolution from a foregoing, but it is carried on through and by means of communities of men and their leaders and guides; and it employs their minds as its instruments, and depends upon them, while it uses them" (*Essay on Development*, p. 38). On p. 75, reflecting on what might be described as the 'vulnerability' of the idea, Willebrands cites Newman again at length (see *Essay on Development*, p. 40: "It is indeed sometimes said that the stream is clearest near the spring. Whatever use may fairly be made of this image, it does not apply to the history of a philosophy or belief, which on the contrary is more equable, and purer, and stronger, when its bed has become deep, and broad, and full. It necessarily rises out of an existing state of things, and for a time savours of the soil. Its vital element needs disengaging from what is foreign and temporary, and is employed in efforts after freedom which become wore vigorous and hopeful as its years increase. Its beginnings are no measure of its capabilities, nor of its scope. At first no one knows what it is, or what it is worth. It remains perhaps for a time quiescent; it tries, as

IV. The Ghost of Newman in Willebrands' Ecumenical Theology

One of Willebrands' most notable contributions to ecumenical theology was his twofold proposal, in lectures delivered in 1970 and 1972[37], to (i) approach the confessional traditions within the church as *typoi* or 'types', "in the sense of general form or character", and (ii) to consider the possibility of "a plurality of *typoi* within the communion of the one and only Church of Christ"[38]. Willebrands' exposition of this notion was in fact rather brief and somewhat opaque, but it attracted (and continues to attract) considerable attention (among others, from Walter Cardinal Kasper who claims to "prefer" Willebrands' notion of *typos* to the approach to non-Catholic churches taken in *Dominus Iesus*)[39].

The *typoi* are the manifestations of particular appropriations of the apostolic tradition, as this has been received and transmitted in different contexts during the course of the Church's history. Willebrands cites the

---

it were, its limbs, and proves the ground under it, and feels its way. From time to time it makes essays which fail, and are in consequence abandoned. It seems in suspense which way to go; it wavers, and at length strikes out in one definite direction. In time it enters upon strange territory; points of controversy alter their bearing; parties rise and around it; dangers and hopes appear in new relations; and old principles reappear under new forms. It changes with them in order to remain the same. In a higher world it is otherwise, but here below to live is to change, and to be perfect is to have changed often".

37. See *A Tribute to Johannes Cardinal Willebrands on the Occasion of His Ninetieth Birthday*, in *Information Service* 101 (1999/II-111) 100-105, 130-134. Both lectures were delivered within the framework of Anglican-Roman Catholic dialogue. The first (pp. 130-134) was delivered in 1970 at Great St. Mary's, Cambridge on January 18, 1970, and entitled *The Notion of 'typos' within the One Church*; the second (pp. 100-105) was delivered on October 4, 1972 at Lambeth Palace and entitled *Prospects for Anglican-Roman Catholic Relations*.

38. Willebrands, *The Notion of 'typos' within the One Church* (n. 36), p. 133; see also *Prospects for Anglican-Roman Catholic Relations* (n. 36), p. 104.

39. See Walter Kasper, *Current Problems in Ecumenical Theology*, 2005 The text is available on the Vatican website: http://www.vatican.va/roman_curia/pontifical_councils/chrstuni/card-kasper-docs/rc_pc_chrstuni_doc_20030227_ecumenical-theology_en.html#_ftn41. In this document, section IV, entitled "Oikoumene with the Churches of the Reformed tradition", Kasper observes that, "In the process of the Reformation – with or without the intention of the Reformers – a new type of church has in fact come into being". In a footnote (note 41) to this text, he explains that he quite deliberately refers to the notion of 'type', and he refers to Willebrands as his source. Kasper writes as follows: "I say deliberately: a new type of church and I prefer this formula of Cardinal J. Willebrands (*The Notion of "Typos" within the one Church* [1970], reprinted in: Information Service 1999/II-III, 130-140) to that of "*Dominus Jesus*" 17, which says that what is meant is not a church in the true sense. That formulation has to be understood in the sense of the scholastic doctrine of analogy. In that sense, it does not say that the churches issued from the Reformation are non-churches or fictitious churches; it does not exclude, or it rather includes that in comparison with the Catholic understanding of the Church they are churches in an analogous sense".

Decree on Ecumenism, #14 to illustrate his point. He quotes the following passage: "… The heritage handed down by the apostles was received in different forms and ways, so that from the very beginning of the Church it has had a varied development in various places, thanks to a similar variety of natural gifts and conditions of life". There is a danger of some confusion here, because this text is describing the reception of the apostolic heritage by the Churches of East and West, and the Council presumes that there is, between these churches, a "communion of faith and sacramental life". Willebrands is aware of this difficulty and he therefore insists that what really interests him is not so much the "communion of faith and sacramental life" (which does not exist to the same degree between the Roman Catholic Church and the Protestant churches), but the fact that the various Churches "went their own ways". In other words, Willebrands is intent on pursuing the implications of the multiplicity of the *typoi* and not the grounding unity[40].

Hence, his next move is to list the features that allow one to identify what he calls "the reality of a *typos*". These features are four in number: (i) "a characteristic theological method and approach"; (ii) "a characteristic liturgical expression", (iii) "a spiritual and devotional tradition"; and (iv) "a characteristic canonical discipline". "Through the combination of all of these", Willebrands argues, "a typos can be *specified*". The use of the word 'specified' here is not unimportant. What interests Willebrands is the 'specificity' of a *typos*, that which distinguishes it from other *typoi*. In short, Willebrands' theory of *typoi* is more about diversity than about unity. When, therefore, he speaks about the *typos* as "a harmonious and organic whole of complementary elements", he is not suggesting that every *typos* is an equally adequate manifestation of the apostolic heritage. Rather, he is suggesting that each *typos* is possessed of its own inner coherence and that it gives expression to a particular experience of the apostolic heritage. Indeed, it is only because each *typos* is, so to speak, a 'partial' expression of the apostolic heritage that the re-establishment of communion between them can be described as a "strengthening and enrichment" of the unity that already exists[41].

---

40. WILLEBRANDS, *The Notion of 'typos' within the One Church* (n. 36), p. 133. Indeed, Willebrands highlights the fact that, "The theological element which must always be present and presupposed is the full 'communion of faith and sacramental life'". He immediately adds: "But the words 'went their own ways' point in the direction of the notion which I would like to develop a little more". He then explains that what is at stake is the nature of these "own ways" and the moment when one can speak of a *typos*. As he expresses it, "What are these 'own ways' and when can we speak of a *typos*"?

41. *Ibid.*, p. 133. See also Willebrands' address to the Ecumenical Patriarchate on November 30, 1969 where he declared that "the unity which we look for … is not a

Commentators tend to see Willebrands' reflections as inspired by notions of church unity that were being developed in the 1960's, including that of 'reconciled diversity' or of the church as a 'communion of communions'[42]. One need not deny this influence in order to point to an even deeper vein of inspiration, namely, Newman's analysis of development as explained above.

At the very least, there is a remarkable coincidence of thought – and even of language – between Newman's reflections on the development of Christian truth – or the Christian 'idea' – and Willebrands' reflections on the *typos*. By way of summing up, I would like to highlight seven of these commonalities. First, for both authors, the root of the Church's life is a grounding *organic* unity. Second, this unity "transcends all human power of organisation"[43]. Third, this grounding unity is a "divine gift" and not "a product of human skill"[44]. Fourth, this grounding unity exists in the fashion of a spirit or 'breath' that permeates the life of the communities. Fifth, this grounding unity is "manifested" (but never exhausted) in a variety of historical forms – 'aspects' of the Christian idea (Newman) or *typoi* (Willebrands) – which are themselves shaped by the permutations of history, and by the diversity of contexts in which the grounding reality takes root. Sixth, these manifestations are the means by which the inexhaustible richness of the grounding unity is disclosed. Hence, it is possible to say that the processes of history are not merely impediments to the disclosure of the grounding unity, but opportunities for its fuller expression. This allows Willebrands to say that the living

question of a uniformity which would reduce all to itself, but o the unity of a body where the harmony consists in the complementarity of the members". See *Tribute to Johannes Cardinal Willebrands on the Occasion of his Ninetieth Birthday* (n. 36), p. 86. See also pp. 90, 92, 95, 96, 98. Speaking to participants in the first meeting of the Catholic-Orthodox Joint Commission for Theological Dialogue in 1980, Willebrands declared (p. 92) that, "Our Churches received the same faith; they have developed this Christian inheritance in different ways and manners".

42. Anton HOUTEPEN, *People of God: A Plea for the Church*, Maryknoll, NY, Orbis, 1985, p. 170; Lorelei F. FUCHS, *Koinonia and the Quest for an Ecumenical Ecclesiology*, Grand Rapids, MI, Eerdmans, 2008, p. 66 n. 49. See also J.A. BURGESS – J. GROS (eds.), *Growing Consensus: Church Dialogues in the United States, 1962-1991*, Mahwah, NJ, Paulist, 1995, pp. 518-519.

43. WILLEBRANDS, *Prospects for Anglican-Roman Catholic Relations* (n. 36), p. 104, where Willebrands invokes five documents of Vatican II (*Lumen Gentium*, *Gaudium et Spes*, *Unitatis Redintegratio*, *Ad Gentes*, and *Dignitatis Humanae*) as supporting the view that "the unity of the Church is a reality which transcends all human power of organisation and is, with its sanctity, its catholicity, its apostolicity, a divine gift which belongs to its mystery rather than being a product of human skill". Of course, for Newman, the 'idea' of Christianity is ultimately the living Christ.

44. See n. 39.

tradition of the Church is actually "enriched" by the variety of *typoi*[45]. Seventh, and last, both Newman and Willebrands insist that the point of the whole dynamic process – and the measure of its success – is the fuller manifestation of Christ. As Willebrands expresses it, the "strengthening and enrichment" of unity among Christians "will manifest itself primarily where it finds its highest motive – in a renewal of witness to Christ, a renewal of mission"[46]. Newman could hardly have said it better[47].

Faculty of Theology   Terrence MERRIGAN
and Religious Studies
KU Leuven
St.-Michielsstraat 4/3101
B-3000 Leuven
Belgium

45. WILLEBRANDS, *The Notion of 'typos' within the One Church* (n. 36), p. 134; see also *Prospects for Anglican-Roman Catholic Relations* (n. 36), p. 105 where Willebrands repeats his claim, made in *The Notion of 'typos' within the One Church*, that "The life of the Church needs a variety of *typoi* which would manifest the full catholic and apostolic character of the one and holy Church".

46. WILLEBRANDS, *The Notion of 'typos' within the One Church* (n. 36), p. 133.

47. See n. 1 of this paper regarding Willebrands' remark to the effect that "Cardinal Newman gave his Oratory an ecumenical spirit". In his address at Lambeth Palace in 1972, Willebrands noted that, "... personally, I attach a great importance to the spiritual nature of ecumenical relationships and the search for unity". See *Prospects for Anglican-Roman Catholic Relations* (n. 36), p. 103.

JOHANNES WILLEBRANDS AND THE CATHOLIC CONFERENCE FOR ECUMENICAL QUESTIONS (1952-1963)

If one would like to have a better understanding of the formative stage of Cardinal Willebrands' commitment to ecumenism, it is not only imperative to carefully study his commitment to ecumenism in the Netherlands[1], but also his period as secretary to the Catholic Conference for Ecumenical Questions (1952-1963)[2]. This responsibility prepared him well for his later task as secretary of the newly created Secretariat for Promoting Christian Unity, for which he obviously was the best candidate. Not only did his position as secretary of the conference allow him to establish close contacts with other, mainly European Catholic ecumenists and to be enriched by their input during the almost annual meetings of the conference, but he also entered in an ever closer contact with the leading voices within the World Council of Churches, especially Hans-Heinrich Harms, Director of the Study Division, and of course also the General Secretary, his fellow Dutchman Visser 't Hooft.

I will first highlight the endeavours of the conference and its spokesperson to be recognized as a legitimate body by the hierarchy of the Catholic Church. Thereafter I will focus on a document which can be considered as a major contribution by the CCEQ. The *Note du Comité Directeur de la 'Conférence Catholique pour les Questions œcuméniques' sur la restauration de l'Unité chrétienne à l'occasion du prochain Concile* was, after its release on June 15, 1959, sent to a number of cardinals, archbishops and bishops of the Catholic Church, but was never published in print. Thirdly, a careful study of the introductions which Willebrands pronounced during each of the nine plenary meetings of the conference makes us better informed about the ecumenical views of one of the major Catholic ecumenists of his generation in the decade preceding the Second Vatican Council. The study of these introductions consti-

---

1. See especially J. JACOBS, *Nieuwe visies op een oud visioen: Een portret van de Sint Willibrord Vereniging 1948-1998*, Tilburg, Valkhof Pers, 1998.
    2. We will regularly use the abbreviation CCEQ in this article. See for a longer version of this article in French: P. DE MEY, *Précurseur du Secrétariat pour l'Unité: Le travail oecuménique de la 'Conférence Catholique pour les Questions œcuméniques (1952-1963)*, in G. ROUTHIER – P.J. ROY – K. SCHELKENS (eds.), *La théologie catholique entre intransigeance et renouveau: La réception des mouvements préconciliaires à Vatican II*, Turnhout, Brepols, 2011, 271-308.

tutes an original contribution to research on Willebrands, even if there exist already some excellent historical studies on the CCEQ on which I could rely, such as the 1991 inaugural lecture of Jan Jacobs, *Naar één oecumenische beweging. De Katholieke Conferentie voor Oecumenische Vragen: een leerschool en gids*[3] and the monograph which Mauro Velati published in 1996 under the title *Una difficile transizione. Il cattolicesimo tra unionismo ed ecumenismo*[4].

I. THE CATHOLIC CONFERENCE FOR ECUMENICAL QUESTIONS AS AN
INSTITUTION LOOKING FOR ECCLESIASTICAL RECOGNITION

The idea to establish a *"Conseil Catholique œcuménique"*[5] was developed by representatives of the Dutch ecumenical association Saint Willibrord, in 1950, as Willebrands recalls during a conversation with father Vodopivec on May 18, 1960.

> The existence of the Conférence [Catholique] is something providential. How did you get this idea? I vividly remember the moment when the thought entered my head. In 1950, in Hotel Noord-Brabant in Utrecht, during the break of meeting of the SWV. I always had the feeling that Divine Providence had given me the idea, yet, I had always felt powerless and worthless to be given such a responsibility. The cooperation of all the members has been fantastic – and the growing importance of the Conférence [Catholique] has not reduced my sense of unworthiness and powerlessness. On the contrary. Although I have grown, through the support and help of so many, the real discrepancies between my own abilities, my preparedness and the task at hand, is only resolved in the Lord Jesus. Therein lies the problem of my trust in Him. Therein lies the core task of everything[6].

An initiative to regularly organise international meetings of Catholic ecumenists only made sense as of that year, in view of the changed

---

3. J. JACOBS, *'Naar één oecumenische beweging': De Katholieke Conferentie voor Oecumenische Vragen: een leerschool en gids. 1951-1965* (TFT-Redes, 4), Tilburg, Tilburg University Press, 1991.

4. M. VELATI, *Una difficile transizione: Il cattolicesimo tra unionismo ed ecumenismo (1952-1964)*, Bologna, Il Mulino, 1996.

5. "Projet d'un Conseil Catholique œcuménique" (FWC). Cardinal Willebrands entrusted the archive of the *Conférence Catholique pour les questions œcuméniques* to the Benedictine abbey of Chevetogne. I thank the abbey and its archivist, Fr. Lambert Vos, for allowing me to consult this material extensively. References to this archival material will be followed by the abbreviation FWC: Fonds Willebrands Chevetogne.

6. T. SALEMINK (ed.), *"You Will Be Called Repairer of the Breach": The Diary of J.G.M. Willebrands 1958-1961*, Leuven, Peeters, 2009, pp. 151-152.

policy within the Vatican. The monitum *Cum compertum* of June 1948 – which in a prohibitive tone had been written in response to the creation of the WCC – was luckily followed in March 1950 – the document, however, was dated December 20 1949 – by the instruction *De motione oecumenica*[7]. As is repeated at the beginning and the end of the document, non-Catholics Christians are invited to come back to the Catholic Church "as to the real and unique Church of Christ". The efforts to promote unity are interpreted by the instruction as taking place "under the inspiration of the grace of the Holy Spirit". Catholic readers are warned, however, that the tendency to focus "on what unites us rather than what separates us" may lead to "a dangerous indifferentism", and the document also expresses its concerns about the regularly heard plea to develop a so-called "irenic spirit". When the history of the Reformation is taught, one should not "exaggerate the Catholic mistakes" or "minimise the guilt of the reformers" – the painful distinction between the *Catholicorum defectus et culpae Reformatorum*[8]. The major goal of the instruction was, however, to give clear instructions to its addressees – the *locorum ordinarii* – on how to deal with "mixed reunions and conferences between Catholics and non-Catholics" in view of "promoting the 'reunion' in the faith" (*ad fovendam in fide "reunionem"*). They should never be organised without the agreement of the competent ecclesiastical authority. The local ordinary should grant permission before local meetings of believers or meetings of theologians should be organised. In the latter case the Holy Office should receive a yearly report "on the issues treated, the persons which took part and on who made the report on both sides". For conferences at an interdiocesan, national or international level the permission of the Holy See should be received before the event can be organised.

Protestant reactions to this document tend to emphasise that "its main thrust was that of warning"[9] and are even more critical of the other events of the same year 1950, the promulgation of the encyclical *Humani*

---

7. SUPREMA SACRA CONGREGATIO S. OFFICII, *Instructio ad locorum ordinarios: 'De motione oecumenica'*, in *Acta Apostolicae Sedis* 42 (1950) 142-147. Father Boyer published a French translation in the French language version of the periodical of the association *Unitas* of which he was the president, in July 1950 (3-7) and added a commentary to it (9-11) in which he insisted that the instruction tried to enforce the Catholic view on unity: "la seule union possible, la seule union légitime est celle du retour des dissidents à l'Église Romaine" (*ibid.*, p. 10).

8. *Ibid.*, p. 144.

9. L. VISCHER, *The Ecumenical Movement and the Roman Catholic Church*, in H.E. FEY (ed.), *A History of the Ecumenical Movement*. Volume 2: *1948-1969 – the Ecumenical Advance*, Geneva, WCC, 1970, 311-351, p. 316.

generis and of the dogma of the assumption of Mary. When, after the death of Pope Pius XII, the French Dominican and director of *Istina* Father Christophe Dumont was asked to write an assessment of the pope's contribution to ecumenism as part of a 1959 volume on *La vie de l'Église sous Pie XII*, he admitted that this pope did not take a great amount of new initiatives as his predecessor had done, but that the instruction *De motione oecumenica* or, according to its first words *Ecclesia Catholica*, "créera des possibilités de rapports que ne laissait pas espérer l'encyclique *Mortalium animos*", that it is "jusqu'à ce jour le document le plus explicite et en même temps le plus positif dont puisse se réclamer l'activité catholique en faveur de la restauration de l'unité chrétienne" and in the conclusion Dumont repeats that "grâce à l'Instruction *Ecclesia Catholica*, le grand travail catholique en faveur de l'unité s'est vu conférer droit de cité parmi les préoccupations générales et primordiales de l'Église"[10]. In his opening speeches Willebrands also regularly made an appeal – often in form of direct quotations – to the instruction and sometimes also to other magisterial documents, to indicate that the Catholic Conference for Ecumenical Questions intended to remain within the boundaries of the magisterial teaching on ecumenism[11].

In his article Dumont mentions the initiative taken by Father Charles Boyer to organise an international meeting of Catholic ecumenists in the Greek-Catholic abbey of Grottaferrata as part of the events of the Holy Year 1950 to have been one of the first fruits of the instruction of the Holy Office, and he deems it also important that the Holy Father granted an audience to this group in Castel Gandolfo. Even if neither Willebrands nor Father Thijssen, Willebrands' close cooperator in the Ecumenical Association Saint Willebrord, took part in the Grottaferrata meeting, their initiative to establish a Catholic Conference for Ecumenical Questions is considered to have been somehow the successor of the Boyer initiative. As Dumont writes in the same article: "Sur l'initiative de deux prêtres hollandais, fut repris le projet qui avait commencé de se réaliser deux ans plus tôt à Grottaferrata"[12]. In his opening speech for the 1952 meeting in Fribourg, which would afterwards appear to have been the first meeting

---

10. C.J. DUMONT, *L'œcuménisme*, in Mgr. G.M. GARRONE (ed.), *La vie de l'Église sous Pie XII* (Recherches et débats, 27), Paris, Fayard, 1959, 90-109. The quotations are found on pages 95, 101 and 109.

11. This is the case for his opening lecture in Fribourg and also for an article which he published soon after his nomination as secretary of the Secretariat for Promoting Christian Unity. Cf. J.G.M. WILLEBRANDS, *Il movimento ecumenico: Sviluppe e speranze*, in *Humanitas* 15 (1960) 263-277, p. 264.

12. DUMONT, *L'œcuménisme* (n. 9), p. 106.

of the CCEQ, Willebrands courteously referred at the very beginning of his speech to the link between the new event and the Grottaferrata initiative[13]. Willebrands and Thijssen succeeded in taking this pan-European initiative because they had visited all major Catholic ecumenists and because the initiative had not been taken in Rome[14].

A first remarkable characteristic of the CCEQ is its endeavour to strictly follow the regulations of the Vatican for the organization of such events and also to seek for ecclesiastical recognition. In fact, they always sought the permission of the local ordinaries of all places where a plenary meeting of the conference would be held: Fribourg (1952), Utrecht (1953), Mainz (1954), Paris (1955), Chevetogne (1957), Paderborn (1959), Gazzada (1960 & 1963) and Strasbourg (1961), and the participants were also asked to obtain the blessing of their ordinaries before participating in the meetings of the conference. The local ordinaries were also asked to assume the presidency of these meetings or to delegate this to someone else in their stead. For that reason Willebrands referred to himself deliberately as secretary. It was considered to be highly relevant when the local ordinaries even accepted to deliver a welcome address to their meetings. In the Chevetogne archives I found the text of one such address. Admittedly, the speech of the co-adjutor from Utrecht, Mgr. Alfrink, during the conference in Dijnselburg, near Utrecht, in 1953, focused especially on the importance of the apostolate of converting non-Catholics, which in his diocese resulted in 1000 conversions a year[15].

The reaction of Father Villain from Lyon is worth quoting in full:

> Quelle surprise et quel choc! "Nous aussi, nous faisons de l'œcuménisme", prononça le prélat dès l'exorde. Mais de quel œcuménisme s'agissait-il? La réponse venait dès la seconde phrase: il s'agissait de convertir les protestants, à commencer par les pasteurs, et l'orateur exposait dans tout leur détail, les diverses méthodes de conversion en usage dans l'archidiocèse.

---

13. WILLEBRANDS, "Introduction à la conférence catholique œcuménique de Fribourg" (FWC), p. 1.

14. Cf. "Projet d'un Conseil Catholique œcuménique" (FWC), p. 7: "Il nous semble désirable que le Secrétariat ne soit pas établi à Rome, mais dans un pays où existe un contact vivant avec les chrétiens séparés: a) car ainsi il sera d'autant plus facile de distinguer entre le Conseil et les autorités ecclésiastiques officielles et de désavouer le Conseil, le cas échéant; b) ainsi il sera d'autant plus facile d'obtenir des informations et d'établir des contacts; c) il sera d'autant plus facile d'exécuter les directives, c'est-à-dire sur place même; d) les frères séparés s'y rapporteront plus commodément. Un petit pays, où existe un contact vécu et vivant avec les chrétiens séparés offrirait peut-être les meilleures garanties pour le siège du Secrétariat général".

15. WILLEBRANDS, "Introduction à la conférence de Dijnselburg par S. Exc. Mgr. B. Alfrink. 6 août 1953" (FWC).

J'étais assis entre le P. Congar et le P. Dumont. À chaque nouveau couplet, nous baissions la tête un peu plus. À la fin, ma tête touchait mes genoux[16].

The consultation with the largest presence of representatives of the hierarchy was undoubtedly the first one which took place on Italian soil, in Gazzada 1960. As Willebrands recalls in his opening address of the Strasbourg conference one year later: "La présence de trois Cardinaux (le Cardinal Alfrink, archevêque d'Utrecht, le Card. Montini, archevêque de Milan et le Card. Bea, Président du Secrétariat pour l'Unité des Chrétiens) lui a donné une splendeur nouvelle, qui a marqué en même temps l'importance du travail œcuménique et l'intérêt qu'y porte la Hiérarchie de l'Église"[17]. It was especially welcomed that Augustin Cardinal Bea, the president of the recently created Secretariat for Promoting Christian Unity, was present and addressed the conference. In his address he recognized that "la 'Conférence Catholique' a été une espèce de préparation officieuse, en même temps d'ailleurs que d'autres institutions similaires, au Secrétariat pour l'Unité des Chrétiens" and he explicitly referred to the fact that many of the members and consultors of the secretariat had been selected out of the active members of the conference[18]. His address also contained personal thanks for the work of "son infatigable secrétaire Monseigneur Willebrands qui désormais pourra se consacrer entièrement à cet important travail pour l'Union en y apportant la grande expérience et la vaste connaissance qu'il a acquises dans sa précédente activité". In the already mentioned opening address of the Strasbourg meeting of the CCEQ, Willebrands highly spoke of this address in the following words: "Le discours du Card. Bea et le dialogue suivant entre Son Eminence et les participants, l'appréciation et la reconnaissance, exprimées par le Cardinal, pour le travail œcuménique des Centres, des Instituts, des Monastères, et pour le travail individuel, ont

16. M. VILLAIN, *Vers l'unité: Itinéraire d'un pionnier 1935-1975*, Lyon, s.d., 208, as quoted in VELATI, *Una difficile transizione* (n. 3), p. 59.

17. WILLEBRANDS, "Strasbourg" (FWC), p. 1.

18. Augustin Cardinal Bea, "Éminence, Excellence, Messeigneurs, Messieurs" (FWC), p. 1. See also the impressive account of the involvement of many members of the Catholic Conference in the work of the secretariat, in THE PONTIFICAL COUNCIL FOR PROMOTING CHRISTIAN UNITY, *A Tribute to Johannes Cardinal Willebrands on the Occasion of His Ninetieth Birthday*, in *Information Service* 101 (1999/II-III) 66-69. Msgr. Radano also mentions the reason why members of the Catholic Conference were obvious candidates for this task: "Some of the CCEQ theologians could bring to it a sense of *commitment* to and support for this new official ecumenical initiative in the Catholic Church, a rich *experience* of study and struggle precisely with ecumenical issues, and in some cases, especially in the years and decades after the Second Vatican Council, a *perspective* on the dramatic ecumenical transition that the Catholic Church had been going through" (*ibid.*, p. 66).

donné un grand encouragement et une joie profonde à tous ceux qui étaient présents"[19]. At this point we can also add a quotation from the newly published diary, from the entry on September 21, 1960:

> Early in the morning, Cardinal Bea arrives, and celebrates the Community Mass. The Cardinal speaks at the first session and responds to an hour and a half of questioning. This gathering is the high point of the Conference. We have never experienced anything like this before. The openness, the caring, the depth of Cardinal Bea makes a lasting impression. How many people are here, who have given their life to work for unity, to work for the separated brothers, without ever receiving any encouragement or gratitude from the hierarchical institutions? Now there is a special blessing from the Holy Father for their work. Later, Père Congar speaks about "un miracle dans l'Église"[20].

The history of the CCEQ also makes it clear that Willebrands, in line with the instruction of the Holy Office, regularly reported in Rome about the work of the conference. Perhaps somewhat remarkable in light of this cardinal's fame, in his diaries Willebrands always has the feeling that Cardinal Ottaviani appreciates his work very much. The entry of March 3, 1959 refers to an audience in which Willebrands receives the request to collect all reactions of non-Catholics to the announcement of the council during which Ottaviani had said: "Tu sei molto bravo!". On June 23 of the same year Willebrands presents the memorandum of the Executive Committee of the CCEQ on the ecumenical tasks of the forthcoming council to Cardinal Ottaviani. The cardinal expressed the hope that "it would serve as a preparation for the Council".

The contacts with the Catholic hierarchy were not always fruitful, however. Willebrands' opening lecture of the 1954 conference in Mainz makes reference to the rather late attempt to obtain the permission of Cardinal Stritch of Chicago to allow for the presence of observers on behalf of the CCEQ at the WCC world assembly in Evanston. Willebrands already feels that the answer might be negative, but acquiesces in the decision of the Catholic hierarchy: "Persönlich glaube ich eine negative Antwort erwarten zu müssen. Aber auch dann haben wir Grund zur Dankbarkeit, dass wir etwas tun durften um dieser Sache zu dienen"[21]. Since 1956 Willebrands was in regular contact with the secretary of the International League for Apostolic Faith and Order (ILAFO), an

---

19. WILLEBRANDS, "Strasbourg" (FWC), p. 1.
20. SALEMINK (ed.), *"You Will Be Called Repairer of the Breach"* (n. 5), p. 209.
21. "Katholische Konferenz für oekumenische Fragen. Arbeitstagung: 21.-24. April 1954, Priesterseminar, Mainz. Einleitung: Prof. Dr. J.G. Willebrands (Sekretär)" (FWC), p. 6.

association of Protestant and Orthodox theologians which had been founded in 1950 to promote the "catholic" tradition in their Churches[22]. The CCEQ received the invitation to participate in the ILAFO meeting in 1957 during which the themes of 'The necessity of the episcopate' and 'The sacrifice of the Holy Mass' would be discussed. After it had been agreed that the CCEQ would delegate six members for this ecumenical encounter, permission was sought from the Bishop of Southwark, who refused by sending a rather vehement letter. Willebrands did not hesitate to express his indignation about this decision in Rome, where he received support from Father Tromp who believed that the ordinary should have referred the decision to Rome, following the procedure for international encounters contained in the 1949 instruction of the Holy Office[23].

II. THE COMITÉ DIRECTEUR'S NOTE ON THE OCCASION OF THE ANNOUNCEMENT OF THE COUNCIL

Even when it is difficult to measure the concrete impact of this initiative, it would seem that the decision by the Comité Directeur of the CCEQ to prepare and disseminate a 'Note sur la restauration de l'Unité chrétienne à l'occasion du prochain Concile'[24], may have been among the most important initiatives taken by Roman Catholic ecumenical bodies in order to promote an ecumenical spirit within the Roman Catholic Church, or at least among its hierarchy, in the decade before Vatican II. In his 1992 contribution "'Mouvements' théologico-spirituels et concile

22. As the statutes indicate: "By 'Apostolic Order' is meant the priestly threefold ministry of bishops, priests and deacons duly consecrated or ordained by bishops in the Apostolic Succession and in the Communion of the Catholic Church". Cf. "International League for Apostolic Faith and Order. Bulletin No 1" (FWC), p. 1.

23. "Réunion du Comité Directeur de la Conférence catholique pour les questions œcuméniques tenue le 14 déc. 1957 à Rome" (FWC), p. 6: "(Le secrétaire a rendu une visite au R.P. Tromp, s.j., le 16 décembre. Le R.P. Tromp s'est montré très étonné, voire même un peu indigné, du refus de l'évêque de Southwark quant à notre participation à la réunion de Pulborough. Il a dit qu'un évêque local ne pouvait pas avoir le mot décisif en la matière d'une réunion internationale. Dans le cas de Pulborough, le refus de l'évêque était certainement contre la tendance et l'avis de l'instruction du Saint-Office de 1949. Pour l'avenir, il a demandé au secrétaire d'avertir à temps le Saint-Office d'une telle réunion, afin de ne pas courir le risque de travailler en vain)".

24. "Note du Comité Directeur de la 'Conférence Catholique pour les Questions œcuméniques' sur la restauration de l'Unité chrétienne à l'occasion du prochain Concile" (15 p.). Quotations in English are taken from the translation revised by Willebrands himself: "Memorandum from the Executive Committee of the 'Catholic Council for Oecumenical Questions' concerning the restoration of Christian Unity on the occasion of the forthcoming Oecumenical Council" (33 p.).

(1959-1962)" Étienne Fouilloux focuses exclusively on this text as illustration of the fact that "le mouvement œcuménique a également le vent en poupe" and his short *laudatio* is worth quoting in full:

> Son principal intérêt est de définir avec précision la position des œcuménistes catholiques avant même la fondation du Secrétariat pour l'unité et la rédaction des schémas préparatoires au concile: on peut donc lui accorder le statut de votum du mouvement œcuménique de souche catholique dans son ensemble[25].

After providing a short summary of the document he concludes:

> Ces vœux seront effectivement retenus par Vatican II. À cet égard, la note est indéniablement, et parmi d'autres, une des sources lointaines, non seulement du décret sur l'œcuménisme, mais d'autres décisions majeures de l'assemblée. Son mélange de modestie, voire de prudence, et d'espoirs réalistes paraît assez représentatif de la phase originale et méconnue qui court de l'annonce du concile à son autonomisation par rapport à la Curie[26].

Before providing a close reading of this document and indicating its potential influence on particular conciliar texts a few words on the history of its composition and dissemination are in order. The recently published diary of Willebrands on the 1958-1961 period will prove to be particularly helpful here. Remarkably there is no diary entry on January 25, 1959, but the report of Willebrands' short trip to Strasbourg on February 7-9 to meet Dom Rousseau and Père Congar to discuss the theme of the next Journées œcuméniques de Chevetogne opens with a surprise. Father Dumont, his co-member in the Comité Directeur of the CCEQ, had made the journey from Paris to Strasbourg as well so that the four of them could have a meeting on the future council. The diary, normally written in Dutch, now switches to French to indicate that Willebrands is transmitting Dumont's reflections in his diary: "Que pourra faire notre Conférence? Il semble qu'elle a une responsabilité et doit prendre une initiative"[27]. The CCEQ, being the "only international group" having "direct relations with the WCC" should prepare the bishops of the Catholic Church and their theologians in view of the coming Council. An urgent meeting of the Comité Directeur was scheduled for February 26, and in the mean-time Father Dumont would draft a text whereas

---

25. É. FOUILLOUX, *'Mouvements' théologico-spirituels et concile (1959-1962)*, in M. LAMBERIGTS – C. SOETENS (eds.), *À la veille du Concile Vatican II: Vota et réactions en Europe et dans le catholicisme oriental* (Instrumenta Theologica, 9), Leuven, Bibliotheek van de Faculteit Godgeleerdheid, 1992, 185-199, p. 197.

26. *Ibid.*, p. 198.

27. SALEMINK (ed.), *"You Will Be Called Repairer of the Breach"* (n. 5), p. 76.

Willebrands would inform Father Boyer and Msgr. Höfer, the other co-members of the Comité Directeur. Boyer and Höfer make no objections[28], and on the first of March Willebrands discusses Dumont's draft and formulates some remarks. The diary expresses some worries: "What will we do with this report? Will the Comité Directeur sign it? P. Boyer? Shall we send it to the Bishops"[29]? The diary reports Father Boyer's "favourable response on the draft of the report" on March 3, but we have to wait till a report of a meeting at *Istina* on May 13, to encounter Willebrands and Dumont discussing the incoming remarks. During this meeting the idea is raised "to present the project to Cardinal Ottaviani, and to Tardini and Tisserant"[30]. Ottaviani had become the Secretary to the Holy Office in 1959, Tardini was Pope John XXIII's Secretary of State, and Tisserant the Dean of the College of Cardinals. The memorandum would also be sent to the archbishops and cardinals of the Catholic Church for discussion "dans les réunions épiscopales de sa province"[31]. The final version of the report was approved during the meeting of the Comité Directeur on June 15-16. Willebrands' diary mentions that Tardini could not receive him because of a visit of Général De Gaulle, but that he was cordially received by Cardinal Ottaviani. His secretary Father Father Paul-Henri Philippe o.p., commissioner of the Holy Office, promised that the Note would be transmitted to the *commissio ante-preparatoria* and would "not be read through 'black glasses'"[32].

The document reflects the results of a decade of intensive study by the CCEQ of the theological positions of the churches issued from the Reformation and their ecumenical relations within the World Council of Churches. Its main drafter, Father Dumont, was director of *Istina* and a specialist of the East. Because all co-authors of the text would soon

---

28. VELATI, *Una difficile transizione* (n. 3), p. 144, quotes from Willebrands' report of this meeting: "Que pouvons-nous faire en ce temps de préparation? La question de la restauration de l'unité chrétienne a été posée. Les futurs participants du concile, les pères abbés et les évêques, ainsi que les théologiens du concile, se sont-ils préparés à cette question? Il faut que nous composions aussi vite que possible un aperçu de la situation: comment l'église orthodoxe se présente-t-elle aujourd'hui à nous et comment la chrétienté protestante et réformée?".

29. SALEMINK (ed.), *"You Will Be Called Repairer of the Breach"* (n. 5), p. 82.

30. *Ibid.*, p. 96.

31. "Projet de lettre d'envoi de la 'Note' de notre 'Conférence' aux Cardinaux et Archevêques" (FWC).

32. SALEMINK (ed.), *"You Will Be Called Repairer of the Breach"* (n. 5), p. 106. Cf. VELATI, *Una difficile transizione* (n. 3), p. 151: "In mancanza di una documentazione certa risulta difficile stabilire se essa giunse anche nelle mani di Giovanni XXIII". Velati knows of one similar initiative of the Swiss ecumenist Otto Karrer, entitled *Pour le Concile Œcuménique*, which was sent in May 1959 to the bishops of Switzerland.

assume important roles within the Secretariat for Promoting Christian Unity, as secretary (Willebrands), voting members (Boyer, Davis) and consultors (Dumont, Höfer), the ideas expressed in this document easily found their way in the work of the secretariat, and above all in the composition of the Decree on Ecumenism, *Unitatis Redintegratio*. Therefore, I will introduce the most remarkable statements of the document while making a small comparison with conciliar documents.

First of all we draw attention to the *title* of the document, which speaks about "the restoration of Christian Unity". In the section after the introduction, 'Some preliminary psychological difficulties' (§§3-9), a plea is made to use the term "return" only in a very careful way since it is easily misunderstood (§5). When the final redaction of the Decree on Ecumenism decided to add an introduction to the decree, the opening words thereof sound very similar to the title of the Note: "unitatis redintegratio inter universos christianos", "the restoration of unity among all Christians"[33]. It is important to understand the prefix 're' in "redintegratio" in the right way. One does not plead for a return to the Roman Catholic Church, but to the common effort among all Christians to reach a new goal, namely the unity among Christians[34]. As to the Note, however, one may wonder how such a carefully selected title and a concern for a politically correct terminology can be harmonized with the regular references in the document to "the problem of reunion" (§3, §20), "attempts at reunion" (§24), or with the document's sympathy for High Church movements in other Christian churches because they foster "harmonious relations" and "reunion" (§37). Bernd Jochen Hilberath for his part starts the concluding section of his theological commentary on *Unitatis Redintegratio* with a subtitle in the form of a question: "Ende der Rückkehr-Ökumene?", especially when he realizes that reunion terminology is not completely absent in a description of his ecumenical dreams by Cardinal Jaeger of Paderborn[35].

33. UR 1 considers "redintegrare" and "restaurare" as synonyms: the paragraph speaks about "unitatis redintegratio", "ad omnium christianorum unitatem restaurandam", "unitatis inter omnes Christi discipulos restaurandae". References to conciliar documents are taken from N.P. TANNER, S.J. (ed.), *Decrees of the Ecumenical Councils*, London, Sheed & Ward; Washington, DC, Georgetown University Press, 1990.

34. Cf. B.J. HILBERATH, *Theologischer Kommentar zum Dekret über den Ökumenismus* Unitatis redintegratio, in P. HÜNERMANN – B.J. HILBERATH (eds.), *Herders Theologischer Kommentar zum Zweiten Vatikanischen Konzil*, Freiburg – Basel – Wien, Herder, 2005, 69-223, p. 109.

35. L. JAEGER, *Das Konzilsdekret "Uber den Ökumenismus": Sein Werden, sein Inhalt und seine Bedeutung*, Paderborn, Bonifacius, 1968, p. 108 as quoted in HILBERATH, *Theologischer Kommentar zum Dekret über den Ökumenismus* Unitatis redintegratio (n. 34), p. 200: "Dabei sagen wir in aller Aufrichtigkeit, dass nach unserem Glauben die

Another psychological counsel is given in the first paragraph of the memorandum: that Catholics should cease giving "an equal importance to that which is essential and to that which is accidental, to the unchangeable substance and to secondary determinations always subject to revision and transitory historic circumstances"[36] (§5). This finds its echo in the famous opening address to the council delivered by Pope John XXIII on October 11, 1962[37]. The CCEQ also anticipates the Council in stating that, when Catholics believe they have to avoid the term "Church" to indicate other Christian bodies, they in turn should avoid using terminology which lacks any ecclesial reference, and ought to use a term such as "communion"[38].

In the next paragraph, 'The unprepared state of people's minds' (§§10-19), the document wonders whether the bishops are sufficiently prepared to make objective statements concerning other Christian churches when gathered in a council. From this paragraph onwards the document addresses "the East" (§11), "the Anglican Communion" (§16) and "the communions stemming from the Reformation" (§19) separately. The council as well decided in the third and last chapter of the Decree on Ecumenism to make a distinction between its reflection on the dialogue with on the one hand 'The Eastern churches' (UR 14-18) and on the other hand the 'Separated churches and ecclesial communities in the west' (UR 19-24). The opening paragraph of this chapter alludes to the bridge function of the Anglican churches when it states that, among the churches of the Reformation and especially "among those in which catholic traditions and institutions in part continue to subsist, the Anglican communion occupies a special place" (UR 13).

Wiederherstellung der Einheit sich durch die Einheit aller Christen in der römisch-katholischen Kirche vollziehen wird, in welcher die einige Kirche subsistiert. Wenn alle Kirchen zusammen ihre Treue gegen den Herrn immer neu prüfen, dann kann in der Zukunft eine Wiederherstellung der Einheit geschehen unter Umständen, die wir uns noch nicht vorstellen können. Die Einheit wird eine Gabe des Heiligen Geistes sein".

36. §5: "Il importe grandement de ne pas laisser croire que tout soit à nos yeux irréformable dans l'Église et que nous attachions une égale importance à l'essentiel et à l'accidentel, à la substance immuable et aux déterminations secondaires, toujours révisibles, fruits de circonstances historiques passagères".

37. Cf. John XXIII's opening speech at the Council *Gaudet Mater Ecclesia*, October 11, 1962 – in French translation in order to allow for an easy comparison with the original French text of the *Note* quoted in the previous footnote: "En effet, autre est le dépôt lui-même de la foi, c'est-à-dire les vérités contenues dans notre vénérable doctrine, et autre est la forme sous laquelle ces vérités sont énoncées, en leur conservant toutefois le même sens et la même portée. Il faudra attacher beaucoup d'importance à cette forme et travailler patiemment, s'il le faut, à son élaboration; et on devra recourir à une façon de présenter qui correspond mieux à un enseignement de caractère surtout pastoral".

38. For the same reason the Council used the term *communitates ecclesiales*. See a.o. LG 15 & UR 19.

Moreover, when referring to "the communions stemming from the Reformation" the Note states: "[I]t is scarcely necessary to emphasize how numerous and profound are the dogmatic and canonical differences that any attempt at reunion would have to overcome"[39]. In the same vein UR 19 reads: "However, since these churches and ecclesial communities, on account of their differences of origin, doctrine and spirituality, differ considerably not only from us but also among themselves, the task of describing them adequately is extremely difficult; and we have no intention of making such an attempt here".

The most remarkable statement of this paragraph is the awareness that till now, in Roman Catholic ecclesiology, "an exact conception of the 'catholicity' of the Church, made up of unity in diversity, ... has not yet been attempted in all its dimensions"[40] (§14). The document then explains that a correct understanding of catholicity implies "the legitimacy of a triple pluralism, liturgical, canonical and theological". We are confronted here with an understanding of catholicity which goes much further than Congar's attempt in chapter three of *Chrétiens désunis* to pay as much attention to the diversity in the unity as to the unity in the diversity[41]. In a paper *De ecumenismo catholico et de opere conversionum* which another (albeit rather irregular) member of the CCEQ Gustave Thils, had presented in August 1961 during a plenary meeting of the Secretariat for Promoting Christian Unity, he almost defended the same idea[42]. One had to wait till the second intersession before this

39. *Note*, §19: "En ce qui concerne les communions issues de la Réforme, il est à peine besoin de souligner le nombre et la profondeur des divergences dogmatiques et canoniques qu'une tentative de réunion aurait à surmonter".

40. *Note*, §14: "Une question, capitale cependant pour une juste conception de la 'catholicité' de l'Église, faite d'unité dans la diversité, n'a pas été abordée jusqu'ici dans toute son ampleur: c'est celle de la légitimité d'un triple pluralisme, liturgique, canonique et théologique".

41. Y.M.-J. CONGAR, *Chrétiens désunis* (Unam Sanctam, 1), Paris, Cerf, 1937, pp. 115-148, here p. 123: "La notion même de catholicité implique un rapport du divers à l'unité et de l'unité au divers". J. FAMERÉE – G. ROUTHIER, *Yves Congar* (Initiations aux théologiens), Paris, Cerf, 2008, pp. 238-242, of course rightly state that catholicity is precisely the notion which forms the red thread throughout Congar's entire work.

42. SECRETARIATUS AD CHRISTIANORUM UNITATEM FOVENDAM, *Sub Commissio III: "De Oecumenismo catholico et de opere conversionum"*, Feria V, 31/8/1961 (FThils 499): "L'Église peut parfaitement intégrer une pluralité de rites, de liturgies, de formes théologiques, de traditions disciplinaires". Cf. P. DE MEY, *Gustave Thils and Ecumenism at Vatican II*, in D. DONNELLY – J. FAMERÉE – M. LAMBERIGTS – K. SCHELKENS (eds.), *The Belgian Contribution to the Second Vatican Council* (BETL, 216), Leuven, Peeters, 2008, 389-414, p. 402.

mature theology of catholicity was eventually introduced in LG 13 and 23, as it is also found in UR 4 and 14-17[43].

The short paragraph entitled 'The need to distinguish without dissociating' (§§20-23) repeats the need to make distinctions between churches if the Council wishes to address the ecumenical question as it should be done. For the Catholic Church it makes a difference whether one is dealing with "a) Christian communions having preserved the form as well as the reality of the sacramental structures of the episcopacy; b) those communions having deliberately rejected this structure; c) those having preserved the form although they have lost the reality"[44]. This is immediately applied to the Eucharist: "What is especially at stake is the reality of the Eucharist, the Lord's Sacramental Body, the significance of which is directly related to that of the Mystical Body, the Church, and the very existence of which depends upon an ontological relationship with it"[45] (§20). The full paragraph is quoted here because it is not improbable that members of the Secretariat for Promoting Christian Unity recalled this text when composing the famous though not undisputed §22 of *Unitatis Redintegratio*: "Though the ecclesial communities which are separated from us lack the fullness of unity with us which flows from baptism, and though we believe they have not retained the authentic and full reality of the Eucharistic mystery, especially because the sacrament of orders is lacking, nevertheless when they commemorate his death and resurrection in the Lord's supper, they profess that it signifies life in communion with Christ and look forward to his coming in glory"[46].

---

43. See e.g. LG 23: "By divine providence it has come about that various churches, founded in various places by the apostles and by their successors, have in the course of time become joined together into several groups, organically united, which, while maintaining the unity of faith and the unique divine constitution of the universal church, enjoy their own discipline, their own liturgical usage and their own theological and spiritual patrimony". UR 4: "All in the church must preserve unity in essentials. But let all, according to the gifts they have received, maintain a proper freedom in their various forms of spiritual life and discipline, in their different liturgical rites, and even in their theological elaborations of revealed truth. In all things let charity prevail".

44. *Note*, §20: "Les réflexions qui précèdent ne font que rappeler, en la précisant, cette constatation élémentaire que le problème de la réunion se présente, historiquement et théologiquement, de façon différente selon qu'il s'agit: a) des communions chrétiennes ayant conservé la forme et la réalité d'une structure épiscopale sacramentelle; b) de celles qui ont délibérément rejeté cette structure; c) ou de celles qui, tout en ayant conservé la forme, en ont perdu la réalité".

45. *Ibid.*: "Ce qui est en cause, en particulier, c'est la réalité de l'eucharistie, corps sacramentel du Seigneur, dont la signification est étroitement apparentée à celle du Corps mystique qu'est l'Église et qui ne saurait être sans relation ontologique avec lui".

46. Cf. WILLEBRANDS, "Introduction à la conférence catholique œcuménique de Fribourg", p. 3: "Les protestants ont conservé la commémoration de la Cène à laquelle ils n'attribuent plus le caractère du sacrifice et dans laquelle beaucoup entre eux nient la

While making these distinctions, the document states almost in passing that "it is not unreasonable to expect that reunion with the Orthodox may be more easily and more rapidly achieved than with the Protestants"[47] (§22). The pathetic tone with which the Council addresses the Orthodox churches in UR 14-18 gives me the impression that the Council fathers five years later were still hoping pretty much for the same[48]. If the Orthodox churches only would embrace one further "element" of Roman Catholic ecclesiology, then the full communion between both churches would soon be celebrated.

The paragraph ends with the warning that an intensification of contacts with the Orthodox from the part of the Catholic Church should not hinder the ecumenical relations of the Orthodox churches with other churches, "whether or no within the framework of the World Council of Churches" (§23). In light of these words it is very much ironical that the main drafter of the Note, Father Dumont, together with Msgr. Willebrands, a few months later would fall in precisely this trap during the so-called Rhodes incident. Willebrands and Dumont had received the permission of Cardinal Ottaviani to attend a meeting of the Central Committee of the World Council of Churches in Rhodes (August 19-27) as journalists. The WCC's Secretary General Visser 't Hooft was furious when he was informed through Radio Vaticana about an informal meeting which had taken place between the two Catholic observers and an unexpectedly large delegation of Orthodox in view of starting bilateral relations between both churches. As a result of this incident, a meeting between the CCEQ and the Division of Studies of the WCC which was scheduled to take place in October 1959 in Assisi – and for which Cardinal Ottaviani had equally given permission – had to be cancelled. According to some interpreters the Rhodes incident accelerated the process of establishing the Secretariat for Promoting Christian Unity[49].

---

realis presentia. Mais ils reconnaissent en elle un instrument de salut et de l'union le plus intime avec le Christ".

47. *Note*, §22: "[I]l est raisonable d'espérer, en effet, que la réunion des Orthodoxes pourra être obtenue plus facilement et plus rapidement que celle des Protestants".

48. See especially UR 16: "To remove all shadow of doubt, then, this synod solemnly declares that the churches of the east, while mindful of the necessary unity of the whole church, have the right to govern themselves according to the disciplines proper to themselves, since these are better suited to the character of their faithful, and more for the good of their souls".

49. JACOBS, *'Naar één oecumenische beweging'* (n. 2), p. 24. In my opinion, however, one can difficultly conclude from the Rhodes incident that the 1957 meeting of the CCQO in Chevetogne was a disaster. Jacobs describes the Rhodes incident as part of a paragraph entitled: 'De conferentie in augustus 1957 te Chevetogne: de mislukking van een veelbelovend initiatief' (19-24). See for a recent detailed account of the incident, K. SCHELKENS,

A final methodological observation (§§24-26) deals with the existence of "basic difficulties" among churches. The document explains that the doctrinal positions of the churches constitute "a fairly coherent whole" which is guided by a "first principle". In UR 11 this insight assumed the form of pastoral advice to Catholic specialists in ecumenism trying to explain the logic of Catholic doctrine to non-Catholics: "When comparing doctrines with one another, they should remember that in catholic doctrine there exists an order or 'hierarchy' of truths, since they vary in their connection with the foundation of the Christian faith"[50]. Of course, when reading this subtitle, one is also reminded of the current discussion among ecumenists who promote 'consensus ecumenism' and others, disappointed with the *Joint Declaration on the Doctrine of Justification*, who plead for an 'ecumenism of difference'[51].

'The present situation' (§§27-41) has convinced the authors of the document that there exists in each of the three mentioned groups of churches with regard to ecumenism a lot of 'unfavorable factors', 'favorable factors' and 'factors with both favorable and unfavorable aspects'. One of the favorable factors mentioned was well remembered in the process of drafting the Decree of Ecumenism, i.e. "the growing conviction shared by an ever-increasing number of the faithful of all denominations, together with their pastors of the harm caused by our divisions, both in the resistance offered by Christians to the forces of evil and to the rising tide of materialism in all its forms, no less than in our common efforts for the spread of the Kingdom of Christ throughout the world"[52] (§32). The introduction to UR states: "Such division is clearly contrary to Christ's will. It is a scandal to the world and damages the sacred cause of preaching the gospel to every creature". Perhaps a bit unwise for

L'*"affaire de Rhodes" au jour le jour: La correspondance inédite entre J. Willebrands et C.J. Dumont*, in *Istina* 54 (2009) 253-277.

50. Cf. already C.-J. DUMONT, *Les voies de l'unité chrétienne: Doctrine et spiritualité*, Paris, Cerf, 1954, pp. 157-161: "Y a-t-il une hiérarchie des valeurs entre les vérités de foi?". The question is answered with a 'yes' but in a very nuanced way: "Du point de vue catholique, ce serait donc une attitude erronée et fâcheuse dans nos efforts de restauration de l'Unité chrétienne que d'envisager la possibilité même en matière doctrinale d'un compromis qui, sous prétexte de hiérarchie des valeurs, sacrifierait les vérités de second plan, les abandonnant à une adhésion facultative. Mais l'attitude inverse ne serait ni moins erronée, ni moins fâcheuse, qui consisterait, prétextant le caractère également obligatoire de toutes les vérités de foi, à ne plus tenir compte, pratiquement, dans notre vie de la nécessaire hiérarchie de leurs valeurs".

51. Cf. U. KÖRTNER, *Wohin steuert die Ökumene? Vom Konsens- zum Differenzmodell*, Göttingen, Vandenhoeck & Ruprecht, 2005. See also M. HIETAMÄKI, *Agreeable Agreement: An Examination of the Quest for Consensus in Ecumenical Dialogue*, New York, T&T Clark, 2010.

52. *Note*, §32.

Protestant-Catholic relationships, strategically speaking, is the remark that the Orthodox churches became better aware of "a fundamental community of opinion with Catholicism in the field of ecclesiology and theology"[53] (§33) precisely through their encounters with Protestant confessions. The memorandum also mentions the growing opinion "that the schism is the perpetuation of a quarrel between the two hierarchies, a quarrel of no direct concern to layfolk and which could easily be brought to an end by a sincere effort at goodwill on both sides"[54] (*ibid.*). This growing awareness culminated, as is well-known, in the lifting of the mutual anathemas on December 7, 1965. The existence of Eastern rite communities in communion with the Catholic Church, however, is mentioned as an example of an ambivalent reality. They are "a positive affirmation in the very bosom of the Catholic Church of her true universal character, open to every legitimate diversity", whereas they also constitute "a menace" to the Orthodox, "even though they carefully abstain from all proselytism"[55] (§38).

The final question raised in this memorandum is: 'How ought the Catholic Church to give expression to her goodwill?' (§§42-55). One of the first things which the CCEQ proposes so that ecumenical progress be made is to focus less on the canonical dimension of the problem of reunion and more on "communion (koinonia)"[56] among churches. This

---

53. *Note*, §33: "En ce qui concerne plus précisément les Églises Orthodoxes: a) le sentiment, acquis à l'occasion des rencontres avec les confessions protestantes au sein du Conseil œcuménique, d'une fondamentale communauté de vues avec le catholicisme en matière ecclésiologique et théologique".

54. *Ibid.*: "c) le sentiment assez répandu dans l'opinion publique que le schisme est une querelle entre nos hiérarchies respectives, querelle à laquelle les simples fidèles ne sont pas directement intéressés et qui pourrait prendre fin avec quelque bonne volonté réciproque".

55. *Note*, §38: "D'une part, une fraction – très minime jusqu'ici – de l'opinion publique des Églises Orthodoxes y voit une amorce et un heureux prototype de l'union rétablie entre l'Église latine et l'Église d'Orient. En outre, sans parler des bienfaits propres que ces communautés tirent de leur communion avec l'Église catholique quant à l'élévation de leur niveau général intellectuel et spirituel, Elles sont au sein de l'Église catholique une affirmation concrète de son caractère universel, ouvert à toute légitime diversité; éventuellement même une revendication en faveur du droit de cité effectif des traditions propres de l'Église d'Orient au sein de l'Église universelle. Ce sont là autant de facteurs favorables. Mais, d'autre part, leur seule existence – a fortiori leur activité, même si elle s'abstient de tout 'prosélytisme' formel vis-à-vis des Orthodoxes – est ressentie par nos frères séparés orientaux comme une menace, une manœuvre déloyale dérigée contre les Églises Orthodoxes afin de leur arracher par ruse leurs fidèles, attitude jugée incompatible avec une recherche sincère et une proposition loyale de réunion". UR 17, for its part, only speaks in a positive way about the Eastern Catholic churches: "This synod thanks God that many eastern daughters and sons of the catholic church, who preserve this heritage and wish to express it more faithfully and completely in their lives, are ready living in full communion with their brothers and sisters who follow the tradition of the west".

56. The reference to the Greek term, which is common in ecumenical literature nowadays, is surprising for a 1959 Roman Catholic document.

communion or "the visible unity of the Church" is being defined as "the re-establishment of that entire communion of faith, discipline, and sacramental life"[57] (§44). The argumentation of the memorandum is worth to be quoted in full:

> There is an obvious psychological advantage to be derived from a theological approach such as this. For if on the canonical level the question of the relationship of a local Church to the one, universal Church may be resolved only by an unequivocal "yes" or "no", the reply to the question concerning communion within the objective content of the faith and sacramental life calls for an infinity of degrees and shades of meaning. Regarding the objective content of the faith every dissident confession preserves some measure of communion with the Catholic Church. As to the sacramental life, communion exists in the sacrament of Baptism where it is validly administered. It also exists in the Eucharist where a valid episcopate and priesthood have been preserved. This Eucharist is not another eucharist [sic] than our own nor another Body of Christ, even though it is neither celebrated nor received in common with us[58] (§45).

The ecclesiology of communion which one encounters here also underscores the first and second chapter of *Lumen Gentium* – emphasising both the vertical dimension of communion, i.e. the relationship between Church and Trinity, and the horizontal dimension of communion, i.e. the relationship between the Catholic Church and the other churches, religions, and eventually the whole world –, even if one

---

57. *Note*, §44: "Ceci peut se faire en rendant à la notion de 'communion' (koinonia) la place première qui lui revient et en présentant le but poursuivi comme étant le rétablissement de l'entière communion de foi, de discipline et de vie sacramentelle en quoi consiste l'unité visible de l'Église". This is clearly the opinion of Dumont himself. See the chapter 'Unité de grâce et Unité visible' (pp. 200-207) in DUMONT, *Les voies de l'unité chrétienne* (n. 49), p. 203: "Pour le théologien catholique l'unité visible n'est réelle et complète que si se vérifient trois conditions: unanimité dans l'adhésion à un même contenu objectif de la foi, appartenance à un unique corps ecclésial hiérarchiquement organisé, participation en commun aux mêmes sacrements et, en particulier, au sacrement du Corps et du Sang du Seigneur". Dumont se rend compte de l'existence d'opinions différentes, surtout dans le protestantisme et dans le Conseil Œcuménique, mais son approche est plutôt 'kontroverstheologisch'.

58. *Note*, §45: "De l'importance de la signification théologique de cette manière de présenter les choses découle un avantage psychologique évident. Car, si sur le plan canonique la question du rapport d'une Église locale à la seule Église-une-et-universelle doit nécessairement être tranchée par le oui ou le non, la réponse à la question de la communion dans le contenu objectif de la foi et dans la vie sacramentelle appelle une infinité de degrés et de nuances. En effet, dans le contenu objectif de la foi, toute confession dissidente conserve quelque mesure de communion avec l'Église catholique. Quant à la vie sacramentelle il y a: communion dans le baptême, là où celui-ci est administré validement, et communion dans l'eucharistie là où un épiscopat et un sacerdoce valides ont été conservés; cette eucharistie n'est pas une autre eucharistie que la nôtre, un autre Corps du Christ, bien qu'elle ne soit pas célébrée ni reçue en commun avec nous".

encounters the term 'communion' less often than the term 'people of God' in *Lumen Gentium*. Just as this memorandum suggests that the notion of communion allows for "an infinity of degrees", *Unitatis Redintegratio* states that "those who believe in Christ and have been truly baptised are in some kind of communion with the catholic church, even though this communion is imperfect" (UR 3). Also the definition of full communion with the Catholic Church in LG 14 may have been partially inspired by this text: "They are fully incorporated into the society of the church who, possessing the Spirit of Christ, accept its whole structure and all the means of salvation that have been established within it, and within its visible framework are united with Christ, who governs it through the supreme pontiff and the bishops, by the bonds of profession of faith, the sacraments, ecclesiastical government and communion". I do not agree with the memorandum when it tends to identify the notion of the "visible unity of the Church" with full communion. Does visible unity not also allow for degrees? In the long citation above the other Christian churches also in a deplorable way seem to have been reduced to "local churches" which relate to "the one, universal Church", i.e. the Catholic Church.

The document also makes clear what greater attention to an ecclesiology of communion would imply, on the one hand, for Orthodox churches and, on the other hand, for Protestant confessions. By way of anticipation of LG 23 we read:

> Many local Catholic churches experience the pressing need of the restoration in law and in practice of intermediate divisions of the hierarchy, ecclesiastical provinces and national groups of provinces; The satisfaction of legitimate claims of this kind would greatly help the prospect of integrating the Orthodox and even the Anglican Churches within the Catholic unity; for they have always been accustomed to such structures[59] (§49).

The insight that "any permanent agreement on controversial points of doctrine" (*ibid.*) with the Orthodox churches requires "a form of theology expressed in biblical and patristic terms"[60] has definitely also been carefully attended to even in the formulation of the conciliar teaching

59. *Note*, §49: "Il faut ajouter que le besoin impérieux, éprouvé par de nombreuses Églises catholiques locales, d'une restauration, dans le droit et le fait, des échelons intermédiaires de la hiérarchie (provinces ecclésiastiques et groupements nationaux des provinces) pourrait contribuer, s'il y était satisfait, à la réintégration dans l'unité catholique d'Églises telle que les Églises Orthodoxes – et même anglicanes – auxquelles une telle structure n'a cessé d'être familière".

60. *Ibid.*: "Ajoutons que si l'on n'admet pas la légitimité d'une forme de théologie d'expression plus purement biblique et patristique, il ne paraît guère possible d'espérer un accord durable sur les points doctrinaux controversés".

itself. Only with regard to the Orthodox churches does our document make the suggestion that "ecclesiastical discipline concerning *communicatio in sacris* should prudently and gradually be arranged to present conditions"[61] (§50). This request is well received by *Unitatis Redintegratio*, which states the following about the Churches of the East, even if it formulates more general criteria for intercommunion as well:

> These churches, though separated from us, yet possess true sacraments, above all, by apostolic succession, the priesthood and the eucharist, whereby they are still linked with us in closest intimacy. Therefore some worship in common, given suitable circumstances and the approval of church authority, is not merely possible but to be encouraged (UR 15).

III. FROM THE WORK OF CONVERSION TO THE WORK OF ECUMENISM: A GROWTH IN ECUMENICAL UNDERSTANDING IN WILLEBRANDS' OPENING SPEECHES

When one realises that the documents of the Second Vatican Council as well reflect signs of theological development in the course of their drafting process, then we should not be surprised to observe a similar evolution in the introductory speeches of the secretary of the CCEQ. The main function of these speeches, however, was to inform the audience about important decisions which the Comité Directeur had made in between two conferences and to introduce the theme of the current one. At some places, however, one is able to sense Willebrands' own theological opinion.

In the initial *Projet d'un conseil catholique oecuménique*, largely drafted by Thijssen in 1951, the work of ecumenism is still believed to be almost identical to the work of conversions, with the only distinction that ecumenism pertains to "collective return".

> Nous avons la conviction que l'apostolat des retours individuels est connexe et même identique avec le travail 'œcuménique' (…) On n'est souvent qu'en apparence que le cas de l'union individuelle se présente moins compliqué que celui du retour collectif[62].

---

61. *Note*, §50: "… la méthode la plus efficace pouvant mener au rétablissement de l'entière et parfaite communion dans ces trois domaines [foi, discipline, vie sacramentelle] pourrait être une méthode progressive comportant une collaboration croissante dans les soucis et les activités pastorales, dans les recherches théologiques et historiques, ainsi qu'un aménagement prudent et progressif de la discipline concernant la 'communicatio in sacris'".
62. "Projet d'un conseil catholique œcuménique" (FWC), p. 2.

In his opening speech during the first meeting in *Fribourg* (1952) Willebrands describes the nature of the CCEQ. A major task of such an association is to contribute to the critical self-evaluation to which extent Catholics in their way of life reflect the catholicity of the Church[63].

> Ce respect nous mène à une introspection sérieuse et profonde au sujet de la question, à quel point nous exprimons par notre attitude et notre vie même la catholicité de l'Église. C'est alors seulement qu'il sera possible de répondre pleinement à notre tâche de catholique, tâche qui consiste à être avant tout un guide pour le frère séparé.

In the further explanation it becomes clear that Willebrands understands catholicity and ecumenicity as almost identical terms pertaining to the universal proclamation of the Christian faith:

> La catholicité est un principe divin, et partant, l'Église n'est pas soumise à des limites de temps et d'espace, ni à celles des nations ou des races. Elle incluse, par suite de sa catholicité, l'homme entier. Les Pères ont toujours compris la catholicité et l'œcuménicité comme étant un tout. La communauté de Smyrna écrit aux Philoméliens: "Polycarpe, ayant rappelé à toute l'Église catholique dans le monde entier…"[64].

The case of Johannes Michael, a former German Protestant theologian who converted to the Catholic Church and whom Willebrands would soon invite to explain a Protestant view on various issues, makes the secretary of the CCEQ praise the ideal of conversion:

> La conversion est un retour d'une personne qui vivait d'une partie seulement de la révélation, à la totalité de la paradosis pour y vivre désormais dans la plénitude du Christ[65].

63. WILLEBRANDS, "Introduction à la conférence catholique œcuménique de Fribourg" (FWC), p. 2.

64. *Ibid.*, p. 3. In his 1960 article *Il movimento ecumenico: Sviluppi e speranze* (n. 10) Willebrands recalls that the concepts of catholicity and ecumenicity were understood by the Church fathers as being almost interchangeable, but have grown apart as a result of the history of schisms. Willebrands approvingly quotes from a 1952 article of the Protestant pastor H. van der Linde. Cf. WILLEBRANDS, *Il movimento ecumenico: Sviluppi e speranze* (n. 11), p. 275: "Purtroppo cattolicità ed ecumenicità non sono ancora identici. Questa è la nostra pena. La futura eventuale coincidenza di questi concetti sarebbe la soluzione del problema ecumenico".

65. WILLEBRANDS, "Introduction à la conférence catholique œcuménique de Fribourg" (FWC), p. 5. The already mentioned 1960 article describes the return of individuals and groups in similar terms: "Già per il passaggio di un individuo alla Chiesa, noi uomini non possiamo essere che uno strumento nella mano di Dio, ci è consentito di dare solo un piccolo aiuto. La grazia di Dio lo muove nel tempo di preparazione, risolve i dubbi, supera le difficoltà. Quando però se tratta di un grande gruppo e di una comunità, quanto più forti sono i legami storici col passato, con la grandezza e la cultura di un popolo! Che radici profonde hanno i vincoli psicologici e sociali! Si parla di quanto è umanamente impossibile". J.P. Michael, representing *Herder-Korrespondenz*, gives an introduction in Utrecht

In the conclusion of his opening lecture during the *Utrecht* conference (1953) Willebrands feels obliged to defend the ideal of ecumenism as *Rückkehr* in response to an objection made by the famous Dutch Reformed theologian van Ruler, who had stated:

> Rom will ökumenisch kein Gespräch, sondern Unterwerfung und Zurückkehr zur einigen wahren Kirche.

Willebrands' answer:

> Wir aber wollen ein Gespräch in vollkommener Freiheit, – wir wollen Unterwerfung und Zurückkehr in vollkommener Freiheit, und auch nur dann wenn der heimkehrende Bruder in freier Ueberzeugung und freier Wahl und im Lichte des Glaubens zur Einsicht gelangt ist, dass Rom wahrlich die Ökumene ist, die Säule der Wahrheit, die alles und allen umfasst[66].

In his introduction to the 1955 meeting in Paris Willebrands again reflects on the meaning of the predicate 'catholic' as ascribed to the

---

(1953) to "La manifestation de l'espérance chrétienne dans la vie chrétienne" and in Mainz (1954), because of the illness of one of the speakers, he treats both about "Die Kirche als Braut Christi in der Protestantischen Theologie" and about "Leib Christi in der protestantischen, vorwiegend lutherischen Theologie". VELATI, *Una difficile transizione* (n. 3), p. 59, quotes a letter by Father Villain sent to Willebrands after the Utrecht conference (FWC), out of which it becomes clear that converts – Michael had been received into the Catholic Church in 1950 – not always reflect a truly ecumenical attitude: "J'ai été frappé (et je pense que tous l'ont été) de l'opposition (je ne dis pas seulement différence) de méthode entre le rapport du P. Dumont et celui du Dr. Michael. Ai-je tort: je considère le premier comme un travail œcuménique, très utile à la fois pour nous-même et pour le Conseil, si on le lui communique. J'ai tendance à penser que le second n'est pas œcuménique du tout, qu'il n'est pas utile pour nous et surtout qu'il serait blessant pour le Conseil si on venait à le lui communiquer". In a letter to the other members of the Comité Directeur dated 12/08/1958 Willebrands decides no longer to invite Michael because of his unfair accusation of the position of the other theologians of the Catholic Conference. Cf. VELATI, *Una difficile transizione* (n. 3), p. 169, n. 75: "Ce qui est pire c'est qu'il parle de 'la part de protestantisme' chez nos théologiens, d'un protestantisme 'rampant et venimeux à l'intérieure de l'Église, se diffusant comme une maladie'. Bien qu'il ne mentionne aucun nom, cette accusation vague est intolérable et n'a aucun fondement réel". According to Velati, it was especially Congar who was envisaged in Michael's criticisms. Michael's 1958 book, *Christen suchen eine Kirche* had been poorly received in WCC circles, as appears from the negative comments by Hans-Heinrich Harms, Secretary of the Division of Studies of the WCC and Willebrands' closest contact within the WCC, in *The Ecumenical Review* 10 (1957-1958) 485-488. The diary entry reports for 17/10/1958: "Leave Mainz to Freiburg im Breisgau, where I held a long and private discussion with Michael concerning the last difficulties. Very personal talk; however, the situation remains professionally and objectively difficult. Provisionally, do not invite to cooperate". Cf. SALEMINK (ed.), *"You Will Be Called Repairer of the Breach"* (n. 5), p. 48 and esp. n. 63.

66. WILLEBRANDS, "Einleitung zur katholisch-oekumenischen Konferenz von Dijnselburg Holland, 6-9 August 1953" (FWC), p. 10.

Church[67]. For him, "the Catholic Church is the oikoumenè" and therefore our separated brethren have to return to her[68]. Willebrands is aware that the concept of catholicity not only pertains to the universal outreach of the Catholic Church but also to the fact "that she has safeguarded the totality of the mystery of salvation of Christ"[69]. The most suitable realisation of catholicity, Willebrands realises, is the communion of the bishop and his priests and faithful within the local church.

The introductory speeches to the Chevetogne (1957) and Paderborn (1959) meetings reveal that Willebrands made great efforts to summarize the current state of reflections within the WCC on the Lordship of Christ and on Unity and Mission, respectively. The last lines of the Paderborn introduction reflect the Catholic Church's great expectation towards the Council. He starts with a quote from the Second Conference on Faith and Order in Edinburgh (1937): "We humbly acknowledge that our divisions are contrary to the will of Christ, and we pray God in his mercy to shorten the days of our separation and to guide us by His Spirit into fullness of unity"[70]. Thereafter Willebrands continues:

> En ce jour d'aujourd'hui, l'absence de l'Église catholique, qui a été longtemps un "se tenir à l'écart", se comble. L'annonce du Concile, et l'esprit dans lequel celle-ci a été prononcée, est un fait libérateur et inspirateur. Des échos d'Italie, des États-Unis, et de partout, montrent comment, tout à coup, l'attitude des catholiques envers leurs frères séparés se transforme. Puisse ce Concile arriver à un moment plus opportun que le Concile de Trente au temps de la Réforme[71].

---

67. The content of his introduction to the Mainz conference is not particularly revealing for our question. One can only hope that Willebrands later on did no longer end ecumenical gatherings in the same way as he concluded this introduction: "Zum Schluss möchte ich dann mit Ihnen zusammen für unsere Arbeitstagung die Fürsprache erbitten der Virgo Mater Maria Assumpta, die die ganze Hoffnung des Alten Israel und des Neuen Israel in sich trug, und der, wie keinem anderen Menschenkinde, die Erfüllung dieser Hoffnung in der Fülle Ihrer Erlöstheit geschenkt wurde, Maria Assumpta, die für uns alle geworden ist: Mater Sanctae Spei".

68. WILLEBRANDS, "Conférence catholique pour les questions œcuméniques. 1-4 août 1955, Cours Dupanloup, Boulogne sur Seine", p. 4: "Ainsi on pourrait espérer que chez nos frères séparés s'accroisse la conviction que l'Église catholique est en vérité le lieu où le Christ a déposé la totalité de la grâce rédemptrice".

69. *Ibid.*, p. 6: "L'Église Catholique n'est pas l'Oicumène uniquement parce qu'en elle tous les hommes peuvent trouver une place, mais aussi parce qu'elle conserve la totalité du mystère du salut du Christ".

70. Cf. also WILLEBRANDS, *Il movimento ecumenico: Sviluppi e speranze* (n. 10), p. 263: "La cristianità soffre del disastro e del peccato delle separazioni nello scisma e nell'eresia, tanto nei paesi dove la Chiesa si è stabilita da secoli, quanto nella sua missione ai popoli che non hanno ancora ricevuto il dono della fede".

71. WILLEBRANDS, "Introduction au thème: Unité et Mission", p. 7. Willebrands repeated the same idea in one of his first published articles with a long quote from Jedin in support. Cf. ID., *Il movimento ecumenico: Sviluppi e speranze* (n. 10), p. 265: "… allora

The Gazzada meeting (1960) dealt with unity in diversity. In his opening speech Msgr. Willebrands again makes it clear that "the great task which we should accomplish in the encounter with separated Christians consists in revealing the catholicity of the Church more and more clearly"[72]. Willebrands exhorts Catholic believers to develop a "notional openness" (*ouverture notionelle*) towards other churches, which thereafter has to be followed by an "existential openness". The work of the Church consists in bringing about "a second Reformation" and he asks himself the question whether such a movement "will orient itself back to Rome", just as the first Reformation had turned its back on Rome. Willebrands knows that the answer will be negative. The churches of the Reformation do not want to return to the historical form of the Catholic Church they left behind in the 16th century. "Ce qu'ils désirent c'est plutôt de vaincre dans l'Esprit du Seigneur ces formes historiques à cause de l'unique Seigneur". Nor would they be willing to return to Rome in the ecclesiological sense, given the new self-understanding of this Church since the first Vatican Council.

Probably due to the huge amount of work Willebrands had to cope with as Secretary of the Secretariat for Promoting Christian Unity, the introductory speeches to the meetings in Strasbourg (1961) and Gazzada (1963) are handwritten. His introduction to the Strasbourg meeting starts with admitting that many members and consultors of the Secretariat had been chosen among members of the CCEQ:

> L'esprit œcuménique qui a inspiré et les discussions et les suggestions de Gazzada, a pu influencer facilement le travail du Secrétariat par le fait qu'un grand nombre de membres et des consulteurs du Secrétariat a été choisi parmi ceux qui participent aux réunions de la Conférence[73].

The most striking element of this introduction is that Willebrands contrasts the attitude of the Anglicans towards the Secretariat and towards the Catholic Church, with the attitudes of the Protestants and the Orthodox. With great sympathy he reads a long quote from an article on

il Concilio di Trento arrivò ben tardi, e troppo tardi per proteggere molti da questo errore". Positively, he pleads in this article for "un dialogo continuo e diretto con i fratelli separati" and he narrates, in a way similar to the introduction to the Paderborn conference, how the dialogue has already begun: "Da questa presa di coscienza il dialogo ebbe inizio, prima timidamente e con esitanza, più tardi rafforzato dalla persecuzione del Nazismo da noi tutti subita, quando teologi cattolici e protestanti, sacerdoti e pastori s'incontrarono nelle prigioni e nei campi di concentramento, dove la loro fedeltà a Cristo ed alla Chiesa li aveva portati. Diversi gruppi interessati a questi dialoghi sono sorti in Germania, Olanda, Francia, Svizzera".

72. WILLEBRANDS, "Gazzada 19.IX.'60" (FWC), pp. 1-3.
73. WILLEBRANDS, "Strasbourg" (FWC), p. 2.

"Canterbury and Rome", published by Dr. Michael Ramsey shortly before his installation as Archbishop of Canterbury:

> Charity demands the speaking of truth in love. It is a fallacy that a dogmatic or exclusive position is necessarily uncharitable: it can be held and commended with humility and charity. It is equally a fallacy that a liberal position is necessarily charitable: it can be held with an uncomprehending contempt for other views. I dissent from, but I respect the conscience of, someone who tells me that the Roman Church is alone the true Catholic Church of Christ and that I am outside it, at best an errant baptized layman, laicus vagans extra ecclesiam. Because I respect the conscience of such a one, I know that his position issues inevitably in policies which hurt and cause friction. On his side, there is all the difference between unchurching me in hatred and contempt and doing so with an attitude of conscientious love for me. In neither of us charity is enhanced by denying that "things are what they are, and the consequence of them will be what they will be". In both of us, charity should enable us to speak of those very matters, and their causes, in friendship as well as frankness[74].

Willebrands continues:

> Ces paroles sont en opposition nette avec les exigences exprimées souvent par des théologiens protestants, répétées également par le métropolite Nikodim de l'église orthodoxe russe. Ils réclament qu'avant tout rapprochement l'Église de Rome devrait abandonner sa position concernant la primauté du Pape et l'Infaillibilité de son enseignement ex cathedra ce qui reviendrait non seulement pour nous à quitter l'obéissance de la foi (Rom. 1,5), mais la demande requête elle-même va directement contre la déclaration de Toronto (1954) du Comité directeur du Conseil Œcuménique des Églises[75].

The last introductory speech made by Willebrands at the start of the Gazzada 1963 conference took place during the first intersession of the Council. The greatest part of this lengthy speech contains of a description of his major responsibilities within the Secretariat. Willebrands describes the mutual visits between church leaders, especially the contacts between Rome and Canterbury[76]. In even greater detail he describes the numerous contacts with representatives of other churches in view of inviting them as observers to the Council[77]. He makes it clear that it was he who had

---

74. *Ibid.*, p. 6; in the handwritten text the quotation is found on a different page than its introduction on page 2.

75. *Ibid.*, p. 2.

76. "Gazzada 1963", pp. 6-9.

77. *Ibid.*, pp. 9-18. Cf. the section on 'The Ecumenical Presence at the Council' in the third chapter on 'The Struggle for the Council during the Preparation of Vatican II (1960-1962)' – written by Joseph Komonchak – in G. ALBERIGO – J.A. KOMONCHAK, *History of Vatican II*. Vol. I: *Announcing and Preparing Vatican Council II. Toward a New Era in Catholicism*, Maryknoll, NY, Orbis; Leuven, Peeters, 1995, 167-356, pp. 318-326.

proposed to Visser 't Hooft and other church leaders residing in Geneva – after reading the second volume of the *History of the Ecumenical Movement* – to address the invitation to attend the Council as observers to the great world federations, in order to avoid having to invite numerous national churches and even sects[78]. He also explains why it was important for the Catholic Church also to send an invitation to the World Council of Churches:

> Le Conseil Œcuménique des Églises était un cas particulier. Il ne représente pas une confession, ni un type ou une structure déterminée d'Église. Mais son importance œcuménique est évidente et reconnue par tous. Si nous voyons la présence des observateurs dans la perspective de l'unité, comment pourrions-nous ne pas reconnaître cette importance et aussi les mérites du Conseil Œcuménique comme tel, et de demander aussi, par cette invitation, sa collaboration dans la perspective de l'unité. Il ne s'en suit pas que par une éventuelle collaboration avec le Conseil Œcuménique nous nous limitons dans tout le travail pour l'unité aux possibilités et aux méthodes du Conseil Œcuménique, mais nous espérons du bien de cette collaboration[79].

Willebrands admits that he has become a bit discouraged about the slowness of the Ecumenical Patriarchate to accept the invitation of the Catholic Church. He cites from a report that he made after his second visit to Constantinople:

> À tout prendre je ne suis pas enthousiaste de l'attitude des Orthodoxes: déjà en février je leur ai fait une visite et j'ai discuté toute la question en détail. À l'heure actuelle leur réponse n'est pas encore prête. Mais aussi ils manquent de force et de conviction: le fait que Canterbéry et le Conseil Œcuménique des Églises réagissent favorablement leur est important pour arriver eux-mêmes à une décision, et encore ils sont hésitants[80].

This section also contains an interesting passage on the relation between the Secretariat and the Oriental Commission. The Secretariat had insisted that it was up to the Oriental Commission to establish the first contacts with the "Patriarcat de Constantinople" but after returning from their visit Archbishop Testa and Father Raes S.J. explained to Willebrands that the Orthodox preferred to have direct contacts with the Secretariat[81].

---

78. "Gazzada 1963", p. 9.
79. *Ibid.*, p. 10.
80. *Ibid.*, p. 13.
81. *Ibid.*, p. 12. Cf. ALBERIGO – KOMONCHAK, *History of Vatican II.* Vol. I (n. 76), p. 324: "The inaction of the OR led the Orthodox to make it clear that they wished their conversations with Rome to be mediated by the Secretariat. Late in 1961, Bea brought this to the attention of Pope John, who granted the request. From then on the Secretariat was in charge of all ecumenical concerns and conversations".

The speech also contains a very honest account of the anti-ecumenical attitude of the Theological Commission. Recalling how the secretary of the Theological Commission rejected all cooperation with the Secretariat in the form of a mixed commission, he describes the disparate ethos between the two curial bodies as follows:

> Or tout le travail du Secrétariat était conçu en fonction du dialogue avec les chrétiens séparés. Le travail de la Commission théologique apparemment était conduit contre les chrétiens séparés, ou, comme ils le disaient, contre les erreurs. On comprend facilement que tout élément œcuménique restait absent de leur travail et qu'y manquait même la compréhension de ceux qu'on voulait réfuter[82].

The most personal pages of the speech are those commemorating the impact which Pope John XXIII made to improve relations between the Catholic Church and other churches with his emphasis on the necessity to combine truth and love:

> Le pape n'opposait, ne substituait point l'amour à la vérité, mais il enseignait la vérité par l'amour et dans l'amour[83]. Il se faisait le serviteur des hommes. Il désirait faire con-naître la vérité. Toute naissance est le fruit de l'amour – la connaissance de Dieu aussi, et la connaissance du Christ et de son Église, de la présence du Christ dans l'Église. Le pape était l'humble serviteur de Dieu et des hommes, il en avait une connaissance profonde et personnelle, il était un témoin de Dieu. Cet appel, a-t-il été entendu? Tout le changement de l'atmosphère, du climat dans les relations entre l'Église et les frères séparés s'explique par cela. Le monde entier l'a aimé comme un frère ou comme un père, comme un envoyé par Dieu. Le Patriarche de Constantinople a exprimé ce sentiment en lui appliquant les paroles de l'Evangile: 'Fuit homo missus a Deo, cui nomen erat Johannes'[84].

I close this account of what in my opinion was the most impressive opening speech which Willebrands gave during the meetings of the

---

82. "Gazzada 1963", p. 5. The relation of the Secretariat with the other preparatory commissions was much better. Cf. *ibid.*: "Nous avons essayé de faire connaître la pensée, les intérêts des chrétiens séparés aux autres commissions préparatoires, afin qu'on en puisse tenir conte [sic], dans la mesure du possible. Cette méthode a été bien acceptée, par certaines commissions, notamment la commission liturgique, la commission pour l'apostolat des laïcs, la commission pour la discipline des sacrements".

83. The following citation of the Pope's Opening Speech at the Council *Gaudet Mater Ecclesia*, October 11, 1962, probably inspired J. Willebrands: "L'Église catholique, en brandissant par ce Concile œcuménique le flambeau de la vérité religieuse au milieu de cette situation, veut être pour tous une mère très aimante, bonne, patiente, pleine de bonté et de miséricorde pour ses fils qui sont séparés d'elle". Cf. AS I/1, 166-175.

84. "Gazzada 1963", p. 6. For reflections on Pope John XXIII and Vatican II see a.o. ALBERIGO – KOMONCHAK, *History of Vatican II*. Vol. I (n. 76); *History of Vatican II*. Vol. II: *The Formation of the Council's Identity. First Period and Intersession. October 1962 – September 1963*, Maryknoll, NY, Orbis; Leuven, Peeters, 1997, pp. 14-21.

Catholic Conference by quoting the opening paragraph which explains
how Pope John believed his Council could become an important instrument serving the goal of Christian unity:

> Concile – Observateurs. Deux mots qui évoquent pour tout œcuméniste
> catholique, le plus grand événement que le S. Esprit ait donné à l'Église de
> notre temps, événement qui, sans doute, n'est pas contraire à l'institution
> mais la déborde infiniment. D'autant plus que le Concile a été conçu et
> consigné par le Pape Jean XXIII sous le souffle du S. Esprit, dans le
> charisme de la prophétie et non comme la conséquence d'une préparation
> élaborée et calculée de l'Institut. Les institutions n'ont pas toujours suivi de
> grand cœur la voix prophétique du Pape. Dès l'origine, dans l'esprit de Jean
> XXIII, l'idée du Concile et les chrétiens non-catholiques étaient liés dans
> la perspective de l'Unité. Ce ne serait pas un Concile d'Union, mais un
> Concile sous le regard de l'Esprit de l'Unité dans la perspective de l'Unité
> de tous ceux qui confessent le Christ, sous un seul Seigneur, par la même
> foi et dans l'unique baptême[85]. L'Église au concile devrait être une invita-
> tion à l'Unité par une réforme intérieure qui la portera à une sainteté plus
> parfaite, à une catholicité plus manifeste, à une apostolicité plus fidèle, à
> une unité plus profonde et plus riche[86].

EPILOGUE

Among the archival material which Willebrands offered to the
Benedictine abbey of Chevetogne, I found one example of a text of a
more spiritual nature which I assume Willebrands himself is the author,
since he added to the typed version the handwritten words: "Gazzada
1963 Willebrands". I would like to end my lecture by quoting this text.
I can imagine Willebrands using it as a homily or a meditation which
formed part of the liturgical gatherings during the Gazzada conference.
Willebrands' meditation on sin and repentance ends with a reflection on
the history of schisms:

> From time to time sin has invaded the Church to such an extent, that there
> have been people who didn't see any longer that the Lord was united to their
> Church, was to be situated in the midst of its members, was co-suffering
> with them. They left the Church in order to seek the Lord. We don't
> need to prove that the Lord is always there. We need repentance and
> penitence. (…) I am not speaking of repentance for things past, of historical
> repentance. What is needed is day to day repentance which reaches back

---

85. Cf. *Gaudet Mater Ecclesia*: "… l'Église catholique estime que son devoir est de
faire tous ses efforts pour que s'accomplisse le grand mystère de cette unité que Jésus-
Christ, à l'approche de son sacrifice, a demandée à son Père dans une ardente prière (…)".
    86. "Gazzada 1963", p. 1.

into the past and is extended towards the future. (…) Repentance forms part of the Christian existence, because it forms part of love. (…) This ecclesial love, this repentant love embraces the Lord, but it embraces at the same time the separated brother who has loved us, because our repentance also implies a return in his direction. This ecclesial love is also the Holy Spirit, who fills the Church with his presence and is its divine structure. That He may complete us, we who are his human structure[87].

Faculty of Theology and   Peter DE MEY
Religious Studies
KU Leuven
Sint-Michielsstraat 4/3101
B-3000 Leuven
Belgium

---

87. "Gazzada 1963", p. 2: "Le péché de temps en temps a envahi l'Église à tel point, qu'il y avait des hommes qui ne voyaient plus le Seigneur uni à Son Église, au milieu de ses membres, compatissant avec eux. Ils nous ont quitté pour chercher le Seigneur. Il ne faut pas seulement démontrer par les preuves que le Seigneur est toujours là, il faut le repentir, la pénitence. (…) Ce n'est pas un repentir pour le passé, un repentir historique, c'est un repentir d'aujourd'hui qui englobe le passé et s'étend vers l'avenir. (…) Cet amour ecclésial, cet amour repentant embrasse le Seigneur, mais il embrasse en même temps le frère séparé, qui nous avait quitté, car ce repentir est aussi un retour à lui. Cet amour ecclésial, c'est aussi l'Esprit Saint. Il remplit l'Église de sa présence, il est sa structure divine. Oh, qu'Il nous remplisse, nous qui sommes sa structure humaine".

WILLEBRANDS' DIARIES AND AGENDAS 1958-1965

A VIEW BEHIND THE CURTAIN

During the Willebrands centenary two books with previously unknown texts from Cardinal Willebrands have been released. The first book contains the diaries of Willebrands from the years 1958-1961, just before the Second Vatican Council[1]. The second book contains his agendas during the Council, between 1963-1965[2]. The Diaries are translated in English, the Agendas are translated in French, both works now contain a rather large scientific annotation and rather large introductions. The Belgian scholar, Leo Declerck, edited Willebrands' Agendas, while I edited the Diaries. In this contribution I provide the reader with some background information about the Diaries and about the Agendas as two important sources for new historical research into the life and work of Willebrands just before and during the Second Vatican Council, but also into the council itself[3].

I. Biographical Notes

During the time that the later Cardinal and Archbishop of Utrecht, Johannes Willebrands wrote his diaries and agendas, he was active as an ecumenist. At the time he was already around fifty years old. In 1934, Willebrands was ordained a priest in the diocese of Harlem, the Netherlands. Later, he wrote his doctoral dissertation in Rome on the renowned 19th century English Catholic convert and Cardinal, John Henry Newman (1801-1890). After some pastoral years in Amsterdam, as a chaplain at the Begijnhof (Beguinage) in central Amsterdam from 1937 to 1940, in 1940, he was appointed professor at the Philosophicum of the Seminary in Warmond, which is located in the diocese of Harlem. In 1945 he was made director. While there, he lectured on the history of philosophy.

---

1. T. SALEMINK (ed.), *"You Will Be Called Repairer of the Breach" : The Diary of J.G.M. Willebrands 1958-1961*, Leuven, Peeters, 2009.
2. L. DECLERCK, *Les agendas conciliaires de Mgr. J. Willebrands, secrétaire du Secrétariat pour l'Unité des Chrétiens*, Leuven, Peeters, 2009.
3. See also the introductions in SALEMINK (ed.), *"You Will Be Called Repairer of the Breach"* (n. 1); DECLERCK, *Les agendas conciliaires de Mgr. J. Willebrands* (n. 2).

Willebrands made his first ecumenical contacts during the Second World War in the so-called 'Larense Kring' or Laren Circle (founded in 1943). This ecumenical group gathered in the house of Lizzy Breman-Schouten (1887-1967) of Laren, the Netherlands.

The formal start of Willebrands' ecumenical work began in 1948 with his appointment as the chairman of the newly established 'Sint Willibrordvereniging' (SWV) or the Saint Willibrord Society. Before the war it had been known as the 'Apologetische Vereniging Petrus Canisius' or the Apologetic Society Petrus Canisius. After the war this new society, however, steered a more open course and rejected the apologetic model that was prevalent since the Reformation and Counter-Reformation. In the 1950s Willebrands as chairman began to set up a dialogue with Protestant, Anglican and Orthodox churches, at first in the Netherlands, and soon afterwards internationally. Willebrands and his life-long friend, Frans Thijssen – who had been excused from his duties to work for ecumenism and who was at that time a member of the governing board of the SWV – travelled throughout Europe to stimulate the cause of ecumenism in Catholic circles and develop a network of Catholic ecumenists. Willebrands received a personal letter of introduction from the Archbishop of Utrecht at the time, Johannes Cardinal de Jong (1885-1955). They visited bishops who showed an interest in ecumenism – like Lorenz Jaeger (1892-1975) of Paderborn – and spoke to ecumenically oriented theologians – like Josef Höfer (1896-1976) from Paderborn; Father Christophe-Jean Dumont o.p. (1897-1991), who was the director of the Study Center for Eastern Churches Istina in Paris; and Dom Theodore Strotmann o.s.b. (1911-1987) from the Monastery of Chevetogne.

Their plan was eventually presented to a few consultors of the Congregation of the Holy Office in Rome. Father Augustinus Bea s.j. (1881-1968), rector of the Pontifical Biblical Institute in Rome, and Sebastiaan Tromp s.j. (1889-1975) were among these consultors. Father Bea was enthusiastic about their plans, although Father Tromp revealed himself to be more reluctant. Finally, in 1952 the Conférence Catholique pour les Questions Œcuméniques (Catholic Conference for Ecumenical Questions) was established based on their efforts. Initially the Conférence was to be called the 'Catholic Ecumenical Council'; however, this name was rejected, because it resembled to closely the model adopted by the World Council of Churches (WCC). Willebrands became its first secretary. The leadership of the organization was held by a Comité Directeur (Governing Board), of which Willebrands was a member.

The first meeting of the Conférence Catholique pour les Questions Œcuméniques took place from the 11th-13th of August 1952. Twenty-five theologians from all over Europe participated in the house of François Charrière (1893-1976), Bishop of Lausanne, Geneva and Fribourg in Switzerland. The Dutch historian Jan Jacobs, who wrote a history of the Conférence and the SWV, mentions that there were about seventy-five theologians who over the years became permanent members. In 1961 the first women became members[4]. These were Dé Groothuizen (1907-1992) of the international Grail Movement and Lydia Simons of the Ladies of Bethany and board member of the SWV.

The Conférence's first task was the organization of 'study days' for theologians who were interested in ecumenism. Its second main activity was the organization of informal meetings with the representatives and associations of other churches. Besides the contacts made with the World Council of Churches (WCC), it also made contacts with the International League for Apostolic Faith and Order (ILAFO), an organization whose members were from the Catholic, Old Catholic, Anglican, Episcopal and Lutheran churches. Willebrands' activities for this Conférence play a great role in his diaries.

II. THE NOTEBOOKS

Until recently it was not known that Willebrands kept a diary of his activities during the period leading up to the Second Vatican Council (1958-1961). The original handwritten notebooks, in which he wrote his diary, are in the possession of the Cardinal Willebrands Archive in Utrecht, the Netherlands.

In 2005 Willebrands' notebooks were discovered in an almost miraculous fashion by Maria ter Steeg, secretary of the Cardinal Willebrands Archive. They were found in a box that had been forgotten in the Dutch College after Willebrands had left Rome (1997). After the discovery of the box, the cooperative Dutch pastor Herman Woorts brought it back to the Netherlands and deposited it in the office of Maria ter Steeg, who was then working for the Archdiocese of Utrecht.

When Ter Steeg searched inside the box, she found three of Willebrands' personal notebooks that had been mixed with tourist guides and other materials. A fourth notebook was empty and had been purchased

---

4. Jan Jacobs' research can serve as background information for Willebrands' 'diaries', J. JACOBS, *De Katholieke Conferentie voor Oecumenische Vragen: Een leerschool en gids 1951-1965*, Tilburg, Tilburg University Press, 1991; J. JACOBS, *Nieuwe visies op een oud visioen: Een portret van de Sint Willibrord Vereniging 1948-1998*, Nijmegen, Valkhof Pers, 1998.

to use later. Two of the notebooks were bound with a red and white speckled cardboard cover and one with a black and white speckled cover. Each is 21 cm wide and 33 cm high, and they were bought in the office supply stores: Brothers Winter in Amsterdam and Mado & Co. in Utrecht. The text was written in Willebrands' own hand, in a very readable script. On the inside cover of the second notebook, Willebrands wrote his name. From notations found in the text, it is clear that Willebrands did not always write in his diary on the same day, but would return to it, sometimes weeks later.

The three notebooks do not cover the entire period 1958-1961. The first notebook begins on the 31st of July 1958. Willebrands began his diary on this date, because on 1st of August, with the approval of the entire Episcopate, he would be appointed as the Episcopal delegate for ecumenical affairs by the Archbishop of Utrecht, Bernardus Alfrink (1900-1987). He completes the first notebook over a year later on the 27th of September 1959. Then, for seven months, there is nothing. It is unknown whether or not a separate notebook exists for this period. Until now, no other diaries, agendas or notes (or even loose pieces of paper) have been found for this intermediary period. More than half a year later, on the 1st of May 1960, he begins the second notebook. Nevertheless, in this second notebook, he leaves the first thirty pages blank, obviously, with the intention to fill it in at a later date. It is probable that he still wanted to fill in the pages with notions from the missing months, but was unable to do so. The second notebook ends on the 28th of August 1960. The third notebook begins on the 1st of September 1960 and ends on the 6th of March 1961. It is unclear whether Willebrands actually kept a diary during the period that followed.

These notebooks (1958-1961), which are now published, contain little or no information regarding his personal emotions and experiences. They are professional 'diaries', which were meant to help him remember information about his international ecumenical (net)work. He often mentions his regular contacts with his parents and family, and also with Dutch friends, including a noticeable number of women. But even here, his personal sentiment is missing. Only here and there does some emotion come through in the text, often through an understatement.

III. THE RHODES INCIDENT

There are many interesting and new topics found in his Diaries. During this lecture I will focus on one in particular. Willebrands encouraged building an open relationship with the World Council of Churches, founded in 1948, and with the Secretary General of WCC, Willem Visser 't Hooft, also a Dutchman. In 1959 Willebrands was invited to the meeting of the Central Committee of the WCC. That represents the first time that a Catholic participated in a meeting of the WCC.

From 19 to 28 August 1959, the 12th gathering of the WCC's Central Committee (CC) took place for the first time in an Orthodox country (Rhodes, Greece)[5]. This happened through the invitation of the Ecumenical Patriarch of Constantinople, the Orthodox Church in Greece and the Greek government. One hundred and eighty-five persons participated. Seventy-two of the participants were members of the CC of the WCC. The Congregation of the Holy Office in Rome, today known as the Congregation for the Doctrine of the Faith, approved the participation of Christophe-Jean Dumont, director of the Centre d'Études Istina (Study Center Istina) in Paris, and Willebrands as 'journalistes accrédités'[6]. They were neither official delegates nor were they official observers. That would have been too radical a step. They were merely 'journalists'. Nevertheless, from Willebrands' diary, it appears that their position was perceived as being more significant, given the ecumenical hope that was awakened due to the announcement of the impending Council.

During this gathering an incident took place that threatened to become an open conflict through sensationalized press releases and the unfortunate intervention of some individuals. Until now, only the public version is known. Willebrands' diary gives us a view behind the curtain. Letters from Willebrands' personal archive dating from this period provide additional background information[7]. At this juncture we will attempt to briefly summarize the main lines of the conflict.

For many years Father Dumont already had contacts with the Orthodox and had led theological discussions at the Study Center Istina. Therefore, in Rhodes they wanted to take the opportunity to meet a number of Orthodox representatives. In fact, the initiative for contact came from the Orthodox.

On Friday evening, the 21st of August, an informal meeting took place at the hotel Mira Mare in Rhodes. In addition to Dumont and

---

5. See *Minutes and Reports of the Twelfth Meeting of the Central Committee of the World Council of Churches, Rhodes, Greece, August 19-27, 1959*, Geneva, WCC, 1959.

6. See Willebrands' report in *Het Schild: Maandschrift van de Sint Willibrord-Vereniging* 36 (1958-59) 157-173.

7. The exchange of letters (mostly in transcript) between Johannes Willebrands and Willem Visser 't Hooft between 23 August – 14 November 1959 can be found in *The Cardinal Willebrands Archive*, inv. no. 111.

Willebrands, three other Catholics were present: Father Theodore
Strotmann (1911-1987), a Benedictine from Chevetogne and editor of
Irenikon; Father Maurice Villain (1900-1977), author of *Introduction à
l'œcuménisme* (*Introduction to Ecumenism* [1958]) and Father Antoine
Wenger (1919), editor in chief of *La Croix* (*The Cross*). These three
persons did not attend the meeting of the Central Committee (CC). To
the great surprise of the Catholic participants, more than fifty Orthodox
representatives came to the informal dinner and meeting, some of whom
were bishops and priests, and also Orthodox members of the CC of the
WCC. Dumont told them about Istina and expressed his desire to organize a new gathering in order to further discuss theological ideas. He also
expressed his personal desire to see the beginning of official relations
between the Orthodox and Catholic churches. The word 'official' would
play a large role in the subsequent crisis. This informal, private gathering
caused a great disturbance among the leadership of the WCC as well as
the press. The impression was created that there was an official meeting
between the two churches, without the knowledge of the leadership of
the WCC.

In ecumenical circles people felt 'used', as the secretary of the WCC,
Willem Visser 't Hooft, later said in his *Memoirs* (1971)[8]. Hans Asmussen (1898-1968) points out in *Das kommende Konzil* (1959) that there
were other initiatives hatched in the Greek Orthodox world during that
period to make contact with the Roman Catholic Church, outside of the
knowledge of the World Council of Churches. This was interpreted
negatively because the Orthodox churches were members of the WCC,
with certain obligations[9]. Their attempts to make contact gave the leadership of the WCC the impression of being double-crossed.

With respect to the 'Rhodes Incident', Willebrands' diaries provide a
surprising and fresh look behind the scenes. According to the diary, Visser
't Hooft, whom Willebrands knew well, blew up in a rage. He felt that what
the Catholic 'journalists' had done was deceptive and unfair. They had
arranged a meeting with the Orthodox without consulting him. He believed
that the Catholic Church, with the blessing of Rome, was busy trying to
build up its own relationship with the Orthodox churches behind his back.
He was led to believe this because the meeting had been arranged with
Orthodox members, who had come as delegates to the session of the

---

8. W. VISSER 'T HOOFT, *Memoires: Een leven in de oecumene*, Kampen, Kok, 1971
(*Memoirs*, Geneva, WCC, 1973), p. 293.
9. H. ASMUSSEN, *Das kommende Konzil: Nach dem Stande vom 10. Nov. 1959*, Mei-
tingen, Kyrios-Verlag, 1959, pp. 17-18.

WCC's Central Committee. The situation was further exacerbated after Willebrands also spoke to the international press. According to the diary entry 23 August 1959, Visser 't Hooft called Willebrands over to him and said: "If you speak to the Press one more time, then, I must ask you to leave Rhodes immediately". He then added: "I thought that I had invited the two most sensible Catholics, but I got the two dumbest ones. Everything has gone the world over; Tisserant and Metropolitan Jakovos have denied the claims. You're a free man, you know what you are doing, but I thought that you were a man of character".

Willebrands remained diplomatic. On the same day he wrote a letter to Visser 't Hooft, in which he attempted to set the record straight and, at the same time, made it known that he regretted the course of events: "I don't think that I have to tell you how much I regret that these difficulties have happened to you and the WCC, but also to me"[10]. On the same day, Visser 't Hooft had an extensive discussion with Dumont in which Willebrands, contrary to Visser 't Hooft's expectations, did not participate. Thereafter, Visser 't Hooft attempted to place the blame on Dumont, but again, Willebrands felt he could not leave this unanswered. Finally, a day later on the 24th of August, the two were reconciled. Willebrands describes in his diary how Visser 't Hooft came over to him and "almost" embraced him, as he offered him his apologies "and asked for forgiveness for the expressions that he had used" in the heat of the moment.

Nevertheless, on the 3rd of September 1959, Radio Vaticana added fuel to the fire by erroneously stating that it had been decided in Rhodes to organize an official Catholic and Orthodox gathering in Venice the following year. In his diary entry made on the 22nd of September 1959, Willebrands reveals how Radio Vaticana really made its 'mistake'. Given the gravity of the situation, Willebrands had to travel to Rome to give a report and to seek the Vatican's support for his performance in Rhodes. Eugène Cardinal Tisserant (1884-1972), who had been the Secretary of the Congregation for Oriental Churches since 1936, supported Willebrands and Dumont's performance, and distanced himself from the announcement made by Radio Vaticana. Eventually Willebrands was able to speak to the journalist responsible for the announcement. He came to the conclusion that the erroneous suggestion of an 'official' relationship was the result of a terrible misunderstanding. The editor, Father Ulrich, had given his text to the secretary of the Congregation of the Holy

---

10. A transcript of the Dutch letter to his compatriot can be found in *The Cardinal Willebrands Archive*, inv. no. 111. The subsequent letters can also be found in the same archive and under the same number.

Office, Cardinal Ottaviani (1890-1979) to read. Ottaviani had deleted the word 'official' at the beginning of the text, but had overlooked the fact that the word 'official' was mentioned a second time later on in the text. Ulrich misunderstood the cardinal's intention and allowed the second 'official' to be read, infuriating Ottaviani.

The announcement of Radio Vaticana, which was seen as the formal voice of the Vatican, created turmoil in the circles of the WCC. On the 9th of September, Visser 't Hooft wrote a letter to Willebrands in English. He said that he had thought that the case was closed, but had great difficulty to convince others within the Central Committee again of Willebrands' previous interpretation: that the meeting was not the result of an 'official' policy of the Vatican. Many members viewed the 'Rhodes Incident' as a "deliberate attempt on the part of Roman Catholics who were our guests to draw the Orthodox Churches toward Roman Catholic Church and, since the Roman Catholic Church is not in the World Council, away from the World Council". There was a great fear that Rome was playing 'divide et impera'. He writes that the Radio Vaticana announcement had brought the whole controversy back to life. Visser 't Hooft then asked Willebrands, but now with more emphasis – "rather bluntly" – for a definitive answer about the correct interpretation.

Willebrands received the letter in Warmond, the Netherlands and responded, after consultation with the Vatican Curia, including Father Bea. In his diary he writes that it was difficult to find the right people in Rome to speak to because of the holidays. Nevertheless, it was obvious, from the people with authority he was able to contact, that the statement that "the Vatican had authorized an 'official' meeting" was erroneous. At first, Visser 't Hooft did not fully accept this interpretation. In the mean time Father Antoine Wenger, one of the Catholic participants who had been involved in the 'incident', gave the impression in his magazine *La Croix* that the gathering in Rhodes was official. On the 21st of September Visser 't Hooft again asks for clarification. After the 27th of September 1959, due to a seven-month gap, we are unable to find out exactly what happened from Willebrands' diary entries. We are, however, able to follow a trail from Willebrands' personal archive. After extensive consultations with Rome again, on the 30th of September, Willebrands responds. He confirmed that neither he nor Dumont had been given a mission by the Congregation of the Holy Office to make 'official' contacts with the Orthodox churches in Rhodes. The announcement made by Radio Vaticana did not accurately portray the Vatican's intentions. In this letter he tried to protect his own relationship with Visser 't Hooft by emphasizing that it was Dumont who had acted and not he.

In the meantime on the 1st of October, in the name of the WCC, H.H. Harms informed Willebrands that, due to the 'incident', the planned study days between the Division of Studies of the WCC and the Conférence Catholique pour les questions Œcuméniques, of which Willebrands was chairman, would no longer take place in Assisi from 26-30 October 1959. On the 3rd of October, Visser 't Hooft again writes to Willebrands to tell him that he is disappointed about Willebrands' letter of the 30th of September. He had expected a more public declaration. Shortly thereafter, in an article on the 8th of October 1958, in the Dutch newspaper *De Tijd/De Maasbode*, Willebrands publicly denied that the gathering in Rhodes was 'official' and that the planned meeting between Orthodox and Catholic Christians, which was to be held in Venice in 1960, would not have an 'official' character.

In order to resolve the issue, the Vatican eventually decided to cancel the theological gathering in Venice. For Visser 't Hooft this was sufficient to consider the conflict settled. On the 22nd of October, he writes that he is happy with the Vatican's decision and makes a plea to work "constructively" together on further ecumenical contacts, even if this would "not be easy" initially. On the 14th of November, Willebrands responds. He is relieved with Visser 't Hooft's reconciliatory tone.

Afterwards all parties concerned put forth a great effort to control the damage of the 'Rhodes incident' in their publications[11]. Willebrands wrote a report on the subject for the Dutch community in the St. Willibrord Society magazine, *Het Schild* (*The Shield*) and in the international Bulletin *Vers l'Unité Chrétienne* of Istina. He emphasized again the informal character of the meeting with the Orthodox in Rhodes and tried to clarify a few of the misunderstandings. In *The Ecumenical Review*, published by the WCC, the usefulness of such informal meetings was underlined, although it expressed regret that there was no consultation with the leadership of the WCC beforehand and that the media had 'sensationalized' the event. Because of this the informal meeting received a 'semi-official image', which was not desired. Similarly, disappointment was expressed with the Radio Vaticana announcement. Dumont also tried

---

11. See the declaration of Johannes WILLEBRANDS in *Het Schild* 36 (1958-1959) 157-173 and in *Vers L'Unité Chrétienne: Bulletin catholique d'Information mensuelle Centre d'Études 'Istina'* 13 (1960) 1/2, pp. 1-4; H.-H. HARMS in *Vers l'Unité Chrétienne* 13 (1960) 1/2; C.-J. DUMONT in *Informations Catholiques Internationales* 106 (15, October 1959) 11-15. The reaction of the WCC in *The Ecumenical Review* 12 (1959-1960) 101-103; VISSER 'T HOOFT, *Memoires* (n. 8), p. 293. Reactions from the Orthodox, O. CLÉMENT, *A Misunderstanding at Rhodes? An Orthodox Viewpoint*, in *The Ecumenical Review* 12 (1959-60) 223-230.

to limit the damage, with some success, in *Informations Catholiques Internationales*. In his *Memoirs* (1971) Visser 't Hooft speaks about a series of misunderstandings and praises Willebrands, who "did much to restore the good relations, by publishing a very objective report on the so-called 'Rhodes Incident'"[12].

Willebrands also expresses great respect for Visser 't Hooft, and on the 13th of January 1961, he writes in his diary: "I defend Visser 't Hooft's position as the Secretary General and admire him, not only as a tactician, but also as a man, who has grown in his understanding of the Catholic Church". In Willebrands' now published 'diaries', unlike Visser 't Hooft's *Memoirs*, it appears that there was far greater tension between the two men than they wanted to reveal in public. Therefore, the diary is of historical importance for an accurate interpretation of the 'Rhodes Incident'.

Moreover, the conflict in Rhodes became one of the reasons for the foundation of the Secretariat for Promoting Christian Unity in 1960[13]. It was argued that a centralized authoritative organization in Rome should be able to prevent incidents like 'Rhodes' and clear up potential confusion about what official agencies mean to say or do not mean to say. Significantly, the 'Rhodes incident' did not damage Willebrands' image, neither in the circles of the WCC nor in Rome, but perhaps even enhanced it. In fact, after the event Cardinal Bea appointed him secretary of the new Secretariat.

The last entry of the first notebook is the 27th of September 1959. Willebrands begins his new notebook almost three quarters of a year later, on the 1st of May 1960. In the second notebook, during the 13th session of the Central Committee (WCC) in St. Andrews, Scotland (16-22 August 1960), he continues to deepen his contacts with the World Council of Churches. Together with Bernhard Leeming s.j. (1893-1971), he attends the conference as an official 'observer' and no longer as a 'journalist'[14]. This time, there are no 'incidents'.

---

12. VISSER 'T HOOFT, *Memoires* (n. 8), p. 293.

13. S. SCHMIDT, *Augustin Bea: Der Kardinal der Einheit*, Graz, Styria, 1989, p. 405.

14. In the official report of the meeting of the Central Committee in St. Andrews 1960, the two Catholic participants were mentioned as 'Roman Catholic Observers', while in the report of Rhodes (1959), there was no mention made of the presence of the Catholic 'journalists'. See *Minutes and Reports of the Twelfth Meeting of the Central Committee of the World Council of Churches* (n. 5); *Minutes and Reports of the Thirteenth Meeting of the Central Committee of the World Council of Churches, St. Andrews, Scotland, August 16-24, 1960*, Geneva, WCC, 1960.

Moreover, Willebrands arranges a meeting between Cardinal Bea and Visser 't Hooft for the 22nd of September 1960, in Milan. Willebrands writes in his diary:

> I bring him to Cardinal Bea. I am present during the meeting. Even though there is no publicity, this is a historical meeting. The Cardinal speaks freely and begins to express his satisfaction with the 5 points, where the reaction of the Central Committee (WCC) at St. Andrews to the establishment of the Secretariat is summarized. [...] The Cardinal will propose the 5 points of St. Andrews to the Holy Father.

Willebrands' good contacts with the World Council of Churches result in the attendance of five official Catholic 'observers' at the Assembly in New Delhi a year later in 1961[15]. Given the nature of his new function at the Secretariat for Promoting Christian Unity, Willebrands could not be an official 'observer' in New Delhi.

IV. THE AGENDAS

In the subsequent years, between 1963 and 1965, Willebrands made short annotations in his personal agenda. During this period he did not keep a diary – at least as far as we know. These agendas were later kept in his personal Archive in the Convent of Denekamp, where he stayed during the last years of his life. After his death they came into the possession of the Foundation 'The Cardinal Willebrands Archive' in Utrecht. As stated, the agendas, which he wrote during the Council from 1963-1965, have been edited by the Belgian historian, Leo Declerck. They are now published in French, entitled *Les agendas conciliaires de Mgr. J. Willebrands, secrétaire du Secrétariat pour l'Unité des Chrétiens* (2009). Declerck achieved an excellent work and made almost 1,500 hundred scientific annotations on persons, organizations, institutions and publications, mentioned in the agendas. Let us take a look at the agendas and the work of Leo Declerck.

These agendas were printed in a fairly large format (12,5 × 17,6 cm). Each day is displayed on a single page, including printed time slots for the hours of the day. Willebrands probably filled in the day's activities on the day itself or on one of the following days. He wrote in a telegraphic style. Often, only the name of the person with whom he had a meeting is

---

15. The Catholic Observers were: Edward Duff, T. Edamaran, Jan Groot, I. Extross, Marie-Joseph Le Guillou. See *The New Delhi Report. The Third Assembly of the World Council of Churches 1961*, London, 1962, p. 393.

mentioned, together with the meeting place. Sometimes he adds a few lines to remind him of the content of the conversation or of the meeting.

The agendas deal with the years 1963, 1964 and 1965. Unfortunately, no agenda for 1962 has been found in the archive. This is a pity, since Willebrands travelled to Moscow that year and managed that the Russian Orthodox Church would send observers to the Council. There are some days (and even weeks) where nothing was written. This might indicate that Willebrands took note of things in another place or on loose sheets of paper. For example, there is an extensive report about the hectic days at the end of the 3rd session of the Council and the *modi* that were included in the last resort by the Pope for *De Oecumenismo* or there are notes that were made during travels.

In terms of content these are not diaries. We can only regret the fact that Willebrands did not find the time to write them. During the Council there were many people who were able to make history, but they were unable to find the time to record it.

Nevertheless, Declerck believes that these agendas are a treasure-house of historical information. Why?

> 1. They are extremely objective: they contain only dates and facts; there are little personal comments, opinions or states of mind.
> 2. They are like a short film of each day and sometimes of every hour of Willebrands' life and work during the Council.
> In this way, we are able to trace a great many activities that concern the Council, the activities of the newly formed Secretariat for Promoting Christian Unity and, of course, of Willebrands himself.

Through the agendas we meet Willebrands' co-workers and get a clearer picture of the Secretariat's work methods (meetings, delegated tasks). We experience the search for appropriate locations as well as Willebrands' many international contacts and travels (sometimes with Bea, often with his colleagues: Duprey, Arrighi and Stransky): to Moscow, for example, for the liberation of Josyf Slipyj, to Geneva for the WCC, to La Petite Église in Lyon and Vendée, to Istanbul (for example, for the lifting of the excommunication between Rome and Constantinople at the end of the Council), to the USA, to Taizé, Bulgaria, Yugoslavia, Kiev, etc.

The agendas also contain new and never before published details about the Council:

First, the agendas provide a picture of the influential role that the observers played at the Council. Their role was made possible especially by the excellent reception and guidance that Willebrands provided for them.

Second, we gain new insights into the genesis of many Council texts. We are informed about Willebrands' three journeys to the Middle East in 1965 to consult with the Eastern patriarchs about the text *De Judaeis*. Willebrands went there to convince them to give up their opposition to the text; a mission he successfully completed. Information is also given about the never-ending discussions on the text *De Libertate religiosa*. The agendas contain information about the incidents with Felici in mid-October 1964 and the improbable manoeuvres of the Council minority in September and October 1965 to block the voting of the text. There is also information about the difficult "cooperation" with the council's commission for the Eastern Churches regarding the redaction of the text *De Oecumenismo*.

Let me focus on the text *Nostra Aetate*.

It is common knowledge that the Declaration *Nostra Aetate* on non-Christian religions had a most eventful history. Especially UR 4, on Judaism, was subject to political pressures. The State of Israel claimed a gesture of reconciliation after the Shoah, and the Arabs (especially the Christian Palestinians) were opposed to a declaration because it could be interpreted as an approval of Zionism. In the council rumour circulated that Patriarch Maximos IV would leave the council if the text on the Jews was approved. It was also known that Pope Paul VI in this case would not promulgate the text. Some more conservative council fathers (as the *Coetus Internationalis Patrum*) persisted to blame the whole Jewish people for the death of Christ.

After the third session, when the text was approved in principle, the Secretariat for Promoting Christian Unity had the difficult task to improve the text. It was also evident that the Secretariat of State and the pope himself were directly concerned about the matter. The role of Willebrands became very important here. He had to elaborate some compromises in the text, be attentive to the press and be prudent with the embassies of Arab nations accredited to the Holy See. Already in March 1965, during the plenary meeting of the Secretariat, he prepared some amendments to the text. But in order to overcome the resistance of the Eastern patriarchs he travelled three times to the Near East.

The first journey to Beirut and Damas was made with Father Duprey from 18 to 23 March, 1965 in order to discuss the matter with the Patriarchs Maximos IV and Meouchi and to meet the Orthodox Armenian, Syrian and Greek patriarchs.

During his second journey Willebrands, accompanied by Duprey, went to Jerusalem, Cairo and Addis Abeba. In Jerusalem they met the Latin Patriarch Gori; the Custos of the Holy Land Foundation, Cappiello, the

Armenian Patriarch Derderian, the Greek Orthodox Metropolitan Basilios and the Anglican Archbishop McInnes. In Cairo they made a visit to Patriarch Cardinal Sidarouss, the Copt Orthodox Patriarch Kyrillos, and the Lebanon ambassador, who was Catholic. In Addis Abeba they were received by Emperor Haile Selassie, Coptic Patriarch Theophilos, Catholic Archbishop Yemmeru and Greek Orthodox Archbishop Nikolaos.

In his extensive report of these journeys sent to Msgr. Dell'Acqua, substitute of the Secretariat of State, Willebrands was deeply impressed by the violent opposition to the Declaration by the Eastern patriarchs and the Arab religious and political personalities. He even proposed that the council should not promulgate the Declaration but that the text should be entrusted to the Secretariat for Promoting Christian Unity and the Secretariat for the Non-Christian Religions as a guide for their further activities. It has to be noted that Cardinal Bea demanded that Willebrands made this proposal only in his personal name.

During the plenary session of the Secretariat in May 1965, some modifications were made in the text. For example, the controversial term "deicidium" was deleted and the word "damnat" was substituted by "deplorat". To explain this new text to the Eastern patriarchs, Willebrands made a third journey to the Near East (Beirut, Jerusalem, Cairo) from 18 to 24 July, 1965, accompanied by Bishop De Smedt, vice-president of the Secretariat, and Father Duprey. This time his efforts were successful. Gori remained opposed, but the other patriarchs agreed to the new text. Even though he still proposed four emendations, Maximos IV promised to support the Declaration.

During the session of the Secretariat of 15 September, 1965, Willebrands and De Smedt successfully introduced three of the four emendations in the text suggested by Maximos. Lastly, on 27 and 28 September, 1965 Willebrands visited the ambassadors of the Arab nations to explain the new version of the Declaration. The pope was reassured, and the Declaration was to be promulgated on 28 October, 1965. Willebrands' agendas illustrate that the creation of this important council text was not solely the work of the council fathers or the members of the council commissions, but was also the fruit of the perseverance and diplomatic qualities of the intelligent secretary of the Secretariat for Promoting Christian Unity.

Finally, the agendas also provide a picture of the man Johannes Willebrands and his close and loyal relationship with family and friends ... His concern for his co-workers in the Secretariat (a visit to their father or mother in the Netherlands or Switzerland; he took them home after they worked all night; he celebrated their birthdays) ... His enormous energy and ability to work (he was at the office at 8:00 in the morning and often worked until late at night, as well as on weekends and during holidays) … The importance that he placed on the spiritual life and pastoral care (his attention to the daily Eucharist, even when travelling to foreign countries; he spent Holy Week in an abbey; the homilies and conferences; his close relationship with the Sisters of Saint Lioba and the Dominican Sisters of Bethany) …. His cultural interests… (visits to churches, museums, monuments, movies and ballet during his travels). His pragmatic and sober approach helped him avoid panic or reacting too emotionally during even the greatest trials.

Of course, after reading the agendas, we remain hungry for more, says Leo Declerck. They provide only a framework and need to be completed by other data. To some extent this has been provided by Leo Declerck's notes that complement the text. The agendas are merely the skeleton, that needs flesh and blood. But it is also a structure that provides stability and solid reference points. Father Stransky's beautiful introduction to the published agendas shows how they give shape to a warm and moving testimony of these agitated years in the life of Willebrands, whom he so accurately characterizes as "a Dutch gentleman".

V. Diaries and Agenda's as a New Source

As discussed, Leo Declerck calls the Agendas "a treasure-house of historical information". I totally agree with this vision. The same could be said of the Diaries. In his Diaries and Agendas, Willebrands carefully mentions many names of persons and organizations. In this sense, we see that he wrote both the diary and agenda as an aide memoire for his work. For him, it was a way to remember the growing list of names and backgrounds of his ever-expanding network of ecumenical contacts throughout the world. The diaries and agendas are a rich source of information for future researchers who are interested in reconstructing the network of ecumenical 'activists' and 'activities' in Protestant, Orthodox and Catholic circles of the day. They provide a view behind the curtain, of areas where most research must content itself with public sources.

The study of the diaries and agendas, in the context of the ecumenical movement, national and international, provides new insights, especially into the relations of the Catholic Church with the Anglican Church and with the World Council of Churches in the period shortly before the Second Vatican Council, and in the role of the Secretariat for Promoting

Christian Unity during the Council. Furthermore, it provides fascinating information about the faction forming within the Vatican before and during the Council.

Tilburg School of Catholic Theology   Theo SALEMINK
Tilburg University
Heidelberglaan 2
NL 3508 TC Utrecht
The Netherlands

II. WILLEBRANDS AND THE DEVELOPMENT OF
THE CATHOLIC VIEW ON ECUMENISM DURING
THE SECOND VATICAN COUNCIL

WILLEBRANDS AT THE COUNCIL

A HISTORICAL APPROACH

When he was named secretary of the Secretariat for Promoting Christian Unity (SPCU), Johannes Willebrands was a foreigner in the milieu of the Roman Curia. The letter of nomination, signed by the Secretary of State Cardinal Tardini, arrived at the wrong diocese, to the Archbishop of Utrecht and not at the Haarlem diocese. Willebrands had the news from the Dutch agency KNP, although he had been prepared by his precedent talks with his friends in Rome, Cardinal Bea *in primis*[1]. Since his first talk with Bea, in May 1960, he had manifested his doubts and so a phase of reflection on the possible acceptance started. He feared possible consequences on his project of the constitution of an Oratorium in Holland. He also feared the negative effects on the position of his friend Frans Thijssen, who was living a precarious situation from the ecclesiastical point of view. But there was another point of difficulty.

The Roman Curia, as seen by some Dutch and other continental ecumenists, appeared at that moment to be a closed circle, dominated by a closed theology which did not give space to dialogue with non-Roman churches. He wrote in his diary: "In any case, I would personally prefer not to live in Rome – and it would benefit the work when I wouldn't get stuck in Rome, with the danger to suffocate and to be suffocated"[2]. Upon personal reflection and consultation with friends, however, Willebrands decided to accept the position. He began his work in the Secretariat in the late summer of 1960. The history of Willebrands' participation in the council is strictly linked with this charge, and it is not a linear or progressive affirmation, but rather represents a winding road, a balance of conflicts and realizations, of notorious victories and hidden pressures from above. It was a turning point in his personal life, as much as in the larger

---

1. "In the afternoon, the KNP calls me: Radio Vaticana has announced my appointment as Secretary of the Secretariat for Christian Unity. I don't know anything about this. It's more than likely that this announcement is true: it fits with the talk that Dr. Thijssen and I recently had with Cardinal Bea and, moreover, Radio Vaticana is usually trustworthy with this type of information" 28.6.1960, in T. SALEMINK (ed.), *"You Will Be Called Repairer of the Breach" : The Diary of J.G.M. Willebrands 1958-1961*, Leuven, Peeters, 2009, p. 172.

2. Note of 3.6.1960, in *ibid.*, p. 164.

range of the history of Catholicism, and after five years, in 1965, the balance was largely positive.

I. The Preparatory Phase

Willebrands was a simple priest when John XXIII announced the council, and he did not participate in the ante-preparatory consultation in 1959[3]. Nevertheless he sent a large document to a number of bishops, the Note of the Direction Committee of the Catholic Conference for Ecumenical Questions (CCEQ). Father C.-J. Dumont had written the first draft of the text, but Willebrands' essential contribution is supported with documentation[4]. These were the vota of a large group of ecumenists in Europe and represented the pastoral and doctrinal bases for a new attitude of the Catholic Church before non-Roman churches[5]. The new charge in the Secretariat gave him the opportunity to work at the centre of the elaboration of some of the texts for the council. The personnel of the Secretariat was named following the indication of the secretary, and we find among them names of theologians and bishops who were involved in different ways in the precedent activities of the Conference. The newly published diaries of this period show also Willebrands' efforts to name as a correspondent member an Italian layman whom he had met in Milan, Franco Falchi. The rigid rules of the Curia did not permit laymen's participation.

The preparatory phase lasted from November 1960 to June 1962 and the Secretariat produced a large number of documents on different subjects[6]. Willebrands' role in the work of the Secretariat was typical. As in the previous times in the Conference, he carried out his activity with a singular capacity to co-ordinate and unify the various members'

---

3. On the general history of the council see G. Alberigo (ed.), *The History of Vatican II*, vol. 1-5, Leuven, Peeters, 1995-2006.

4. "1 March 1959, Morning, P. Dumont at Dutch College. Went through the draft of Dumont's report, with my remarks. What will we do with this report? Will the Comité Directeur sign it? P. Boyer? Shall we send it to the Bishops?" Notes of 1.3.1959, 2.4.1959 and 13.5.1959 in Salemink (ed.), *"You Will Be Called Repairer of the Breach"* (n. 1), pp. 82, 89 and 96. Willebrands' notes to the document can be found in Willebrands' archives in Chevetogne.

5. An Italian version of the text was published in G. Alberigo, *Agli albori dell'ecumenismo cattolico*, in E. Curzel (ed.), *In factis mysterium legere. Miscellanea di studi in onore di Iginio Rogger in occasione del suo ottantesimo compleanno*, Bologna, EDB, 1999, 216-233.

6. See M. Velati, *Dialogo e rinnovamento: Verbali e testi del segretariato per l'unità dei cristiani nella preparazione del concilio (1960-1962)*, Bologna, Il Mulino, 2011.

contributions. The minutes of the Secretariat's meetings during this phase contain relatively few interventions by the secretary on the matters discussed. Nevertheless these rare interventions show an attentive consideration of the subjects, not only in the realm of theological signification but also on the level of effects on pastoral care. They also provide a little catalogue of Willebrands' opinions on some of the most discussed problems in the Church at the eve of the council. He declares himself favourable to the introduction of the vernacular in liturgy instead of Latin, not only for a better "intellectual understanding" but rather for the creation of a way of "communication" between the people and the priest[7]. He approves the return to receiving holy communion under two species and the reintroduction of permanent diaconate[8]. On the other hand, he rejects the praxis of the rebaptism of a convert to Catholicism. During the debate over the question of the membership in the Church Willebrands insists for letting go the traditional language of "members" and adopting instead the new terminology of "elements of the Church", as it will also be in the definitive text of *Unitatis redintegratio*[9].

One of the main problems of the debate on ecumenism was that of the relationship between conversion work and dialogue with the separate churches. In Holland Willebrands lived through the difficult transition from the old way of seeking conversions to the new way of dialogue which emerged from the development of an ecumenical theology in Europe. He saw no radical opposition between these two elements. The experience of conversion has a deep spiritual dimension, but beyond it there is place for dialogue. For Willebrands ecumenism is not only a sort of "corporate reunion". It has its roots in the dimension of ecumenicity that the Belgian theologian Gustave Thils had defined in texts produced during the preparatory phase. In debating these texts Willebrands outlined the specificity of this notion, whose importance is basic for the Catholic understanding of ecumenism: "Ecumenicity is not linked with separation. Ecumenicity includes centuries, times, places and all mankind. We cannot forget the difference between catholic and protestant

7. "*Mgr. Willebrands*: il ne s'agit pas seulement de la compréhension intellectuelle du texte; il s'agit de créer par la langue une sorte de communication entre le peuple et le prêtre", *ibid.*, p. 435.

8. *Ibid.*, pp. 436 and 662.

9. "*Mgr. Willebrands* souligne que 'membrum' et 'filium' se réfèrent à des personnes. L'expression élément indique quelque chose de constitutif et indique que ce n'est qu'une partie de la totalité, alors que 'organum' peut désigner toute l'Eglise 'organum salutis'", *ibid.*, p. 330.

ecumenism, as the second is conceived as interconfessionalism"[10]. Following this distinction Willebrands was very attentive to avoid every confusion or superficiality.

During the preparatory phase the Secretariat produced thirteen texts on doctrinal and pastoral subjects. Most of them regarded the ecumenical field, but the main idea of the work was that of the transversal quality of the ecumenical dimension. For this reason some of the texts touched internal subjects of Roman doctrine (the role of the laity in the Church, liturgy, ecclesiology, etc). The drafting of the texts was committed to some of the consultants of the Secretariat, but the work proceeded in a strict link with the staff of the Secretariat, particularly the secretary. The distinctive sign of Willebrands' contribution to this work is his skill to manage the collective work in sub-commissions. At least in two cases his intervention was decisive for the conclusion of the work. The third sub-commission on "Catholic ecumenism" was divided due to the eccentric presence of Father Edward Hanahoe who was not integrated in the global "ecumenical" perspective of the Secretariat's work. Willebrands' intervention in July 1961 released the brake on the work with the insertion of two of his most reliable collaborators (F. Thijssen and G. Thils) in the sub-commission and the choice of a new "pastoral" approach for the subject. In the same way he intervened for a better definition of the work of sub-commission 9 on the "prayer for unity". In the first months different projects had been presented, but a clear opposition between the two traditional lines in this field emerged. On one hand was the Franciscan congregation of the Friars of the Atonement, of which Hanahoe was a member. On the other hand was the French priest Paul Couturier, represented in the Secretariat by the Dominican priest Christophe Dumont, a good friend of Willebrands. After the presentation of two different texts of a prayer's formulation which had not received the agreement of the members, Willebrands suggested to revise the aim of the work, rather than watching towards the drafting of a generic exhortation on prayer, without fixing the formula[11].

A certain influence of Willebrands' thought on the work of the sub-commissions is clear also in the case of *De Iudaeis*. The draft presented in August 1961 at the plenary session of the Secretariat had two different parts, one dedicated to theological principles, and the other to practical

10. *Ibid.*, p. 552. Thils also wrote one of the most important books on the ecumenical movement for the time, G. THILS, *Histoire doctrinal du mouvement oecuménique*, Louvain, E. Warny, 1955.
11. VELATI, *Dialogo e rinnovamento* (n. 6), pp. 460-461.

proposals. In debating the text Willebrands intervened to express his doubts on the proposal of extending to the universal Church the feasts of some saints and prophets of the Old Testament, already revered by the local church of Jerusalem. At the same time he declared resolutely that the question of the recognition of the State of Israel was not in the agenda. The result of the discussion was to cut out the practical part of the document and to develop the first part of theological principles with the rejection of anti-Semitism[12]. Willebrands had a clear conscience of the singularity of the Jewish question and of the deep differences with the ecumenical one. In November 1961 in a subsequent discussion he noticed in the text the use of the words "fratres separati" as improper for addressing the Jewish people. He also participated in the enlarged commission charged with the drafting of a new version of the decree *De Iudaeis*[13].

II. The Non-Catholic Observers at Vatican II

Apart from the sub-commission's work in the Secretariat, the only direct responsibility of the secretary was related to the non-Catholic observers' invitation at the council. Willebrands seized the opportunity of a hint in John XXIII's announcement of the council on January 25th 1959, and prepared a proposition to be approved by the Secretariat during the preparatory phase[14]. The matter was difficult because of its novelty and because of the opposition it received from some cardinals and prelates of the Roman Curia. Willebrands realized that the main problem was secrecy. The presence of observers might jeopardize confidentiality. However, on the other hand, it met the need for the Church itself to be more open and clear. In his report to the Secretariat Willebrands wrote: "(…) il ne faut pas perdre de vue le grand bien que poursuit l'Église en admettant les frères séparés à une présence d'Observateurs. Nous n'avons pas à cacher ou à dissimuler, au contraire nous devons nous montrer nous-même tels que nous sommes et l'Église telle qu'elle est"[15]. Another

---

12. The minutes say: "L'après-midi lors de la reprise du travail à 15 h. 30, Son Éminence ajoute ceci: en modifiant les vota, il vaut mieux parler de choses doctrinales et citer quelques points sans donner d'applications pratiques. Ces applications pratiques pourraient passer dans un Directoire qui serait à préparer ultérieurement, mais après le Concile", *Dialogo e rinnovamento* (n. 6), pp. 645-652.

13. *Ibid.*, pp. 741-744.

14. On the important discourse of the pope see A. MELLONI, *L'annuncio del Vaticano II*, in *Papa Giovanni. Un cristiano e il suo concilio*, Torino, Einaudi, 2009, pp. 195-225.

15. *Dialogo e rinnovamento* (n. 6), p. 305.

problem was the choice of the partners. Who will be the addressees of
the invitation? As the diaries show, Willebrands spoke with various
people engaged in Catholic ecumenism. The easiest solution was that of
an invitation to public events such as the inauguration ceremony of the
council, addressed to the representatives of bishops and authorities of
various Churches. In Willebrands' mind this was a superficial approach,
at the same time too optimistic and too little pretentious. He reflected in
his diary commenting a talk with Father Stephanou and a precedent proposal of a German ecumenist, Dr. Albert Brandenburg:

> My difficulties with this, at least my questions about this remain: Can we
> request such a demonstrative presence of the leaders of the separated
> churches at the opening of the Council of the Catholic Church, without them
> knowing about the approaching decisions of the Council? Doesn't their
> presence imply their involvement in what follows, in the coming decisions,
> about which they would rather raise protest? Can we promise them that
> such decisions, against which they must protest, will not be made, that we
> will take their objections into consideration, at least negatively? That is, we
> will do nothing that will cause a new fundamental protest (e.g. new Marian
> dogmas, etc.). Moreover: is such a demonstrative presence the most useful
> at this moment? Is this type of presence and encounter that we need and
> should request now for the restoration of unity? Shouldn't we search for a
> presence and cooperation that isn't demonstrative, more modest, but none-
> theless, more realistic? If we ask professors, then, the questions about prec-
> edence fall away; then, we get people, who are theologically prepared for
> a discussion with Catholics; who are able to understand us, at least to some
> extent. They are capable of observation and then of reproducing what they
> observed for their religious communities. They must be given the opportu-
> nity to receive information; explanations about the questions that concern
> us; the opportunity to ask questions, to request an explanation, etc. Of
> course not at the meetings, where they are unable to speak, but at gatherings
> that have been organized for them, on the margin of the Council, where
> competent persons are able to respond to their questions. They must receive
> a good seat at the meetings and be able to follow the discussions. They need
> to have more access than journalists[16].

In these lines the core of Willebrands' project for the observers at the
council was already set up. After the approval by the Pope of the final
document of the Secretariat (*Votum propositum a secretariatu ad christianorum unitatem fovendam*), Willebrands began to contact a number of
churches and church federations to test their willingness to send a delegation to Rome. In a few months, between January and September 1962,
he played the role of an 'ecumenical globetrotter' visiting most of the

---

16. SALEMINK (ed.), *"You Will Be Called Repairer of the Breach"* (n. 1), p. 232, note
of 23.11.1960.

authorities of non-Roman churches. Willebrands relied on the General Secretary of the World Council of Churches, Dr. Willem A. Visser 't Hooft, who introduced his Catholic fellow-countryman into the Protestant circles of ecumenical relationships. The result of this tiring and complex activity went beyond all expectations. In October 1962 when the council was opened a group of churchmen from various origins sat in Saint Longinus' tribune before the presidency table of the council and not far from the papal throne[17]. The presence of a Russian delegation was the most talked about. Willebrands, and through him the Secretariat, had been able to renew the face of Catholicism, creating the "address ... in Rome" which Visser 't Hooft missed already in the 1950s[18]. Willebrands' diplomacy was different from traditional Catholic approaches, based on church-state relations. It distinguished itself even from the local Catholic churches' points of view which were generally in conflict with Protestant or Orthodox majoritarian churches. He searched for a direct church-to-church relationship, based on common faith elements. Here lies the secret of his good outcome.

When at the council the debate began the observers were immediately involved in the bishops' internal conflicts and dynamics. Willebrands and Bea asked them to express their opinions and requests on the matters of debate during a weekly meeting that was a real "parallel council", formed by the representatives of all the most important Christian churches[19]. The passive attitude of the "observer" was transformed into a passionate attitude that took some of the Protestant observers to make an alliance with the most progressive parts of the episcopate. The observers' opinions were reflected and diffused by international newspapers and progressively won the confidence of large parts of the catholic world.

---

17. The list of official observers at the first session of the Council in *Observateurs-délégués et hôtes du Secretariat pour l'unité des chrétiens au deuxième concile oecuménique du Vatican*, Città del Vaticano, Typis polyglottis vaticanis, 1965, pp. 11-15. Cf. T. STRANSKY, *The Observers et Vatican II: A Unique Experience of Dialogue*, in *Centro Pro Unione Bullettin* 63 (2003) 8-14.

18. "I had so often complained that although we had many contacts with individual Roman Catholics, there was no address or office in the Roman Catholic Church to which we could turn to discuss problems of relationship at an ecclesiastical and representative level" in A.W. VISSER 'T HOOFT, *Memoirs*, London, SCM, 1973, p. 328.

19. There is no complete series of the minutes of these meetings, conceived at the beginning as informal discussions on the conciliar matters. The personal archives of Charles Moeller at the Centre Lumen Gentium in Louvain-la-Neuve keep the copies of the 1963 and 1964 minutes, so as the Fondo Concilio Vaticano II in the Vatican Secret Archives. A useful complement is Douglas Horton's diary published in four volumes (D. HORTON, *Vatican Diary*, 4 vol., Philadelphia, PA – Boston, MA, United Church Press, 1965).

Willebrands was the secret director of this relationship and he found himself repeatedly at the centre of ticklish communication cases. At the end of the second session the representative of the Evangelische Kirche in Deutschland (EKD) Edmund Schlink protested against a wrong interpretation of his words during a press conference, and Willebrands had to mediate between Schlink and the journalists of the *Deutsche Pressezentrum*. The observers felt very acutely the risk of a propagandistic exploitation of their presence in Rome, in the direction of the unionist activity.

At the same time a large part of Catholic bishops, supported by some cardinals of the Roman Curia, became more and more annoyed by the growing influence of the observers. At the end of the first session a bitter saying circulated among these groups of bishops: "If you want to have credit at the council you have to be a cardinal or an observer". The climax of this hidden conflict was reached in November 1964 when the Decree on Ecumenism was voted on definitively by the council fathers. In a final intervention the pope inserted nineteen amendments that had not been considered by the bishops – some of which touched neuralgic points of division between Catholics and Protestants. The observers were troubled by the fact, not only for the pejorative amendments but also for the procedure. The pope's imposition was seen as the last example of Roman authoritarianism. The reactions were very hot and Willebrands found himself at the very centre of the storm. The observers did not know that the secretary of the SPCU in the precedent hours had been the protagonist of a close negotiation with the pope and his collaborators which had the effect to considerably reduce the number of the amendments requested[20]. At the weekly meeting of the observers, the same day of the announcement, Willebrands was pressed by the requests of explanation and his reply left many of the observers' eyes wet by tears. He called his fellow Christian brothers to unity and asked for a strong common engagement in prayer. This is the report of Douglas Horton, an American representative of the International Congregational Council:

> Bishop Willebrands' reply left us with wet eyes. He too was sorry that the change had been made. In fact, more than one of the events of the morning had filled him with regret. (And regret did indeed speak for him in the very tone of his voice.) In the midst of the present strained circumstances, in which misunderstandings could so easily develop, he hoped that we would look past the temporary setbacks to the great gains that had already been established in the field of ecumenicity and which were registered in many paragraphs of the schema; and then, still speaking in French in response to

20. See M. VELATI, *L'ecumenismo al concilio: Paolo VI e l'approvazione di Unitatis redintegratio (1964)*, in *Cristianesimo nella Storia* 27 (2005) 427-476.

Dr. Cullmann, he said the equivalent for "Don't give up us!" This became suddenly a moment of rededication. We observers saw, as by a flash of light, where the knife cut deepest – in the red flesh of the Secretariat. These men, dedicated to church unity, had unexpectedly had their plans scotched by brethren of their own household. Observers could sit loose to these events, but not they, whose loyalty to their church is closer than breathing. We on our side were determined not to be separated from them in thought or word. [...] bishop Willebrands himself now having to take his leave, the Bishop of Ripon [J. Moorman, Anglican representative] rose and, in behalf of us all, thanked him for his unfailing courtesy and his innumerable acts of hospitality[21].

After the end of the third session the revolutionary fact of the promulgation of the ecumenical decree *Unitatis redintegratio* enlightened also the trouble of the last weeks under a new, positive light, but the presence itself of the observers at the council was progressively discussed by some eminent cardinals of the Roman Curia.

In April 1965 the Pope informed Bea that some "voci che corrono" ("running rumours") asked to discontinue having observers, not to renew the invitation for the fourth session of the council[22]. Cardinal Cicognani had already expressed his doubts, but the most vigorous pressures on the pope probably came from the secretary of the council Pericle Felici. Willebrands' diary quotes Cicognani's synthetic comment after the delivery of a note signed by a group of observers relating to the question of mixed marriages. He said to Willebrands who was the courier: "Sono osservatori" ("They are observers")[23]. Willebrands defended till the end of the council the presence of the observers and their right to speak on conciliar subjects. His final masterpiece was probably the prayer for unity held in the Basilica of Saint Paul Outside the Walls on the 4th of December 1965 at which the pope presided, surrounded by the council fathers and observers. It was, in fact, Paul VI's idea that, in a first phase, met the opposition of some Protestant observers (like L. Vischer and

21. D. Horton, *Vatican Diary 1964: A Protestant Observes the Third Session of Vatican Council II*, Philadelphia, PA – Boston, MA, United Church Press, 1965, pp. 187-188.
22. See T. Stransky, *Paul VI and the Delegated Observers/Guests to Vatican Council II*, in *Paolo VI e l'ecumenismo: Colloquio internazionale di studio Brescia 25-26-27 settembre 1998*, Rome, Istituto Paolo VI, 2001, 118-158, pp. 147-148.
23. Even at the end of October 1965 Willebrands' diary registers a Cicognani's bitter comment on the liberty of the Council: "Ensuite, il fait une remarque générale sur le concile: le concile n'est pas libre: 'noi siamo nelle mani di coloro che non comandano: le donne, gli osservatori, la stampa!'" (note of 24.10.1965, in L. Declerck [ed.], *Les agendas conciliaires de Mgr. J. Willebrands, Secrétaire du Secrétariat pour l'unité des chrétiens*, Leuven, Peeters, 2009, p. 247).

E. Schlink), but in the following weeks grew as a project strongly
supported by Willebrands. In this case Willebrands had to negotiate for
dissolving the observers' fears and doubts. An act of prayer with the pope
could produce in Protestant communities a very strong reaction, but the
event was prepared with great care. The presidency of the pope was very
discrete. He sat on a simple elevated chair, not on the papal throne. The
resounding in the great basilica (the same place where John XXIII had
announced the council) of the notes of a Lutheran chorale were a clear
sign of the ecumenical engagement of the Catholic Church[24].

III. THE TEXTS

In 1960 many people in Rome considered the new Secretariat a simple
'information office', a sort of complement of the *Osservatore Romano*,
specialised in relationships with other Christians. For Bea and Willebrands the stake was considerably higher. The council was the prospect
for a true renewal of Catholicism, of which the Secretariat's contribution
could be very significant. The work program had been decided during the
first meeting of the Secretariat in November 1960, through a unique procedure. There were no indications from above but a free discussion, with
the contribution at the same level of the Secretariat's members and
consultants. In this way some of the most important subjects of the
desired renewal were emerging: valorisation of the laity, liturgical
reform, renewal of ecclesiology, a new attitude of the Church towards
the Jewish people and a new ecumenical engagement[25]. The Secretariat
did not want to compete with the theological commission. However,
inaugurating ecumenical dialogue – which was its specific goal – had
some terms, among which the most important were theological renewal
and the gradual rapprochement between the Catholic Church and the
other churches. The same perspective had driven the work of the Catholic Conference on Ecumenical Questions in the precedent years. In
Willebrands' opinion ecumenism was not a pastime for snob ecclesiastics
but a real need of the Catholic Church in the present time, a recall to its
truest 'catholic' nature.

---

24. On the preparation and the development of this historic event see M. VELATI,
Separati ma fratelli: Gli osservatori non cattolici al Vaticano II, publication forthcoming.
    25. See J. KOMONCHAK, *The Struggle for the Council During the Preparation of Vati-
can II (1960-1962)*, in ALBERIGO (ed.), *The History of Vatican II* (n. 3), vol. 1, 227-300.

When the Secretariat began to write some texts on some different subjects Willebrands had the difficult task to look for a collaboration by the other preparatory commissions. Already at the very beginning of his charge, talking with Bea, he realized the problems. And he noted in his diary: "The difficulties that we should expect: with the Roman Curia, the Holy Office and the Congregation for the Oriental Churches"[26]. The diary also shows the deceptive contacts with Father Tromp, secretary of the theological commission, and those with the liturgical commission and the commission on Oriental Churches. In Rome the Secretariat in a short time was considered an inconvenient presence. Tromp wrote in his diary after a long meeting with Willebrands: "Vult omnia facere"[27]. The impression of an uncontrolled activism is not far from the real truth. The enthusiasm of neophytes was certainly a distinctive character of the Secretariat's men but Tromp did not understand the real dimensions of Willebrands' idea, that of ecumenism as a key for renewal, expanding itself to most of the branches of catholic doctrine and praxis. The Secretariat was an "information office" but paradoxically the secretary of the council Felici reproved Willebrands for his press contacts and his writing some articles on ecumenism. The new style of communication of the Secretariat and Willebrands' open attitude to the press contrasted with the Roman tradition of secrecy, or better introduced a modern interpretation of this tradition.

During the preparatory period the Secretariat produced some documents which did not reach the bishops. Only the events of the first session and the surprising attitude of the bishops, rejecting most of the documents proposed by the theological commission, threw in the Secretariat's contribution. At the same time John XXIII had confirmed the Secretariat as a conciliar commission pulling it out from the limbo of an uncertain juridical legitimation. The Secretariat became the leader of the so-called "second preparation" and Willebrands found himself at the

---

26. SALEMINK (ed.), *"You Will Be Called Repairer of the Breach"* (n. 1), p. 175, note of 8.7.1960. Willebrands had a strong collaboration with the German Jesuit and cardinal, based on a common vision of ecumenical fundamentals: cf. S. SCHMIDT, *Agostino Bea: il cardinale dell'unità*, Roma, Città Nuova, 1987.

27. "Vespere longum colloquium cum Mgr Willebrands, secr. Secr. pro unione: Dicit se addere debuisse plures paginas in Const. de Oecumenismo de Protestantibus, ita volente Cardli Secr. Status, et se non habuisse tempus monstrandi mihi Schema. Vult omnia facere, ut non obstante responso Secretarii Status agatur de libertate et tolerantia religiosa. Dixi ei ubi iacent difficultates theoricae et practicae quaestionis. Sed mansit in suo proposito, ita tamen ut redactio committatur secretariis Comm. doctr. et Secr. pro unione", S. TROMP, *Diarium Secretarii Commissionis Theologicæ Concilii Vaticani II, adiunctis documentis variis*, ed. A. VON TEUFFENBACH, versionem germanicam confecit B. Wegener, Romæ, Editrice Pontificia Università gregoriana, 2006.

centre of an extended net of relations and conflicts[28]. The ecumenical dossier was the reason of a lasting tension with the conciliar Commission for the Oriental Churches. This commission had prepared a text *De unitate ecclesiae ut omnes unum sint* which had received the approbation of the secretary of the council and of Cardinal Cicognani, who was the president of the same commission. The Secretariat for Promoting Christian Unity had prepared its own text *De oecumenismo catholico* of which the third chapter, divided into two parts, paid attention to the divisions which occurred in history in the body of Christianity. Cicognani wanted this chapter to focus exclusively on Protestantism. At the same time Willebrands was aware of the unity of the ecumenical movement. If the council had to make a statement on the relationships with Orthodox Churches, it would be necessary to do it in the larger context of a decree on ecumenism rather than in a document primarily regarding the Oriental Catholic churches. In a first phase of common work, a new text was written. Willebrands relied on his friend and fellow-countryman J. Witte, a member of the conciliar theological commission. In September 1963 the secretary of the Commission for the Oriental Churches, the Ukrainian priest A. Welicky, attacked Willebrands for his work with the Secretariat, rejecting his idea of unity in an ecumenical approach[29]. Conflicts of competences hindered this activity, but the real legitimation of the Secretariat's work came from the bishops who were gradually convinced by its 'modernisation' program.

The most discussed texts of the Secretariat were nevertheless *De libertate religiosa* and *De Iudaeis*. The first was the result of a long negotiation which tried to unify the different texts of the preparatory phase[30]. It was written in a sub-commission guided by the bishop of Bruges, Mgr. De Smedt. The ideas in this text stood in tension however with chapter 10 of *De Ecclesia*, regarding relationships between church and state, a text prepared by the Theological Commission. The theological approaches were very different. Willebrands was at the very core of the negotiations, with his continued relationships with Father Tromp and Cardinal Ottaviani. He knew the importance of the matter. In one of the first meetings with Visser 't Hooft, after the announcement of the

28. Jan Grootaers used the term of "second preparation" referring to the period of the first intersession when many of the texts of the council were revised or created anew (see *History of the Vatican II* [n. 3], vol. 3).

29. *Les agendas conciliaires* (n. 23), pp. 58-59.

30. The history of the text in S. SCATENA, *La fatica della libertà: L'elaborazione della dichiarazione "Dignitatis Humanae" sulla libertà religiosa del Vaticano II*, Bologna, Il Mulino, 2003.

council, he became aware of the fact that Protestants considered religious liberty a decisive "test" for the appreciation of the expected Catholic renewal in the council. In view of the fact that Protestant communities had been discriminated in Spain and Columbia, the ecumenical way passed also through a mitigation of Catholic traditional doctrine on the "Catholic state" and a limited acceptance of the principle of religious liberty. The first project of the text appeared during the second period as an *appendix* to the ecumenical scheme. The effort of the secretariat in the following time was that of keeping the responsibility on the matter, against different attempts to remove it from the agenda of the council or to put it under the closed sovereignty of the theological commission of card. Ottaviani.

One of the most dramatic moments occurred at the beginning of October 1964 when the secretary of the council Felici tried to impose the formation of a *commissio mixta*, whose members were some of the strongest opponents of the declaration (for example, the French bishop Marcel Lefebvre). The manoeuvre was stopped by a coordinated effort of the leaders of the secretariat. Immediately Bea wrote a letter to the Pope. Willebrands' diary shows the close exchange between the secretary of SPCU and Mgr. Dell'Acqua of the Secretariat of State, who had repudiated Felici's solitary enterprise[31]. The creation of an experts' group was decided but – interpreting also the will of Paul VI – the secretary of state reaffirmed the full responsibility of the SPCU on the matter. At the end of the third period the announced promulgation of the declaration was postponed, thus showing once more the force of the opponents in the conciliar assembly and most of all in the strict interlacement of relations between the presidency of the council and the Roman congregations. Willebrands' specific contribution to the declaration was not at theological level, where a growing influence came from the American theologian J.C. Murray, but in a sort of motherly service of surveillance, with the attention to preserve a place of "freedom" inside the secretariat for bishops and theologians. During the fourth period he also placed the matter on the agenda of the weekly meetings with the observers, collecting some concrete proposals for the emendation of the text. The observers were not officially members of the council but their proposals passed through the collaboration of the secretariat and of some friends-bishops like Hermann Volk or the Swiss prelate H. Vonderach.

---

31. See *Les agendas conciliaires* (n. 23), pp. 137-143.

The question of *De Iudaeis* was not less complex[32]. There played a role not only theological elements but even diplomatic factors coming from the political situation of the Middle East. The conflict between tradition and reform was complicated by the interference of parallel conflicts between the Latin church and the Eastern Catholic churches, living in Islamic countries, and finally between the opponent interests of the two diplomacies of the Arab Countries and of Israel, both pressing on the Vatican for a preferential treatment. Willebrands found himself at the very core of these conflicts. The first draft of *De Iudaeis* was presented in the second period as an appendix of the ecumenical scheme. As in the case of *De libertate* this was the only way to preserve the Secretariat's entire responsibility on the matter. The opposition of the Secretary of State Cicognani towards the possibility of putting the matter on the agenda of the council was well known. Willebrands had to confront himself with a rather different approach from the ecumenical one, i.e. the world of Vatican diplomacy. His principal partner was Mgr. Dell'Acqua, substitute at the Secretariat of State, an Italian prelate who was very far from him from the point of view of culture and education, but with whom Willebrands was able to build a personal relationship based on confidence and respect[33].

In Willebrands' diary the numerous quotations from meetings and contacts with Dell'Acqua reflect the absence of conflicts or incomprehension, so frequent in the relations with other members of the Curia. Dell'Acqua was one of the few prelates of the Roman Curia whose attitude was sympathetic with the Secretariat's effort to renew the public image of the Roman Catholic Church. He had also a key-role in the communication with Paul VI, ensuring a direct line between the Secretariat and the Pope, also in the most dramatic moment of conciliar history. He was for example the channel in the negotiations between Willebrands and Montini for the 19 amendments to *Unitatis redintegratio* in November 1964. As for *De Iudaeis* Willebrands had to keep some contacts also with the first section of the Secretariat of State, which had competence for the relationships with States and was directed at that time

---

32. On the history of *Nostra Aetate* see J.M. OESTERREICHER, *Waking the Dawn*, in *The New Encounter between Christian and Jews*, New York, Philosophical Library, 1986, 103-295; N. LAMDAN – A. MELLONI (eds.), *Nostra Aetate. Origins, Promulgations and Impact on Jewish-Catholic Relations*, Münster, LIT Verlag, 2007.

33. See for example the annotation of 12.7.1963: "Au sujet du communiqué de presse de ce matin, on a oublié d'en parler à la Secrétairerie d'État. J'ai téléphoné à Dell'Acqua. Celui-ci dit qu'il suffit que le P. Duprey vienne l'apporter 'per conoscenza'. Cela est un heureux exemple de confiance", in *Les agendas conciliaires* (n. 23), p. 41.

by mgr Samorè[34]. The affaire had a great impact on mass media and Willebrands had to organise a sort of "media strategy" of the Secretariat to reassure the Arab public opinion and in the meantime to sustain the level of the declaration before the Jewish world. In March 1965 Willebrands made a long journey to Middle East and North Africa to meet the Eastern Catholic Patriarchs and have an adjourned photograph of the situation in the Arab countries. Willebrands had studied some days before a dossier of the Nuncio Angelo Felici which contained some critical outlines on the strategy of the Secretariat. The short circuit between diplomacy and Willebrands ecumenical approach produced some fire after the journey, with the strange situation of Vatican diplomats writing dispatches on the Secretariat's envoy! Willebrands wrote in his diary: "10 h: Chez le card. Bea avec le P. Long. Après notre arrivée, le cardinal nous fait lire les deux rapports des nonces à Beyrouth et à Damas au sujet de mon voyage du 18 au 23 mars. Ces rapports sont rédigés à la demande de la Secrétairerie d'État. La réaction du cardinal est vive. C'est nettement une méfiance envers moi. On me fait suivre et on fait rédiger des rapports à mon sujet. Puis-je, dans ces conditions, encore entreprendre un voyage à Jérusalem et au Caire?"[35]. Willebrands did not give up the second journey but the case is significant of the tangled situation in the relationships among the organs of the Holy See.

After his journeys Willebrands wrote a report in order to orient the future of *De Iudaeis*, which is very interesting also to discern the personal convictions of the Dutch prelate. Willebrands was not a radical supporter of the declaration. He tried to explain to the assembly that in the strange situation created on *De Iudaeis* a special mental quickness was needed:

Les raisons en faveur d'une promulgation du paragraphe sur les juifs se situent sur le plan de la théologie et de l'apostolat de l'Église. Les raisons contre la promulgation se posent sur le plan de l'opportunité et des conséquences graves pour la vie des Églises. Les raisons pour et contre ne s'opposent donc pas directement et ne s'excluent pas les unes les autres. On peut être d'accord avec les idées exprimées et en même temps être convaincu de l'inopportunité du moment pour les manifester. L'inopportunité pourrait même rendre impossible, en cas de promulgation, d'atteindre le but visé. Les raisons d'opportunité sont très graves[36].

34. Note of 28.11.1963 in *ibid.*, p. 80. For Willebrands' engagement in the preparation of *De Iudaeis* see M. LAMBERIGTS – L. DECLERCK, *Msgr. Willebrands and* Nostra Aetate *4: Diplomacy and Pragmatism*, in this volume, pp. 245-259.

35. Note of 15.4.1965 in *Les agendas conciliaires* (n. 23), p. 171.

36. See the minutes of the meeting *Secretariatum ad christianorum unitatem fovendam, Sessio Feria IV, 12 maii 1965, 9 h. a.m.*, p. 3, in De Smedt archives, KU Leuven. A detailed analysis of this debate in M. LAMBERIGTS – L. DECLERCK, *Mgr. E.J. De Smedt et*

He then indicated two alternative solutions. On one hand, the emendation of the current text of the schema, trying to reach a very improbable large consensus. On the other hand, the definitive cancellation of the text from the agenda of the council with a vote for entrusting the two Vatican secretariats (Secretariat for Promoting Christian Unity and the newly established Secretariat for non-Christians) with the task to study the matter of relationships of the Church with other religions, "in the sense and with the spirit of the principles enounced in the declaration *De Ecclesiae habitudine ad religiones non-christianas*, voted and approved by the majority of the bishops of the Council"[37]. The proposal was a risk and Bea asked his secretary to present it as a "personal opinion", imaging possible strong reactions by several conciliar fathers and also by members of the Secretariat. This way the proposal reached the plenary assembly of the SPCU in May 1965. Willebrands explained the situation referring to his journeys. One of the most important concerns emerging from his intervention was that for Catholic-Orthodox relationships. The affaire of the *De Iudaeis* had created a strong negative opinion among Orthodox churches before the council[38]. Nevertheless the first interventions after Willebrands' introduction at the plenary session made clear that a strong majority in the Secretariat did not accept a postponement of the question. Too great were public opinion's expectations, especially in Europe and the USA.

The text of *Nostra Aetate* went on in its way and was promulgated by the Pope at the end of October 1965. Willebrands put aside his doubts and was very active in managing the different reactions from all over the world. Until the very day before the promulgation, attempts to modify or to block the text went on. Between the end of September and the beginning of October 1965 Willebrands visited some of the Arab Legations in Rome and organised a meeting with orthodox observers in Rome to explain the real intention of the catholic Church in promulgating the text of *Nostra Aetate*.

---

le texte conciliaire sur la religion juive (Nostra Aetate, n° 4), in *Ephemerides Theologicae Lovanienses* 85 (2009) 341-384.

37. Minutes of the meeting *Secretariatum ad christianorum unitatem fovendam, Sessio Feria IV, 12 maii 1965, 9 h. a.m.*, p. 3, in De Smedt archives, KU Leuven.

38. "Dans ces conditions le paragraphe sur le juifs risque d'opposer orthodoxes et catholiques, même sur un plan purement religieux et de provoquer chez tous une opposition au concile. Les orthodoxes nous reprochent d'avoir fait tout seuls cette déclaration, dont ils subiront avec nous les graves conséquences. Pour affirmer d'une part leur fidélité arabe, et d'autre part leur fidélité à la tradition spirituelle orientale, ils attaquent les catholiques et surtout les concile. Beaucoup de catholiques sont confus et suivent les orthodoxes dans leur opposition au concile sur ce point", *ibid.*, p. 2.

IV. MAN OF CONTACTS

Willebrands became bishop in June 1964 and as a bishop he had the right to intervene in the conciliar debate, but he did not use this right during the council. The only written intervention by his name was a text on the Marian chapter of *De Ecclesia*, arguing the danger of new Marian dogmas from an ecumenical point of view[39]. His position was rather that of "inspirator" of a strategy of interventions than a direct protagonist of debate. During the second period Willebrands' diary notes his personal engagement in preparing the texts for the intervention of mgr. Mansourati in the matter of laity and of Msgr. Van Velsen on the *De Ecclesia*. Both were members of the Secretariat and their participation to the debate was a part of a co-ordinate strategy. In the same October 1963 Willebrands wrote some notes for Cicognani's report on *De Oecumenismo*. It was an attempt to reduce the unionistic tenor of the speech of the secretary of State and to influence his thinking towards an ecumenical vision.

These are only some traces of a "ghost writer" activity that Willebrands exercised even though in a limited measure. He was primarily a "man of contacts" and during the council this ability was exalted by the context of an international and ecumenical gathering. There is an underground level of the conciliar history in which Willebrands had a central role. This is the level of relationships between churches. The personal contacts built with the invitation to the observers needed a more official recognition and Willebrands paved the way to the definitive entrance of the Catholic Church into the ecumenical movement. It was not an easy task because the situation of Catholicism was unique. The traditional doctrine of the Church implied a sort of "monologue" attitude which was well represented by the teaching of Pius XI's encyclical *Mortalium animos*[40]. Willebrands' presence at the reunions of the WCC at Rhodes and St. Andrews and the subsequent invitation to the WCC to send a delegation of observers at the council, primed a reciprocity mechanism whose consequences were bound to become very important. The key role of Visser 't Hooft in this connection is unquestionable. The telephone line between Rome and Geneva was often busy in the most important moments of the council. Willebrands had arranged the first meeting between the general secretary of the WCC and Bea in September 1960. Four years

39. T. STRANSKY, *Memories of J. Willebrands at Vatican II: An Insider's Story*, in *Les Agendas conciliaires* (n. 23), p. XVII.

40. On the general attitude of Catholicism towards the ecumenical movement is still valid E. FOUILLOUX, *Les catholiques et l'unité chrétienne du XIXème au XXème siècle: Itinéraires européens d'expression française*, Paris, Le Centurion, 1982.

later, again in Milan, he prepared the first bilateral meeting between the two parts, whose goal was to put some bases of a system of stable relationships.

Willebrands walked over a very narrow bridge. The multilateral approach of the WCC seemed to exclude a free activity on the bilateral level. Since the Rhodes meeting in August 1959 to Paul VI's pilgrimage to the Holy Land and the meeting with patriarch Athenagoras in January 1964 there were a series of falls and rebirths in the relationships between the WCC and the catholic church, for the suspicion of a catholic exploitation of the WCC services[41]. Willebrands was able to balance the opposite necessities to satisfy the request for a new partnership with the WCC and in the same time to guarantee the Catholic church's freedom of movement in the relations with the single churches. He spent a lot of time during the conciliar periods in a daily contact with the observers. Lunch meetings, excursions, the weekly meetings at the secretariat were only some of the places where a new relationship was taking shape. Within four years Willebrands reached the goal to open a dialogue with the most important churches or churches' federations. In his diary, he notes in the fourth period the contact with the president of the World Methodist council, bishop Fred Pierce Corson, together with the patient negotiations with the secretariat of State and the Congregation of the doctrine of Faith to have approved the composition of the Catholic delegation at the first meeting of the bilateral dialogue with the Lutheran World Federation. Willebrands also helped the realization of the personal desire of the Pope to have a visit from the Anglican archbishop of Canterbury. At the end of the council the Catholic Church was engaged in direct bilateral conversations with some Protestant groups. But the most important progress was made in the relationships with the Orthodox churches, particularly with Constantinople. In the last days of the council the ceremony of the cancellation of the excommunications of 1054 took place, and its impact on public opinion was very high: although it had no practical or juridical consequences it was the symbol of a new era in East-West relationships. Willebrands' role in these events was not marginal. He was one of the members of the Catholic delegation at the Istanbul consultation in

41. Lukas Vischer, one of the WCC observers at Vatican II, had declared in a meeting with catholic partners: "The World Council is a tool which is helping the Churches to show their unity. But it is also a community of Churches. The Roman Catholic Church is inclined to treat the World Council only as a tool. However it cannot close its eyes on the fact that in the World Council a new community is already grown. The Roman Catholic Church cannot only use the tool. It has to recognize the community which is behind it". Cf. *Separati ma fratelli* (n. 24).

November 1965. A similar picture of facts was unexpected only some years before, at the time of the beginning of the council. The vision of reconciliation that Willebrands was cultivating in previous time began suddenly a reality. The general secretary of the WCC Visser 't Hooft defined the major gift of the Dutch prelate as a "fine combination of vision and realism"[42]. Vision was clear in his mind but he had also the capacity to realize, to search for a concrete way to the goal. He was well aware that "ecumenical policy, like every other policy, must be the art of the possible and not a castle built in the air"[43].

Anyhow he was not a solitary hero. The work's style and methodology in the Secretariat was that of a large collaboration. Willebrands' way of direction was very discrete but precise, very friendly and not authoritative. Bea took himself at some distance from his collaborators and was at the vertix of the pyramid of consultation. In the case of the beginning of bilateral conversations with Lutherans he signed the formal request to the Pope for permission. In a lower level Willebrands and the members of the staff were at the very centre of all these personal contacts. There was a sort of specialization, a division of commissions and Willebrands stood at the centre of co-ordination. Duprey had the responsibility of relationships with the Orthodox world while the French J.F. Arrighi (who came from the Congregation of the Oriental Churches) was a landmark for Anglicans. Father Thomas Stransky, aided by some other consultants, took care of the relations of the Secretariat with the WCC and the complex landscape of American Protestantism. This collective work represents a unique experience in the history of recent Catholicism, in a very fluid situation when some of the secular division walls were crumbling.

Willebrands' first and sole public appearance on the scene of the council was during the ceremony of the 7th of December 1965, when he read the text of the common declaration of Pope Paul VI and Patriarch Athenagoras on the removal of sentences of mutual excommunications of 1054. Behind this figure stood a great and tiring work for unity, almost unknown by the majority. Willebrands' central role in this history was recognized by the pope who invited him at the table on the last day of the council. This is also the last annotation of the Agenda ("Session de clôture du concile. 13h30: Déjeuner chez le Saint-Père: présents: Mgr Felici, Mgr

---

42. VISSER 'T HOOFT, *Memoirs* (n. 18), p. 323.

43. Visser 't Hooft wrote also in his memoirs, referring to Willebrands: "I liked his frankness and I appreciated especially that he was at once a progressive ecumenist looking for ways of making a real advance towards unity and a realist who knew that, in order to have results, an ecumenical policy, like every other policy, must be the art of the possible and not a castle built in the air", *ibid.*, p. 329.

Carlo Colombo, Mgr Willebrands, Don Macchi, Don Bruno")[44] together
with the evening appointment with the Russian bishop Nikodim.
Willebrands and Montini had had their first meeting in May 1960 when
the secretary of the CCQE was in Milan to give a lecture and to contact
some of the theologians of the diocese, for the organisation of the meeting
of the Conference at Gazzada[45].

Pope Paul VI did not have a close relation with the secretary of the
SPCU, and the agendas confirm that he had not a complete understanding
of the activity of the secretariat for conciliar texts. The request of the pope
to the secretary reported by Stransky ("Help me by being completely
honest and frank") is an illustration of the willingness of Paul VI to accept
the help of the SPCU in ecumenical matters[46]. Willebrands' report on one
of the first audiences by the Pope shows Montini's sincere concern for the
situation of the observers, with some suggestions for their best reception.
The pope also showed a prudent attitude towards the activity of the secretariat and, at Willebrands' request for strengthening the Secretariat's position within the Roman Curia, he said: "Patience! Il faut gagner, conquérir
le terrain, avant d'en fixer les frontières. Si on commence par fixer les
frontières, le terrain est trop étroit, et peut-être le Droit actuel ne permet
pas suffisamment d'élargir les frontières"[47]. The Pope in this first phase
had not many occasions to appreciate Willebrands' qualities. He had some
periodic audiences with the president of the Secretariat, Cardinal Bea.
Willebrands often entered the papal rooms with some members of the
group of the observers but the atmosphere in these cases was very official
and his presence very discrete. In June 1965 Paul VI asked the secretary
of the SPCU to return to him with more time to discuss some matters
regarding his ecumenical journeys but we have no following news on the
meeting[48]. Montini and Willebrands came from different human and
religious experiences but probably the pope recognised in the Dutch prelate, beyond all differences, the light of an authentic vocation to unity. And
day by day he learned to appreciate it for the good of the entire Church.

Via Bonomelli 5   Mauro VELATI
I-28100 Novara
Italy

---

44. Note of 8.12.1965, in *Les agendas conciliaires* (n. 23), p. 269.
45. Note of 11.5.1960, in SALEMINK (ed.), *"You Will Be Called Repairer of the
Breach"* (n. 1), p. 145.
46. STRANSKY, *Memories of J. Willebrands* (n. 37), p. XVII.
47. *Audience privée du Saint Père, le Pape Paul VI, le 18 septembre 1963*, dt, fr., p. 3,
in Vatican Secret Archives, *Conc. Vat. II*, 1424.
48. Note of 22.6.1965, in *Les agendas conciliaires* (n. 23), p. 197.

WITH PASSION FOR UNITY

APPROACHES TO THE ECUMENICAL THEOLOGY OF
JOHANNES WILLEBRANDS

Alongside Augustin Cardinal Bea, Johannes Cardinal Willebrands is known to be one of the most influential early Catholic ecumenists before and during the Second Vatican Council. His long experience, as well as numerous contacts and encounters, enabled him to receive, analyse and foster the cause of ecumenism. Not only as an observer to the Council, but already as co-founder of the Catholic Conference for Ecumenical Questions, thereafter as secretary and later as president of the Secretariat for Promoting Christian Unity (currently Pontifical Council for Promoting Christian Unity) did Willebrands contribute constitutively to the preparation of the opening of the Catholic Church towards ecumenism. The Second Vatican Council then took this step in an authoritative manner, and it was Willebrands in particular who helped shaping it during the Council itself and who would give support to and deepen this project in the decades that followed. His modesty and benevolence, as well as his deep piety, not only made him an authentic witness for the search of the Catholic Church for unity in faith, but also conduced to the success of his efforts. Willebrands undoubtedly belongs to those grand figures, who truly shaped the ecumenical movement and whose heritage is and remains an obligation, especially in current times.

Besides this passion for unity, Willebrands possessed a clear view of the realities of the ecumenical movement. Unlike anybody else, he saw the deep connection between the dogmatic constitution on the church, *Lumen Gentium*, and the requirements for the ecumenical dialogue, which are expressed in the decree on ecumenism, *Unitatis Redintegratio*. Whoever reads his considerations on the teaching of *subsistit* in *Lumen Gentium* no. 8 today will undoubtedly realise the clarity in distinction with which the philosopher and theologian Willebrands was able to face the decisive challenges in that regard. As little as the teaching of *subsistit* puts the case for a relativisation of the unique quality of the Catholic Church, so distinctly did he argue that this expression may only be understood properly within the context of the renewed teaching on the Church. It is precisely this context of conciliar renewal, which was emphasised by the Council itself, that leads to a correct and pursuable interpretation of the term *subsistit*. In that regard the hermeneutical connection between

text and context, which Willebrands mentions, is of particular importance.

The following presentation is based on some of his writings that originated shortly after the Council[1]. They tell us about the motifs, background and challenges, and also about the occasional struggle for the
proper expressions in the documents of the Second Vatican Council. His
remarks give a relevant and still convincing account of the various contexts of meaning. Willebrands undoubtedly belongs to the exceptionally
gifted theologians, who are able to present highly complex matters precisely and straightforwardly in just a few theses. I am going to concentrate on the search for a synthesis of his thoughts. If I am correct, both
Willebrands' line of thought and his actions during the years of the
Council revolve around three elements of ecumenical theology: hermeneutics, conversation[2], and ecclesiology.

I. UNDERSTANDING THE COUNCIL:
INSIGHTS INTO CONCILIAR HERMENEUTICS

1. *The Council as Event*

In order to understand the Council, one must first stress the intention
of Pope John XXIII. Cardinal Willebrands had a particular instinct for
exploring the historical origin of the Second Vatican Council. According
to Willebrands' experience, the summoning of the Second Vatican
Council cannot be ascribed to activities of the Roman Curia, but is
closely affiliated with the personality of Pope John XXIII. The Council
is inseparably bound to the pope's motifs, concerns, expectations and
hopes. Pope John was well prepared for the Council – both spiritually
and pastorally. As shepherd, he clearly saw the necessity for a renewal
of the Church, unlike the curia, which is said to have rather striven for
thwarting the Council in the first place. From the first day of his

1. Cf. in that regard the two collections of essays, which contain partially identical
contributions in different languages: J. WILLEBRANDS, *Oecuménisme et problèmes actuels*,
Paris, Cerf, 1969; ID., *Mandatum Unitatis: Beiträge zur Ökumene* (Konfessionskundliche
Schriften des Johann-Adam-Möhler-Instituts, 16), Paderborn, Bonifatius, 1989.

2. A remark on the translation: It would have been possible to translate the German
term "Dialog" with the English equivalent "dialogue". The term "conversation" stresses,
however, that the ecumenical gatherings and their respective deliberations regularly
involve more than two parties, thereby also mirroring the rather complex nature of
ecumenism as a whole. Throughout the text, the German term "ökumenischer Dialog"
therefore reads "ecumenical conversation".

pontificate on, John made very clear that he personally wanted that Council to take place. At the same time, the pope was at all times well aware of the scope of his announcement[3]. According to Willebrands, the tremendous initiative to summon a Council originated from a deliberate decision of the pope. Of course, there is no need for Willebrands to deny that the preparations for a council had started already, even though a formal decision had not yet been taken. Hence he as an eye witness does not make the mistake of having to differentiate strictly a time before and one after the Council, which then break apart little by little. Precisely this way of reasoning apparently had become quite common shortly after the Council. With this in mind, it is clear that none of the eyewitnesses and advocates of the Council, among them Willebrands himself, intended to break with the tradition of the Church.

Whoever wants to gain access to the Council must see it as an event in the life of the Catholic Church. The Church herself is an event. "The Church is not primarily a teaching; being the Church is living in Christ"[4]. 'Event' in this sense therefore does not mean the same as the term in its modern connotation. Rather, 'event' explicitly signifies the coming of Jesus Christ into our time and age, effective in the Holy Spirit. In this particular historical context, the category of event indicates that the wish for a council, which many believers shared, had finally come true. There-with Willebrands belongs to those figures who contributed greatly to the proper understanding of the Council.

From the outset, the pope understood the Council as the means to assert anew the message of the Church of today. The pope gave the Church the task to undertake the renewal of faith for the Church as a whole. Namely the Church's mission in and to the world was of particular importance in that regard. Whenever the pope spoke of renewal, of *aggiornamento*, he did not primarily mean the opening of an ecclesial institution, that was widely considered to be rigid and frozen in structure, towards all kinds of influences from the modern world. Rather the pope wanted the Church to go into the world in order to proclaim the gospel of Jesus Christ. Against this background it is a misinterpretation to infer that the initial motivation for summoning a council was solely to open the Catholic Church to the modern world. Pope John was never ambiguous about what the Church had to tell the world of today. On the

3. Cf. *Inhalt, Ziel und Aufgabenbereich möglicher Kontakte und Zusammenarbeit zwischen Römisch-katholischer Kirche und Lutherischem Weltbund. Rückblick und Hoffnung*, in *Mandatum Unitatis* (n. 1), 15-28, pp. 19-24.
4. Cf. *ibid*, p. 20.

contrary, for the time right after the Second World War, it was essential that the Church, in accordance with her apostolic tradition, brought the people in touch with the good news again and did not keep them from hearing it. The Church, however, must not be one with the world, but must be the salt of the earth and the light on the path of humankind and the peoples. This task, which has been outlined in these few sketches, is of fundamental importance. It can be explained more clearly with reference to the gospel[5].

In order to emphasise this concern of the Church's mission, Willebrands clarifies a few points. One can talk properly about the dignity of the human person once the human being recognises God and worships him. The prerequisite for the human being's turning towards God is the atonement with God, which is fully accomplished in Jesus Christ. The emancipation or liberation of the human being means to be free of all kinds of mundane constraints. This process of emancipation or liberation, however, must not only be understood in a negative sense, but also needs to be seen as a dis-closure of new possibilities and options. From the outset, the aim of the Council is oriented towards these core aspects of the gospel. Against this background it becomes immediately clear that any interpretation of the Council as being defensive and self-centred in nature is to be rejected. On the contrary, it is in this sense that the pope speaks of a pastoral council from the very beginning on, with "pastoral" meaning that the Church is sent into the world by Christ[6].

Against the backdrop of this fundamental idea of "mission" the Council has to be interpreted as encounter or meeting. Within the Catholic Church, such an encounter or meeting takes place with other churches and communities. For this reason, the missionary nature of the Church is intrinsically bound to the ecumenical intention of relating the gospel not only to the Catholic world, but to the whole of Christianity. The ties to the other Christian churches and ecclesial communities, which slowly began to emerge after the Council, as well as the contacts, which were established with the various denominational federations or alliances, and the beginning of a substantial ecumenical conversation with the different ecclesial traditions all implement the initial aim of Pope John XXIII, which led him to summon the Second Vatican Council in the first place. In this respect, the Council develops an extraordinary dynamics which does indeed seem to break with the former tradition of the Church at first sight, but which never really makes this distinction. Concerning the

---

5. Cf. *ibid*, pp. 20-25.
6. Cf. *Gesandt in die Welt*, in *Mandatum Unitatis* (n. 1), 112-125, pp. 112-118.

tradition of the Church, one also has to note, of course, that there never was and never will be simply an organic growth with regard to keeping the tradition of the Church. Rather there always was and will be change and reform. Willebrands consequently puts great emphasis on the assessment that the renewal with regard to the mission of the Church must not be interpreted as break or rupture with her tradition.

2. Christian Unity through Reform

In Willebrands' view, Pope John XXIII. put an ecumenical orientation onto the Council from the start. He cautiously avoided to use the term "return", in order not to suggest any notion of inflexibility, or to purport the idea of lacking willingness for a reform of the Church. With this, Willebrands emphasises a second, fundamental aim of the Second Vatican Council. A close look into the history of reformation makes quite clear that the loss of the unity of the Church was mainly due to a lack of renewal in the Church. Whoever wants to regain the unity of the Church must therefore discover the Second Vatican Council with regard to the on-going need for reform of the Church and of religious life[7]. Consequently, it almost amounts to a revolution to understand the notion of *ecclesia semper reformanda* as something other than a heresy. With the Church as institution having been more or less explicitly counter-reformational in her overall orientation over the past centuries, there was simply no room for any such notion of reform. Long before the Second Vatican Council, however, different movements evolved within the Church, such as the biblical movement, the liturgical movement, as well as the intense research activities with regard to ecclesiology and the New Testament. They all opened the way for the reforms of the Second Vatican Council. In that sense, the Second Vatican Council is even more of a reform-council than the Council of Trent. Accordingly the constitution on the Church states that the Church needed to renew herself at all times. In fact, the Church on her pilgrimage is called by Christ to this on-going reform.

But is the Church able to reform herself? What is the Council's understanding of reform? It is decisive to pay close attention to the wording, which Willebrands stresses. In the Catholic sense, reform does not imply a complete rupture with the past, simply because Christ is with his Church at all times and will never allow his Church to fall into a state of betrayal or infidelity. At the same time, however, reform does not only imply the negative task to work against all sorts of maldevelopment and

7. Cf. *Reformation und Reform heute*, in *Mandatum Unitatis* (n. 1), 29-47, pp. 35-47.

grievances. It also implies the positive task to expand the Church. In this respect, the initial aim of the Second Vatican Council, to proclaim the gospel, shines through once again. The experience of the Church therefore does not mean to change, leave or completely give up her tradition, but to fulfil the mission that has been given to the Church by the apostles. This very mission is the concern of the Church as such. As it is always one and the same gospel, there must not be a mistaken adjustment to the world, as if the gospel itself was in need of renewal. If interpreted correctly, *aggiornamento* means to permeate the world by means of the gospel, and not to change the gospel according to the world. In that regard, Willebrands takes up the intention of the ecumenical movement, to couple the proclamation of the gospel and the willingness to return to the unity of the Church. In that sense the reforms of the Church refer to her unity. Consequently, Willebrands is able to incorporate the ecumenical notion of the Second Vatican Council into the intention of the World Council of Churches. This results in the image of the Catholic Church not only being opposite the ecumenical movement, but truly existing as an integral part of it.

II. CHARACTER AND NATURE OF THE ECUMENICAL CONVERSATION

1. *Overcoming Denominational Distinction and Polemics*

Each reform of the Church is of ecumenical importance[8]. What exactly, however, is the scope of the reforms of the Second Vatican Council? The theology of the Catholic Church seems to have been rather apologetic in the past. This apologetic orientation always corresponded to a strong confessionalism. This resulted in certain distortions with regard to presenting the official teaching of other Christian traditions, to constrictions in the life of the Church, and to the exclusion of other denominations[9]. At least the decisions of the Holy Office from the beginnings of the ecumenical movement to the encyclical of Pope Pius XI, *Mortalium Animos*, in 1928 give this impression. Consequently, all members of the people of the Church, the theologians as well as the bishops, were called to contribute to overcoming this exclusion. The renewal of both theology and the entire religious life already began during the pontificate of

---

8. Cf. *Ökumenische Aspekte und Perspektiven des Zweiten Vatikanischen Konzils*, in *Mandatum Unitatis* (n. 1), 98-111, pp. 99-101.
9. Cf. *Inhalt, Ziel und Aufgabenbereich möglicher Kontakte und Zusammenarbeit zwischen Römisch-katholischer Kirche und Lutherischem Weltbund* (n. 3).

Pius XII. It was not the Second Vatican Council initially which allowed for overcoming the confessional exclusion. The reforms of the Second Vatican Council therefore are aimed at overcoming confessionalism.

For the schism of Christianity in the western world both sides are to blame. Today we know, that Luther is not the only culprit for the division among Christians. Numerous factors contributed to the schism of the Church[10]. Be it the general state of the Church, erroneous forms of piety, a lacking or misguided orthopraxis of the people – all these factors contributed to the complex development of the Reformation. It was very important for Willebrands to point to the pontificate of Pope Adrian VI, which admittedly only marks an interim period and left everything but a mature religious impression (1522-1523)[11]. To his contemporaries, Pope Adrian made a public confession of guilt of the Catholic Church. Although a genuine abundance of intellectual force existed at that time, it turned out impossible to identify the defining aspect of that era. The world was in upheaval, not only with regard to religious matters, but also in other regards. Even though Adrian saw Luther's mistakes very clearly and demanded his obedience to him as pope on the one hand, he felt the profound necessity for a reform on the other. He identified with great clarity the causes for the crisis within the clergy, especially with regard to the so-called moral issues. This was the very point where Luther's criticism of the state of the Church of his time was rooted, the disturbing experience of the squalor of human beings. Adrian did not succeed, however, to use the various movements within the Church for a reform thereof.

2. A New Evaluation of the Reformation

It took a long while until the churches of the Reformation entered into conversation with the Catholic Church again. As late as 1917, the last grand jubilee of the Reformation, controversial theology dominated the Catholic perspective on Luther's personality and character. Since then, the ground has been cleared in Catholic theology as well for a theological discussion with Luther. Today, also Catholic theologians can deal with Luther's theological concerns in an unbiased manner. It is very important for Willebrands to fully understand the initial and whole concern of the Reformation. "Luther's only interest is to see what God does"[12]. Luther is

---

10. Cf. *Reformation und Reform heute* (n. 7).
11. Cf. in detail: *Hadrian VI. und die katholische Reform*, in *Mandatum Unitatis* (n. 1), 291-301.
12. *Reformation und Reform heute* (n. 7), p. 32.

primarily interested in our being before God. The Church is subordinated
to the Word of God; she is no doctrine of faith herself. Consequently, the
necessity of reform is focused on the religious thinking, for Luther was not
interested to reform rather petty or minor grievances. That the gospel be
preached correctly seems to be his primary concern. Against this background one also has to view the differentiation between law and gospel as
theological instruction. One can certainly understand Luther's concern for
a reform as such that he wanted anew to pave the way for theology against
a philosophy that had become rather overwhelming. In that regard, further
research is necessary to determine whether or not the theological aspects
are exclusive or if they indeed refer to one another. In this respect and
within the context of a new evaluation of the Reformation, Willebrands has
seen the tasks of an ecumenical theology at a very early stage already.

3. *Conversation and Truth*

A subject of the ecumenical conversation are the differences that have
arisen between both the theologies and the official teachings of the
churches. Differences with regard to the official teaching do not allow for
an honest conversation. It is the achievement of the Second Vatican
Council to have placed both the character and the nature of the ecumenical conversation at the centre of the renewal of the Church. Following
Willebrands, the junction from a polemical attitude to a conversational
one can therefore be identified as one of the major achievements of the
reforms initiated by the Council. The prerequisite of such a conversation
is, first of all, the methodological insight formulated by Pope John XXIII
at an early stage already, namely the differentiation of the unalterable
deposit of faith on the one hand and the alterable formulations or language
on the other, in which theological statements are expressed in a specific
and historical manner. With regard to this, the ecumenical conversation is
a struggle for truth at all times. The conversation must add to both a common understanding and a common establishment of the truth. In that sense
the conversation is a mutual quest. In the process of the ecumenical conversation we seek to discern what precisely is the content of each doctrine
that causes problems in our understanding of each other. To this extent,
the point today is to mutually promote the knowledge of our faith.

Therefore the conversation strives to gather together the different theologies[13]. Faith shall be interpreted jointly with respect to the entire

---

13. Cf. *Überlegungen zum ökumenischen Dialog*, in *Mandatum Unitatis* (n. 1), 179-
197; *Der ökumenische Dialog: Zwanzig Jahre nach dem Zweiten Vatikanischen Konzil*,
in *ibid.*, 243-256.

teaching of the Church. To this extent, the ecumenical conversation is nothing else than the mutual effort to reacquire a common theological language. Of course, there is a number of theological problems behind this opinion, which Willebrands mentions but which he cannot solve. At least he asserts that the theological attitude is not independent of language. The connection of faith with Christ is always in need of a binding statement. Consequently, one would have to look for agreements in order to account for the causes that led to the schism. By means of a conversation one would have to discern a new way of expression and a new lingua franca, so that the faith may be expressed in a common fashion. With these remarks Willebrands seeks to identify the hermeneutical question of the ecumenical conversation. It should be clear in that regard, however, that the point is not to simply agree on and exchange compromised formulae. Alternatively the ecumenical conversation is always more than the theological discourse on theological differences. Conversation means meeting each other in faith, for faith surpasses mere knowledge. According to Willebrands, the nature of the ecumenical conversation is rooted in the urge of love.

4. *Mission and Proselytism*

The ecumenical conversation desired by the Second Vatican Council does not merely originate from an intuition of our time. It is rooted in the very concern of the Church herself. It is very important for Willebrands to integrate the ecumenical conversation into the lived reality of the Church. Even the opponents' intention was quite obvious: they argued that the dialogue between the separated churches and communities was just an ephemeral phenomenon, a mere whim of a century desperately seeking peace. The cardinal is convinced, however, that the conversation is clearly directed towards the common witness of the Church. With regard to this, he can include the substantial propositions on the mission of the Church, i.e. the fundamental concern of the Second Vatican Council that the Church is sent to proclaim the gospel of Jesus Christ. Methods that intend to coax the addressee of this good news, however, are contrary to such a proclamation[14].

A fruitful understanding within the ecumenical conversation requires in the first place the acknowledgement of certain principles which rule out any kind of proselytism. Common wtiness and proselytism mutually exclude one another. Common witness is directed towards a relationship

---

14. Cf. *Gemeinsames Zeugnis und Proselytismus*, in *Mandatum Unitatis* (n. 1), 86-97.

of mutual respect and esteem among the Christians. A number of aspects are to be observed in that regard, which Cardinal Willebrands brings forth with determination: renunciation of denominational pride, authenticity of one's own belief, willingness for conversation, elimination of temporal benefits, a clear view of the margins, within which the support of the state is compatible to true freedom of religion. All these regulations can actually be summarised in one sentence: the Christians' attitude among themselves must correspond to the good news they proclaim. Proselytism is diametrically opposed to the conversation of truth. This touches upon the problem of freedom of religion, a matter which Cardinal Bea and Cardinal Willebrands have already given their attention to at a very early stage.

5. *No Conversation Without Freedom of Religion*

There is no real ecumenical conversation without a proper conception of freedom of religion[15]. With this introductory aphorism, which originates from a draft version of the decree on ecumenism, Willebrands opens his precise and far-reaching remarks on the ecumenical significance of freedom of religion. With regard to its ecumenical significance in particular it will most certainly take quite a long while still to integrate freedom of religion into the ecumenical conversation. Of course, the declaration on freedom of religion addresses all people. Given the democratic precondition of today, it seeks to shape anew the relationship between state and church. But the declaration on freedom of religion amounts to more than that.

In the eyes of the ecumenical observers of the Second Vatican Council, the initial attitude of the assembly – identifiable already at an early stage – to approach the requests of the representatives of the ecumenical movement by means of a declaration on freedom of religion was a decisive factor for the Council's overall credibility. Only if such a foundation is laid, would a conversation *par cum pari* be possible. In this respect, the World Council of Churches made seven claims with regard to the question of freedom of religion in July 1965:

1. The problem of religious freedom shall be regarded from a specific Christian point of view.
2. Religious freedom includes the right of every human being to change one's religion or creed.
3. Everybody has the right to express one's faith.

---

15. Cf. *Religionsfreiheit und Ökumenismus*, in *Mandatum Unitatis* (n. 1), 54-69, p. 57.

4. Everyone should be able to live in certainty that he or she may give witness to one's religious conviction both individually and in communion with others.
5. Freedom of faith includes the individual and collective right to be associated with other religious communities across national borders.
6. There should be internationally accepted standards on the conception of freedom of faith.
7. The exercise of the right of freedom of faith should only be restricted by law under certain preconditions, i.e. if the restriction is necessary to maintain public order.

It goes without question that such principles of freedom of faith were an important stimulus for the declaration on freedom of religion. Accordingly the effort for a Catholic declaration on this matter were monitored with great interest. The declaration on freedom of religion forms the indispensable ground to heal relations among the churches. Precisely for this reason the declaration was received with such great satisfaction.

Cardinal Willebrands, therefore, is among those theologians who recognised the significance of the declaration of freedom of religion both within the context of the Second Vatican Council and beyond. New relations with other Christian churches and communities may only be established if the declaration avoids all misconceptions of the fundamental task of the Christian Church. Christian faith always includes the freedom to choose. There is no forcing in matters of faith. Only if these issues are resolved clearly and definitely will the way to an ecumenical conversation be open. Willebrands indicated the internal preconditions for this decision. The declaration on freedom of religion was only possible thanks to the clarification of the ecclesiological foundations. For Catholic theology it was important at all times that the confirmation or acknowledgement of freedom of religion would not include any kind of relativism with respect to ecclesiological matters. It goes without saying that this is exactly the point, which many bishops feared.

III. THE ECCLESIOLOGY OF THE COUNCIL

From its very beginnings Willebrands' theological oeuvre is devoted to the genesis and the shape of the ecumenical conversation. He knew how to scrutinise the preconditions and requirements of the ecumenical conversation and to present them time and again in articles and lectures. As much as the preconditions of the conversation seek to overcome both the polemics and the demarcations caused by theological differences, the motifs and driving forces behind the ecumenical conversation seek to renew Catholic ecclesiology. The Second Vatican Council itself pointed out this connection in the Decree on Ecumenism. Willebrands confirms this connection by referring to the foundational principles of Catholic ecclesiology[16].

The Council itself can be interpreted as a council of the Church on the Church. To this extent, the Constitution on the Church forms the basis for the Catholic Church's openness towards other churches and ecclesial communities. Namely the Decree on Ecumenism then defines the specific relation between them. But ecclesiology is not only in a formal sense the prerequisite for ecumenism. Particularly the definition of the Church as *mysterium* constitutes the decisive foundation for engaging in the ecumenical quest of unity. In that regard, already the encyclical *Mystici Corporis* of Pope Pius XII turned out to be of crucial importance. The mystery of the Church is readily affiliated with the mystery of the trinity. Whoever speaks of the Church as mystery, always has an eye on the deepest mystery of faith, i.e. the unity of the Father, the Son and the Holy Spirit. Hence not only is the Church described as mystery, but also is her unity. Against this background one may then discern the ecumenical issues in a specific manner.

The concept of mystery is particularly linked to the idea of communion. Already long before the Council can one identify an ecclesiology of communion within Catholic theology, which is then received by the Council. The notion of communion is of central importance for the further development of ecumenism. What does the term *communio* mean? It corresponds to the Greek term *koinonia* in the New Testament. *Koinonia* essentially means to have a share in all things. This sharing creates a bond among the participants, who then form a community on the basis of this mutual sharing. In its original sense in the New Testament, this sharing implies common faith, life and witness. Community members confess the same faith, celebrate the same sacraments and participate in mission. With this image of the Church as communion, one can face the ecumenical challenge.

A deepened understanding of the ecclesiology of communion forms a clear perspective for ecumenism. Although it is not possible here to outline specific suggestions which would describe the communion among the churches, it is obvious that it has elements ready for the unity of the

---

16. Cf. *Die ökumenische Bewegung: Ihre Probleme und Antriebskraft*, in *Mandatum Unitatis* (n. 1), 165-178; *Die Zukunft der ökumenischen Bewegung*, in *ibid.*, 198-215.

churches. Even against the background of this fundamental notion of communion it cannot be foreseen, however, how perfectly or imperfectly this communion is going to be realised in the end. In this respect, Willebrands early on keeps an eye on the development of the World Council of Churches. Quite early he puts emphasis on the understanding of *communio*. Indeed, one could even argue in a prophetic sense that it is Willebrands who crafted the very idea of a communion of churches.

This very notion consequently forms the background against which Willebrands then unfolds the relevance of the teaching of *subsistit* with even greater clarity[17]. In a number of contributions Willebrands pondered an authentic interpretation thereof. By shifting from *est* to *subsistit*, the Council by no means intends to break with the encyclical *Mystici Corporis*. At the time Willebrands explicitly mentions this point in order to avoid any later reinterpretation. As a matter of fact, the Council fathers rather wanted to deepen the basic ideas of the encyclical. For a correct interpretation of *subsistit*, it is therefore necessary to consult both the constitution on the Church and the encyclical of 1943, *Mystici Corporis*. Already in this encyclical Pius XII intended an opening of the Church, so that one can interpret accordingly the *subsistit* in *Lumen Gentium* No. 8 as an opening clause. Admittedly, Willebrands does not use this term, but his overall interpretation allows for this conclusion.

The correct interpretation of the term *subsistit* can by no means be derived from one single sentence or passage of the Constitution on the Church alone. The *subsistit* is stronger and more expressive than *existit* or *adest*, or *inest*, all of which were suggested as well, but were rejected in the end. Neither it is necessary to make use of the scholastic term *subsistentia*. Willebrands rather opts for an interpretation which allows for a dynamic understanding. "Dynamic" in this context means that it refers to the idea of communion. Unity among Christians needs to grow. Precisely in that sense the *subsistit* seeks to foster the growth of the relations. One cannot draw the conclusion, however, that one would rather make the case for a plurality of churches and ecclesial communities. A Catholic ecclesiology does not permit a separation of the Church, even though it accepts the schism of Christianity. In order to close the gap between the schism of Christianity and the unity that subsists in the Catholic Church, a process of growth of the relations between the Catholic Church and the non-Catholic churches and ecclesial communities is necessary. In that sense, the *subsistit* brings into view the elements and goods of truth, which

---

17. Cf. *Die Communio-Ekklesiologie des Zweiten Vatikanischen Konzils*, in *Mandatum Unitatis* (n. 1), 341-356.

Christians share among themselves. This connection is crucial for the interpretation of the *subsistit*. Elements that Christians share are the confession of faith, the sacraments and the single office in the communion of the Church. In conjunction with the concept of communion, this notion of elements can be interpreted as a link between the reflection on the mystery of faith on the one hand and the gradual growth of ecclesial communion among the churches and communities on the other.

IV. Conclusion

This condensed overview of the conciliar theology of Johannes Cardinal Willebrands mediates some fundamental insights in order to understand the ecumenical intentions of the Second Vatican Council: the ecumenical conversation is not subject to negotiation, but is rather a vivid process involving all of the participating churches. The acceptance of this conversation includes the idea of a reform of the Church. This requires a reform hermeneutics at the same time. The ecumenical conversation seeks to overcome the schism of Christianity. The renewed ecclesiology of the Second Vatican Council forms the basis for this aim, as its conception of communion already points to the future unity among the Christian churches.

Both Willebrands' thinking and actions are guided by certain prerequisites and principles. That is why he did not yet have a realistic idea of the communion among the churches. Nonetheless his theology offers a brilliant commentary on the intentions and statements of the Council. Even though the Council intends a clear renewal of ecclesiology, this does not imply a rupture with the tradition of the Church. Sure enough, the past is abandoned in one single respect: the attitude of controversial theology, which manifested itself in polemics and differentiation, is indeed bettered for good.

Johann-Adam-Möhler-Institut   Wolfgang THÖNISSEN
für Ökumenik
Leostrasse 19a
D-33098 Paderborn
Germany

Translation: Sven Christer Scholven

CARDINAL WILLEBRANDS AS AN EXPONENT OF
CATHOLIC ECUMENICAL THEOLOGY

Johannes Willebrands gave nearly forty years of active service to the cause of ecumenism in the Catholic Church, beginning with his coordination from 1952 to 1963 of the Conférence catholique pour les questions œcuméniques. As secretary (1960-1969) and then as president (1969-1989) of the Vatican Secretariat for Promoting Christian Unity (SPCU), he was remarkably generous in responding to invitations to give lectures to various groups in Europe and increasingly in North America[1]. From the published texts of these lectures, I draw together here four significant theological themes which Cardinal Willebrands put into circulation in his role as a major spokesman for the Catholic Church in her ecumenical engagement.

Johannes Willebrands's doctoral studies, at the Angelicum in Rome, had been in philosophy, with a thesis on the illative sense in Newman. As professor at Warmond Seminary in his diocese of Haarlem, his courses surveyed the history of philosophy. When his ecumenical activities began in the early 1950s, he began laying a solid basis by extensive reading and careful study, as his diary records for 1958, as he prepared a two-week course on Catholic ecclesiology at the World Council of Churches' Ecumenical Institute at Bossey, Switzerland[2]. Willebrands had a receptive mind and a notable talent for setting forth concisely what he read and heard from the theologians of the Catholic Conference and later from the theologian-consultants of the SPCU. The rest of this text presents four themes which Willebrands gleaned from his reading and personal contacts which he then articulated in a number of texts of notable theological richness.

---

1. Some of Willebrands's lecture texts have been come out in collections, notably, *Œcuménisme et problèmes actuels*, Paris, Cerf, 1969; *Mandatum Unitatis: Beiträge zur Ökumene*, Paderborn, Bonifatius, 1989; and Pontifical Council for Promoting Christian Unity, *Information Service*, no. 101 (1999/II-III). But many texts remain scattered in journals and in collaborative volumes published by those who sponsored his lectures. See the Willebrands bibliography assembled by Maria ter Steeg for this volume.

2. T. SALEMINK (ed.), *"You Will Be Called Repairer of the Breach" : The Diary of J.G.M. Willebrands 1958-1961*, Leuven, Peeters, 2009, pp. 42-56. Willebrands was the first Catholic lecturer at the Institute of Bossey.

I. WILLEBRANDS CONTRIBUTES TO A
GLOBAL INTERPRETATION OF VATICAN II

From 1965 to 1973, in different venues, Willebrands regularly called attention to the Second Vatican Council's approval and appropriation of movements of renewal which had begun among Catholics before Pope John XXIII announced, on January 25, 1959, that he was going to convene Vatican Council II. Willebrands had first-hand experience of just such a renewal movement in the Conférence catholique pour les questions œcuméniques. This experience became a part of his early interpretation of the Council's outcomes. He would recall pioneering individuals and small groups of Catholic theologians who took fresh initiatives, which the current teaching and practice of the time did not support, but which the Council in time validated and made centrally important for the whole Church. In this, Willebrands offers a way to read Vatican II as a whole and makes a point that can well be connected with recent global characterizations of the Council, for example, as advanced by Giuseppe Alberigo[3], Agostino Marchetto[4], John O'Malley[5], and Peter Hünermann[6].

3. G. ALBERIGO is the general editor of *History of Vatican II*, 5 vols., Maryknoll, NY, Orbis; Leuven, Peeters, 1995-2003, in which Alberigo writes interpretive conclusions of each volume, with emphasis on the intuitions of Pope John XXIII, the Council as "event", and the only imperfect realization of renewal in the formulated Vatican II documents. In compact form, see G. ALBERIGO, *A Brief History of Vatican II*, Maryknoll, NY, Orbis, 2006, which offers some key interpretive passages from Alberigo's mentor, Fr. Giuseppe Dossetti.
4. *Il Concilio ecumenico Vaticano II: Contrappunto per la sua storia*, Vatican City, Libreria editrice Vaticana, 2005, which collects in one volume fifty-two texts, including many previously published reviews, mostly critical, of works by Alberigo and his collaborators both in *The History of Vatican II* and in related symposia volumes. Marchetto's watchword is continuity, as between previous councils and Vatican II, between John XXIII and Paul VI, and between tradition and renewal. An English translation, in preparation at the University of Scranton Press, is expected in April 2010.
5. *What Happened at Vatican II*, Cambridge, MA, Harvard University Press, 2008, a volume distinctive by setting Vatican II in relation to currents of Catholic thought and life from ca. 1800 to 1958 and by regularly noting the Council's unclear delineation of decision-making responsibilities. O'Malley attends to the rhetorical style – of respectful invitation, idealism, and esteem for others – adopted in the Vatican II documents.
6. *Der Text: Werden – Gestalt – Bedeutung. Eine hermeneutische Reflexion*, in P. HÜNERMANN – B.J. HILBERATH (eds.), *Herders Theologische Kommentar zum Zweiten Vatikansichen Konzil*, 5 vols., Freiburg, Herder, 2004-2006, vol. 5: *Die Dokumente des Zweiten Vatikanischen Konzils: Theologische Zusammenschau und Perspektiven*, 3-101. Hünermann sees Vatican II's sixteen documents as a textual corpus arising from a gradually clarified intention which Paul VI expressed in his opening address of the Council's Period II (September 29, 1963). Along with differences, Vatican II shows similarities, in the occasion, the working methods, and level of generality, to the constitutional bodies that produced the Italian Republican Constitution in 1946-1947 and the German Federal Republic's *Grundgesetz* of 1949. The Council's documents are "constitutional" for living

Their interpretations can be tested by the degree to which they honor and incorporate what Willebrands grasped as he reflected on the Council in which he had participated intensely and as he regularly connected Vatican II's decisions and teachings with creative proposals made in the ca. twenty-five years before the Council.

As early as 1965, in introducing a volume of conferences given in Naples, Willebrands wrote that the decree *Unitatis Redintegratio* fulfills Pope John's prayer that a something like a "new Pentecost" take place. The decree ends a time of fear and hiding behind closed doors (Acts 1,13-14). It carries Catholics out to meet others in repentance, friendship and readiness to fill in their own *lacunae* in teaching and life. Willebrands noted, however, that the change was prepared over thirty years before the Council, for example, by Yves Congar's *Chrétiens désunis*, published in 1937[7]. Also in 1965 Willebrands cited another work by Congar that prepared Vatican II, namely, an essay of 1950 treating the ecclesial character of bodies separated from the Catholic Church[8].

At an exposition of French religious books in Rome in 1966, Willebrands listed the ecumenical pioneers who laid bases for the Council's decree: Card. Mercier, Dom Lambert Beauduin, Abbé Couturier, Père Congar, and Père de Lubac. Willebrands said, "The dynamism of their personalities, their personal contacts, and their work prepared many minds and souls over the last forty-five years. (...) They have contributed to the formation of a mentality, a spirituality; they have given a new

the Catholic faith, because, with a remarkable internal breadth of outlook, they aim to promote a reformed basic ordering of Catholic teaching, worship, and life of service in the world. P. Hünermann developed his proposal in *Der 'Text': Eine Ergänzung zur Hermeneutik des II. Vatikanischen Konzils*, in *Cristianesimo nella storia* 28 (2007) 339-358.

7. J. WILLEBRANDS, *Cattolicesimo aperto ed ecumenismo*. Introduction to Y. Congar, R. Schutz, J. Hamer, and F. Sheen, *L'unità dei cristiani*, Napoli, Edizioni domenicane italiane, 1965, 23-30. Later in 1965, at the first meeting of the group assembled to plan Lutheran/Catholic world-level dialogue, Willebrands also spoke of the mystery of the Holy Spirit's presence in the event of Vatican Council II, *Inhalt, Ziel und Aufgabenbereich möglicher Kontakte und Zusammenarbeit zwischen Römisch-katholischer Kirche und Lutherischem Weltbund*, in *Mandatum Unitatis* (n. 1), 15-28, p. 21. On this theme, see T. HUGHSON, *Interpreting Vatican II: 'A New Pentecost'*, in *Theological Studies* 69 (2008) 3-37.

8. J. WILLEBRANDS, *Le mouvement œcuménique à l'heure du Concile*, in *Vers l'unité Chrétien* 18 (1965) 17-23, p. 20. The reference is to Y. CONGAR, *Note sur les mots 'Confession', 'Église' et 'Communion'*, in *Irénikon* (1950) 3-26, reprinted in *Chrétiens en dialogue. Contributions catholiques à l'œcuménisme*, Paris, Cerf, 1964 and translated in *Dialogue Between Christians*, Westminster, MD, Newman Press, 1966, pp. 184-213, esp. pp. 200-202, listing references in official Catholic texts to separated eastern bodies as "churches". Congar's dossier of papal and conciliar references to Orthodox "churches", entered Vatican II in the draft schema *De ecclesia* of 1962, in a note to Ch. XI on ecumenism. *Acta Synodalia*, I/4, pp. 88-89.

depth to the *sensus fidelium*. In this way, one can say that they made possible the Council's work"[9].

Similarly, on *Dignitatis Humanae*, Willebrands once listed the pre-conciliar Catholic writers on religious liberty: John Courtney Murray, Albert Hartmann, Joseph Lecler, Albert Dondeyne and the contributors to the 1951 work, *Tolérance et communauté humaine*[10].

Beyond noting individuals, Willebrands wrote appreciatively in 1973 of a pioneering group, namely, the German Ecumenical Working Group of Evangelical and Catholic Theologians, which had begun dialogue sessions in 1946, thirteen years before Pope John announced the coming Council[11]. By 1962 the Group had met twenty-two times and ninety papers had been presented and discussed by the Working Group's Lutheran and Catholic ecumenical pioneers[12]. *Unitatis Redintegratio* 11 gave guidelines for theological dialogue, which could be written because what it proposed was already being practiced in the German working group. Willebrands modestly omitted mention of the group he had himself coordinated, the Conférence catholique pour les questions œcuméniques, which drew the Catholic ecumenical theologians out of isolation and laid important bases for the Council work of the secretariat and for the documents it saw through the Council's processes of redaction, exposition, and incorporation of comments and amendments.

Just two months after the promulgation of *Unitatis Redintegratio*, Willebrands formulated his thesis on the forerunners and the Council in this way.

> By its Decree on Ecumenism, the Church did not only acknowledge and approve the ecumenical vocation of certain Catholic specialists and theologians, but she adopted their vocation as the vocation of the whole Church, that is, of the people of God in its entirety. (...) A current of Catholic theology has become the doctrine of the Church. What was the effort of a few

9. J. WILLEBRANDS, *The Present Orientation of the Ecumenical Movement*, in *Unitas* 19 (1967) 83-89, citing p. 88. The lecture was given on December 5, 1966, and includes Willebrands's testimony that those who worked on the schema and revisions of *Unitatis Redintegratio* know how much the document owes to Congar's *Chrétiens désunis*.

10. J. WILLEBRANDS, *Ökumenische Aspekte und Perspektiven des Zweiten Vatikanischen Konzils*, in E. SCHILLEBEECKX – J. WILLEBRANDS, *et al.*, *Christentum im Spannungsfeld von Konfessionen, Gesellschaft und Staaten*, Freiburg – Basel – Wien, Herder, 1968, 37-58, cited from WILLEBRANDS, in *Mandatum Unitatis* (n. 1), 98-111, p. 106.

11. J. WILLEBRANDS, *Der evangelisch-katholische Dialog: Tatsächliches und Grundsätzliches*, in *Ökumenische Rundschau* 22 (1973) 182-202; reprinted in *Mandatum Unitatis* (n. 1), 133-154.

12. A valuable overview, is E. SCHLINK, *Pneumatische Erschütterung? Aus der Zusammenarbeit eines evangelischen und eines römisch-katholischen ökumenischen Arbeitskreises*, in *Kerygma und Dogma* 8 (1962) 221-235.

theologians ought now to become the attitude and direction of the people of God[13].

Another affirmation of the Council's preparation came in Willebrands's Reformation Day lecture in 1967 at Lund, Sweden, e.g., "Long before the Second Vatican Council a new understanding of the church was being prepared. (…) Before the Council, a sizeable Catholic reform literature was circulating, out of which I mention only the works of Yves Congar and Karl Rahner as examples"[14].

Willebrands' point about the pioneering forerunners can and should be applied across the wider span of Vatican II's teaching and insistence on new attitudes and practice[15]. Willebrands can contribute today to the ongoing discussion over what happened at the Council, in which options and preoccupations of present-day interpreters at times leave in the shadows the pre-conciliar pioneers and their initiatives, to which Willebrands referred. The pioneers had an impact on the Council and on its renewal program in ways going far beyond what they could ever have foreseen as they wrote, spoke and discussed during the pre-conciliar period.

II. Willebrands on the Complementary Unity of Diverse *Typoi* of Church Life

The cardinal's address at Great St. Mary's, Cambridge, England, in January 1970, on different "types" of church life within a larger unity, is rightly considered the articulation of a significant ecumenical theological theme[16].

---

13. Willebrands, *Le mouvement œcuménique à l'heure du Concile* (n. 8), p. 18. This lecture was delivered at Lyon and nearby cities during the Week of Prayer for Christian Unity in January 1965.

14. *Reformation und Reform heute*, in *Mandatum Unitatis* (n. 1), 29-47, pp. 36-37.

15. In work on Vatican II's Dogmatic Constitution on Divine Revelation, I found Pieter Smulders anticipating the doctrine of *Dei Verbum*, Ch. 1, in his critical notes on the Preparatory Theological Commission's schema *De deposito fidei pure custodiendo*, given in September 1962 to the Vatican Nuncio in the Netherlands. J. Wicks, *Pieter Smulders and* Dei Verbum, *1. A Consultation on the Eve of Vatican II*, in *Gregorianum* 82 (2001) 241-297, pp. 267-272. In this Smulders was drawing extensively on pioneering French and German biblical theologies of revelation set forth in books of the 1940s and 1950s.

16. J. Willebrands, *The Notion of 'Typos' Within the One Church*, in *Information Service* 101, 130-134. In Lorelei F. Fuchs' wide ranging study of ecumenical ecclesiology, we read, "The ecumenical task is not to eliminate the different '*typoi*' which give variegated expression to ecclesial faith, life, and witness, but rather to make visible their legitimacy and to preserve them as facets of church fellowship". *Koinonia and the Quest for*

Earlier, in 1965, Willebrands had anticipated the topic of different "types" of church life, which express catholicity within unity, in his paper at Strasbourg during the first meeting of the working group for planning the Lutheran/Catholic bilateral dialogue that followed and continues today. There, he foresaw a dialogue which would heighten our sense of what is Christian and ecclesial in the partner's tradition. He said:

> We will become able to realize a diversity containing nothing which destroys unity or is incompatible with it. May the one Lord and one Spirit so lead us. One could develop a typology of the Christian reality and of the churches, working, to be sure, not from abstractions but from historical realities and concrete givens. The typology would explain and show as legitimate the diverse traditions, theological statements and methods, spirituality, and the form of church life, even if one's own tradition lacks certain elements proper to the other, which however are reconcilable with what Christ has given. That would enrich both diversity in unity and the catholicity and unity of the Church of Christ[17].

Moving on from this proposal made at Strasbourg in 1965, at Cambridge in 1970 Willebrands appealed to Pope Gregory the Great's instruction given to St. Augustine of Canterbury that he, Augustine, not simply import the customs of Rome – for example, the form of the mass – into "the church of the English". Augustine should instead carefully select customs from the different churches, whether of Rome, Gaul or other realms, and make them into a coherent bundle to be inculcated in the still young church in England[18].

At Cambridge, a pointer toward diverse ecclesial "types" was the passage in *Lumen Gentium* on how, under divine providence, the churches of the apostles and of later founders have "in the course of time coalesced into several groups, organically united, which, [while] preserving the unity of faith and the unique divine constitution of the universal church, enjoy their own discipline, their own liturgical usage, and their own theological and spiritual heritage" (LG 23)[19].

Willebrands stated his concept in this way:

an Ecumenical Ecclesiology, Grand Rapids, MI, Eerdmans, 2008, p. 325, based on the Lutheran-Catholic world-level commission's statement *Facing Unity* (1984), no. 43.

17. Presentation by J. WILLEBRANDS on August 25, 1965, at Strasbourg, *Inhalt, Ziel und Aufgabenbereich möglicher Kontakte und Zusammenarbeit zwischen Römisch-katholischer Kirche und Lutherischem Weltbund* (n. 7), p. 26.

18. Given in BEDE, *Ecclesiastical History of the English People*, I, 27, 2, trans. J. McCLURE – R. COLLINS, Oxford, Oxford University Press, 1994, 43; and in Bede's Latin in *Sources chrétiennes*, no. 489, Paris, Cerf, 2005, 210-212.

19. To this he added, from the Decree on Ecumenism, how for centuries Eastern and Western churches "went their own ways, although communion in faith and sacramental life bound them together" (UR 14).

> Where there is a long coherent tradition, commanding people's love and loyalty, creating and sustaining a harmonious and organic whole of complementary elements, each of which supports and strengthens the other, you have the reality of a *typos*.

The fields of a recognizable type of church life are (1) theology, in approaching from a particular perspective the single mystery of Christ; (2) liturgy, in a classic language and music of worship, in a dominant tone of sacramental celebration and rite, and in a "flavor" arising from how a people experiences God and responds to him; (3) spirituality, drawing on preferred biblical sources and classic works on prayer and the devotional or ascetical life; and (4) a canonical discipline laying down norms of order and procedures giving basic shape to church life. Willebrands concluded, "Through the combination of all these, a *typos* can be specified".

Today, after diverse types of worship and life have sadly grown asunder, the ecumenical movement is by God's grace creating bonds of affection and fresh understanding between them. But the Cardinal looked beyond healing divisions in his conclusion. "The life of the Church needs a variety of *typoi* to manifest the full catholic and apostolic character of the one and holy Church". A variety of complementary types "multiplies the possibilities of identifying and celebrating the presence of God in the world". Here is the boon to be gained, the blessing that lies beyond reconciling doctrines and church orders, namely, the recognition of several valid ways of knowing God and different ways of being enveloped by him who is with us to save. So the Cardinal argued for the imperative that ecumenical theology work further on a typology of cohering traditions.

What Willebrands stated at Cambridge in 1970, he repeated two years later in an address at Lambeth Palace, with emphasis on how full communion between churches of different types does not of itself demand unity of organization, but does require oneness and coherence in the faith professed – on which the theologians of ARCIC, the Anglican Roman Catholic International Commission, were then beginning to show areas of agreement between the Anglican and Roman Catholic traditions[20].

But who gave the cardinal the stimulus to speak as he did on different "types" of church life? Part of the answer may lie in the papers presented and the discussions held during the September 1960 meeting of the Conférence catholique pour les questions œcuméniques, held at Gazzada

---

20. J. WILLEBRANDS, *Prospects for Anglican-Roman Catholic Relations*, Address at Lambeth Palace, October 4, 1972, given in *Information Service* 101, pp. 100-105.

in the Archdiocese of Milan, where the central topic was the differences compatible with the unity of the church[21]. At Gazzada, Dom Emmanuel Lanne of Chevetogne, gave a historical paper on differences accepted as compatible with unity which did not fracture communion between families of churches during the first twelve centuries[22]. Willebrands did draw on this 1960 study by E. Lanne in a text of late 1967 on "diversity in unity"[23]. However, Lanne did not propose the notion of a variety of ecclesial "types" in his Gazzada paper. But there is another source of "typological" thinking in Willebrands's ecclesiology on which he may well have been drawing in his proposal at Strasbourg in August 1965.

During the third period of Vatican II, on November 14, 1964, a week before the promulgation of *Unitatis Redintegratio*, Willebrands brought Dr. Lukas Vischer, a council observer for the World Council of Churches, to see Pope Paul VI. We know the content of their half-hour conversation from Dr. Vischer's detailed report, composed shortly after the audience and sent to the World Council's General Secretary, Dr. W.A. Visser 't Hooft. Dr. Vischer and Paul VI spoke in French, but the former's report is in English, for circulation among the heads of the World Council's departments.

At one point, Paul VI spoke of the ecumenical goal and the present new dynamism, which however has to be combined with patience. The pope continued on the ideal outlook and approach, including a notion of ecclesial typology, which Dr. Vischer recorded as follows:

> The true attitude toward the other Churches did not want to enforce victories on them. On the contrary, it should aim at the victory of the other Churches. He [Paul VI] then went on to emphasize the importance of what he called the "typology" of the Churches. He said that every tradition should maintain its characteristic features. There was no need for uniformity. He mentioned the Anglican Communion. They would not have to give up the *Common Prayer Book*, if they wanted to enter into the one Church of Christ. He praised the respect of the Lutherans for the Bible. If they would join the one fold (*le bercail*) they could still develop their particular

---

21. M. VELATI, *Una difficile transizione: Il cattolicesimo tra unionismo ed ecumenismo (1952-1964)*, Bologna, Il Mulino, 1996, pp. 151-155.

22. *Les différences compatibles avec l'Unité dans la tradition de l'Église ancienne (jusqu'au XIIe siècle)*, published in *Istina* 8 (1962) 227-253, and now in Lanne's collected articles, *Tradition et communion des églises* (BETL, 129), Leuven, Peeters, 1997, 359-385.

23. J. WILLEBRANDS, *Diversité dans l'unité*, in *Œcuménisme et problèmes actuels* (n. 1), 115-129, in which pp. 119-124 draw on Lanne's paper, with proper acknowledgment. One reference that then came back at Cambridge in 1970, was to Gregory the Great's advice to Augustine of Canterbury on combining different liturgical practices for use in England. *Œcuménisme et problèmes actuels*, p. 121, from LANNE, *Les différences* (n. 22), p. 239.

tradition. He finally referred to the Orthodox liturgies and to the place of the eastern liturgical tradition in the Church. At this point he [Paul VI] turned to Mgr. Willebrands and asked him whether he agreed with this idea. Of course Willebrands agreed and just added that this idea of typology should first be lived out within the Roman Catholic Church[24].

Thus Pope Paul VI, in a conversation of November 1964, sowed a seed of the concept of varying "types" of church life[25]. Willebrands first developed the notion embryonically in 1965 at Strasbourg to give a perspective on the Lutheran-Catholic dialogue then being planned.

Later, but still before Willebrands' Cambridge lecture of 1970, Dom Lanne published a paper elaborating the possibility of diverse ecclesial typologies in one church[26]. From this, the Cardinal moved on to his more developed account at Cambridge in 1970, with his own concise definition of an ecclesial *typos* and his account of why the Church needs a variety of *typoi*. The ecumenical goal is a unity which is inclusive of different types (*typoi*) of worship, spirituality and church order. But, within the variety of types, what is to be the form of their unity?

III. WILLEBRANDS EXPOUNDS THE ECCLESIOLOGY OF COMMUNION

In 1975 Cardinal Willebrands set forth in two lectures, one in Vienna, Austria, and the other at Eichstätt, Germany, what for him was an essential

---

24. L. VISCHER, *Report on a Private Audience with Pope Paul VI*, 14 November 1964, 12:30-1:00 PM. In copy in the World Council of Churches Archive, Geneva, in L. VISCHER, *Letters and Other Papers Concerning the Second Vatican Council*, vol. 3A. I gave the text, with Dr. Vischer's permission, as Appendix I of *Collaboration and Dialogue: The Roman Catholic Presence in the Ecumenical Movement during the Pontificate of Paul VI*, in *Paolo VI e l'ecumenismo*, Brescia, Istituto Paolo VI; Rome, Studium, 2001, pp. 215-267, esp. pp. 259-262, from which I cite here p. 261.

25. One can only surmise who or what prompted Paul VI to imagine a church unity embracing different types of church life. One occasion could have been the 1960 Gazzada meeting of the Conférence catholique pour les questions œcuméniques, at which Cardinal Montini was present since Gazzada was within the Archdiocese of Milan.

26. *Pluralisme et Unité: Possibilité d'une diversité de typologies dans une même adhésion ecclésiale*, in *Istina* 14 (1969) 171-190. This was Lanne's contribution to the study of catholicity and apostolicity by a group commissioned by the Roman Catholic–World Council of Churches Joint Working Group, which met in 1967-1968. On November 19, 2009, at the Willebrands Colloquium in Rome, Abp. Rowan Williams attributed the notion of "diversity of types of communion", adopted by Willebrands at Cambridge in 1970, to Dom Lanne. The address is given at http://www.archbishopofcanterbury.org/Articles, Interviews & Speeches/Archbishop's Address at a Willebrands Symposium in Rome, accessed November 22, 2009.

condition of ecumenical progress toward visible church unity[27]. Progress will depend on conceiving the church as a *communio* at its different levels of existence, both in spiritual transcendence and in earthly ecclesial visibility. The notions of partial and full communion enter here for conceiving ecumenical progress as a development from real but only partial communion to full communion, that is, to a re-integrated unity in being possessed together by God's self-communication as he gives this through mediations provided by Christ and animated by the Holy Spirit.

Both at Vienna and at Eichstätt, Willebrands acknowledged his debt to three others who had gone ahead of him in presenting the ecclesiology of communion, namely, Père Jérôme Hamer, O.P., Franjo Cardinal Šeper, and Dr. Pier Cesare Bori[28]. Drawing on their work, he then offered his own sketch and application of what he had appropriated about ecclesial *communio*, doing this in five points.

First, a terminological clarification had to be made, to indicate that "communion" (*koinonia, communio*, fellowship) is the relationship arising from a reality in which several or many persons have been given to share in common. What is shared unites individuals both to a gift and its giver and to each other, for the gift creates between them, as co-participants, the bond of community. The relation is not due primarily to their voluntarily deciding to associate, as in a Rotary Club, but it arises essentially from the reality that opens itself to participation in itself by persons who are thereby drawn together. The quality of their relationship depends on and is determined by the reality in which they share[29].

---

27. J. WILLEBRANDS, *L'avenir de l'œcuménisme*, address of February 3, 1975, to the Pro Oriente Foundation in Vienna, published in *Proche-Orient Chrétien* 25 (1975) 3-15, from which an English translation appeared in *One in Christ* 11 (1975) 310-323, and in *Information Service* 101, 134-140. Then, *Die Zukunft der ökumenischen Bewegung*, was given on June 30, 1975, at the Catholic University of Eichstätt, being first published in A. BAUCH (ed.), *Zehn Jahre Vaticanum II*, Regensburg, Pustet, 1966, 76-94, and reprinted in *Mandatum Unitatis* (n. 1), pp. 198-215.

28. J. HAMER, *L'Église est une communion*, Paris, Cerf, 1962, in English as *The Church Is a Communion*, London, Geoffrey Chapman; New York, Sheed and Ward, 1964; F. ŠEPER, Opening *relatio* at the 1969 Extraordinary Synod of Bishops on collegiality, given in Giovanni CAPRILE, *Il Sinodo dei vescovi: Prima assemblea straordinaria (11-28 ottobre 1969)*, Rome, La Civiltà cattolica, 1970, 455-466, esp. pp. 456-459; P.C. BORI, *Koinonia: L'idea della comunione nell'ecclesiologia recente e nel Nuovo Testamento*, Brescia, Paideia, 1972.

29. J. Hamer had written, "When we consider the New Testament use of the word, we must beware of reducing *koinonia* to mere friendly relationships between man and man. The vertical dimension is the primary one: *koinonia* is founded wholly on Christ and on the Spirit. (...) The horizontal dimension in *koinonia* must thus be regarded as resulting from a vertical relationship and can only be explained through this". *The Church Is a Communion* (n. 28), p. 162.

Second, the New Testament witnesses to this communion center, ultimately, on the Risen Christ, as when St. Paul speaks of God having called believers "into the *koinonia* of his Son, Jesus Christ" (1 Cor 1,9). St. John declares, "our *koinonia* is with the Father and with his Son Jesus Christ" (1 Jn 1,3). In and from Christ believers receive *bona divina*, and thereby come into communion with the Father, in the Holy Spirit. The Risen Christ conveys the graces of salvation. By these, people live in God in an intimate personal relationship, and by this communion in divine life (2 Peter 1,4) they are joined together in sharing in God's saving mystery[30].

The Scriptures of Israel offered gradual but significant preparations for this Christian theme, for example, when Moses begs that the Lord will take Israel as his "inheritance" (Ex 34,9), so the people may benefit from his mercy and steadfast love (34,6) by belonging to the Lord in an intimate way. From another perspective this is the covenant-relation between the Lord who chose Israel as "my people" for whom he is their God (as in Jer 24,7). In New Testament developments, believers come to share in a complex of divine gifts, indicated by the "kingdom" (Mt 25,34) and "eternal life" (Mt 19,29).

> The members of the new people of God are heirs of God and co-heirs with Christ (Rom 8:17). The Father gives all he has to his Son, risen from the dead, and through him to his faithful. The inheritance is participation in the life of the Risen Christ (cf. 1 Cor 15:49-50). Even now we live by the promised Spirit who has been given to us and we hope from him to reach the fullness of possession (cf. Eph 1:14)[31].

Believers relate to God by his gifts imparted through Christ and thus they are "holy," while being drawn together in community because they have these gifts in common. In their union, the eschatological "communion of saints" is present and at work in human history. The goal is the complete number of the elect (Rev 6,9-10), the Church in its fullness, when it will be perfect in the profound unity of a people made one by

---

30. Bp. Pierre Duprey, M.Af., Secretary of Unity Secretariat/Pontifical Council from 1983 to 1999, developed Willebrands's thought in *A Catholic Perspective on Ecclesial Communion*, in G.R. EVANS (ed.), *Christian Authority: Essays in Honour of Henry Chadwick*, Oxford, Clarendon, 1988, 7-19. Duprey characterized saving spiritual communion with God as that from which everything in the Church more or less immediately derives and toward which it is ordered. Second Corinthians 13,14 expresses this, which is the intended end of the whole economy of salvation, as communion of the Holy Spirit, manifesting the Father's love, in the grace of the Lord Jesus. This also indicates that profane models are not adequate to explain it (Duprey, pp. 7-9).

31. J. WILLEBRANDS, *The Future of Ecumenism*, in *One in Christ* 11 (1975) 310-323, at p. 314, and in *Information Service* 101, 134-140, at p. 136.

the unity of Father, Son, and Holy Spirit, as indicated in *Lumen Gentium* 4, which cites St. Cyprian[32].

A third aspect of Willebrands' account of ecclesial communion is that for us who live on earth before Christ's second coming, the transcendent spiritual communion, just sketched, comes about and develops through mediations and ministries on our human level. This follows from the principles of incarnation and sacramentality.

Fundamental mediations, after the humanity of Christ, are the Gospel word of good news and the assembled people who themselves embody the Gospel in a witness which invites the world to be gathered out of dispersion into one people (cf. John 11,52). Acts of the Apostles tells of the particular mediations, especially baptism in the name of the risen Christ for forgiveness of sins and the outpouring of the Holy Spirit (Acts 2,38). Further mediations appear in the account of those who "devoted themselves to the Apostles' teaching, to the common life, to the breaking of the bread, and to the prayers" (Acts 2,42). Thus, God mediates saving communion through "holy things," the *sancta*, namely, the word of faith confessed, the sacraments celebrated, and especially the Eucharist for *koinonia* in the blood of Christ and in the body of Christ (1 Cor 10,16). By these, persons are gathered and further served by ministers who are themselves established sacramentally for serving God's gifts and the people assembled by those gifts.

In another vocabulary, used in central Vatican II passages, the mediations are the "elements of truth and sanctification" by which God takes people unto Himself. In our bodily realm, God assembles believers through their partaking in and holding to the mediations or elements that the Holy Spirit has adopted as instruments for giving and deepening the transcendent spiritual communion.

Cardinal Willebrands spoke emphatically of communion that is realized by the Eucharist and is served by ministers carrying on the apostolic mission.

---

32. Archbishop Rowan Williams treated this transcendent theological foundation of ecclesiology in no. 1 of his November 19, 2009, address (as in n. 26, above), taking it as the outcome of being restored to life with God in the filial relation of those incorporated into Christ by the Holy Spirit, by which believers have a mutual human communion among themselves. "The sacramental life and the communal disciplines of the Church exist to serve and witness to this dual fact of communion with the Father and with all believers". The primacy of this filial communion, the Archbishop recognized, has deep roots in Vatican II, was central for Cardinal Willebrands, and has been featured in the ecclesiology set forth in several ecumenical dialogues, as synthesized in W. KASPER, *Harvesting the Fruits: Basic Aspects of Christian Faith in Ecumenical Dialogue*, London – New York, Continuum, 2009.

> The Eucharist (...) is the great sacrament of communion with Christ and, in consequence, of communion between the faithful (1 Cor 10:16). In the eucharistic synaxis there is already the realization in the present through the Spirit of that eschatological communion we sketched a little earlier. For the eucharistic synaxis does not only gather together in unity the assembly of the faithful in communion with the eternal life of the triune God through the body and blood of Christ; in and through the Spirit, the celebrating communion is also identified with the community contemplated by the seer of the Apocalypse, (...) that of the believers of all ages reunited with the apostles in the presence of God and Christ for the eternal heavenly liturgy[33].

Then on the service of ministers:

> The Christian community is gathered together for a life of holiness by those and around those who continue to exercise in its midst the mission which the apostles received from the Lord, so far as this mission was to be continued through time[34].

Thus, the faithful are united among themselves not only spiritually on the level of the transcendent mystery of God, but as well through the visible, quite human, realities which, while served by ministers, are the means that the Holy Spirit has adopted as ways of building them up in truth and holiness.

Fourth, ecclesial communion in the mediations has its levels of local, regional and universal communion. Local communion is of baptized persons assembled by the Gospel word proclaimed and for Eucharist under the presidency of their bishop (Vatican II, *Christus Dominus* 11). But other communities hold to the same Gospel and celebrate the same Eucharist, the "synaxis" which gathers them together. Thus, a trans-local communion appears, based on common mediations and ministers sharing in the continuing apostolic mission.

A bishop, while serving in his local or particular presidency, brings the local church into communion with other churches through his communion with other bishops. At the same time, his belonging to a collegial episcopal body brings the wider communion into the local church. An essential factor here is *conciliarity*, which is not the task-oriented union of a commission but a reality of communion between local churches through their bishops, by reason of their sacramental episcopal ordination by other bishops.

Intermediate episcopal groups make manifest the communion of several local churches and serve its maintenance and deepening. But

---

33. *The Future of Ecumenism* (n. 31), p. 316 / p. 137.
34. *Ibid.*, p. 317 / p. 137.

every conciliar or synodal body of bishops has its *protos* or head, according to the rule of the canons of the early *Apostolic Constitutions*, of which the cardinal cited Canon 34.

> The bishops of each nation must know who among them is the first (*prōton*) and consider him as their head (*kephalēn*). They must do nothing of importance without his agreement, even though each one is responsible for the affairs of his own diocese and its dependent territories. But no more must he (that is, the one who is first) do anything without the agreement of all the others. Thus peace will reign, and God will be glorified through Christ in the Holy Spirit[35].

For the universal communion on a world-wide level, there is the headship of the bishop of the primatial see of Rome, which has a "more excellent origin" (*potentiorem principalitatem*, Irenaeus) from its founding by Peter and Paul. The Catholic conviction about the primacy, thus, concerns the presidency of the Bishop of Rome among the bishops of the world in the conciliarity of the universal church. This has its place in a network of churches in communion, where the primacy serves to link episcopally-led churches in communion within the sacramental structure of mediations given by Christ.

A fifth aspect of ecclesial communion is the difference between full or partial communion. Between the churches, the relation is "full" when it is "participation together in all that the Lord has given to his church"[36]. This is sacramental and ministerial completeness, not a fullness of perfect sharing in what the sacraments mediate, that is, divine life realized in holiness. Sharing in the spiritual gifts opens upon ongoing personal growth through purification and communal deepening, with moments of reforming change aimed a more fervent reception of the mediated gifts.

Willebrands made the further point that when Catholics work out this communion ecclesiology, they do not take their own Church as an independent measuring rod, for all the ecclesial elements and ministries, whether they operate in incomplete configurations or in their sacramental-structural fullness in the Catholic Church, come from Christ and by him mediate life in himself[37]. This, for the cardinal, explains why the Doctrinal

---

35. *Ibid.*, p. 319 / p. 138. The canon is given, in Greek and French, in M. METZGER (ed.), *Les Constitutions apostoliques* (Sources chrétiennes, 336), vol. 3, Paris, Cerf, 1987, 284-285. The larger collection dates from 340 A.D., but Willebrands follows the view that this canon is considerably older, possibly reflecting the practice that emerged during the regional councils held to deal with the late second century quarrel over the date of Easter.

36. *The Future of Ecumenism* (n. 31), p. 320 / p. 138.

37. In January 1965, Willebrands emphasized that the Catholic Church does not explain itself in and by itself. "Le source et le centre de notre communion, dans la mesure

Commission at Vatican II revised an initial assertion that the one Church of Christ is (*est*) the Catholic Church to "subsists in" (*Lumen Gentium* 8), because many of the mediations coming from Christ are present and operative in churches and communities outside the Catholic Church[38].

Partial or imperfect communion, the decisive ecumenical challenge, rests on an incompleteness in a church's possession of mediations and ministries established by Christ and taken into the Holy Spirit's operation. To be more concrete, Cardinal Willebrands gave a short catalogue.

> We speak of partial or imperfect communion between the divided Churches according to the way in which they participate in these gifts of the Spirit; in these realities which are gifts of the Spirit; the way in which they are in agreement as to the content of their profession of faith; the way in which they celebrate the sacraments and the eucharistic liturgy; the way in which they benefit from the apostolic ministry and its holding together of catholic unity[39].

The cardinal added a warning about quantitative measuring of the mediations and ministries, since, while they are visible aspects of our human world, they are also taken up into the work of the Holy Spirit which escapes the reach of quantitative analysis. In illustration of considering the mediations and ministries in their spiritual depth, Willebrands adduced Paul VI's "charter-text" of 1967 for Catholic-Orthodox relations. The Pope speaks of how the shared gifts of the apostles' witness, baptism, apostolic succession, the priesthood, and the Eucharist serve to bring Catholics and Orthodox into oneness in Christ (Gal 3,28) as sons in the Son in all truth (1 Jn 3,1-2). Thus the mystery of divine love works in each local church, which tradition calls sisters of each other, and this holds despite the obstacles still to be overcome on the way to the fullness of the already existing communion[40].

Thus a first ecumenical task is to work through differences in faith, sacraments, and ministries, as in the bilateral dialogues, which were beginning when Willebrands spoke in 1975. Through them, the aim is the kind of mutual understanding in unity that was reached between the Apostle of the Gentiles and the Jerusalem "pillars", who then extended

---

où elle existe réellement bien que de manière imparfaite, est le Christ". *Le mouvement œcumenique à l'heure du Concile* (n. 8), p. 20.

38. *The Future of Ecumenism* (n. 31), p. 321 / p. 139. The fourth part of this presentation will present Willebrands's interpretation of *subsistit in*.

39. *Ibid.*, p. 321 / p. 139.

40. *Ibid.*, pp. 321-322 / p. 139, drawing on the Letter *Anno ineunte*, read out by Cardinal Willebrands and given by Paul VI to Patriarch Athenagoras at the end of a joint prayer service in the Latin Cathedral of Istanbul, July 25, 1967. The text is given in *Towards the Healing of Schism*, ed. and trans. E.J. STORMON, New York – Mahwah, NJ, Paulist, 1987, pp. 161-163.

to Paul and Barnabas "the right hand of fellowship" (of communion, that is, *koinonia*, Gal 2,9).

The cardinal added an observation which anticipated John Paul II's *Ut unum sint* of 1995 when he said that the principle of sacramental episcopal leadership and of papal primacy among bishops is one thing, but the exercise of both is another thing, being in fact an area of liberty, because the exercise unfolds in history amid contingencies which permit renewal and development[41].

In both lectures on *communio*, Cardinal Willebrands concluded by warning against a theology which becomes so engrossed in discussing the mediations that it relegates to unimportance the spiritual and saving communion with God in faith, hope and love. But he remained convinced that *communio* was the essential framework for ecumenical ecclesiology. It should be deepened, but always presented in a balanced manner[42].

IV. Willebrands Interprets *subsistit in* (*Lumen Gentium* 8)[43]

In 1974, at Princeton Theological Seminary, Cardinal Willebrands insisted that the Catholic Church's recent entry into the ecumenical movement was a consequence of its own redesigned self-understanding

---

41. *The Future of Ecumenism* (n. 31), pp. 322-323 / p. 139.

42. He also noted realistically that such an ecclesiological concept does not provide everything that is needed, as he sensed in the mid-1970s when new issues on moral questions, such as abortion, were arising and posing new obstacles to agreement.

43. On this term, Gerard Philips's prediction is now being amply fulfilled, namely, that "rivers of ink would flow" over the meaning of *subsistit in* in LG 8. *L'Église et son mystère au II° Concile du Vatican*, 2 vols., Paris, Desclée, 1967, Vol. 1, p. 119. See, for example, J. RATZINGER, *Das neue Volk Gottes*, Düsseldorf, Patmos, 1969, pp. 235-237, and *The Ecclesiology of the Constitution Lumen Gentium*, in *Pilgrim Fellowship of Faith: The Church as Communion*, ed. S.O. HAHN – V. PFNÜR, San Francisco, CA, Ignatius Press, 2005, 123-152, esp. pp. 144-149; F.J. SULLIVAN, *The Significance of the Vatican II Declaration That the Church of Christ Subsists in the Roman Catholic Church*, in R. LATOURELLE (ed.), *Vatican II: Assessment and Perspectives*, 3 vols., New York – Mahwah, NJ, Paulist Press, 1989, Vol. 2, pp. 233-287; A. VON TEUFFENBACH, *Die Bedeutung des subsistit in in LG 8: Zum Selbstverständnis der katholischen Kirche*, Munich, Herbert Utz, 2002; K.J. BECKER, *An Examination of Subsistit in: A Profound Theological Perspective*, in *l'Osservatore Romano* (Weekly English Edition), December 14, 2005, reprinted in *Origins* 35 (January 19, 2006) 514-522, and under the title *Ecclesia Christi – Ecclesia Catholica*, in *Studia Missionalia* 55 (2006) 63-83; F.J. SULLIVAN, *A Response to Karl Becker, S.J. on the Meaning of Subsistit in*, in *Theological Studies* 67 (2006) 395-409; *The One Church in Current Ecclesiology*, in *Ecumenical Trends* 38 (2009) 4-16, and *Further Thoughts on the Meaning of subsistit in*, in *Theological Studies* 71 (2010) 133-147; K. SCHELKENS, *Lumen Gentium's 'subsistit in' Revisited: The Catholic Church and Christian Unity after Vatican II*, in *Theological Studies* 69 (2008) 875-893; L.J. WELCH – G. MANSINI, O.S.B., *Lumen Gentium No. 8, and Subsistit in, Again*, in *New Blackfriars*

as Vatican II set this forth[44]. After long emphasis on social visibility and juridical relationships with authority, Catholic ecclesiology now brings to the fore spiritual and sacramental themes. As a work of the Triune God, the Church has to present herself through numerous biblical images. The Church is sacramental, since in it visible and social elements are instruments of the Holy Spirit for the growth of the Body of Christ.

Speaking at a Presbyterian school, Willebrands then took up the way in which Catholic ecclesiology understands other Christians and relates the Catholic Church to their churches and communities. *Communio* gives the overarching Catholic conception of God's saving grace and its mediations by word and sacrament served by ministries on earth. But the cardinal concentrated on *Lumen Gentium* 8, which states that the Church of Christ *subsists in* the Catholic Church, while many elements of sanctification and truth are found outside. The "outside" are the other churches and communities in which baptized believers benefit from Scripture and live their Christian faith by elements or mediations which unite them to Christ.

A first point concerns the successive changes during Vatican II from a draft saying, "the Church of Christ is (*est*) the Catholic Church" to an intermediate Commission draft saying "is present in" (*adest in*), and then to the final "subsists in" (*subsistit in*) of *Lumen Gentium* 8. This, according to Willebrands, has to be first understood from the Council no longer basing the theological status of other Christians on their sincere good will (a *votum* of following God's call), but instead on "the real fact of being baptized in Christ and confessing faith in the Trinitarian and Christological doctrines". Their life in Christ has objective ontological bases, namely, the mediations by which God brings them into communion with himself. Several (*plura*) of the same mediations which operate in the Catholic Church are also at work outside her boundaries[45].

Second, *subsistit in*, concerning the Church, denotes a relation of the vital source of grace and life to the social reality of the Catholic Church,

---

90 (2009) 602-617; and D. VALENTINI, *Subsistit in*, in G. CALABRESE – P. GOYRET – O.F. PIAZZA (eds.), *Dizionario di ecclesiologia*, Rome, Città Nuova, 2010, 1393-1408.

44. *The Ecumenical Movement: Its Problems and Driving Force*, in *One in Christ* 11 (1975) 210-223; given in German translation in *Mandatum Unitatis* (n. 1), 165-178.

45. *The Ecumenical Movement: Its Problems and Driving Force* (n. 44), pp. 218-219. Here the cardinal followed the *Relatio* in which the Vatican II Doctrinal Commission explained why it substituted *subsistit in* for *est*, namely, "so that the expression might better agree with the affirmation about the ecclesial elements which are found elsewhere", in *Acta Synodalia*, III/1, p. 177. So, the main clause affirming *subsistit in* coheres with a contrasting or concessive *licet* clause about *plura elementa*. The pattern is: "This is definitely the case", (A subsisting in B), "but this does not exclude that this other is also the case", (particular *elementa* constitutive of A being also present in C, D, E, etc.). As is often true, God's economy results in a paradox.

to which the source is united in an ongoing way. This continuity denoted by *subsistit in*, according to Willebrands, is not what classical dogma affirms about the Word Incarnate, that is, that the eternal Son subsists hypostatically in an assumed human nature. Nor does the term refer to a static substance (*substantia*). But *subsistit in* differs from the earlier draft, on the Church of Christ *being* the Catholic Church, which, according to the cardinal, indicated a complete or exclusive relation which would not cohere well with the affirmation that saving elements are at work outside the Catholic Church.

Third, the broader context in Vatican II indicates that "subsists in" means to affirm that the full complement of sacramental and ministerial means of saving grace are present in the Catholic Church. However, their effectiveness has been limited by mediocrity in Catholic life. The Catholic endowments do make up a complete system and structure, but without being completely effective. Consequently the Decree on Ecumenism adds its striking words on ongoing reformation[46].

Fourth, the cardinal emphasized that Vatican II does not see other Christians benefiting from mediations of life in Christ as isolated individuals, for they receive God's gifts in and through their own communities, as the Constitution on the Church affirms in no. 15. To be sure, the communities, in the Catholic view, suffer from defects, but still "they have been by no means deprived of significance and importance in the mystery of salvation. For the Spirit of Christ has not refrained from using them as means of salvation" for their members (UR 3). So Catholics should esteem the endowments preserved and cherished by the other communities and should be edified by the Holy Spirit's work through them (UR 4).

Thus, while the Church of Christ is present in structural-sacramental completeness in the Catholic Church in which it subsists, the Church of Christ nonetheless has a saving presence and impact through ecclesial mediations beyond that Church. So far, Willebrands in 1974.

Thirteen years later, in 1987, Willebrands returned to *subsistit in*, at a meeting of ecumenists in Atlanta[47]. Here the cardinal made extensive use

---

46. "Although the Catholic Church has been endowed with all divinely revealed truth and with all means of grace, yet its members fail to live by them with all the fervor that they should. As a result, the radiance of the church's face shines less brightly in the eyes of our separated brothers and of the world at large, and the growth of God's kingdom is retarded" (UR 4). This leads to saying that "Christ summons the church, as she goes her pilgrim way, to that continual reformation (*ad hanc perennem reformationem*) of which she always has need" (UR 6).

47. *Subsistit in. Address to the National Workshop for Christian Unity*, in *One in Christ* 23 (1987) 179-191, and in *Origins* 17 (May 28, 1982). Reprinted in *Information*

of a twenty-page study of Vatican II's *subsistit in* which he had requested from Père Jean-Marie Tillard, O.P., of Ottawa[48].

A new consideration in Willebrands' 1987 lecture is the documented practice of the Holy See over centuries of referring to separated Eastern bodies as "churches", in spite of their not being in communion with the Catholic Church. Thus if Vatican II were to strictly identify God's Church with the Catholic Church, it would not be honoring an established Catholic tradition[49].

Another innovation in 1987 was Willebrands's use of the *Acta Synodalia*, which allowed him to formulate the imperatives arising from Vatican II's members to guide revision of earlier drafts of *De ecclesia*. Cardinal Achille Liénart, president of the French Episcopal Conference, opened the debate on the first ecclesiological schema on December 1, 1962, by calling for a revision in which the Catholic Church would not say it is simply identical with the Mystical Body of Christ, for Christ's Body is not confined within the Catholic Church[50]. The German bishops proposed an alternative text, in February 1963 which said that the other communities make the elements central to their lives, and thereby they come close to the Church of Christ[51]. The Coadjutor-Archbishop of Strasbourg, Leon-Arthur Elchinger, affirmed a point to be made, namely, that

---

Service 101, pp. 142-149.

48. Projet pour le cardinal Willebrands, Doc. B 7/13 of the Tillard papers at the monastery of Chevetogne, Belgium. This hand-written text is not dated, but Tillard says that he is revisiting the meaning of *subsistit in* twenty years after Vatican II promulgated the text, which indicates composition in late 1984 or during 1985. I am grateful to Lic. theol. Adam Strojny, who discovered the text during research on his dissertation at the Pontifical University of St. Thomas (Angelicum) in Rome and to the dissertation moderator, Prof. James Puglisi, S.A., who kindly gave me a copy of the Tillard *Projet*. J.-M. TILLARD made his own use of what he provided to Cardinal Willebrands in the final pages of *Church of Churches: The Ecclesiology of Communion*, Collegeville, MN, Liturgical Press, 1992, pp. 307-318 (French original, 1987).

49. The evidence of this unreflective practice was presented in 1950 by Y. CONGAR in *Note sur les mots 'Confession', 'Église' et 'Communion'*, in *Irénikon* (1950) 3-26. In the translation in *Dialogue Between Christians*, see pp. 200-202 for a long series of citations of official Catholic references to separated eastern bodies as "churches". This evidence appeared at Vatican II in the 1962 draft schema *De ecclesia*, in Ch. XI, *De oecumenismo*, where it left a tension in that draft between Ch. XI, and Ch. I, no. 7, which said that only the Roman Catholic Church is rightly called "church". It is from this unresolved tension that there began the evolution in the drafts through *est* and *adest in* to *subsistit in*. The *elementa* present and operative in the other bodies had also been in the ecumenism chapter of 1962, from which they moved to have their place in the *licet* clause tied paradoxically to the basic affirmation about the Catholic Church.

50. *Acta Synodalia*, I/4, 126-127, which is cited by Willebrands, in *Information Service* 101, p. 147, with the claim that this first address set the tone for the council debate on *De ecclesia*, Dec. 1-6, 1962.

51. *Acta Synodalia*, I/4, pp. 618-619.

the Church of Christ is the Catholic Church, but the former stretches itself (*se prolonge*) to those of good will who by faith and baptism are united to Christ[52].

These proposals by Council members were not pious wishes, but amounted to directives which the Doctrinal Commission and its *periti* were to follow in revising *De ecclesia*. At Vatican II, the revision of schemata was not an arena of freedom in which Commission members and *periti* might formulate the texts in the light of their own theology, no matter how brilliant this might be. The revision was to follow the oral and written comments of Council members on the earlier draft, so that the Council members would later find their own proposals realized in deletions and new texts in the next draft, leading to the text they would eventually vote to make the teaching of the Catholic Church[53].

For Willebrands in 1987, the formulation *subsistit in* indicated the way in which Christ's Church is in the Catholic Church integrally and uniquely, but it also opens upon a prolongation of the Church of Christ beyond this Catholic fullness, so that other communities also make sanctifying use of endowments of word and sacrament. The cardinal noted that in some of these other communities, the full substance of the Eucharist is lacking and their pastors are not united through the college of bishops in communion with the bishop of Rome. But still, they often take important Christian steps with utmost seriousness by welcoming the word of God in faith, by sealing this welcome by baptism, and by their zeal in witnessing to Christ. Here, he says, "we are in the field of *koinonia*, already associated with the reality of ecclesial being. We are not (...) 'outside the church of God'"[54].

---

52. *Acta Synodalia*, II/1, p. 657.

53. This "ethic" of revision work was clear to Y. CONGAR, who formulated it insistently in his Vatican II diary, *Mon Journal du Concile*, Paris, Cerf, 2001, Vol. 2, pp. 406-407 and p. 460. A counter-example was the revised schema *De libertate religiosa* of 1964, in which the *periti* P. Pavan and J. C. Murray had inserted many of their own ideas, going beyond what Council members had called for, *Mon Journal*, 2, 202. Consequently, *De libertate* has held over for further discussion, emendation, and voting in Period 4 of 1965. This is relevant for evaluating the recent proposal that *subsistit in* really means *est*, advanced by A. von Teuffenbach and K.J. Becker (see footnote 43). They work from the discovery in the Council archives that *subsistit in* entered *De ecclesia* with almost no discussion at the Doctrinal Commission meeting of November 26, 1963. The evidence is clear that this was an emendation suggested by the Commission's Secretary, Fr. Sebastian Tromp, who himself held the full identity of the Church of Christ and the Catholic Church – in contrast to what Card. Liénart had called for.

54. *Subsistit in*, in *Information Service* 101, p. 149.

God's economy of saving grace is vast, working through chosen mediations throughout Christianity. Just before concluding his 1987 lecture, Cardinal Willebrands said this:

> *Subsistit in* thus appears, in an ecclesiology of communion, as an attempt to express the transcendence of grace and to give an inkling of divine benevolence. It is then that the traditional view of ecclesial *koinonia* as the sacrament of God's design takes on a new depth[55].

This is no relativizing of the Catholic Church, but instead a recognition of further degrees of ecclesial reality, given objectively and ontologically by a gracious and saving God, in other Christian bodies. The affirmation of *subsistit in*, with its *licet extra* of *plura elementa*, would give an "inkling of divine benevolence", which also expands our ecclesial horizon of thought in a salutary way.

These, then, are four significant contributions to ecumenical theology put into circulation by Cardinal Johannes G.M. Willebrands. Together they make up a legacy of considerable value. Willebrands offers us a valuable insight into a central drama that unfolded within the event of Vatican II, namely, the appropriation of pioneering pre-conciliar renewal proposals. He sketches an engaging vision of diversity of types of ecclesial life within the longed-for unity of one Church. He presents the ecclesiology of communion with a profundity which can enrich the many contemporary adherents of this conception. He grapples in an exemplary way with one of Vatican II's most widely discussed affirmations, namely, that the Church of Christ subsists in the Catholic Church, but in a way that does not ∢to preclude that many of Christ's "elements", given for human salvation, are present and operative in other Christian bodies.

Willebrands drew his ideas out of works of the best Catholic theologians of his day, welding their insights into the proposals that he made accessible to his many hearers and readers. This was theology presented with spiritual sensitivity and acute judgment, amid an admirable engagement for God and the Church. The legacy should not be forgotten.

John Carroll University   Jared WICKS, s.j.
University Heights OH 44118
USA

---

55. *Subsistit in*, in *Information Service* 101, p. 149. This was especially emphatic in J.-M. Tillard's preparatory *projet*, as hinted at in *Church of Churches* on the ample scope of the work of the Holy Spirit (pp. 313-314).

III. WILLEBRANDS AND ECUMENISM

JOHANNES CARDINAL WILLEBRANDS
AND THE EASTERN CHRISTIAN CHURCHES

At the end of his life Johannes Cardinal Willebrands wrote the preface to a collection of tributes to the man who for nearly thirty years was one of his closest collaborators, Bishop Pierre Duprey. These are his words: "He was concerned to promote mutual understanding between East and West, so that each should travel together the road that leads to *rapprochement*"[1]. This sentence, written in the twilight years of his life, is quite characteristic of the cardinal's own attitude: listening respectfully to the Eastern churches, journeying together, and unity as a gift of the Spirit that the churches must learn to receive.

Anyone who undertakes studying Msgr. Willebrands' relations with Eastern Christianity, whether it be Orthodox churches or Eastern Catholic churches, will soon see that one clearly needs to distinguish two periods: the one which precedes his arrival in Rome in 1960, and the one which stretches from 1960 to the later years. His contacts with the Christian East appear to be rather sparse in the pre-1960 period, but are correspondingly numerous and intensified in the second period.

There are two possible approaches to the available documentation. The first can be classified as historiographic. It consists of an enumeration and evaluation of the countless contacts that he had. This is not the focus of this essay, but it will prove indispensable for any future research. The second approach can be classed as theological. While it notes important dates and ecumenical events, it seeks to highlight the motivations and the ecclesiological reflection which inspired Cardinal Willebrands' activities. When appropriate, citations in this essay will be in his own words[2].

---

1. *Agapè: Études en l'honneur de Mgr Pierre Duprey*, Chambésy-Genève, 2000, pp. 13-15, esp. 15.

2. We dispose of three collections of texts. They are occasional discourses which have later on been published in a collective volume. One encounters many repetitions that invite the reader to sense the profound ecumenical convictions the cardinal had, and which he also hoped to see them spread among the churches. In 1969 he published in Paris "*Œcuménisme et problèmes actuels*" (henceforth: *Œcuménisme*). In 1989 the J.-A. Möhler Institut in Paderborn edits a number of his conferences under the title "*Mandatum Unitatis: Beiträge zur Oekumene*" (henceforth: *Mandatum Unitatis*). Later on still, in 1995 appears in Italian "*Una sfida ecumenica, la nuova Europa, Discorsi*" at Verucchio (henceforth: *Sfida ecumenica*). Other articles will be mentioned as the present study develops.

Here a methodological difficulty comes to mind. Immediately upon his arrival in Rome, Msgr. Willebrands worked within the Secretariat, that is to say, in a team. He was Cardinal Bea's right hand man[3], and both men had the gift of being able to attract co-workers who were both competent and sincerely committed to the ecumenical cause. Their convictions had sometimes matured together, in the first instance in the Conférence Catholique pour les Questions Œcuméniques. Let us mention at random, and at the risk of leaving out quite a few, Msgr. Pierre Duprey, Fr. John Long, Fr. Thomas Stransky, Msgr. Paul-Werner Scheele, Fr. Emmanuel Lanne[4], Fr. Jean-Marie Tillard, Fr. Christophe Dumont, Fr. Jerome Hamer, Msgr. Jean-François Arrighi, and Msgr. Eleuterio Fortino. The bonds of friendship and confidence that Willebrands built up were his great strength, but they make it more difficult to evaluate his personal contribution. For him as for Bea this was of but little importance. He saw himself as a servant of God and of his church.

There is a little anecdote which illustrates well the magnanimity and humility of Msgr. Willebrands, though it does not shed such a positive light on my monastery. In August 1951 Willebrands and his inseparable friend, Msgr. Frans Thijssen, went on a grand tour to survey the ecumenical scene. Having arrived at Chevetogne in a little car, they announced to one of the first great Catholic ecumenical theologians, Fr. Clément Lialine[5]: "You have the ideas, we have the means". They got a frosty reception. Happily, Fr. Théodore Strotmann recovered the situation and later started up a cordial collaboration.

---

3. The relationship between Cardinal Augustin Bea and Cardinal Willebrands was a very close one, as Willebrands explains in the Foreword of S. Schmidt's monumental biography (*Augustin Bea, der Kardinal der Einheit*, Graz, 1989, pp. 7-11). The first contacts date from 1951, at J. Willebrands' initiative, who was in search for Roman support for his future Catholic Conference for Ecumenical Questions. A. Bea chose him as the first Secretary of the Secretariat for Promoting Christian Unity, and thus as his closest collaborator. Willebrands will succeed Bea as President of the same Secretariat. The "dedication" of S. Schmidt's book on Bea expresses wonderfully the relationship between the two cardinals: "Dedicated to Johannes Cardinal Willebrands, who, together with Cardinal Bea, was the architect of the Secretariat for Christian Unity, and who assumed the cardinal's legacy and developed it further".

4. See, e.g., E. LANNE, *Le rôle du monastère de Chevetogne au deuxième concile du Vatican*, in D. DONNELLY – J. FAMERÉE – M. LAMBERIGTS – K. SCHELKENS (eds.), *The Belgian Contribution to the Second Vatican Council* (BETL, 216), Leuven, 2008, 361-388, pp. 382-387.

5. Cf. M. VAN PARYS, *Dom Clément Lialine, théologien de l'unité chrétienne*, in *Irénikon* 76 (2003) 240-269.

I. The First Contacts with the Christian East (1934-1960)

We know little about the contacts that Father Willebrands had with the Eastern churches during the first years of his ordained ministry. According to an oral source (Evert de Jong), he had said on several occasions, while he was professor and director of the department of philosophy of the Great Seminary of Warmond (Diocese of Harlem), that he was learning Russian. Where did this interest come from?

1. There are several plausible answers, and a range of influences may have been concurrently at work. Had he read the books of Piotr Hendrix[6]? He certainly knew the *Apostolaat der Hereeniging* (Apostolate of Reunion) founded in 1927, fruit of the visit of Metropolitan André Szeptytskyj of Lviv to the Netherlands in April 1921. The perspective was clearly "unioniste", to borrow the vocabulary of the historian E. Fouilloux. In 1941 his fellow student at the Seminary of Warmond, Cornelius Bouman, later professor at the University of Nijmegen, who had lived for a year at Amay as a candidate for the monastic life (1938-1939), published two little volumes in a collection from the *Apostolaat*[7]. These monographs can be distinguished from the others by the real sympathy they show towards the Orthodox Church. In all settings Willebrands, like any Catholic priest in the Netherlands, was aware of this "unionist" movement and of its goals.

What contacts did he have with the "Russian Mission" of the Capuchin Fathers? The *Pokrof* initiative (the Protection of the Mother of God) was present in the Baltic States before the war and was very active among the Russians and Ukrainians after the war. In 1954 it launched a monthly revue entitled *Pokrof* whose aim was to inform Catholic sympathizers about the situation of Christians in Russia, and to "support the victory of Christianity in Russia"[8]. The proselytising aims of *Pokrof* would change towards the end of the Second Vatican Council.

Other more open Eastern initiatives came into being after the war. The best known and most meritorious is that of the Assumptionist Fathers who in 1945 founded in Nijmegen a Byzantine Institute and in 1948 a

---

6. *Russisch Christendom: Persoonlijke herinneringen*, Amsterdam, 1937 (with a rather critical preface by Fr. Ildephonse Dirks, monk of Amay-Chevetogne), and *Het schoone Pascha: Indrukken over het Russisch-Orthodoxe Paaschfeest*, Leiden, 1940.
7. *De breuk tussen Oost en West* (vol. 1) and *Theotokos* (vol. 7).
8. Editorial of the first issue of March-April 1954.

periodical *Het Christelijk Oosten en Hereniging* (The Christian East and Reunion)[9].

2. Nevertheless Father Willebrands' focus of interest moved essentially towards the Churches of the Reformation. After the war the mentality in certain Catholic milieus in the Netherlands changed. The strategy moved from one of individual conversations to a timid attempt at inter-confessional dialogue. Willebrands' friend Frans Thijssen was one of the main pioneers of this[10]. However the general climate remained one of conquest and proselytism.

It is worth mentioning here the ecclesial climate in which Father J. Willebrands began his ecumenical initiatives. Let us read the outline of Father Maurice Villain, a disciple of Father Paul Couturier and one of the very first ecumenists. In February 1947 he made an initial journey to the Netherlands. At Leiden he met Prof. Hendrik Kraemer, missiologist and friend of Dr. W. Visser 't Hooft, and the first director of the Ecumenical Institute at Bossey. There he also met a few scarce Catholics more open to the ecumenical cause. Did he on this occasion have any contact with Fathers Willebrands and Thijssen? This is what he notes in his memoirs:

> Finally here are the names of two priests who may be counted among the most influential in the history of ecumenism in the Netherlands. One was vicar of the parish St. Martin of Utrecht when I visited him in 1943, before meeting him again in the Rozemond's sitting room. A colorful figure if ever there was one, a veritable force of nature, a good man, agreeable, amusing, explosive, with a thunderous voice! – I am speaking of Dr Thijssen. The second is the complementary image of the first: shy, discrete, silent – I am speaking of Father Jan Willebrands, professor of philosophy at the Seminary of Warmond near Leiden. We had hardly made acquaintance when he invited me to come and speak at his Institute. I was the first to present the ideas of my teacher to the future cardinal Willebrands and I have every reason to believe that they fell on fertile ground[11].

On another occasion, several years later, he notes the following: "Our friend Jan Willebrands was doing the groundwork for an international Catholic conference on ecumenical questions – a courageous and

---

9. J.Y.H.A. JACOBS, *Continuïteit en discontinuïteit bij de vormgeving aan een ideaal: Enkele reflecties bij 70 jaar Aktie en Ontmoeting Oosterse Kerken*, in *Het Christelijk Oosten* 49 (1997) 259-281.

10. J.Y.H.A. JACOBS, *Een beweging in verandering: De inzet van Belgische en Nederlandse katholieken voor de eenheid der kerken*, 1921-1964, in *Trajecta* 1 (1992) 67-91.

11. M. VILLAIN, *Vers l'unité: Itinéraire d'un pionnier, 1935-1975*, Dinard, 1976, p. 207. Unfortunately, he does not note the date of the meeting.

inspired initiative – and he invited ecumenists from all over, including four or five from France. The inauguration was to be in Utrecht, where the suffragan bishop, Msgr. Bernard Alfrink, offered the use of the recently restored Great Seminary, and as was fitting, the prelate himself led the opening meeting in the chapel he just had built. What a surprise and a shock! "We also do ecumenism", announced the prelate at the start of his introduction. But what kind of ecumenism was he referring to? The answer came in the next sentence: it was about converting Protestants, starting with the pastors, and the speaker went on to elaborate in great detail the different methods of conversion that were employed in the diocese. I was seated between Fr. Congar and Fr. Dumont. At each new declamation we lowered our heads a little further. By the end my head was touching my knees. In the closing session I tried to express my disappointment; a waste of time: "You are always in favour of the simplicity of the dove", the suffragan bishop fired at me, "but you need to know that when up against Protestants – and we know them well in this country – you need the wisdom of a serpent!" Should I add that on the program of this session not one moment of prayer had been included? Our president contented himself with a brief invocation of the Virgin at the start of the sessions. Our group, still learning the ropes it is true, was unaware of the role of *metanoia*, which ought to be written on the first line of every ecumenical directory. And the worst is that I found the typewritten text of the opening speech in Geneva on the desk of Dr Visser 't Hooft!"[12].

3. The progress towards a more ecumenical attitude regarding the churches of the Reformation led to the transformation of the Apologetische Vereniging Petrus Canisius (Apologetic Society of Peter Canisius) into the St Willibrordvereniging (Society of St. Willibrord) in 1948[13]. Fr. Willebrands was elected in his absence as its first secretary. He had been chosen for those same qualities which were to distinguish him in his service for ecumenism "(...) At Warmond he showed himself to be a subtle professor and an organizer who was as efficient as he was careful, capable of gathering together people of very diverse opinions"[14].

---

12. *Ibid.*, p. 208. Here too the date is missing.
13. See J.Y.H.A. JACOBS, *Nieuwe visies op een oud visioen: Een portret van de Sint Willibrord Vereniging, 1948-1998*, Tilburg, 1998.
14. *Ibid.*, p. 25.

This does not mean that the views of Willebrands at that time were at odds with common Catholic doctrine. On 14 June 1950 Willebrands elaborated his conclusions drawn from the Study Days of the Society of St Willibrord, stating: "From the very first moment of her existence the Catholic Church has possessed unity in diversity without being touched by schism or heresy. This is the reason why we can no longer speak in the strict sense of the 'becoming one' of the church. But in this matter the Church possesses an eschatological orientation, just so long as in receiving the Eastern Orthodox and the Protestants within the already existing unity – and also in the receiving of the rest of humanity – she becomes a clearer sign of unity in the Holy Spirit"[15].

Two years later the Society of St Willibrord organized a symposium on the theme "The ecumenical question in contemporary Christianity" (3-5 June 1952). Dom Theodore Strotmann from the monastery of Chevetogne argued that the ecumenical question formed a whole and that dialogue, conducted with a proper concern for historical truth, had to be taken forward with all the churches, without dogmatizing over things which were not essential to Catholic dogma[16].

The following month (6 July 1952), on the occasion of the silver jubilee of the Apostolate of Reunion, another Dutch ecumenist whom we have already mentioned, C. Bouman, gave in the presence of Eugene Cardinal Tisserant a speech for the occasion: "Separation and Reunion in the Perspective of History". He too noted that the ecumenical question was one, in East and West[17].

4. We may suppose that this broadening of the ecumenical question rapidly bore fruit in the mind of Fathers Willebrands and Thijssen. At all events it coincided with the preparations for the launching of the Catholic Conference for Ecumenical Questions[18].

---

15. In *Binnenlands Apostolaat* 1 (1950) 148-158, pp. 156-157.

16. *De huidige situatie van het oecumenische vraagstuk*, in *Binnenlands Apostolaat* 3 (1952) 179-199. Already a year beforehand, in a contribution to a collective volume dedicated to the Catholic-Protestant dialogue, he stressed the importance of the impact of Orthodoxy on the ecumenical movement: *Katholieken en protestanten in de twintigste eeuw*, in *Geloofsinhoud en geloofsbeleving*, Utrecht, 1951, 26-113.

17. Cf. *Kerkelijk Archief* 7 (1952) 737-744.

18. J.Y.H.A. Jacobs' title sounds correct: *Naar één oecumenische beweging: De Katholieke Conferentie voor Oecumenische Vragen: Een leerschool en gids, 1951-1965*, Tilburg, 1991 (*Towards One Ecumenical Movement: The Catholic Conference for Ecumenical Questions: A School and a Guide*). In French see E. FOUILLOUX, *Les catholiques et l'unité chrétienne du XIXe au XXe siècle: Itinéraires européens d'expression française*, Paris, 1982, pp. 711-716.

We need to speak of the participation of Willebrands and Thijssen in the Chevetogne Ecumenical Days[19]. If we think only of the Orthodox participants they met over the days of the conference, we could mention the future metropolitan Emilianos Timiadis (1916-2008, Patriarch Athenagoras' representative to the WCC from 1959 to 1984), professors H. Alivisatos, N. Nissiotis, A.-E. Tachiaos, and several professors from the St. Sergius Institute in Paris[20].

In 1958 Willebrands, who was then the episcopal conference's delegate for ecumenism, had a first contact with representatives of the patriarchate of Moscow in Utrecht (7-9 August) when the latter were meeting with a delegation from the WCC. This first opening was an influential factor in the Russian Orthodox Church becoming a member of the World Council of Churches in 1961[21]. At the same time his attention was drawn towards the Melkite Catholic Church of the Near East. Patriarch Maximos IV had sent him a booklet *On Safeguarding the Rights of the Eastern Church*. In a letter to Fr. Theodore Strotmann (27 October 1959, in the archives at Chevetogne) he asked for the patriarch's address, to thank him for this "particularly precious" gift. It is true that in 1958 the periodical *Irenikon* had drawn attention to the dismal fate reserved for the Eastern Catholic churches[22].

Finally let us say a word about the famous "Rhodes incident" of August 1959[23]. From 19 to 28 August the meeting of the WCC Central Committee was being held on this Greek island. Fr. J. Willebrands and Fr. Christophe Dumont (of the journal *Istina*) were participating as "accredited journalists". An informal meeting between the few Catholics present and a few dozen Orthodox provoked Dr Visser 't Hooft's keen displeasure. Some erroneous information in the press had aggravated the conflict. Willebrands' efforts and calm finally restored the peace. What needs to be underlined is the fact that this painful incident made Willebrands understand how delicate multilateral ecumenical relations

---

19. Cf. O. ROUSSEAU, *Les journées œcuméniques de Chevetogne* (1942-1967), in *Au service de la Parole de Dieu. Mélanges offerts à Mgr A.-M. Charue, évêque de Namur*, Gembloux, 1969, 451-485.

20. Cf. A. VERDOODT, *Les Colloques œcuméniques de Chevetogne (1942-1983) et la réception par l'Église catholique de charismes d'autres Communions chrétiennes*, Chevetogne, 1986.

21. Cf. *Irénikon* 31 (1958) 500-501.

22. *Irénikon* 31 (1958) 221-234; 235-245; 352-357.

23. Brief summary in J. GROOTAERS, *Actes et Acteurs à Vatican II*, Leuven, 1998, p. 488. Official version by J. WILLEBRANDS in *Het Schild* 36 (1958/9) 157-173. Cf. *Irénikon* 32 (1959) 454-463, by F. Théodore Strotmann.

were and to what extent the official entry of the Catholic Church in the dialogue was turning into a major issue at stake.

II. THE PREPARATION OF VATICAN II (1960-1962)

On 28 June 1960 Johannes Willebrands, proposed by Cardinal Bea, was appointed secretary of the Secretariat for Promoting Christian Unity, which was created on 5 June. His life took a decisive turn, and henceforward the Eastern churches would have a very special place in his heart and in his activities. However, it was only in June 1962 that the responsibilities of the Secretariat were extended to include relations with Orthodox churches. Up to that point these were the responsibility of the Eastern Commission which in reality came under the Congregation for the Eastern Church. On 22 October of the same year the Secretariat for Promoting Christian Unity was raised to the same rank as the other conciliar commissions[24].

In August 1959 John XXIII had already decided to invite observers to the Council. Msgr. Willebrands thus became the chief architect of these invitations, taking and making many initiatives and visits. It is not necessary here to retell the story of the presence of Orthodox observers at Vatican II. It is sufficiently well known. The process of learning about ecumenical relations with the churches of the East was difficult. After many disappointing setbacks, it bore fruit that lived on well beyond the Council[25]. Bea and Willebrands favoured discreet contacts and visits to ecclesial authorities. It was a way of honouring these ancient churches, who for centuries had been waiting to be recognized by the Church of Rome for what they were.

For the secretary of the Secretariat for Promoting Christian Unity these were visits of discovery. In February 1962 J. Willebrands went to Istanbul for the first time. There he met Ecumenical Patriarch Athenagoras in order to advise him of the preparations for Vatican II and to discuss the possibility of Orthodox observers being present at the Council. In a few pages of memoirs, published in 1987, he gives us his impressions and also reflects retrospectively on a theme which was very dear to him, that of the relationship between a dialogue of charity and theological dialogue.

---

24. For the entire period here under discussion, we refer the reader to M. VELATI, *Una difficile transizione: Il cattolicesimo tra unionismo ed ecumenismo (1952-1964)*, Bologna, 1996.

25. *Ibid.*, pp. 275-318.

This was my first meeting with Patriarch Athenagoras (...) I was deeply impressed by his personality. It was as if his lively eyes looked through history to see the future. His heart had the openness of an ecumenical patriarch, embracing the world of humankind; his heart burned with the fire of what he would later call the dialogue of charity. He did not set the dialogue of charity in opposition to theological dialogue, as has sometimes been thought and said. He considered it to be its foundation. Indeed to speak of God and his mysteries without charity is but a clanging gong or a resounding cymbal. He embraced the emissary of ancient Rome, the first after so many centuries because he had been waiting for his sign as a watchman who sees a new dawn approaching. Although the Holy Synod was divided and his wish could not be fulfilled straight away, the dialogue of charity had begun and the theological dialogue would follow soon after. The latter sometimes came up against serious difficulties and not always for theological reasons. These difficulties could surface because there was some element of charity missing, or of mutual confidence which reveals the truth through people and over time[26].

The other mission led Willebrands to Moscow. In August 1962 he had already been to Paris to see Msgr. Nikodim, then archbishop of Yaroslavl and of Rostov, and head of the Department of External Relations, on the occasion of a session of the Central Committee of the WCC. This meeting was followed by an invitation from Msgr. Nikodim to come and explain the aim of Vatican II in Moscow to qualified representatives of the Russian Orthodox Patriarchate[27].

Willebrands was therefore in Moscow from 27 September to 2 October. The memoirs of Fr. Vitalij Borovoj[28], who participated in the unofficial negotiations, give a good account of the impact of the personality and method of Willebrands on his Orthodox interlocutors.

Around the end of September to the beginning of October the second meeting between Nikodim and Willebrands took place. The latter had made the journey especially in order to meet up with representatives of the patriarchate and talk about the Council. The meetings took place at the Church's Department of External Relations with Mgr Nikodim and the members of the Department (among whom were metropolitan Nikodim's suffragan,

26. J. WILLEBRANDS, Rome-Konstantinopel: Ontmoeting en herkenning, in Het Oosten nabij: Aspecten van de Oost-christelijke wereld, Kampen, 1987, 9-12, p. 10.

27. Cardinal Willebrands evoked the memory of these events in 1995: La rencontre entre Rome et Moscou: Souvenirs, in A. MELLONI (ed.), Vatican II in Moscou (1959-1965) (Instrumenta Theologica, 20), Leuven, 331-338. The entire volume should be consulted, especially the contributions of A. ROCCUCCI, Russian Observers at Vatican II (pp. 45-69) and E. LANNE, La perception en Occident de la participation du Patriarcat de Moscou à Vatican II (pp. 111-128).

28. The archpriest V. Borovoj (1916-2008) was a key figure in all the ecumenical initiatives of the Russian Orthodox Church. A biographical note may be found in Irénikon 81 (2008) 413-417.

Mgr Aleksij Ridiger...). The exchanges were very fruitful. As well as pastoral and theological questions, they broached political questions (peace,
reconciliation, the problems of relations between Church and State, materialism and atheism). Willebrands explained very calmly and in a convincing
manner that all these questions would be examined at the Council at a
general level and would not run counter to the interests of any State. No
political system would be spoken of either in its favour or against it (...)
On the basis of the discussions and reports of discussions from the meeting
it was clear that there was no formal agreement which would prohibit the
Council from taking an anticommunist position, though such a prohibition
could have ensured the presence of Russian observers. But Mgr Nikodim
did not ask these questions as conditions for the presence of our observers[29].

A few days later the Russian Orthodox Church, with the *placet* of the
Party, decided to send two observers to the first session of Vatican II,
Fr Vitalij Borovoj and Archimandrite Vladimir (Kotljarov), now Metropolitan of Saint-Petersburg.

From these two less well-known testimonies we may retain those
elements which were characteristic of all of Willebrands' initiatives:
attentive listening and sympathy with the other church, a peaceful calm
in the face of all trials, and faultless loyalty to the theological positions
of his own church. He inspired confidence, because he really believed in
the ecumenical ideal. Many testimonies bear witness to the singularly
high regard in which he was held in Orthodox circles. The survey should
also be extended to include his numerous visits to other Byzantine and
Eastern Orthodox churches.

III. VATICAN II

1. It is not easier to delineate the part played by Willebrands in the
elaboration of the constitutions and decrees of the Council or in the place
given to the observers from the Orthodox churches than to delineate his
part in the preparation of Vatican II. Ecumenism became an essential
component of the Council. It inspired its texts. It brought forth a new
attitude towards other churches and ecclesial communities. It opened the
way to dialogues between churches.

Bea and Willebrands were men in whom John XXIII and Paul VI
placed their trust. The role of the Secretariat grew as the months and

---

29. Published in a volume in memory of Metropolitan Nikodim of Leningrad, edited
by Metropolitan JUVENALIJ under the title *Čelovek Cerkvi* (Vir Ecclesiae), Moscou, 1998.
Father Borovoj's contribution "And he was faithful unto death", is found at p. 108
(pp. 91-120).

years went by. The constitutions on the Church (*Lumen Gentium*) and on revelation (*Dei Verbum*), the Decree on Ecumenism (*Unitatis Redintegratio*) and the Declaration on Religious Freedom (*Dignitatis Humanae*) marked a readjustment towards an ecclesiology of communion and of collegiality, towards a right balance between Scripture and Tradition, towards a more tranquil relationship between the Church and the State.

The Decree on Ecumenism became the Magna Charta of the Catholic Church's commitment to the ecumenical movement[30]. J. Willebrands followed it with all his heart, and in his capacity first as secretary and then president of the Secretariat for Promoting Christian Unity, he indefatigably made it known and put it into practice. It was his vocation, his *mandatum unitatis* to borrow the title of one of his books. *Unitatis Redintegratio* 14-18 deal with the Eastern churches. Willebrands constantly drew from these and sought to elaborate their theological and ecclesiological implications. He also did all he could so that the ecumenical vision of these paragraphs would state the concrete attitudes of the Catholic Church with regard to the Christian East. To quote just one example from many: the (honorary) Latin patriarchs of eastern patriarchal sees were suppressed and the titular bishops no longer carried the title of a see in canonical Orthodox territory.

Elaborated under the leadership of Willebrands, the Decree on Ecumenism, which, of course, forms a whole along with the other documents of Vatican II, did not only modify the Catholic Church's attitude and conduct with regard to the Eastern churches. It stipulated an ecumenical conversion. Msgr. Willebrands came back to this almost every time he gave a lecture. For Catholics ecumenism means the renewal and reform of the Church, the acceptance of legitimate diversity, a spirit of penitence and humility, prayer, and getting to know Christians of other churches. Before being about theological or pastoral competence, ecumenism becomes a way of being Catholic.

2. Two events during the Council left an indelible mark on the heart of Msgr. Willebrands: the meeting of Pope Paul VI and Patriarch Athenagoras I on 6 January 1964[31], and the lifting of the mutual anathemas between the churches of Rome and the churches of the New Rome on 7 December 1965. Moreover, for him these were not only events; they

---

30. Cf. Cardinal G. LERCARO's conference from the end of 1964 (prepared by Fr. Emmanuel Lanne): *La signification du Décret 'De Oecumenismo' pour le dialogue avec les Églises orientales non catholiques*, in *Irénikon* 37 (1964) 467-486.

31. VELATI, *Una difficile transizione* (n. 24), pp. 414-427.

were works of the Holy Spirit. Later Willebrands would speak of the "Holy meeting"[32] between Paul VI and Athenagoras I. The two church leaders met in Jerusalem while on pilgrimage.

Let us speak finally of the three meetings between Pope Paul VI and Patriarch Athenagoras 1st. Some may have seen nothing but spectacular even theatrical gestures, without any lasting significance. Those who think this way think perhaps that nothing of import can be done unless it be by discussion, seated around a table. In the West particularly there are those, worthy sons of Descartes, who tend to see the exchange of ideas and discussion as the highest form of dialogue. But in life there exist realities that are greater than discussion. In his address to the Pope in Istanbul the Patriarch said: "Let us apply ourselves then, by reciprocal gestures between the Churches, wherever possible, to the reuniting of what is divided" (1967). In the written document which he gave to the Patriarch, the Pope expressed himself in these words: "We are listening to the message that John, the beloved disciple sent from Ephesus to the churches of Asia: That which we have heard we declare to you, so that you may have fellowship with us. Our fellowship is with the Father and with his Son Jesus Christ (1 John 1,3). All the reciprocal gestures made by the Churches were made listening to this word from the apostle John and with a view to creating communion between them. Everything in the Church is oriented towards communion with the Father, by his Son Jesus Christ". The Pope mentioned the preaching of the gospel, the sacraments, especially baptism and Eucharist, and the apostolic succession within the priesthood: "Such is the deep and mysterious communion which exists between us: in participating in the gifts of God to his church we are placed in the Holy Spirit. Having actually and in reality become sons in the Son (cf 1 John 3,1-2), we have also really and mysteriously become each other's brothers. The Churches are communities of life. These acts and gestures are manifestations of life: I am quite convinced that they have done more to revive the awareness of communion among the people than any study or discussion could have done.

The lifting of the mutual anathemas between Rome and Constantinople at the end of Vatican II was another action with extraordinary symbolic power, bearing the weight of a future as yet unaccomplished. This is what the secretary of the Secretariat for Promoting Christian Unity said:

On several occasions Patriarch Athenagoras had expressed the wish that this symbolic act be nullified, and that its consequences be put right. Paul VI made this desire his own and during the Council wished to make a new gesture, together with the patriarch, to make good what had formerly been undone. On 7th December 1965 at Saint Peter's in Rome and in the cathedral of Phanar simultaneously, the public reading of the joint declaration was made, in the presence of delegates from the two churches, and in Rome in the presence of all the Council Fathers. The declaration refers to excom-

32. *Œcuménisme* (n. 2), pp. 38-39.

munication in respect of all its remaining consequences. The crucial sentence is the following one: "Pope Paul VI and the patriarch Athenagoras 1st ... declare ... with common accord ... that they regret in equal measure and remove from common memory and from the midst of the Church the sentences of excommunication (...), whose memory right up to our days constitutes a kind of obstacle to our coming together in charity, and we consign them to oblivion".

The expression "the midst of the Church" (*medium Ecclesiae, to méson tes ekklesias*) is borrowed from the Latin liturgy and means the life and tradition at the heart of the Church. It goes without saying that this declaration does not remove the present day differences between the two Churches; it is part of the dialogue of charity. Moreover it is stated in the first paragraph that after their meeting in Jerusalem the Pope and the Patriarch decided 'henceforward to omit nothing of those acts which are inspired by charity and which could facilitate the development of fraternal relationships'[33].

IV. The Reception of Vatican II in the Catholic Church

The steps to be taken after the Council in order to enact the conciliar decisions were no less important than the work done during the Council. The work after the Council needed no less wisdom and perseverance that that done during the Council. That work had twin goals: developing contact with the other churches and ecclesial communities which had been established during the Council, and setting in motion the conciliar decisions which would engage Catholics in the ecumenical movement[34].

Johannes Willebrands was the kingpin, firstly alongside Cardinal Bea, then as president of the Secretariat for Promoting Christian Unity, of the opening up of the Catholic Church to the Christian East. One is constantly amazed by the multiplicity of his ecumenical commitments in Rome and elsewhere with the Orthodox Churches. They would dwindle slightly once he became archbishop of Utrecht in 1975.

In the interest of clarity I will distinguish three sectors: the Byzantine Orthodox churches, the Eastern Orthodox churches, and the Eastern Catholic churches. Here again it is only possible to provide a brief outline

---

33. *Ibid.*, pp. 41-42 [my translation].

34. *Il Cardinale Agostino Bea: Il suo contributo al movimento ecumenico, alla libertà religiosa e all'instaurazione di nuove relazioni con il popolo ebraico*, in *Atti del Simposio Card. Agostino Bea* (1981), Roma, 1983, 1-23, p. 20.

of the main facts before speaking of the extent and influence of the cardinal's contribution.

1. *The Byzantine Orthodox Churches*

Vatican II raised great ecumenical hopes within the Catholic Church, hopes of an occasional ingenuous quality. Sometimes one forgets that the contacts, visits and exchanges were not limited simply to the patriarchs of Constantinople and Moscow. One should certainly remember the key moments: the visits of Paul VI to Constantinople and of Athenagoras to Rome in 1967; the publication of the first Ecumenical Directory (1967 and 1970); the annual visits of a Catholic delegation to Constantinople for the feast of St. Andrew and an Orthodox delegation from Constantinople to Rome for the feast of St. Peter and St. Paul; and the speeches given during these visits, the exchanges of letters and messages[35], the restitution of relics to the Orthodox churches.

The other Orthodox churches were not forgotten: contacts multiplied, though not without difficulties on occasion. A series of five separate theological conferences between the Russian Orthodox Church and the Catholic Church took place: Leningrad (1967), Bari (1970), Zagorsk (1973), Trent (1975) and Odessa (1980).

On 30 November 1979 Pope John Paul II and Patriarch Dimitrios I announced the start of an official theological dialogue between the Catholic Church and the Orthodox Churches[36]. The dialogue effectively began the following year on the Greek islands of Patmos and Rhodes. It was slow in getting going, and since 1989 it has suffered due to the legalization of Greek Catholic churches in Eastern Europe. But this nonetheless remains a major event in the recent history of the Church. Cardinal Willebrands' tenacity had a lot to do with it.

Thus far five documents in common were drafted by the Joint International Commission for Theological Dialogue between the Roman Catholic Church and the Orthodox Church. Three of them were produced under Willebrands' leadership on the Catholic side: in Munich in 1982 *The*

---

35. All the documents of the first years have been gathered in *Tomos Agapis. Vatican-Phanar (1958-1970)*, jointly published by the two Churches in 1971.

36. See the fundamental article of Msgr. E. FORTINO, *Impostazione del dialogo teologico tra la Chiesa cattolica e la Chiesa ortodossa*, in *Divinarum rerum notitia: La teologia tra filosofia e storia. Studi in onore del Card. W. Kasper*, Rome, 2001, 449-476. In appendix he publishes the plan of the theological dialogue established in 1978. For the English translation of the plan, see J. BORELLI – J.H. ERICKSON (eds.), *The Quest for Unity: Orthodox and Catholics in Dialog*, Crestwood, NY, 1996.

Mystery of the Church and of the Eucharist in the Light of the Mystery of the Holy Trinity[37]; in Bari in 1987 *Faith, Sacraments and the Unity of the Church*[38]; and in Valamo in 1988 *The Sacrament of Order in the Sacramental Structure of the Church, with Particular Reference to the Importance of Apostolic Succession for the Sanctification and Unity of the People of God*[39].

2. *The Eastern Orthodox Churches*

The Eastern Orthodox Churches accept the faith confessed by the first three ecumenical councils. Today a consensus has been established between historians and theologians that their disagreement with the Council of Chalcedon (451) was over the formulations used rather than over the faith confessed in the incarnate Word. The *"Pro Oriente"* foundation of Vienna in Austria did some remarkable work in promoting some unofficial conferences for representatives of the Eastern Orthodox Churches and the Catholic Church. These encounters prepared the ground for a variety of common statements on the common faith. The first was signed by Pope Shenouda III of the Coptic Orthodox Church and Pope Paul VI in 1973. It was followed in 1984 by the one signed by Patriarch Ignace Zakka I of the the Syrian Orthodox and Pope John Paul II. Other agreements followed[40].

One can readily understand the importance of such doctrinal agreements for the cause of rapprochement between Christian churches. The cardinal had thought about this, as we shall yet see, and began a process of reflection on the councils held after the ruptures in communion.

3. *The Eastern Catholic Churches*

Two texts from Vatican II, the decrees on ecumenism and on the Eastern Catholic churches, were promulgated on the same day, the 21 November 1964. The sensitivity towards the Christian East displayed by the two decrees is not identical, even if the conclusion of the decree *Ecclesiarum Orientalium* inserts a clause of great ecumenical significance: "All these juridical dispositions are taken with the present circumstances

---

37. Pontifical Council Promoting Christian Unity, *Information Service* 49 (1982/II-III) 107-112.

38. PCPCU, *Information Service* 64 (1987/II) 82-87.

39. PCPCU, *Information Service* 68 (1988/III-IV) 173-178.

40. Presentation and texts in: R. ROBERSON, *The Eastern Christian Churches: A Brief Survey*, Rome, [7]2008, pp. 193-220.

in view, until the Catholic Church and the separated Eastern Churches unite in the fullness of communion"[41].

The third pan-Orthodox conference at Rhodes had just finished (1-15 November 1964), and had left it up to each Orthodox church to decide whether or not to send observers to Vatican II. But it had also brought up what in its eyes constituted a stumbling block – the existence of Eastern Catholic churches (improperly called "uniate")[42].

It is true that the Catholic Church, due to the theological significance it ascribes to communion with the church of Rome, found itself and still finds itself in an ambivalent position. The Orthodox churches see this ambivalence as an ambiguity, if not to say a duplicity. It is not our task here to go into the very diverse history of the Eastern Catholic churches nor to take sides regarding the events of the last two decades. What matters to us is to take into consideration the way in which Willebrands faced up to this fiery ordeal in the relations between the Catholic Church and the Orthodox churches. Let us try to sketch an outline of his convictions and activity.

At the start of the summer of 1959 the Catholic bishops were officially required to send their *vota* to the Holy See regarding themes to be dealt with by the proposed Council. Although not asked to respond, Patriarch Athenagoras had several articles published in the periodicals of the Ecumenical Patriarchate in September 1959. In them he expressed the expectations of the Orthodox Church with regard to the Catholic Church. The question of Uniate churches was also mentioned. "Let adequate attention be paid to such problems as proselytism, the perversion of the *Ounia* which for centuries has wounded the Orthodox Church and has created and creates tensions in relationships between the two worlds (...) We are expecting a gesture from the new Pope"[43]. Might Msgr. J. Willebrands have known of these *vota*? It is unlikely that he did in the immediate term. Later however he was not slow to realize the deep hurt that the very existence of the Uniate churches were for the Orthodox East.

Let us remember that Msgr. Willebrands played a centre stage role in the liberation after eighteen years of detention of Metropolitan Joseph Slipyj, archbishop of the Ukrainian Catholic Church (10 February 1963). This liberation brought to light the persecution to which this church had been subject in the USSR, and in the eyes of most Catholics it had been

---

41. E. LANNE, *L'Orient chrétien dans la perspective de Vatican II*, in «*Con tutte le tue forze*»: *I nodi della fede cristiana oggi. Omaggio a G. Dossetti*, Genua, 1993, 197-221.

42. O. ROUSSEAU in *Irénikon* 37 (1964) 487-507 and 516-519.

43. Voir V. MARTANO, *Athenagoras il Patriarca (1986-1972): Un cristiano fra crisi della coabitazione e utopia ecumenica*, Bologna, 1996, pp. 408-413.

with the assent of the Orthodox Church. The bishops of the united Ukrainian Church of the diaspora had been offended by the presence of observers from the Russian Orthodox Church at the first session of the Council. The liberation of the metropolitan, followed the same year by the elevation of his metropolis to a major archbishopric, put in question the good relations which had been reinstated with Moscow. There was a total imbroglio among ecumenism, religious freedom and political interests[44].

At the start of the second session, after the death of John XXIII, the election of Paul VI and the "exile" of Msgr. Slipyi in Rome, the Russian observers had the impression that the Vatican was changing its policy regarding the Soviet Bloc[45]. They felt a certain reserve, if not to say embarrassment towards them. In Ukrainian Greek Catholic circles (bishops of the diaspora and political figures) there was a push to establish their own Ukrainian patriarchate and to legalize their Uniate church in the USSR with its primatial seat in Kiev. Willebrands tried to calm Borovoj. The Russians got the impression that there was a two-sided politics. Many Ukrainians feared they would become victims of the Vatican's ecumenical openness, and Msgr. Willebrands was to suffer much acerbic criticism. The problem would follow him right to the end of his mandate as president of the Secretariat[46].

However the cardinal's thinking was clear: fundamentally the anomaly lay in the ruptured union between the Eastern and the Western Church. While speaking of Eastern Catholics who were obliged to be integrated into the Russian Orthodox Church, he said in an interview that he had republished in the *Information Service* of the Secretariat[47]:

---

44. With regard to this V. Borovoj writes: "One must remark (Mgr) Nikodim's personal implication in the liberation of Metropolitan Slipyi and the collaboration with Willebrands during the visit to Moscow in order to take Metropolitan Slipyi with him to Rome", in JUVENALIJ, *Čelovek Cerkvi* (n. 29), p. 110.

45. A recent Orthodox historical study illustrates the sensibilities still existent as to this topic: H. PETROUCHKO, *La 2ᵉ session du concile Vatican II et la question de l'érection du patriarcat uniate de Kiev* (en russe), www.sedmitza.ru/index.html?sid=619adid=3443 apcomment=belief. The study is based on Fr. Vitalyj Borovoj's unpublished report.

46. To illustrate this we would like to refer the reader to the documents published by the Pontifical Council for Promoting of Christian Unity, *Information Service* N° 71 (1989), pp. 135-140. An excellent overview of the question can be found in K. ROUSSELET, *Histoire du christianisme*. T. XIII: *Crises et Renouveau (de 1958 à nos jours)*, ed. J.-M. MAYEUR, et al., Paris, 2000, pp. 460-464. Already in 1979 a letter sent by Pope John Paul II to Archbishop Joseph Slipyj had worried the Moscow Patriarchate: cf. *Irénikon* 52 (1979), pp. 265-267 et 386-389. It has been followed by an exchange of letters between Metropolitan Juvenalij and Cardinal Willebrands (*ibid.*, pp. 532-544).

47. This is the *Sobor* which has elected Patriarch Pimen; see the Pontifical Council for Promoting Christian Unity, *Information Service* 15 (1971/III), pp. 8-10.

The Council has noted the annulment of the unions of Brest and of Uzhorod of the XVI and XVII centuries. We know that in 1946 and 1949 these two unions were unilaterally declared to be abolished, and consequently these communities were placed under the jurisdiction of the Patriarchate of Moscow. It is quite certain that we cannot share the view which holds that by the annulment of these acts of union the ecclesial situation of our Eastern Catholic brothers in the Soviet Union was resolved. The Catholic Church is certainly happy that in the last few years, with the help of God, significant progress has been made in her relations with the Russian Orthodox Church. However, in this dialogue of charity which is in the process of developing, we continue to be resolutely convinced, as we have always been, that such intractable problems cannot be resolved unilaterally". And he closed the interview with: "To conclude, I would like to add that in our contacts with the Russian Orthodox Church, we never lose sight of our brothers in the Eastern Catholic Churches".

In another interview, deliberately republished by the *Information Service*, he responded with great clarity to a journalist who posed a question about the obstacle of "uniatism".

For the Catholic and Orthodox Churches, the fact of not being in full communion creates an abnormal and unnatural situation between them. Two Churches living by the same Christ, having the same Lord, cannot be divided among themselves. The scandal is even more pointed, becomes intolerable, when the reality of this situation is seen in one same location, between Christians of the same culture, of the same ecclesial tradition, whose way of prayer and celebration of the liturgy are the same. This is the situation with regard to Eastern Catholic communities whose existence and presence make us painfully aware of this scandal, the scandal of division between Christians. This awareness is not an obstacle to the reestablishment of unity, but should be an incentive to bring to an end the scandalous and unnatural situation which our division constitutes. The reestablishment of full communion is the only real solution. So long as we are divided, the Catholic Church cannot refuse the request for communion addressed to her by the demands of conscience, and the conviction of an obedience to the Holy Spirit, of people or communities. And this Catholic communion is in no manner asking that this or that person or community should abandon the legitimate Christian traditions into which they were received and have lived out the gospel. How much more would she not ask for an abandonment of these Eastern traditions of which the Vatican Council said: "they have their roots in holy scripture, they are nurtured and given expression in liturgical life, they derive their strength from the living tradition of the apostles and from the works of the fathers and the spiritual writers of the eastern churches, and they promote the right ordering of life and, indeed pave the way to the full contemplation of Christian truth" (*Unitatis Redintegratio* 17). These communities must not be seen as an attack or a challenge to the Orthodox Church. They are the inevitable consequence of an abnormal situation of division, as well as of the respect for the freedom of every person or group to choose their own ecclesial belonging. The present existence of these Churches, whatever the past may have been, does not disguise any intention to proselytize. The Pope and the patriarch were categorical, and said in their joint declaration that they wished to see a selfless collaboration develop between Catholics and Orthodox, one of mutual respect and a faithfulness of each respectively to their own Church[48].

In Egypt too the fruitful and promising dialogue with the Coptic Orthodox Church suffered from the expansion of the Coptic Catholic Church. The Secretariat succeeded in setting up in 1973 a joint commission for consultation. That led to somewhat of a lessening of tensions[49].

We must however note a particular situation within the Catholic East which contrasts with the picture we have drawn up to this point. It concerns the monastic Congregation of Mekhitarist monks (Armenian Catholic). I shall explore this subject further as it gave Msgr. Willebrands the opportunity to develop a positive view of the collaboration between Eastern Orthodox and Eastern Catholics.

On 22 October 1977 Cardinal Willebrands gave a lecture in Venice at the celebration of the third centenary of the birth of Father Mekhitar of Sebaste (1676-1749)[50]. This Armenian monk and *vartapet* (doctor), founder of a monastic order whose main centres are still today located in Venice and in Vienna, was a reformer of Armenian monasticism and the chief architect of the cultural renaissance of his nation. Having joined the communion of the Church of Rome, in 1701 he founded a religious congregation in Constantinople, which later moved to Venice (1715). A keen defender of the traditions of the Armenian Church and at the same time deeply convinced of the unique place that the Church of Rome held within Christianity, he distinguished himself by what we might already call an authentic ecumenical spirit.

The solemn commemoration gave Willebrands the opportunity to deal in a calm way with the thorny problem of the place of the Eastern Catholic churches in the *rapprochement* between the Orthodox churches and the Catholic Church[51].

Let us give a *résumé* of this conference. The rather unenlightened zeal of the Latin missionaries after the Council of Trent was at the root of

48. N° 13 (1971/1), pp. 16-18.
49. Cf. Pontifical Council Promoting Christian Unity, *Information Service* 24 (1974/2) 14-17. The problem remained, however, a cause of continuous frictions: see *Irénikon* 52 (1979), pp. 321-322 et 374-379, et *ibid.* 61 (1988), pp. 250-252.
50. See B.L. ZEKYAN, *Mékhitar de Sébaste*, in *Dictionnaire de Spiritualité* X (1980), col. 940-950.
51. The conference has been published in the journal of the mekhitarist monastery of Venice, *Bazmavep* 135 (1977) 417-436.

the attempts at latinisations of the ecclesial patrimony of the Eastern churches, in particular the Armenian believers. In place of the search for unity between churches as at the Council of Florence (1438-1439), there came a proselytism of individual conversions. But Mekhitar had a different vision of the restoration of the unity of the Church. The first task, he believed, was to resource the indigenous ecclesial tradition of the Armenian Church: the liturgy, the Armenian fathers, the Greek and Latin Syriac fathers of the ancient church. This revitalization of their own tradition had also to reach the believing people. Thus in 1725 Father Mekhitar published a catechism in the Armenian language as spoken in his day. This servant of God was persuaded, on the other hand, that the faith of his people should be attuned to that of the Church of Rome, while still keeping its own traditional formulations. Besides, the Armenian Church's deep and conscious rootedness in the tradition allowed Mekhitar to open himself up freely to the spiritual traditions of the Latin church without distorting the specificity of his own ecclesial patrimony. Finally and most importantly, Father Mekhitar did not wish entry into communion with the Church of Rome to interrupt the *communicatio in sacris* between Armenian Orthodox and Armenian Catholics. They formed a single church. He considered that communion between the churches was "weakened" without being broken (p. 435). He was deeply saddened too by the creation of an Armenian Catholic Patriarchate in 1742.

Cardinal Willebrands later reflected on the current state of Mekhitar's ecumenical ideal in the post-conciliar period. With slightly exaggerated optimism he believed that Vatican II had fully accepted the claims of the great Eastern tradition. The essential contribution of Vatican II in his eyes was to have shown the importance of an *ecclesiology of communion*[52]. The Eastern churches and the Catholic Church found themselves sister churches once again. "From this perspective there is no longer room for one church to want to absorb another, or to want to impose on another church her own culture or her tradition. A latinisation of the East thus becomes inconceivable. On the contrary there is only room for continuing and profound exchanges, so that the churches may respond to the fresh demands of today, each church in her own way, and in conformity with her own style and tradition, in communion of faith and of sacramental life with Peter's successor" (p. 433).

---

52. His reference is at Cardinal Seper's report to the Synod of Bishops from October 1969. [*Documentation catholique* 66 (1969), pp. 960 s.]. At the same time he returns to his article in *Proche Orient Chrétien* 25 (1975), pp. 3-15: «*L'avenir de l'œcuménisme*».

From all this the Catholic Church must draw the practical conclusions and that requires a deep conversion (p. 434). The Eastern Catholic churches have their role to play in the remaking of unity (p. 435). They must follow the example of Father Mekhitar and his deeply felt love for the individual tradition and its liturgical expression (p. 434).

V. MATERIAL FOR EVALUATION

In his vision of the Christian East and in his ecumenical action Msgr. J. Willebrands consciously leaned on the ecclesiological positions of Vatican II, as they were written in the Constitution on the Church (LG) and in the Decree on Ecumenism (UR). There, for him, lie the foundations. On these foundations one had, with the help of God, to build the ecumenical project.

Willebrands was the closest collaborator of both Paul VI and of John Paul II in the Catholic Church's engagement in ecumenism. He represented the official position of his church, and did so with perfect loyalty. Did this always correspond with his personal feelings? Whether or no, and purely by way of example, it is certain that he identified completely and with conviction with the papal brief "Anno ineunte" of Paul VI (25 July 1967)[53], just as he was quite at home with the later encyclical *"Ut Unum Sint"* of John Paul II.

Looking forward from Vatican II ecumenism must also learn from contacts with other churches, deepen its understanding of the mystery of the faith, and act and witness together in the service of humanity. Either ecumenism is a movement or it is nothing. "It is the urgent wish of this holy synod that the measures undertaken by the sons and daughters of the catholic church should in practice develop in conjunction with those of our separated sisters and brothers, so as to place no obstacle to the ways of divine providence and to avoid prejudicing the future inspirations of the holy Spirit" (UR 24).

On 3 February 1975, on the occasion of the tenth anniversary of the foundation *Pro Oriente*, the president of the Secretariat for Promoting Christian Unity gave a lecture entitled "The future of Ecumenism"[54]. In it he worked out the ecclesiological convictions which underlay his ecumenical actions towards the Orthodox East. What were those convictions? The necessity for renewal of the Church, communion (koinonia)

---

53. *Tomos Agapis* (n. 35), pp. 386-393.
54. Published in *Proche-Orient Chrétien* 25 (1975) 3-15.

in the church and between churches, the decisive importance of baptism and Eucharist, a correct reciprocity between local church and universal church, conciliarity, the meaning of *subsistit in* (LG 8), and the different forms of the exercise of ministries.

Let us look again at these elements and try to assess them.

1. *Conversion and Renewal*

> We cannot speak of *the* ecumenical movement, of its development and of its perspectives without speaking of conversion *of the heart* and of renewal of the Church (...) Ecumenism will make progress only to the extent that the renewal of theological reflection on the Church deepens, that it more truly impregnates the mentality of pastors and faithful, and that it inspires the gradual renewal of the entire life of the Church[55].

This is a leitmotif taken from the invitation to "continual reformation" in *Unitatis Redintegratio* 6. In a chapter entitled "Reform and reformation today"[56] he concluded: "'if (reform) means conversion to the totality of the message of the New Testament and an adaptation of its message to the world of today, then it alone can bring the different Churches and Christian communities together in any substantial way'. Together we must bear witness to the gospel of salvation"[57].

2. *The Church Is a Communion*

The rediscovery of the Church as communion resumes in a few words a central idea of Vatican II. Communion, which is a multi-faceted reality, "establishes the Christian in a new relationship with God and (...) establishes between believers themselves a new, mysterious and spiritual relationship, as truly and as mysteriously as they have become sons in the Son, they become brothers one of the other"[58]. Baptism unites us as members of the same Body of Christ[59]. Baptism turns us towards the fulfillment of participation in the same Eucharist.

This is the tragedy of our separations. "It is precisely the ecclesiology of communion, communion which can be perfect but can also be imperfect, which has enabled us to understand better the terrible situation

---

55. *Ibid.*, p. 6.
56. *Œcuménisme* (n. 2), pp. 91-113.
57. *Ibid.*, p. 113. Cf. also p. 18, and *Mandatum Unitatis* (n. 2), p. 71.
58. *L'avenir de l'œcuménisme* (n. 52), p. 9.
59. Cardinal Bea's great intuition! Cf. E. LANNE, *La contribution du Cardinal Bea à la question du baptême et l'unité des chrétiens*, in *Atti del Simposio Card. A. Bea*, Roma, 1983, pp. 159-185.

which exists between Christians who see one another as separated and at the same time as brothers and sisters in Christ"[60].

The Holy Spirit builds this communion, and arouses the desire for full communion.

> The notion of *communio* in the first instance goes back to community in Christ by the Holy Spirit. This community is realised in word and sacrament, by faith and through new life in Christ. One would only imperfectly understand this community if one was to see it as a gathering of believers in Christ. It is only through the sending of the life-giving Holy Spirit that this community of believers becomes the Church of Christ, in the same way as Christ glorified in Spirit is the head of the Church and continually pours out his Spirit on her. This community in Christ by the Holy Spirit also creates community between the brothers in the same Spirit and creates the Church with her diverse charisms and her institutions by which the Lord is with us. Here is the unity of the church as gift and mystery of salvation. It does not coincide with what we men see of the Church with our eyes and our intelligence (organization, structure and doctrinal edifice). It is only by faith that it may be recognized[61].

This vision of the mystery of the church has a particular application to relationships between the Orthodox Churches and the Catholic Church. Cardinal Willebrands expressed his conviction in a speech in Constantinople on 30 November 1977:

> Is it not sacramental reality which makes this communion solid and incorruptible in its substance? Indeed we Catholics and Orthodox believe that the Church is the great sacrament of salvation, the pillar and the ground of truth. This deep conviction is the basis on which relations between our two Churches – sister Churches – are built. The Church, over the course of its journey through the history of humankind, has met and lived through many difficulties, both interior and exterior. Among these difficulties, the divergences and divisions which have struck at the seamless robe of Christ are those from which she has suffered the most.
>
> In patience and love she strives to overcome them by the power of the Spirit which the risen Christ has given her. She must overcome them to be able to proclaim her mystery to the world. In her and by her the Kingdom of God is built. The Spirit, the definitive eschatological reality, is communicated to man. The community of the faithful redeemed by the blood of Christ and incorporated in him is led progressively by the sacraments to transfiguration and divinization. There lie the deep life and reality of our Churches. There is knit together this mysterious communion which unites them, mysterious yet real and efficacious, as is every work of God.

---

60. *Il dramma della divisione* (Bologne 1990), in *Sfida ecumenica* (n. 2), p. 64.

61. *Mandatum Unitatis* (n. 2), p. 109 (paper delivered in 1968). See also *Œcuménisme* (n. 2), pp. 132-135.

In the East and in the West, the implementation of these gifts, the development of the sacramental life of the Church, the expressions given to this
common faith, have been diverse, rich and complementary in their variety.
This sacramental reality which we live from is at the foundation of the solid
relationships which are being established between our Churches. It gives
substance to the rich dialogue of hope which is opening up. It must allow
us to confront with Christian realism and to clarify definitively all the points
which remain as sources of difficulties and which yet prevent us from con-
celebrating the holy Eucharist. It must be located at the very heart of this
mystery, at this central point where the multiplicity and variety of the surface are expressed as one. It is there, in that light, that we discover ourselves
and we recognize each other truly as brothers that we discover and recognize that our Churches are truly sister Churches[62].

Communion does not mean uniformity, but *diversity* full of pastoral and
cultural promise for a common future ... This legitimate diversity in unity,
which the ancient Church knew, about which Saint Irenaeus, Saint Basil,
Saint Augustine, Saint Cyril testified and which points the way towards
unity reestablished between the Churches[63].

3. *Local Church and Universal Church*

With an eye to the unity to be restored between the churches of the
East and the Catholic Church, Willebrands showed a concern that the
functioning of the local and universal levels of the Church should be well
integrated. The bishop of any particular church had to watch over the
unity of his church and serve the unity of the local churches. The Bishop
of Rome had a special and unique responsibility for the unity of the
entirety of the local churches and for the Catholic Church. He saw this
as an essential component, part of the apostolic faith. The mode of implementation of this twin service however, could vary according to times
and circumstances: councils or local synods, metropolses, patriarchates
... The phenomenology of relations between the bishop of Rome and the
diocesan bishops, and between the bishops could also vary and could still
develop further[64].

The primacy however must be exercised in conciliarity (or collegiality)[65].
In this context the cardinal referred to canon 34 of the Apostles, and this

---

62. *Service d'information* N° 37 (1978/2), p. 1.
63. Discourse to Patriarch Athenagoras on 30 November 1969 in *Tomos Agapis* (n. 35),
pp. 590-598. Compare it with Paul VI's discourse in Phanar on 25 July 1967 (*ibid.*,
p. 374).
64. *Mandatum Unitatis* (n. 2), pp. 212-213 (paper delivered in 1975).
65. *L'avenir de l'œcuménisme* (n. 52), pp. 9-12.

is significant, as a model to be imitated[66]. Was he remembering a sentence of Paul VI at Phanar in 1967? "We thus see more clearly that it is up to the leaders of the Churches, to their hierarchy, to lead the Churches on the road that leads to the rediscovery of full communion. They must do this recognising one another and respecting each other as pastors of Christ's flock which has been entrusted to them"[67]. If globalisation is taken into consideration, the effective application of this openness could lead us to major steps forward in ecumenism.

4. *Sister Churches*

On 20 September 1963 the newly elected Pope Paul VI sent a handwritten letter to the patriarch Athenagoras[68]. The revue *Apostolos Andreas* of the Ecumenical Patriarch reacted with the big headline "The Two Sister Churches"[69]. And thus began the story of this expression of great symbolic power, whose reception in the Catholic Church and in the Orthodox Churches is not yet finished[70].

This is how Willebrands spoke about this matter in his 1975 lecture[71].

> During his visit to Phanar in July 1967, Paul VI gave Athenagoras a brief, his intention being that this should be the great charter for our future relationships with the Orthodox Churches. All that I have just said is no more than a clarification and interpretation of this important text from which I will now read you the central passage. "It has been given to us by God to receive by faith that which the apostles saw, heard and declared to us. In baptism we are one in Christ Jesus (Gal 3,28). Through the apostolic succession, the priesthood and the Eucharist unite us more closely; participating in the gifts of God to his Church, we are placed in communion with the Father, by the Son, in the Holy Spirit. Having truly become sons in the Son (cf. 1 Jn 3,1-2), we have equally truly and mysteriously become each other's brothers. In each local Church this mystery of divine love is at work, and is this not the reason why we have the beautiful traditional expression according to which local Churches loved to call each other sister Churches?

---

66. "The bishops of each province must recognize the one who is first amongst them, and consider him to be their head, and not do anything important without his consent; each bishop may only do what concerns his own diocese and its dependent territories. But the first cannot do anything without the consent of all. For in this way concord will prevail, and God will be praised through the Lord in the Holy Spirit".

67. *Tomos Agapis* (n. 35), pp. 375-376.

68. *Ibid.*, pp. 82-85.

69. *Irénikon* 36 (1963), pp. 541-542.

70. Fr. John Meyendorff's Orthodox reflection and Fr. Emmanuel Lanne's Catholic reflection encounter brotherly under the common title *Églises-Sœurs. Implications ecclésiologiques de Tomos Agapis*, in *Istina* 20 (1975), pp. 35-46 and 47-74.

71. *L'avenir de l'œcuménisme* (n. 52), p. 13.

(...) Now (...) the Lord allows us to rediscover ourselves as sister Churches, despite the obstacles which were at that time raised between us. In the light of Christ, we see how urgent is the need to overcome these obstacles in order that we may bring to fullness and perfection the communion that exists between us and which is already so rich[72].

Dimitrios I and John Paul II followed this line when they together proclaimed the opening of theological dialogue between the Catholic Church and the Orthodox churches. "The goal of this theological dialogue is not simply to move towards the reestablishment of full communion between the Catholic and Orthodox Sister Churches, but further, to contribute to the many dialogues which are developing within the Christian world as it seeks its unity"[73]. Let us note the hope for a mutual enrichment from the many bilateral dialogues undertaken by the two churches.

5. *"Subsistit in"*

The Constitution on the Church of Vatican II defined the presence of the Church of Christ with the Latin verb *subsistere* (LG 8; cf UR 4). Was this a simple stylistic modification or a theological correction?

The position of Willebrands is quite clear: "we do not judge Churches or ecclesial communities in relation to ourselves; we judge both them and ourselves in relation to Christ and his mystery. This Christological approach seems to me to be the underlying reason for the change made by the Fathers of the theological commission of the Vatican Council in the draft of the 8th paragraph of *Lumen Gentium*. The first draft said that the unique Church of Christ (...) is the Catholic Church. The final version said: 'the unique Church of Christ subsists in the Catholic Church'"[74]. In any case the question concerned him greatly[75].

---

72. *Tomos Agapis* (n. 35), pp. 389-391. Already at the time of the meeting of the Mixt Commission charged with the preparation of the declaration on the mutual elevation of the anathemas (Istanbul, 22 November 1965), he declared: "The Church of the Ancient Rome became aware of the sentiments and wishes of its sister, the Church of the New Rome, as to the tragic incidents from 1054...". ("L'Église de l'ancienne Rome a pris connaissance des sentiments et des désirs de sa sœur l'Église de la nouvelle Rome concernant les incidents tragiques de 1054...") (*Tomos Agapis* [n. 35], p. 266).

73. *Irénikon* 52 (1979) 513-531.

74. *L'avenir de l'œcuménisme* (n. 52), pp. 13-14. He continues by saying that he has consecrated a conference on the topic in November 1974 in Princeton.

75. See a paper delivered on 20 February 1983, *Der ökumenische Dialog: Zwanzig Jahre nach dem Zweiten Vatikanischen Konzil*, in *Mandatum Unitatis* (n. 2), 243-256, pp. 244-245.

In fact this question seemed so crucial to him in order correctly to situate Catholic ecumenism, that he came back to it in a lecture given in 1988[76]. It is the interpretation of *subsistit in* by which stands or falls the conviction of the Catholic Church, rooted in a secular Latin tradition, that the Orthodox churches are authentic churches. In the lecture one finds an approach which is very nuanced, yet which insists on the full sacramental ecclesiality of the Orthodox churches.

6. *Theology within Ecumenism*

Willebrands had a high view of the ministry of the theologian in the Church and within ecumenism. Ecumenism in the Catholic Church is entrusted to the bishop and to the theologian. The theologian must "develop and deepen the knowledge of the mystery of salvation as a service to the people of God"[77]. The bishop and the theologian are complementary. Following St Thomas Aquinas, Willebrands even speaks of two seats of truth.

> The theologians involved in ecumenism should therefore pay attention to both aspects. An ecumenism which did not take into consideration the teachings of the Episcopal *cathedra* would be an 'untamed' ecumenism. An ecumenism which did not pay attention to the teachings of the *cathedra* of the theologians would be a "blind" ecumenism. But as far as faith is concerned, those who would not wish to follow the *regula fidei* that the authority of the Church proclaims and makes known – this authority possessed by those who are seated in the Episcopal cathedra – they would be without excuse[78].

Theology must stay with a primarily pastoral orientation, without however renouncing the necessary conceptual and hermeneutical tools[79].

Willebrands recognized all that Vatican II owed to the theologians. He said as much in a lecture delivered at Toronto on 26 April 1990:

> It is clear that ecumenism sprang to life in the Catholic Church following Vatican II. This happened thanks to the Decree *Unitatis Redintegratio* and to the two great documents from which it may not be separated, *Lumen Gentium* and *Dei Verbum*. Without paragraph 8 *of Lumen Gentium* (and in particular the famous *subsistit in*) the Catholic Church would never have been capable of leaving behind the old notion of an ecumenism of return into which the great Pope Leo XIII had tried to breathe new life. And

76. *La signification de « subsistit in » dans l'ecclésiologie de communion*, in *La Documentation catholique* 85 (1988) 35-41.
77. *Œcuménisme* (n. 2), p. 78.
78. *Ibid.*, p. 79.
79. *Ibid.*, p. 59.

without the reflection on *koinonia* we would never have possessed the necessary tools for dialogue with the other Christian communities embodying both deep respect and a correct appreciation of their diversities when these latter are compatible with the apostolic tradition. Without the words of *Unitatis Redintegratio* about the *elementa Ecclesiae* which the Holy Spirit has preserved in the communities separated from the Church of Rome, it would have been difficult to resist the temptation to triumphalism and self-sufficiency which other Christians have reproached us for in the past, above all when we have rejected their pressing invitation to participate in their ecumenical movement. Without the clarifications in *Dei Verbum* on Scripture and Tradition we would still be implicitly engaged in polemic with the Churches of the Reformation. And if Vatican II had not completed and reinterpreted the constitution *Pastor Aeternus* of the first Vatican Council, we would be incapable of rethinking the nature of the ministry of unity of the bishop of Rome and its place with regard to ecclesial communion[80].

7. *Councils and General Synods*

On the occasion of the celebration of the sixteenth centenary of the Council of Constantinople (381), which defined the consubstantial divinity of the Holy Spirit, Willebrands reflected on the task allotted to councils, and perhaps that of a future council of union. He formulated a threefold conclusion. In the first place the Creed of Nicea-Constantinople and the confession of the divinity of the Holy Spirit was the fruit of a consensus between the East and the West. The Church of Rome had played a decisive role (the *Tomus Damasi*). The 'economy' which the Council subsequently practiced was an attempt to hold together the greatest number possible, while avoiding terms which would seem unacceptable to some, and yet unequivocally confessing the faith of the Church. This 'economy' followed in the footsteps of St Athanasius of Alexandria (Synod of Confessors in 362), of St Hilary of Poitiers, of St Eusebius of Vercelli, of St Basil of Caesarea and other Church fathers. In short, the formulation of the confession of faith was based on the sacramental life of the Church, baptism and Eucharist.

It seems clear that these same principles were those that were the most important in the Christological agreements signed by the popes and the heads of the Eastern Orthodox churches.

This raises a fresh question: what binding power should be ascribed to the different councils and synods held by the divided churches after the schisms? Paul VI alluded to this problem in a letter addressed to the

---

80. *La teologia nel movimento ecumenico: Il suo contributo ed i suoi limiti*, in *Sfida ecumenica* (n. 2), 71-82, p. 74. Paper delivered in Toronto in April 1990.

cardinal on the occasion of the celebration of the seventh centenary of the Second Council of Lyon (1274), which addresses the question of union. He wrote: "(…) the Council of Lyon, reckoned as the sixth of the general councils held in the West"[81]. In his homily in the cathedral church of Lyon Willebrands referred to this and wondered if the Latin church should not take the path of repentance for her centuries-old failure to understand the Christian East[82].

8. *Dialogue of Charity and Theological Dialogue*

Willebrands tried to understand the things he encountered in the day to day experiences of the various dialogues that were undertaken. A good example of this thoughtful approach is the report presented to the Johann-Adam-Möhler Institute at Paderborn on 13 March 1975. It was entitled: "Reflections on the ecumenical dialogue". The cardinal emphasized the change in mentality of the Catholic Church, thanks to Vatican II, from polemic to dialogue: "Certain dialogues have drawn us into a deep experience. We are only just beginning to be aware and to see what the consequences will be when we go further, always of course in such a way that motivated by love we hold firm in the truth" (c.f., Eph 4,15)[83].

In an article in 1981 he expressed his views on the necessary relationship between a "dialogue of charity" and "theological dialogue". "We know that where relations between Orthodox and Roman Catholics are concerned, the emphasis was long put on charity. The Orthodox-Catholic dialogue has been called a dialogue of charity. Some have interpreted this nomenclature as a sentimental expression which rather cleverly masks the impossibility of a theological dialogue. In reality to speak of a dialogue of charity was a very profound inside view of Christian and ecclesial relationship. For many centuries there had been neither dialogue nor charity between Orthodox and Catholics, even though one could always find notable exceptions here and there. Without charity there is no dialogue. Between Orthodox and Catholics charity more than doctrine had been offended and wounded. Above all else esteem, mutual confidence and charity had to be restored. In rebuilding confidence, in giving signs of esteem and trust, in expressing charity in a concrete way, we did theology. The achievements of twelve years of relations between the Church of Rome and the Church of Constantinople, and more particularly

---

81. *Service d'information*, n° 25 (1974/3), pp. 10-11.
82. *Ibid.*, pp. 11-13.
83. *Mandatum Unitatis* (n. 2), pp. 179-197, p. 180.

between Patriarch Athenagoras and Pope Paul VI – correspondence, exchange of documents, personal visits and meetings – were published under the title *Tomos Agapis. The Book of Charity*. This was an event which left its mark, exceptional, of fundamental importance for the dialogue between the churches. Most far reaching in its effect, one of the manifestations of this charity was the gesture made by Pope Paul VI on 14 December 1975. He kissed the feet of Metropolitan Meliton of Chalcedon, who led the delegation from Constantinople which came to Rome for the commemoration of the tenth anniversary of the lifting of the mutual excommunications between the churches of Rome and Constantinople. Relations with the other Orthodox churches developed in a similar way, in particular with the Russian Orthodox Church"[84].

Thus the churches will never be able to turn away from this dialogue of charity, which can but involve costly sacrifices for which the pastors must prepare the faithful.

CONCLUSION

'Veritatem in caritate' is the episcopal watchword of Msgr. Jan Willebrands. He explained his own ecumenical vocation in the following way. "Saint Paul wrote to the Ephesians: "veritatem autem facientes in caritate..." (Eph 4,15), which goes beyond saying truth with charity. It is rather a question of doing, of creating truth in charity"[85]. A dialogue of charity *and* of truth. Willebrands was careful in his audacity[86]. "Go forward with prudence and audacity towards the unity that the Lord wants for us", he said to Patriarch Athenagoras on 30 November 1969 at the Phanar[87]. With audacity and prudence, in brotherly relationships with the churches of the East he deepened and broadened the openings springing from Vatican II. Some of these accomplishments have little by little entered into the life of the Catholic Church. Others have yet to do so, and we set ourselves to dreaming of what we had hoped to be already ours. His tenacity will be an example for us.

---

84. *Réflexions sur les vingt années de travail du Secrétariat pour l'Unité des chrétiens*, in *Irénikon* 54 (1981) 5-24, p. 14.

85. *La teologia nel movimento ecumenico* (n. 80), p. 76.

86. This is already the portrait sketched by J. GROOTAERS in 1970: *Jan Cardinal Willebrands: The Recognition of Ecumenism in the Roman Catholic Church*, in *One in Christ* (1970) 23-44.

87. *Tomos Agapis* (n. 35), p. 598.

On the topic of Willebrands and the Christian East, we conclude with the testimony that he himself gave of Patriarch Athenagoras: "Some three weeks before his death he gave to one of the co-workers of our Secretariat one of those pithy little statements which he had the gift of making, on the subject of the long awaited day of reestablishment of full communion between the Catholic Church and the Orthodox Churches: 'The day will come, because we believe in it'"[88].

Monastère bénédictin   Michel VAN PARYS
B-5990 Chevetogne
Belgium

---

88. *Mandatum Unitatis* (n. 2), p. 215.

WILLEBRANDS, THE CHURCHES OF THE WEST, AND THE WORLD COUNCIL OF CHURCHES

A ROMAN-CATHOLIC ASSESSMENT

My task here is to give a Catholic assessment of Johannes Cardinal Willebrands' ecumenical work as it related to the churches of the West and to the World Council of Churches (WCC). This is no easy task because the cardinal helped to launch the new relationships of the Catholic Church with many Western communions which had begun with their observers at the Second Vatican Council, and which started to flourish right after the Council. As an official of the Secretariat for Promoting Christian Unity (SPCU) he participated in the first meetings, in the 1960s, of various bilateral planning groups that organized the new international bilateral dialogues with Lutherans, Methodists, Anglicans, Reformed, and in the 1970s, with others such as Disciples of Christ. As the dialogues were beginning, he gave addresses as SPCU's Cardinal President either at major assemblies of the dialogue partners, or in other significant settings which supported the dialogues, or he sent messages afterwards helping to promote good relations and a healing of memories. In the late 1960s he also raised the question of dialogue with conservative Evangelicals and Pentecostals, at that time further away on the ecumenical horizon, but whose phenomenal growth today offers a great challenge to mainline churches and to the ecumenical movement. Catholic dialogue with Pentecostals began in 1972, and with some Evangelical leaders in 1977. He promoted work with the United Bible Societies. And, of course, his work with the World Council of Churches began even a decade before the beginning of Vatican II[1].

In this presentation, from the various relationships just mentioned, I will focus specifically on some of Willebrands' contacts and activities with the World Council of Churches, with the Lutheran World Federation (LWF) and with the World Alliance of Reformed Churches (WARC).

---

1. Much information about the variety of these early activities of the Cardinal can be found in *A Tribute to Johannes Cardinal Willebrands on the Occasion of His Ninetieth Birthday*, The Pontifical Council for Promoting Christian Unity, Vatican City, *Information Service* [=*IS*] 101(1999/II-III).

I. WILLEBRANDS AND THE WORLD COUNCIL OF CHURCHES
EARLY CONTRIBUTIONS

There is a very good relationship today between the Catholic Church and the World Council of Churches. Willebrands, starting even before Vatican II, helped plant the seeds for good relations between the WCC and the Catholic Church which began even during the Council, developed rapidly soon after the Council and continue today.

While the Catholic Church is not a member of the WCC, the two have fashioned a partnership which keeps them in close contact, and in some ways helps them to contribute together to the whole ecumenical movement. A Joint Working Group between the Roman Catholic Church and the World Council of Churches (JWG), begun in 1965 and continuing today, has promoted widespread contacts between the two. The JWG has produced study documents which have been of service to the larger ecumenical movement. Since 1966, the Secretariat (from 1988, Pontifical Council) for Promoting Christian Unity and the WCC's Faith and Order Commission have together prepared the materials used throughout the Christian world for the Week of Prayer for Christian Unity. There has also been consistent cooperation with the WCC Faith and Order Commission (since 1968, Catholic theologians have served as full voting members of that commission), in mission concerns (since 1984, a Catholic missionary has served on the staff of the WCC mission unit), in ecumenical education (for decades a Catholic professor has served on the staff of the WCC's Ecumenical Institute at Bossey), in social concerns and many others. There has been continuing contact and cooperation between offices of the WCC with comparable offices in the Vatican. The eight reports of the JWG have documented this ongoing cooperation at length[2]. In 2008 Pope Benedict XVI described the relationship between the Catholic Church and the WCC as a "fruitful ecumenical relationship dating back to the time of the Second Vatican Council. The Joint Working Group, which began in 1965 (…) has given vivid expression to the communion already existing between Christians and has advanced the cause of ecumenical dialogue and understanding"[3].

This fruitful ecumenical relationship was already taking shape before the initial session of the Second Vatican Council. Augustin Cardinal Bea,

2. The most recent one is: *Joint Working Group between the Roman Catholic Church and the World Council of Churches: Eighth Report 1999-2005*, Geneva – Rome, WCC Publications, 2005.

3. *To Members of the Joint Working Group between the World Council of Churches and the Catholic Church, January 25, 2008*, in *IS* 127 (2008) 2.

first President of the SPCU, and Dr. W.A. Visser 't Hooft, first General Secretary of the WCC, met for the first time in 1960. In 1961 Catholic observers attended the WCC Assembly at New Delhi, and other important contacts took place shortly thereafter[4]. The intense and constructive contacts of Catholic theologians with the WCC in the previous decade had paved the way for this. While there were important contacts between WCC leaders and Catholic ecumenists earlier[5], the establishment in 1952 of the Catholic Conference on Ecumenical Questions (CCEQ), by Johannes Willebrands and Frans Thijssen opened a new chapter for Catholic relations with the WCC. Though an unofficial body, the conference brought together Catholic theologians engaged in ecumenical studies, in close relationship with numerous Catholic bishops, with consistent contacts with the Holy See, and giving priority to working with the World Council of Churches. In his memoirs, Dr. Visser 't Hooft observes that this development "was to have far-reaching consequences for the ecumenical movement". When the two co-founders came to see him shortly afterwards, Visser 't Hooft describes that "as an important moment in the relations between the World Council and the Roman Catholic Church"[6]. Though the CCEQ had no official status, Visser 't Hooft considered it as a great advantage for the WCC to be in conversation with a responsible body of Roman Catholic ecumenists[7].

The Catholic Conference continued until 1963, and its history has already been well documented[8]. The new situation created by Vatican II allowed the Catholic Church from that time forward to engage more formally in relations with the WCC. But here, let us recall just some aspects of the conference's work. Because not only was it historically important, but also, in some ways, the spirit in back of the conference's work in the 1950s is reflected in the Catholic Church's relations with the WCC afterwards and today.

---

4. In 1963 Catholic observers attended the WCC World Mission Conference in Mexico City; in 1963, for the first time, a Catholic speaker gave a major address at a WCC sponsored World Conference when biblical scholar Raymond Brown, addressed the 1963 World Conference on Faith and Order in Montreal; WCC observers attended four sessions of Vatican II, 1962-65.

5. For example, Visser 't Hooft describes important contacts in 1949 with the Catholic ecumenists of the *Istina centre* in Paris. W.A. VISSER 'T HOOFT, *Genesis and Formation of the World Council of Churches*, Geneva, World Council of Churches, 1982, pp. 74-76.

6. W.A. VISSER 'T HOOFT, *Memoirs*, Geneva, WCC Publications, 1973, p. 323.

7. *Ibid.*

8. Mauro VELATI, *Una difficile transizione: Il cattolicesimo tra unionismo ed ecumenismo (1952-1964)*, Bologna, Il Mulino, 1996.

The method of cooperation adopted was that the Catholic Conference would study and develop a Catholic theological commentary on important themes on which the WCC was working. It did this in a way that emphasized solidarity with the WCC. And at certain points the WCC gratefully acknowledged its contribution.

The CCEQ undertook, especially, two major projects in the course of the decade. The first had to do with the theme of the WCC's Second Assembly at Evanston, Illinois (USA) 1954: "Christ-the Hope of the World". The WCC chose this theme for the assembly because, in its view, it "touched a nerve centre of human need, both within the churches and outside", and raised more vividly perhaps than any other "the whole range of areas touched by Christian thought in general. The destiny of the individual and the human race, and the character of man and the effectiveness of his own efforts to control his destiny", and in light of this "God's purpose and the meaning of his revelation in Christ, were fundamental starting and finishing points in the entire discussion", raising in turn "questions concerning the nature of His Kingdom on earth, and the place of the church in relation to it"[9].

WCC discussion of this theme had already begun in 1950[10]. The newly founded CCEQ, in solidarity with the WCC, decided in 1953 to develop a memorandum on this theme to be made available to Geneva as a contribution to the Evanston meeting, and did so[11]. Though it arrived too late to allow its use in the preparatory phase of the assembly, Visser 't Hooft made it available to the assembly participants[12], and he also commented on its value in his narrative account of the Evanston assembly:

> (...) it is significant that a number of well known Roman Catholic theologians in Western Europe have issued a substantial memorandum on the main theme of our Assembly which is a valuable contribution to our discussion. Introducing that document the review *Istina* expresses its sentiments of fraternal sympathy with the effort made in the ecumenical movement to render a common witness to Christ as the only Hope of the world. Good to know that in spite of deep divergences there remains this precious link[13].

---

9. *The Evanston Report. The Second Assembly of the World Council of Churches 1954*, New York, Harper and Brothers Publishers, 1955. Introduction, pp. 5-6.

10. *Ibid.*

11. Congar was the primary drafter, but all members of the CCEQ had a chance to comment on it. It was published in *Istina* 2 (1954) 132-158 under the title "Le Christ, l'Église et la grace dans l'économie de l'espérance chrétienne (Vues catholiques sur le theme d'Evanston)". Cf. VELATI, *Una difficile transizione* (n. 8), pp. 62-67.

12. VISSER 'T HOOFT, *Memoirs* (n. 6), p. 323.

13. *The Evanston Report* (n. 9), pp. 27-28: "The Narrative Account".

Lukas Vischer, too, commented on the quality of this contribution. Because it was late in coming it could only be duplicated and distributed at Evanston, "otherwise", he said, "it would certainly have left an even deeper mark on the discussion and reports"[14].

In 1955, Willebrands, with the hope of contributing again to WCC work, consulted Visser 't Hooft as to what burning issues could be studied. Visser 't Hooft proposed, as the central theme of theological discussion within the WCC, "The Lordship of Christ over the Church and Over the World". It was somewhat in continuity with the Evanston theme. It became from 1955 the object of reflection of the WCC Division of Studies. It was taken up by the Catholic Conference in its meetings over the next several years[15], again in solidarity with the WCC. Willebrands and Dr. Hans-Heinrich Harms, Director of the WCC Division of Studies, kept in touch with each other concerning progress of their respective studies. In its report to the WCC Central Committee meeting of 1957, the Division of Studies pointed to the Catholic Conference's efforts, and to the significance of this study:

> There has been wide interest in this study. Even a very representative Roman Catholic group has taken it up and has already worked out substantial contributions. It is apparent that the theme of the study points to the centre of the problematic of Christian life today, of churches and of individuals, and is being understood in that sense[16].

By mid-1959 the CCEQ sent its text on this question to the WCC Division of Studies in Geneva as a contribution to its work and published it in *Istina*[17]. As mutual trust developed, plans for a joint meeting of the CCEQ and the Division of Studies on this theme were undertaken. In Rome, Cardinal Ottaviani gave Willebrands his approval of this, and both sides prepared for an eventual meeting in Assisi 26-30 October 1959. Ottaviani agreed, also, to Willebrands and Père C.J. Dumont attending a Central Committee meeting on Rhodes 19-28 August 1959. But a serious misunderstanding took place at that Rhodes meeting, when an encounter between the Orthodox participants and the Catholics at the Central

14. L. VISCHER, *The Ecumenical Movement and the Roman Catholic Church. The Ecumenical Advance: A History of the Ecumenical Movement*, Volume 2, 1948-1968, ed. H.E. FEY, Philadelphia, PA, The Westminster Press, 1970, p. 321.

15. VELATI, *Una difficile transizione* (n. 8), pp. 73-79.

16. *Minutes of the Central Committee of the World Council of Churches, July 30-August 7, 1957*, Report of the Division of Study, p. 18.

17. *"La seigneurie du Christ sur l'Église et sur le monde" par un groupe de théologiens de la 'Conférence catholique pour les questions œcuméniques'*, in *Istina* 2 (1959) 131-166. Cf. VELATI, *Una difficile transizione* (n. 8), p. 89 n. 45 and n. 47. As in the previous contribution Yves Congar was the main drafter.

Committee was organized without informing the WCC leadership, and the motivation for the meeting was misunderstood. The time it took to clarify the whole thing, and the bitter feelings caused by the incident, led to the cancellation of the meeting by the WCC[18]. But after clarification, contacts were picked up again shortly afterwards, and especially after the establishment of the Secretariat for Promoting Christian Unity by John XXIII in 1960.

The recently discovered Willebrands' diary of 1958-61[19] underscores the consistency and growing intensity of this relationship in the late 50s. Just in the first year accounted for by notebook one of the diary, from August 1958 through July 1959, there are entries every month, usually several, concerning the World Council of Churches. References are made in seven of the twelve months to Dr. Visser 't Hooft, often showing ample discussion periods with him. Thus: 9 August 1958 "to Utrecht..., 2-4 o'clock: discussion with Dr. Visser 't Hooft (Père Dumont is present)"; 4 November 1958 "Meeting with the WCC staff in Geneva, (including) Dr. Visser 't Hooft, Dr.Harms, Dr.Bridston, Dr.Wolf, Dr.West, Weymarn et al. (...) The meeting lasted from 14:30-17:30 (...) In the evening, at Dr. Harms' home, met with Dr. Visser 't Hooft, Dr. Wolf and his wife". 11 November 1958 in Geneva "spoke with Dr. Visser 't Hooft for an hour"[20].

The importance of the theological work concerning the "Lordship of Christ" is reflected by citations in nine of the twelve months of the first year of the diaries. Four of these are contacts with WCC's Dr Harms, with whom Willebrands was preparing a joint meeting. In one of these (12 December, 1958) Harms told him that he had spoken about this project at the Central Committee meeting in Nyborg-Strand 1958 and "Everyone was pleased with this form of contact". The greatest number of these entries is contacts with Catholic theologians, concerning the draft Congar was preparing about the theme[21] or preparations for the meeting, and contacts with theologians to discuss the study[22]. Six other entries relate to contacts with people in Rome about the study, including, several

---

18. T. SALEMINK (ed.) *"You Will Be Called Repairer of the Breach" : The Diary of J.G.M. Willebrands 1958-1961*, Leuven, Peeters, 2009, pp. 7-12. For Willebrands' request to Ottaviani about the joint meeting, and Ottaviani's approval of the joint meeting and of Willebrands and Dumont attending the central Committee meeting at Rhodes see the entries of 21 November 1958, pp. 59-60, 5 December 1958, pp. 62-63, 21 June 1959, p. 105, and 23 June 1959, p. 106.

19. See note 18.

20. Other similar references: 6 September 1958; in 1959: 8 February, 23 February, 25 February, 13 June, 17 June.

21. 10 January, 8 February and 13 May, 1959.

22. 7 December 1958, and, in 1959: 9 February, 7 April, 8 May, 29 May.

times, Cardinal Ottaviani, who had granted him permission to go ahead with the project and whom he kept informed[23], and also, Father Bea, SJ[24] and Father Tromp, SJ[25]. And at a meeting in Istina (Paris, 13 May 1959) with Père Dumont, he states that "We think that it is best if we present the project to Cardinal Ottaviani, and to Tardini, and Tisserant as well (...)".

The intense theological work involved in the Catholic Conference's contributions to the WCC is important in itself. But it can be seen also as a prelude to what would happen after Vatican II. The Secretariat/ Pontifical Council for Promoting Christian Unity has shown solidarity with the WCC in a variety of activities mentioned earlier. At the same time, reminiscent of the Catholic Conference's focus on theological reflection on WCC themes, SPCU/PCPCU has given a certain priority to supporting the theological work of the WCC, particularly of Faith and Order. In a 1983 address, Cardinal Willebrands, making clear that the Secretariat gives "full importance to these many sided activities of the Council", said nonetheless that "the Catholic Church observes with the closest attention ... what importance is given to Faith and Order in the World Council of Churches, and what is the role played by that commission. On this importance and this role will depend largely, I think, the success of the Council in achieving its aim which is to call the churches to unity (Constitution, art. 3)"[26]. Cardinal Willebrands and his successors, Cardinals Cassidy and Kasper, have given priority to the theological work with WCC's Faith and Order Commission and its task of fostering a common understanding of the apostolic faith. A recent example concerns the project on the nature of the church undertaken by Faith and Order, a project suggested by the responses of many churches to the 1982 convergence text *Baptism, Eucharist and Ministry* (BEM). So far this study has produced two volumes, in 1998[27] and 2005[28]. The Pontifical Council, working with a number of Catholic theologians, has contributed

---

23. 3 March and 23 June 1959, *cf.* also 21 November and 5 December 1958. Also, Msgr Crovini, Ottaviani's co-worker, tells Willebrands that they are satisfied with the work and are following it with great interest (5 December 1959).

24. 20 November 1958.

25. 17 November 1958.

26. *The Role of Faith and Order: Excerpt from the Cardinal President's Opening Address at Plenary meeting of the Secretariat, January 31-February 5, 1983*, in *IS* 101 (1999/II-III) 129.

27. *The Nature and Purpose of the Church: A Stage on the Way to a Common Statement* (Faith & Order Paper, 181), Geneva, World Council of Churches/Faith and Order, 1998.

28. *The Nature and Mission of the Church: A Stage on the Way to a Common Statement* (Faith & Order Paper, 198), Geneva, World Council of Churches, 2005.

lengthy theological evaluations of those two volumes as they were published, and suggestions, with the hope now of helping Faith and Order in
its goal of achieving an even better version of the text in the future.

The diaries show another foreshadowing of the future work of the
SPCU/PCPCU, namely, in reference to the WCC's Ecumenical Institute
at Bossey. As Willebrands in October-November 1958 was the first Catholic lecturer in Bossey, along with Thijssen, there are numerous references in the diary to Bossey, especially in September, October, November, 1958. Many entries say only "Study, Preparation Bossey". But
Willebrands' experience at Bossey also helped him to see Bossey's
ecumenical potential, when several Protestant participants indicated that
at Bossey they gained a different view of Catholicism compared with the
stereotype they had previously (entry of 1 November 1958). He also
notes that Dr. Wolf, the Director of Bossey, told him that the ecclesiological part of the course Willebrands had given was very enriching,
showing him that it was possible to discuss potentially difficult issues
such as Mariology and Primacy (24 February 1959). Perhaps these experiences contributed, years later, to the SPCU, under Willebrands'
leadership, undertaking serious collaboration with the WCC on ecumenical education, not only by appointing a Catholic professor to Bossey on
an ongoing basis, but also, since the late 1970s until today, by inviting
its whole student body with some professors to spend a week in Rome
each year as part of its semester. For this week, the SPCU/PCPCU sets
up a program, including meetings with various offices of the Roman
Curia, with leaders of men's and women's religious orders, with visits to
Pontifical universities, contacts with various Catholic movements, and
often including a private audience with the Pope, or special mention at
his general audience on Wednesday. The purpose of the program is to
show the students, who are from Protestant, Anglican and Orthodox
churches, various aspects of the Catholic Church and Catholic life at first
hand. Willebrands' own experience at Bossey in 1958 illustrated the
value of ecumenical contacts in education, and of ecumenical education.

As I look at these various contacts with the WCC and others seen also
in the diary, the image that comes to me is that of Willebrands as an
architect of trust, continually working to fashion bonds of trust, a circle
of trust, between the CCEQ and the WCC, between himself and Visser
't Hooft, between the CCEQ and Vatican officials, between the Catholic
theologians and the bishops within the CCEQ. The trust that was built
enabled these contacts to go ahead and was basic for the good relations
that would develop during and after Vatican II. Willebrands' role in the
continuing and fruitful relations between the WCC and the Catholic

Church mentioned by Pope Benedict in 2008, relations which have developed over decades, has been significant from the 1950s up to the time when he left the PCPCU in 1989. His good relations with the WCC before Vatican II, helped relations between the Catholic Church and the WCC develop quickly during Vatican II and immediately after the Council.

II. WILLEBRANDS AND THE LUTHERAN WORLD FEDERATION

Cardinal Willebrands had important contacts with the Lutheran World Federation and other Lutheran bodies from the time of Vatican II. These included helping to organize the international Lutheran-Catholic dialogue which began in 1967, addressing two LWF general assemblies (at Evian, 1970 and at Budapest, 1984), being present at the LWF fortieth anniversary celebration in 1987, and addressing important Lutheran gatherings in Germany and the USA. Some of these addresses had a significant impact.

The *Joint Declaration on the Doctrine of Justification*, officially signed by the Catholic Church and the Lutheran World Federation in 1999, is the most important result of decades of international and national dialogue between Catholics and Lutherans which began after Vatican II. It claims consensus on basic aspects of the doctrine of justification, the central theological issue at the heart of Luther's conflict with church authorities in the sixteenth century. When the LWF and PCPCU made a decision in 1993 to seek a joint declaration on justification, Willebrands had already been retired from the PCPCU for four years, and he was not part of that. When they signed the *Declaration* in Augsburg, Germany in 1999, he had been retired from the PCPCU for ten years, and he was not present. Yet, in some ways, his activity from the 1960s through the 1980s helped to create the level of mutual trust which forms part of the background of that achievement. In important ways he was a herald of the reconciliation reflected in the *Joint Declaration*. Three factors suggest this: his statements about justification, his statements about Luther and his concern about ecumenical reception of the results of dialogue[29].

---

29. Many of the details describing these three factors here, are found also in J.A. RADANO, *Lutheran and Catholic Reconciliation on Justification*, Grand Rapids, MI – Cambridge, Eerdmans, 2009.

1. *Willebrands and Justification*

First: justification. Willebrands, as SPCU Secretary, served on the Lutheran and Catholic joint working group, newly created while Vatican II was still in session, which met in 1965 and 1966 to explore ways to deepen the new relationship between the LWF and the Catholic Church, and to identify issues to be undertaken in a dialogue that would begin in 1967. In its report the JWG identified seven general areas for dialogue. The fifth was "Justification and Sanctification", including as subtopics "Law and gospel", "Baptismal Faith and Justification", and "Sacraments as means of Grace"[30]. Writing in *L'Osservatore Romano* in July, 1966, to explain this joint report about future dialogue, Willebrands illustrated that there was now a different context in which to assess theological problems that had divided Lutherans and Catholics since the Reformation. While these problems are still with us, "the manner in which they present themselves today is very different". Without mentioning justification, he said that "the classical problems are presented in a completely new context. The progress of the natural sciences, of history and scripture has from time to time modified their terms"[31].

He did mention justification in 1970, in an address to the LWF Fifth Assembly at Evian, France, in a way that would encourage the dialogue on that issue then taking place. Willebrands, now Cardinal President of the SPCU, referring to the Lutheran-Catholic International dialogue, said that there can be no doubt that many controversies of the sixteenth century "appear in a new light today".

> Many questions, which at that time stood at the very center of controversy, have today been partly pushed towards the periphery and are now barely felt as controversial. An example of this is to be found in the doctrine of justification as such. It has been shown that extensive misunderstandings came into play on both sides and that these made a factual discussion impossible. The ecumenical dialogue has now been going on for some decades and the situation has been substantially improved[32].

The results of the first phase of dialogue reflected this judgment. A description of the final meeting of that phase published by the SPCU in 1971 already indicated the participants' "general agreement that the

---

30. *First Official Report of the Joint Working Group between the Roman Catholic Church and the Lutheran World Federation*, in *IS* 3 (1967) 26-28.

31. Cited in *The Roman Catholic Church and the Lutheran World Federation*, in *IS* 1 (1967) 6.

32. *Sent into the World*, Address of Cardinal Willebrands at the Assembly of the Lutheran World Federation, Evian, France, 1970. Reprinted in *IS* 101 (1999) 107-113, p. 111.

long-standing controversial issue of justification need no longer divide our churches"[33]. The dialogue's 1972 report, *The Gospel and the Church* (Malta Report) itself indicated that:

> Today, however a far reaching consensus is developing in the interpretation of justification. Catholic theologians also emphasize in reference to justification that God's gift of salvation for the believer is unconditional as far as human accomplishments are concerned. Lutheran theologians emphasize that the event of justification is not limited to individual forgiveness of sins, and they do not see in it a purely external declaration of the justification of the sinner. Rather the righteousness of God actualized in the Christ event is conveyed to the sinner through the message of justification as an accompanying reality basic to the new life of the believer (no. 26).

The Malta Report's claim of a "far reaching consensus developing" would be tested by further Lutheran-Catholic dialogue, both international and national, over the next two decades, to the point in which an adequate theological basis existed on which to develop the *Joint Declaration on the Doctrine of Justification*[34]. The earlier misunderstandings on justification, to which Willebrands had referred, were being cleared up.

2. *Willebrands and Luther*

Second, Willebrands also spoke of Luther at Evian and later in other settings. Some of what he said about Luther at Evian[35] was later included in the dialogue about justification. The joint research of Catholic and Evangelical theologians, he said, has shown that "In Luther's sense the word 'faith' by no means intends to exclude either works or love or even hope. We may quite justly say that Luther's concept of faith, if we take it in its fullest sense, surely means nothing other than what we in the Catholic Church term love". This statement was cited in the 1986 report of the German ecumenical study group, *The Condemnations of the Reformation Era. Do they Still Divide?*[36], one of three major resources later

33. *Roman Catholic / Lutheran Relations*, in *IS* 14 (1971) 9-10.
34. For example, the USA dialogue's *Justification by Faith* (1985) which cites (in n.2) the Malta report statement as challenging it to give further treatment to justification, which it did. The report of the third phase of international Lutheran-Catholic dialogue, *Church and Justification: Understanding the Church in the Light of the Doctrine of Justification* (1994) also tested the Malta Report's claim of a "far-reaching consensus" (see its Foreword). These studies along with the German study on the condemnations of the sixteenth century (see note 36 below) were basic sources later used in formulating the *Joint Declaration*.
35. Cf. *Sent into the World* (n. 32), pp. 111-112.
36. *The Condemnations of the Reformation Era: Do They Still Divide?*, ed. K. LEHMANN – W. PANNENBERG, Minneapolis, MN, Fortress, 1990. Original German *Lehrverurteilungen-Kirchentrennend?*, Freiburg im Breisgau, Herder, 1986.

used in the drafting of the *Joint Declaration*. After a lengthy analysis arguing that the old condemnations do not apply today, the German group cited Willebrands' statement, making it their own. It then immediately summarized its argument:

> If we take all this to heart, we may say the following: if we translate from one language to another, then Protestant talk about justification through faith corresponds to Catholic talk about justification through grace; and on the other hand, Protestant doctrine understands substantially under the one word 'faith' what Catholic doctrine (following 1 Cor. 13:13) sums up in the triad of 'faith, hope, and love.' But in this case the mutual rejections in this question can be viewed as no longer applicable today – that is, cans. 9 and 12 of the Decree on Justification (*DS* 1559 and 1562) and the corresponding condemnations in the. Formula of Concord SD III, first group of rejections 1-2 (*BC* 547f.); cf. HC, esp. 20[37].

Willebrands' statements about Luther at Evian show the importance, for Lutheran and Catholic reconciliation on justification, of a common appreciation or healing of memory relating to Luther. It is good, he said in the same address, to "recall to mind a man for whom the doctrine of justification was the 'articulus stantis et cadentis Ecclesiae'. In this we could all learn from him that God must always remain the Lord, and that our most important human answer must always remain absolute confidence in God and our adoration of him"[38].

And seeking a common understanding of the reformer, the cardinal asked "is it not true that the Second Vatican Council has even implemented requests which were first expressed by Martin Luther, among others, and as a result of which many aspects of Christian faith and life now find better expression than they did before? To be able to say this in spite of all the differences is a reason for great joy and much hope". The cardinal underlined here the importance of Holy Scripture which, for Luther, was the starting point of theology and Christian life, and which the Vatican Council has inserted even more profoundly into the life of the Church[39]. On the other hand, along with these positive statements, he also suggested his criticisms of Luther. He said that he preferred "to say nothing about certain particularly sharp attacks that Martin Luther made against the Roman Pontiff; they sadden my heart and I feel sure that you, too, regard them as a burden"[40].

The Lutheran-Catholic international dialogue's 1983 statement, *Martin Luther – Witness to Jesus Christ*, during the "Luther year", also cites

---

37. *The Condemnations of the Reformation Era* (n. 36), p. 52.
38. *Sent into the World* (n. 32), p. 112.
39. *Ibid.*
40. *Ibid.*

Willebrands. It underlines this connection between Luther and the doctrine of justification. The Gospel, as the "doctrine of the justification of the sinner through faith alone" was, for Luther, "the central point of his theological thinking and of his exegesis of Scripture"[41]. Luther research and biblical studies on both sides, and other factors, have "contributed to the widespread recognition among Catholics that Luther's ideas, particularly on justification, are a legitimate form of Christian theology" (no. 11). As a result of the intensive Catholic re-evaluation of Luther the man and of his Reformation concerns, it is widely recognized that "his fundamental belief – justification given to us by Christ without any merit of our own – does not in any way contradict genuine Catholic tradition, such as found, for example, in Saint Augustine and Thomas Aquinas" (no. 22). Taking the lead from Willebrands' address at Evian, and citing it twice, this document first expands and illustrates further the cardinal's statement that "the Second Vatican Council has even implemented requests which were first expressed by Martin Luther" (no. 24, cf. no. 23) by listing a number of ways in which this is the case. And in the spirit of the cardinal's efforts to seek common ground, a closing fifth section of *Witness* entitled "Luther's Legacy and Our Common Task" is introduced by the cardinal's statement that "we could all learn from him that God must always remain the Lord". It expands on this too, illustrating a number of ways in which this can be done (no. 26).

Willebrands continued in the years ahead to speak of Luther, stressing how Lutherans and Catholics together can learn from him. He did this during the Luther year (1983) in his address in Leipzig, and during the following year in his address in Toronto at the assembly of the Lutheran Church in America (1984), and in an address at a "Day of Dialogue" in South Carolina (1987). Furthermore, during the Luther year, Pope John Paul II used the vehicle of a letter to Cardinal Willebrands on that occasion to speak of Luther in a way reflecting contemporary research, and calling for the necessary further theological dialogue and historical research in order to resolve remaining conflicts, and to deepen common understanding. The pope's gestures were acknowledged with appreciation by Lutherans and Catholics[42]. The statements and gestures of the pope and of Willebrands helped create the good will that was later helpful to the Lutheran and Catholic partners as they moved toward the

---

41. *Martin Luther – Witness to Jesus Christ: Statement by the Roman Catholic/Lutheran Joint Commission on the occasion of Martin Luther's 500th birthday* (1983), no. 9, cf. no. 8. Further references to this document will be made in the text.
42. *Address to the Holy Father of Prof. Dr. George Lindbeck, Lutheran Co-Chairman,* in *IS* 54 (1984) 11. Lindbeck referred here especially to those gestures and other activities of John Paul II.

mutual commitment involved in accepting together the *Joint Declaration on the Doctrine of Justification* in 1999.

3. *Willebrands and Reception*

Third, Cardinal Willebrands gave significant attention to reception of dialogue reports, sometimes speaking to this in contexts involving Lutheran church bodies or the Lutheran-Catholic dialogue.

As reports of international dialogues, including the Lutheran-Catholic dialogue, were being published in the early 1970s, Willebrands began to address the question of the reception of these reports. He did this first, in Catholic circles, in his address to the 1973 SPCU Plenary meeting[43] and also in his address to the 1977 assembly in Rome of the Synod of Bishops, giving perspectives in light of the teaching of Vatican II, especially of *Unitatis Redintegratio* (no. 5 and 11). Addressing the Synod of Bishops he asked "*[h]ow do we deal with the results*, the final reports of the dialogues?" He explained that, with publication, critical study by specialists can be invaluable for revision or for the examination of the same theme in subsequent dialogue. At the same time, since dialogue is an instrument of reconciliation of the partners, "publication is an aid, at the various levels of the Church's life, in the task of assimilation of the process of convergence in practice, of understanding the method used, and the language used". He then gave some specific examples of dialogue, indicating how dialogue is intended to foster, among the faithful, the task of restoring unity[44].

In 1973 the SPCU was involved in initial efforts towards evaluation of the report of the first phase of International Lutheran-Catholic dialogue, *The Gospel and the Church* (Malta Report 1972). It was sent to study centers of both confessions, as well as by the LWF to its member churches and by the Catholic Church to Catholic Episcopal conferences in countries where Lutherans were most represented[45]. Some emphasis was put on evaluating the present relations between Lutheran and Catholic churches in light of the Malta Report including the question of the consequences of agreements achieved for the common life of the churches

---

43. *Opening Address by His Eminence Cardinal Willebrands,' at the SPCU Plenary, November 6-14, 1973*, in *IS* 23 (1974) 3-6. While focusing on dialogue, in different ways he also spoke of its concrete realization among Christians.

44. *The Activity of the Secretariat for Promoting Christian Unity: Report to the Synod of Bishops, October, 1977*, in *IS* 36 (1978) 7 [emphasis original].

45. SPCU Plenary session, February 17-24, 1975, *Dialogue with the Lutherans on the International Level*, in *IS* 27 (1975) 22.

at the local level[46]. By 1976 there were twenty-two Catholic responses and ten Lutheran responses[47]. The Lutheran-Catholic joint commission studied these responses and determined that it was too early to determine "whether the substance of the 1972 report has gained acceptance or been rejected by the churches"[48]. But by this initial effort of reception of this report, the sponsors made clear that one purpose of the dialogue was to help change attitudes of Lutherans and Catholics toward each other.

Willebrands spoke of reception in the 1980s on three occasions involving contacts with Lutheran church bodies. His most extensive presentation on it came in his address to the Lutheran Church in America convention in Toronto, July 3, 1984[49]. He illustrated a Catholic understanding of reception rooted in the teachings of Vatican II and involving the whole People of God within the hierarchical sacramental structure given to it by the Lord. He gave several examples of reception taking place between Lutherans and Catholics, referring twice to events related to the 1983 Luther year, but also to the 1980 commemoration of the Augsburg Confession. Many Catholics sought, together with Lutherans, to draw up a differentiated and truthful picture of Luther and his present day importance within Christendom. Pope John Paul II made important gestures, both his letter addressed to Willebrands in which he reflected the scientific research of Catholic and Lutheran scholars giving a more complete and differentiated picture of Luther, though raising critical questions as well, and by his visit to the Lutheran church in Rome in 1983[50]. The cardinal mentioned his own address in Leipzig in 1983, stressing important aspects of Luther. He then drew the conclusion that these examples are signs "of the efforts the Catholic Church is making to promote the reception of insights that are of great importance for the rapprochement and mutual recognition of our churches and their communions. Today we must continue to build on them and collect new elements that will pave

46. SPCU Plenary session, November 6-14, 1973, *General Report by Msgr Charles Moeller*, in *IS* 23 (1974) 12; and *Lutheran/Roman Catholic Joint Commission, Geneva, March 21-24, 1973*, in *IS* 21 (1973) 15.
47. *Dialogue with Lutherans at the International Level: A Report of the SPCU Plenary of November 10-18, 1976*, in *IS* 33 (1977) 21.
48. *Lutheran/Catholic Joint Commission, Liebfrauenberg, France, March 15-21, 1976*, in *IS* 31 (1976) 11.
49. *Address of Johannes Cardinal Willebrands to the Convention of the Lutheran Church of America*, Toronto, Canada, July 3, 1984. New York, Department for Ecumenical Relations, Lutheran Church in America, 1984.
50. For details on John Paul II's ecumenical addresses during the 1983 Luther year as well as the 1980 commemoration of the Augsburg Confession see J.A. RADANO, *Lutheran and Catholic Reconciliation on the Justification*, Grand Rapids, MI – Cambridge, Eerdmans, 2009, pp. 66-79.

the way to full church communion". Referring the second time in his Toronto address to the importance of the "recent rapprochement in the assessment of the Augsburg Confession and the historical judgment of Martin Luther", he concluded, perhaps prophetically, "By the grace of God, this first brief history of reception in the ambit of Lutheran-Catholic relations is going to have its sequel both in the present and in the future"[51].

The cardinal reflected on reception again in an address to the LWF Seventh Assembly in Budapest in 1984. He referred to it briefly, recalling a statement of the Malta Report (n. 73) which said that what we are engaged in is a "process of gradual rapprochement (...) in which various stages are possible". Commenting on this, he spoke of the urgency of reception. "If this process is really to be anchored in the life of the churches, the question of 'reception' acquires great significance and urgency, increasingly so today"[52].

The cardinal again spoke of reception in an address given in Columbia, South Carolina in 1987 at a "Day of Dialogue" co-sponsored by the Lutheran Church in America, the Lutheran Theological Southern Seminary and the Bishops' Committee on Ecumenical and Interreligious Affairs of the U.S. Conference of Catholic Bishops. He could now describe an actual process of formal response by the Catholic Church to a dialogue document, namely, the Catholic response to *BEM* which had been sent to Faith and Order that year. This first official reception of an ecumenical document by the Catholic Church took place during his presidency of the SPCU. He also spoke of the third phase of Lutheran-Catholic international dialogue which had, as one task, to assess whether the "far reaching consensus" on justification affirmed by the Malta Report could now be claimed by all. The dialogue was working with other dialogue reports from the USA and Germany which supported the

---

51. *Address of Johannes Cardinal Willebrands to the Convention of the Lutheran Church in America*, Toronto, Canada, July 3, 1984. The cardinal's presentation of reception had an impact. In the early 1990s, as the LWF and the PCPCU were discerning the best way to approach reception of the reports produced by the dialogue since 1967, they published together a brief statement called *Strategies for Reception, Perspectives on the Reception of Documents Emerging from the Lutheran-Catholic International Dialogue* (1991). While not mentioning Willebrands, the document points to some examples of Lutheran-Catholic reception that he had mentioned in Toronto, especially the Pope's statements on the occasion of the Luther Year and the Augsburg Confession anniversary (no. 13).

52. *Ecumenical Commitment: A Roman Catholic Perspective*, in C.H. MAU, JR. (General Editor), *"In Christ – Hope for the World"*, *Official Proceedings of the Seventh Assembly of the Lutheran World Federation, Budapest, Hungary July 22-August 5, 1984*, Geneva, Lutheran World Federation, 1984, p. 135.

Malta Report's claim. But this third phase of international dialogue would only be completed in 1993.

At the "Day of Dialogue" in 1987, after reviewing various dialogues in progress and indicating that they are all important, Willebrands then commented on the specific importance of the Lutheran-Catholic dialogue: "But the Lutheran-Catholic dialogue is important especially for Western Christianity because at the heart of the Reformation in the sixteenth century was the conflict between Martin Luther and the authorities in Rome. Reconciliation between Lutherans and Catholics would therefore be highly symbolic as well as significant. I believe there is a special ecumenical responsibility here"[53]. It goes without saying, then, that reception of the dialogue's results would therefore be important.

In his address in Toronto in 1984 as seen above, Willebrands had pointed to the brief history of reception concerning Lutheran-Catholic relations up till then, and predicted that this, "by the grace of God ... is going to have its sequel both in the present and in the future". Although he could not envision it in 1984, a major sequel did come in the reception of dialogue results by Lutherans and Catholics which led to the conclusion in the 1990s that they had achieved consensus on basic truths of the doctrine of justification. It was in 1988, while Willebrands was PCPCU president, that the LWF and the PCPCU began to make together the firm decision to engage in the reception of dialogue results, focusing a few years later on the dialogue's results concerning justification[54]. They brought this to a successful conclusion on October 31, 1999, signing together the *Joint Declaration on the Doctrine of Justification* in Augsburg, Germany. This was an important step in responding to what the cardinal called in 1987, this "special ecumenical responsibility" of this particular dialogue.

Willebrands' contributions to Lutheran-Catholic understanding were also acknowledged by the LWF. In 1987 Pope John Paul II wrote a letter of congratulations to the LWF on the occasion of its fortieth anniversary, which Willebrands brought to the celebration. Writing in response to the pope, LWF General Secretary Gunnar Staalsett said that the LWF values highly the theological dialogue with the Roman Catholic Church. And saying that "[t]he efforts of many dedicated persons have opened doors

53. *The Catholic Church and the Ecumenical Movement: An Address by Johannes Cardinal Willebrands. A Day of Dialogue* (Booklet) produced by Department for Ecumenical Relations, Lutheran Church in America, New York, 1987, p. 16.

54. For details on this mutual process from 1988 forward see J.A. RADANO, *Lutheran and Catholic Reconciliation on Justification*, Grand Rapids, MI – Cambridge, Eerdmans, 2009, pp. 113-142.

that we had for too long shut against one another", he gave a special mention and "deep appreciation" of Cardinal Willebrands[55].

III. WILLEBRANDS AND THE WORLD ALLIANCE OF REFORMED CHURCHES "SOME FUNDAMENTAL CONVICTIONS"

In the period after Vatican II until today, there has been an important international dialogue between the Catholic Church and the World Alliance of Reformed Churches[56], and cordial relations and contacts. Cardinal Willebrands, as SPCU Secretary helped to plan the first phase of dialogue which began in 1970, and was President during two of its three phases. There have been important dialogues as well in several national settings, including one in the Netherlands.

It has been said that "[c]ompared with other international bilateral dialogues the Reformed-Roman Catholic debate is less spectacular. It has produced considerably fewer documents than the Anglican-Roman Catholic and the Lutheran-Roman Catholic conversations"[57]. Perhaps that is true. But that dialogue has also made an impact. In the Netherlands, for example, an ecumenical group studied the 1990 report of the second phase of the international Reformed-Roman Catholic dialogue, *Towards a Common Understanding of the Church*, intending to "publicize the results of the international dialogue and make a critical contribution to its reception". It did so with an impressive volume published in 1998[58].

Concerning Willebrands' contacts with WARC, the following is a timely example. During the year 2009, the Reformed are commemorating the 500th anniversary of the birth of John Calvin. In 1986, on the occasion of another Calvin Year, the 450th anniversary of John Calvin's arrival in Geneva, Willebrands wrote a brief letter to the President of the World Alliance of Reformed Churches, Dr. Alan Boesak[59], acknowledging the importance of that event, especially in light of Calvin's influence on the western world, and his impact on church history. Indicating that

---

55. *Celebration of the Fortieth Anniversary of the Lutheran World Federation, July 4-5 (1987)*, in *IS* 64 (1987) 62.

56. In 2010 the WARC and REC (Reformed Ecumenical Council) merged and created the World Communion of Reformed Churches (WCRC).

57. "Introduction", in M.E. BRINKMAN – H. WITTE (eds.), *From Roots to Fruits: Protestants and Catholics Towards a Common Understanding of the Church*, Geneva, World Alliance of Reformed Churches, 1998, p. 6.

58. *From Roots to Fruits* (n. 57), quote on p. 15.

59. *Letter on the 450th Anniversary of John Calvin's Arrival in Geneva, May 13, 1986*, in *IS* 101 (1999/II-III) 115-116.

Catholics and Reformed view the results of Calvin's coming to Geneva differently, the cardinal said that he wanted to voice, nonetheless, "some fundamental convictions" which have meaning for our relationship today and express a vision of Christian hope for the future". These 'convictions' are worth recalling today.

First, despite our divisions, there are basic ties binding Reformed and Catholics together. "Even after the separation basic ties of faith and love bind us together (…) (which) have not always been acknowledged and lived by our communities". We have "rediscovered in faith 'the profound, even though imperfect, communion already existing among those who have been justified through faith in Jesus Christ, who are incorporated in Him through baptism and are enlivened by the Holy Spirit (John Paul II, June 28th, 1985)'. It is our intention to deepen these ties". It is especially through dialogue that this can be done.

Then, he raises the question of renewal with the intention also of commenting on the divisions of the past. "Another conviction is the vital importance of renewal in continuing conversion to the Word of God and the Spirit of truth". We both believe that achieving unity "requires renewal in truth, growth in love, in the life of every Christian and in the life of the Church as a community". This challenges us to look at the divisive events of the past in a new perspective. In the 15th and 16th centuries, he said, the "intention of renewal was common to all Christians". "It was against the original intention that division has come over us. We cannot leave the situation at this point".

Reflection on renewal also challenges us to appreciate the restoration brought about by the ecumenical movement itself. A third conviction relates to the ecumenical movement in which Reformed and Catholics, along with others, are partners. Is it not, he asked, reshaping relationships among separated Christian communities in basic ways? In common prayer, through dialogue, "we seek theological convergence or agreement between communities on significant issues long considered church-dividing". Considering "this movement as a 'grace of the Holy Spirit' (UR 1)", he suggested, in regard to the divisive events of the past, "that Christians today might well look at the events of both Reformation and the 'Counter-Reformation' of the sixteenth century from the perspective of this ecumenical movement taking place in the twentieth". The ecumenical movement of today should now be the perspective in which to look at the divisive conflicts of the past.

Finally, a challenge to common mission. In light of today's great problems and deep social needs "our communities are called to collaboration as Christians and to common witness to the Gospel of Jesus Christ".

Recalling that for Calvin "concern for society was specific", the cardinal suggests that "Common reflection on the teaching of Holy Scriptures, on the lessons of history and tradition, may lead us to further cooperation and common witness in the world to which Christ has sent his disciples".

After presenting ideas that could help Catholics and Reformed to look at their relationships in a very new way, he ends with a commitment. "[W]e renew our commitment to the dialogue and collaboration which have been developing among us, praying with the hope that will not disappoint, that through God's grace our common search for unity will continue to bear fruit".

Important Common Statements of Faith

In fact that commitment, of which the cardinal spoke, of the Catholic Church to dialogue with the World Alliance of Reformed Churches as a way of deepening the ties that already "bind us together", has continued, and has brought some important results. Unlike the official Lutheran-Catholic *Joint Declaration*, there have been no official agreements between the Catholic Church and the World Alliance of Reformed Churches. But three phases of dialogue have produced important common statements concerning the apostolic faith which are offered for the consideration of the two sponsoring bodies. The 1990 report *Towards a Common Understanding of the Church* mentioned above includes a chapter entitled "Our Common Confession of Faith". Although it is made clear that this "is neither a confession in the ecclesial sense, nor a complete statement of faith ... the importance of what we are able to say together merits such a title" (no. 64). Furthermore, they understand that "[t]his confession involves ... the recognition of the authority of the Scriptures" and that "[t]he teaching of the Church ought to be an authentic explanation of the Trinitarian and Christological affirmations of the early confessions of faith and the early councils" (no. 67).

In this light, "we announce the death of the Lord (cf. 1 Cor 11,26) and proclaim his resurrection from the dead (cf. Rom 10,9; Acts 2,32; 3,15). In that mystery of death and resurrection we confess the event which saves humanity (...)" (no. 68). "We therefore confess together that Christ, established as Mediator, achieves our reconciliation in all its dimensions" (no. 71). "We confess together that just as God is unique, the Mediator and Reconciler between God and humankind is unique and that the fullness of reconciliation is entire and perfect in him" (no. 72). They say together that "the work of Jesus, the Son, reveals to us the role of the Spirit of God who is common to him and to the Father: it reveals to us that God is Triune" (no. 74). They say together that "[b]ecause we believe in Christ, the one Mediator between God and humankind, we believe that we are justified by the grace which comes from him, by means of faith which is a living and life-giving faith (...) justification is a totally gratuitous work accomplished by God in Christ" (no. 77). And "[t]ogether we confess the Church, for there is no justification in isolation. All justification takes place in the community of believers, or is ordered toward the gathering of such a community" (no. 80).

In addition to this powerful confession of faith, another particularly important contribution of the dialogue, over two phases, was to illustrate, after intense study, that two visions or conceptions of the church as "creatura verbi" (Reformed tradition) and as "sacramentum gratiae" (Catholic tradition), are not contradictory. *Towards a Common Understanding of the Church* concluded that these two conceptions "can in fact be seen as expressing the same instrumental reality under different aspects, as complementary to each other or as two sides to the same coin" (no. 113). The 2007 report of the third phase of dialogue, *The Church as the Community of Common Witness to the Kingdom of God*, went further saying that "... in light of our investigation both of the kingdom and of the patristic literature, not only are these visions ... complementary, but that neither is fully adequate without the other. A 'sacramental' church that does not give proper place to the Word of God would be essentially incomplete; a church that is truly a creation of the Word will celebrate that Word liturgically and sacramentally" (no. 193).

There are other significant results of this dialogue. While the dialogue needs to continue reflection on important issues, such as the nature of the church, and ministry, what it has produced is significant. Willebrands helped initiate this dialogue in the late 1960s. And as he stated in his letter to the president of WARC in 1986, the commitment of the Catholic Church to dialogue and collaboration with the Reformed continues today.

IV. CONCLUSION

The Second Vatican Council was a great event for the Catholic Church, bringing renewal to it in a variety of ways. But Vatican II was also, in itself, an ecumenical event, in that it contributed to the broadening of the ecumenical movement and led to some new ecumenical developments. Cardinal Willebrands was a primary participant in some of these new developments.

The modern ecumenical movement has had to deal with the impact of centuries of separation among Christians characterized by long-standing mutual hostility, mutual misunderstandings resulting from lack of contact, and the unfortunate willingness to allow those conditions to continue century after century, generation after generation, with all the bitter memories attached. The modern ecumenical movement, beginning with the 1910 Edinburgh World Missionary Conference, opened new doors to separated Christians, and opened other doors after Vatican II. Nonetheless, establishing the new relationships necessary to reconstitute unity required trust. Cardinal Willebrands' effectiveness in ecumenical work included his ability to foster trust in building new ecumenical relationships.

Concerning the World Council of Churches, the Catholic Church had not been part of the Faith and Order and Life and Work movements which developed after Edinburgh 1910, and led to the creation of the WCC in 1948. Nor did Catholic authorities permit Catholics to attend the WCC's first (Amsterdam, 1948) or second (Evanston, 1954) general assemblies. It was only after John XXIII's call in 1959 for Vatican II and his establishment in 1960 of the Secretariat For Promoting Christian Unity, that the Vatican sent five observers to the WCC's third assembly (New Delhi, 1961), and more formal relations with the WCC began. Willebrands' informal work with the WCC in the previous decade, starting in 1952 with the Catholic Conference on Ecumenical Questions, giving attention to WCC theological concerns and providing Catholic theological perspectives on them, was deeply appreciated by the WCC. During that decade, as suggested above, Willebrands can be described "as an architect of trust", fashioning "bonds of trust, a circle of trust, between the CCEQ and the WCC, between himself and WCC general secretary Visser 't Hooft, between the CCEQ and Vatican Officials, between Catholic theologians and the bishops within the CCEQ". In the 1960s, when more formal relationships with the WCC could be developed through the SPCU, during and after Vatican II, there was already a level of trust on which to build because of the work that Willebrands (and others with him) had already done.

In relationships with Lutherans and Reformed, new contacts began during Vatican II. But mutual trust needed to be established after centuries of separation. With Lutherans, the conflicts between Luther's and church authorities in the sixteenth century left bitter memories. Willebrands took advantage of significant opportunities to promote trust. Towards the end of Vatican II, he helped organize a dialogue with the LWF which began in 1967. In his address to the 1970 LWF Assembly in Evian, Willebrands expressed a positive appreciation of Luther on the basis of contemporary research, and continued to do this afterwards, also making clear that he did not agree with everything Luther said, especially his attitude toward the papacy. At Evian he also pointed to the possibility of resolving issues, including differences over the doctrine of justification, which led to division in the sixteenth century. He thus encouraged the dialogue on this question which led eventually to the 1999 Catholic-Lutheran *Joint Declaration on the Doctrine of Justification*. In his efforts, the Cardinal helped to promote the mutual trust necessary for promoting ecumenical achievement.

With the Reformed, an important international dialogue developed with the World Alliance of Reformed Churches starting in 1970. It has been very effective, producing important reports. There were not as many opportunities to shape new relations with WARC as there were with Lutherans. Nonetheless In 1986, Willebrands used the occasion of the 450th anniversary of Calvin's coming to Geneva to write a letter to President of the WARC. He stressed that despite their divisions, "basic ties of faith and love bind us together", and that it "is our intention to deepen these ties". In light of today's great problems and deep social needs, he said, "our communities are called to collaboration and to common witness to the Gospel of Jesus Christ". He ended by stating that we "renew our commitment to the dialogue and collaboration which have been developing among us".

In these three ecumenical relationships, and in others not mentioned here, Willebrands fostered trust. This was reflected in the comments of W.A. Visser 't Hooft, WCC general secretary, who had worked with Willebrands since 1952. In his *Memoirs*, he recalls that he was glad when he heard in 1960 that Willebrands had been appointed secretary of the new Secretariat for Promoting Christian Unity. "He and I had been cooperating since 1952 and we had no difficulty in understanding each other. I liked his frankness and I appreciated that he was at once a progressive ecumenist looking for ways of making a real advance toward unity and a realist who knew that, in order to have results, an ecumenical policy, like every other policy, must be the art of the possible and not a castle built in the air"[60].

Willebrands was a trusted partner in the great work of promoting unity.

Seton Hall University   John A. Radano
400 South Orange Avenue
South Orange, New Jersey 01019
USA

---

60. Visser 't Hooft, *Memoirs* (n. 6), p. 329.

CARDINAL WILLEBRANDS AND THE RELATIONS BETWEEN ROME AND THE WORLD COUNCIL OF CHURCHES

In July of 1985, Cardinal Willebrands travelled to Geneva to attend the funeral of his old friend, Dr. Willem Adolf Visser 't Hooft, who had served as the General Secretary of the World Council of Churches (WCC) for its first twenty years, from 1948-1968. At the funeral, Willebrands recalled the day when he took Visser 't Hooft to St. Peter's Basilica to attend a session of the Second Vatican Council. They stopped at the back of the church, at a spot where they could see the entire assembly, and gazed for a long moment, during which Visser 't Hooft appeared to be profoundly moved. Finally, he simply pronounced the Latin words: "Nostra res hic agitur", (what is going on here concerns us [too]). During the funeral Willebrands went on to say: "I was not the first or the only Roman Catholic friend that Visser 't Hooft had, but right from the start our friendship had a special, unique quality. What I mean is that it went beyond a purely personal relationship; it was part of his, of our, ecumenical faith and hope"[1].

The friendship between these two great pioneers in the cause of Christian unity seems a valid point of departure for considering the overall relationship between the Catholic Church and the World Council of Churches. Perhaps only personal friendship can set up and guide such a complex and diversified relationship. Willebrands himself noted on several occasions that these two partners are not strictly speaking comparable; one is a federation or council of independent churches and ecclesial communities, each with its own autonomy and particular tradition somewhat tied to a specific geographical setting, while the other is a single church whose self-understanding and sense of pastoral responsibility are in a special way attuned to the universal, catholic unity of the whole body of Christ. The essential differences between the Roman

---

1. J. WILLEBRANDS, *Un pioniere dell'ecumenismo*, in *L'Osservatore romano* 125, no. 161 (15-16 luglio 1985) 4. In his *Memoirs*, London, SCM Press, 1973, p. 329, W.A. Visser 't Hooft wrote the following about Willebrands: "I was of course glad to hear that Father Jan Willebrands had been appointed as executive secretary of the new Secretariat for Unity. He and I had been co-operating since 1952 and we had no difficulty in understanding each other. I liked his frankness and I appreciated especially that he was at once a progressive ecumenist looking for ways of making a real advance towards unity and a realist who knew that, in order to have results, an ecumenical policy, like every other policy, must be the art of the possible and not a castle built in the air".

Catholic Church and the World Council would necessarily condition how they related to one another[2]. What was Willebrands' role in the establishment and unfolding of this relationship? Because it is so multi-dimensional and because Willebrands' contribution to it spans a lengthy period of nearly forty years, it is not easy to summarize the relevant data, which consists of many hundreds of letters, contacts, visits, meetings and celebrations. Nevertheless, I believe that it is possible to sketch out the main lines of Willebrands' role by trying to answer accurately, even if not exhaustively, two simple questions. First, what did he do to establish and sustain the relationship between the Catholic Church and the World Council of Churches? And, second, what do his writings reveal about how he understood this relationship?

I. JOHANNES CARDINAL WILLEBRANDS' ACTIVITIES RELATIVE
TO THE RCC-WCC RELATIONSHIP

Willebrands' efforts to bring about positive relations between the Catholic Church and the WCC go back to a time prior to Vatican II and prior even to the establishment of the Secretariat for Promoting Christian Unity on June 5, 1960. Perhaps it would be best to allow him to tell the story in his own words. I quote:

> The foundation and work of the World Council of Churches reminded the Catholic Church also of its ecumenical responsibility. [...] It was above all an exhortation to the hierarchy. But there were no contacts, no channels, to transmit the messages from one side to another. In 1948, a "monitum" from the Holy Office forbade participation by Catholics in ecumenical conferences, without the explicit permission of the Holy See. In 1949, an Instruction from the same Office, '*Ecclesia Catholica*', brought about a change: Catholic participation at ecumenical conferences at the local level became possible with the agreement of the local bishop, and prayer in common was allowed in principle[3].

Willebrands goes on to recount that this Instruction of 1949 led him and his friend Frans Thijssen to come up with the idea of establishing an informal association of Catholic Bishops, institutes and theologians

---

2. See J. WILLEBRANDS, *Origine e fine del "Gruppo misto del lavoro"*, in *L'Osservatore romano* 106, no. 45 (24 febbraio 1966) 1 and, especially, J. WILLEBRANDS, *Letter of Cardinal Willebrands, July 4, 1983* [written to the WCC General Secretary Philip Potter, accompanying the Fifth Report of the JWG], in The Secretariat for Promoting Christian Unity, *Information Service* [hereafter *IS*], 53 (1983/IV) 119-121, p. 120. Hereafter this letter will be referred to as *Letter on the Fifth JWG Report*.

3. J. WILLEBRANDS, *40 Years of the World Council of Churches*, in *IS* 70 (1989/II) 62.

interested in ecumenism, with the aim of allowing its members to share experiences and coordinate efforts, to communicate regularly with ecclesiastical authorities, and to establish contacts with representatives of other churches, especially with the newly founded World Council of Churches. In 1951 Willebrands and Thijssen toured various European countries, making contact with Catholics interested in ecumenism but also visiting Rome for the purpose of seeking advice and approval for such a new Catholic ecumenical organization[4]. They received encouragement from Fr. Augustin Bea, rector of the Pontifical Biblical Institute, but also consulted with other figures on the Roman scene such as professors Charles Boyer, Jan Witte and Sebastiaan Tromp of the Gregorian University and Cardinal Ottaviani, the head of the Holy Office[5]. The draft of their proposal for the Catholic Conference for Ecumenical Questions" (CCEQ) – as this new association would be called – quoted the 1949 Instruction, thus indicating the intention to act in line with Vatican directives[6]. In 1952, the first meeting of the CCEQ took place in Fribourg, Switzerland, and the group continued to meet about once every year under the guidance of Willebrands and a small steering committee[7]. Over the course of the next ten years some 170 different theologians and bishops participated in these meetings, many of whom were eventually to play an important role in the foundation and work of the Secretariat for Promoting Christian Unity and in the deliberations at Vatican II[8].

4. The Editor [= John A. Radano], *I. Some Aspects of the Catholic Church's Involvement in Ecumenism, 1951-1999: The Ecumenical Ministry of Johannes Cardinal Willebrands. A. 1951-1963, Johannes Willebrands and the Catholic Conference for Ecumenical Questions*, in *IS* 101 (1999/II-III) 62-69, p. 63. Hereafter, this work will be cited as J. RADANO, *Johannes Willebrands and the CCEQ*.

5. *Ibid.*; see also VISSER 'T HOOFT, *Memoirs* (n. 1), p. 323. According to very well documented study by M. VELATI, *Una difficile transizione: Il cattolicesimo tra unionismo ed ecumenismo (1952-1964)*, Bologna, Il Mulino, 1996, p. 28, the European tour by Willebrands and Thijssen began in August, 1951; after visiting Catholic ecumenists in Germany (pp. 29-31), France (pp. 31-34) and Belgium (pp. 34-35), they arrived in Rome ("la fossa dei leoni", pp. 35-44) in October of 1951 and visited there again six months later in April, 1952.

6. Cf. VELATI, *Una difficile transizione* (n. 5), p. 38. Willebrands himself gives a brief account of the work of the CCEQ in his *40 Years of the World Council of Churches* (n. 3), pp. 62-63. Cf. also E. FOUILLOUX, *Les catholiques et l'unité chrétienne du XIXme au XXme siècle: Itinéraires européens d'expression française*, Paris, Le Centurion, 1982, 711-717, and J.Y.H.A. JACOBS, *"Naar één oecumenische beweging" : De katholieke Conferentie voor Oecumenische Vragen: Een leerschool en gids*, Tilburg, Tilburg University Press, 1991.

7. Cf. J. RADANO, *Johannes Willebrands and the CCEQ* (n. 4), p. 64, especially n. 29.

8. The enumeration of "around 170" comes from VELATI, *Una difficile transizione* (n. 5), p. 166. The important role of the members of the CCEQ in the eventual work of

Various proposals had been considered for the activities of this new association, but it seemed prudent to begin with the relatively modest role of providing Catholic theological reflection on themes that were being discussed generally within the ecumenical movement. The first topic discussed by the CCEQ was the theme chosen for the Second Assembly of the World Council of Churches, to be held in Evanston, Indiana, USA, in 1954: "Christ the Hope of the World". The Catholic discussions resulted in a paper on this theme which was made available to the delegates at the 1954 WCC assembly and acknowledged by its general secretary in his subsequently published *Report*[9]. Evanston provided the occasion for the first meeting between Willebrands and Visser 't Hooft, during which they discussed the possibility of Catholic observers at that up-coming assembly, an eventuality which never came to pass[10]. But this first contact led Willebrands to consult the WCC general secretary concerning further themes that the CCEQ might usefully pursue, which put on the conference's agenda such topics as "The Lordship of Christ", "Religious Freedom" and "Mission", this latter of special relevance for the Third Assembly of the WCC to be held in New Delhi in 1961 at which the International Missionary Council would be integrated into the WCC[11]. One of the distinctive features of these Catholic studies was their tendency to highlight the role of the Church with regard to the topic under consideration, such as Christian hope or Christ's Lordship. Thus a heightened sensitivity to ecclesiology seemed to be the special contribution that Catholics brought to reflection within World Council circles[12].

While there were certainly other ecumenical initiatives within the Catholic Church during the 1950s, the most direct Catholic contact with other Christian communities was the approved but unofficial activity of the Catholic Conference for Ecumenical Questions. This activity was directed almost entirely toward the World Council of Churches, and Johannes Willebrands was its principal facilitator. As just noted, one issue under consideration was the possible presence of Catholic observers

---

the Secretariat for Promoting Christian Unity, along with many of their names, is outlined by RADANO, *Johannes Willebrands and the CCEQ* (n. 4), pp. 64-69.

9. See RADANO, *Johannes Willebrands and the CCEQ* (n. 4), p. 65, and VISSER 'T HOOFT, *Memoirs* (n. 1), p. 323. The Catholic paper on "Christ the Hope of the World" was drafted by Yves Congar and published in *Istina* 2 (1954) 132-150, as reported by VELATI, *Una transizione difficile* (n. 5), p. 65.

10. That this was the first meeting between Willebrands and Visser 't Hooft and that Catholic attendance at Evanston was not approved by the local ordinary, Cardinal Stritch, see VELATI, *Una transizione difficile* (n. 5), pp. 68-72.

11. Cf. *ibid.*, pp. 73-75; 104-105; 121-122.

12. Cf. *ibid.*, pp. 55-61 and p. 90.

at World Council events. While the plans for observers at the Evanston Assembly did not come to fruition, five years later Johannes Willebrands and the French Dominican Christophe Dumont attended the WCC Central Committee meeting at Rhodes in August 1959 as observers, with the approval of the Vatican[13]. This occasioned the notorious "Rhodes incident" which, in hindsight, turned out to be a *felix culpa*, in that it contributed to the establishment of the Vatican's official organ for ecumenical relations – the Secretariat for Promoting Christian Unity[14]. At Rhodes, Dumont and Willebrands met for dinner with what turned out to be, to them, a surprisingly large number of Orthodox bishops and theologians in order to discuss informally the possibilities for continuing dialogue between representatives of the two churches. Now this particular WCC central committee meeting was the very first to be held in a predominantly Orthodox environment; moreover, it occurred shortly before a number of Orthodox churches planned to enter the WCC as full members during the General Assembly to be held in New Delhi two years later (1961). In light of these facts, the dinner discussion between the two Catholic observers and the Orthodox gave the appearance to the other members of the central committee of the WCC, especially to its general secretary Visser 't Hooft, that the Catholic Church had come in the guise of invited guests for the hidden purpose of weaning the orthodox away from the World Council. Subsequent reports in the press, even in *L'Osservatore Romano*, not only did not clear up the misunderstanding but even seemed to confirm this suspicion[15]. In the aftermath of the "Rhodes incident" Willebrands played a crucial role in explaining to WCC leaders that the Catholic Church had no intention to "divide and

---

13. Cf. *ibid.*, p. 106.

14. On this incident, see the well documented account in Chapter Four of VELATI's *Una difficile transizione* (n. 5), pp. 101-135, which provides further bibliography in its notes. A fascinating first-hand account is the notebook diary of Willebrands, recently published, T. SALEMINK (ed.), *"You Will Be Called Repairer of the Breach" : The Diary of J.G.M. Willebrands 1958-1961*, Leuven, Peeters, 2009; for the "Rhodes incident" see pages 85-99 of the section entitled *Notebook One: August 17-September 26, 1959*. Hereafter this work will be referred to as *The Diary*.

15. Cf. the account by VISSER 'T HOOFT in *Memoirs* (n. 1), pp. 327-328, and that by Willebrands mentioned above in note 14. An excellent summary of this event is provided by T. SALEMINK in his *Introduction* to *The Diary* (n. 14), pp. 8-12. Particularly interesting is the contrast Salemink points out between the accounts here indicated. That of Willebrands, written at the time of the Rhodes meeting, registers some of the angry feelings expressed by members of the WCC; the version by Visser 't Hooft, written some years later, is more serene, displaying perhaps that mellowing that can come with the passage of time.

conquer" by tempting the Orthodox away from the WCC[16]. He was also instrumental in interpreting to Vatican officials the true meaning of initiatives of the WCC at the time, such as Visser 't Hooft's article criticizing the idea of a "super-church" or the plan to integrate the International Missionary Council into the WCC at New Delhi. Both of these had been misinterpreted as suggesting a certain anti-catholic sentiment in the WCC, even by such an ecumenically sympathetic figure as Cardinal Bea[17]. The actual establishment of the Secretariat for Promoting Christian Unity was due to a range of factors, including its foreseen necessity in facilitating the presence of non-Catholic observers at Vatican II. But among those factors, the need for an official agency that could speak clearly and authoritatively about Catholic ecumenical intentions was a significant motive[18]. This need was made glaringly evident by the "Rhodes incident" and, again, Willebrands was at the center of that event.

After the establishment of the Secretariat for Promoting Christian Unity, the good personal relations between Willebrands and various members of the WCC made it possible for the Catholic Church to receive advice concerning the best way of inviting observers to Vatican II and coming up with a *modus operandi* for their participation at the council. In addition, even before the promulgation of the Decree on Ecumenism, *Unitatis redintegratio*, on November 21, 1964, representatives of the Secretariat and of the WCC had begun to look beyond the council to explore the possibilities for their continued relationship in its aftermath. Discussion had proceeded to the point that the WCC central committee meeting in Enugu, Nigeria, of January 1965, proposed the establishment of a Joint Working Group between the Roman Catholic Church and the World Council of Churches, almost a year before the close of Vatican II, and Cardinal Bea flew to Geneva to visit the WCC in February, 1965, to accept the proposal[19]. The first meeting of the Joint Working Group took place in May 1965, at the Ecumenical Institute in Bossey, near Geneva, under the co-chairmanship of the two Dutchmen, Visser 't Hooft, General Secretary of the WCC, and the newly consecrated Bishop

---

16. Cf. VELATI, *Una transizione difficile* (n. 5), pp. 116-120. VISSER 'T HOOFT, *Memoirs* (n. 1), p. 328, wrote that "Father Willebrands helped greatly to restore the good relations by publishing a very objective account of the so-called 'Rhodes incident'".

17. Cf. VELATI, *Una transizione difficile* (n. 5), p. 95.

18. This point is argued convincingly by SALEMINK, *Introduction* (n. 15), pp. 11-12.

19. Cf. J. WILLEBRANDS, *Cardinal Augustin Bea: His Contribution to the Ecumenical Movement and to Religious Liberty*, in *IS* 101 (1999/II-III) 76; WILLEBRANDS, *Origine e fine del "Gruppo misto del lavoro"* (n. 2), p. 1; and J. WILLEBRANDS, *Introduction*, in A. BEA – W.A. VISSER 'T HOOFT, *Peace among Christians*, New York, Herder & Herder, 1967, 24-26.

Willebrands, Secretary of the SPCU. Thomas Stransky outlined its original mandate in the following three points: 1) the JWG was to be a consultative forum, initiating, evaluating and sustaining collaboration between the WCC and the RCC and reporting to the competent authorities in the parent bodies; 2) it was to be flexible, keeping "new structures to a minimum while concentrating on ad hoc initiatives"; and 3) it was not to limit its work to the administrative aspects of collaboration but also prayerfully to discern the will of God in the contemporary ecumenical situation and to offer its own reflections in studies[20].

The very first report of the JWG, from February, 1966, described the wide range of possible collaboration between the Catholic Church and the WCC – including the theological work of the Faith and Order Commission, common prayer for Christian unity, mission and evangelization, the relation of Church and society, laity, women, charitable-social-emergency-development assistance, common translations of the Bible, agreement on a common date for the celebration of Easter, liturgical renewal, ecumenical formation, the doctrine and practice of baptism, mixed marriages, religious freedom, proselytism and youth[21].

Willebrands noted that, at this initial stage, the JWG saw its work as provisional. Once its evaluations and proposals had been made, the competent authorities could decide on their implementation and the working group itself, having fulfilled its task, could pass out of existence[22]. As things turned out, the JWG was able to celebrate its 40th anniversary in 2005 and the sequence of the eight reports that it has so far issued serve as a history of the ever developing and multidimensional relation between the Catholic Church and the World Council of Churches. In addition to overseeing and fostering the wide range of contacts and collaboration between the two partners, the JWG has also produced a series of important study documents on themes, such as, ecumenical dialogue and its reception (1967 and 2004), common witness and proselytism (1971 and 1995), "Catholicity and Apostolicity" (1971), "The Church: Local and Universal" (1990), "The Hierarchy of Truths" (1990), ecumenical dialogue on moral issues (1995), the ecclesiological and ecumenical implications of a common baptism (2004), and Roman Catholic participation in national and regional councils of churches (2004).

20. Cf. T. STRANSKY, *The History of the RCC/WCC Joint Working Group*, in *IS* 97 (1998/I-II) 76.

21. See the *First Official Report of the Joint Working Group between the Roman Catholic Church and the World Council of Churches*, in *IS* 1 (1967/I) 18-22.

22. WILLEBRANDS, *Origine e fine del "Gruppo misto del lavoro"* (n. 2), p. 1.

Cardinal Willebrands stepped down as co-chairman of the Joint Working Group in 1969, at its first meeting after he had been named the President of the Secretariat for Promoting Christian Unity in succession to Cardinal Bea[23]. In his twenty years as President of that Vatican dicastery, Willebrands continued to foster the relation between the Catholic Church and the World Council of Churches. He regularly reviewed the activities of the Joint Working Group during the many plenary meetings of the Pontifical Council for Unity over which he presided, in particular, writing letters to the General Secretaries of the WCC with personal reflections about the 4th and 5th Reports of the Joint Working Group, which appeared during his tenure as President[24]. He arranged for Philip Potter who, prior to becoming General Secretary of the WCC, had led its "Commission on World Mission and Evangelization" to speak to the Synod of Bishops in 1974 dedicated to the theme of evangelization[25] and later organized other World Council participation at other Catholic synods of bishops, most notably that in 1985 on the 20th anniversary of the conclusion of Vatican II[26]. He delivered important addresses on the occasion of significant World Council Anniversaries: the 25th of its foundation in 1973, the 50th of the foundation of the Life and Work movement in 1975 and the 40th of Amsterdam Assembly in 1988[27].

His fostering of the relation between the Catholic Church and the WCC also included many fraternal visits, perhaps the most important being the two papal visits he organized to the World Council in Geneva by Paul VI in 1969 and by John Paul II fifteen years later in 1984[28].

During the second of these, together with the Rev. Dr. Philip Potter, then Secretary General of the WCC, Willebrands issued a joint declaration that both sides fully shared the goal of "visibile unity in one faith and in one Eucharistic communion expressed in worship and in common

23. Cf. *IS* 11 (1970/III) 19.

24. Cf. J. WILLEBRANDS, *Appendix I*, to the *Fourth Official Report of the Joint Working Group (RCC/WCC)* [= a Letter addressed to Dr. Philip Potter, General Secretary WCC, Nov. 21, 1975] in *IS* 30 (1976/I) 1; and *Letter on the Fifth JWG Report* (n. 2), pp. 119-121. Hereafter the letter of Nov. 21, 1975 will be referred to as *Letter on the Fourth JWG Report*.

25. Cf. *Dr. Philip Potter at the Synod of Bishops in Rome*, in *IS* 25 (1974/III) 1-7.

26. Cf. *IS* 60 (1986/I-II) 19-22 on ecumenical aspects of the extraordinary synod of 1985 at which ten non-Catholics were present as invited observers.

27. J. WILLEBRANDS, *Twenty-five Years of the World Council of Churches, 1948-1973*, in *IS* 22 (1973/IV) 26-27; J. WILLEBRANDS, *Addresses for the Celebration of the fiftieth Anniversary of the Stockholm Conference on "Life and Work"* in *IS* 28 (1975/III) 1-9; WILLEBRANDS, *40 Years of the World Council of Churches* (n. 3), pp. 61-65.

28. The 1969 visit to the WCC by Paul VI is presented in *IS* 8 (1969/I) 3-6; the 1984 visit of John Paul II is documented in *IS* 56 (1984/IV) 114-115.

life in Christ"[29]. They recalled many of the positive results of the collaboration between the two partners, especially the doctrinal convergence represented by the Faith and Order text on *Baptism, Eucharist and Ministry* (*BEM*), which had been completed only two years earlier. They expressed confidence that the Joint Working Group would continue to serve the two partners in making progress toward greater unity, common witness, social collaboration and ecumenical formation at all levels.

Thus we can conclude that the principal activities of Cardinal Willebrands in bringing to life and sustaining the rich, multidimensional relationship between Rome and the World Council of Churches unfolded in three phases: first, an informal phase with the "Catholic Conference for Ecumenical Questions" (1952-1960); second, a conciliar phase leading to the establishment and initial activity of the Joint Working Group (1960-1969); and, third, a phase of interventions in the role of President of the Pontifical Council for Promoting Christian Unity (1969-1989). Each phase was marked by many and various initiatives on his part to foster, guide and promote this relationship. This is what one sees from the outside. But fortunately we also have access through his writings to what he thought about the World Council and about the Catholic Church's relation to it. To this I will now briefly turn.

II. JOHANNES WILLEBRANDS' REFLECTION ABOUT THE WCC AND CATHOLIC RELATIONS WITH IT

Willebrands once called the foundation of the World Council of Churches "a turning point in the history of the Church"[30]. It is not surprising, therefore, that he attached great significance to the Catholic Church's relation to it. During the 1977 Synod of Bishops, Willebrands noted that "One of the Catholic Church's most important ecumenical undertakings is its relationship to the World Council of Churches"[31]. He was convinced of the importance of the origins of any movement or institution. On the occasion of the 40th anniversary of the WCC he stated: "The way in which something comes into being determines its later development. This is even more so if in this birth the Spirit is seen

---

29. For this quotation and the material which follows in this paragraph, see the *Common Declaration with the WCC*, in *IS* 55 (1984/II-III) 42-43.

30. WILLEBRANDS, *Twenty-five Years of the World Council of Churches, 1948-1973* (n. 27), p. 26.

31. J. WILLEBRANDS, *The Activity of the Secretariat for the Promotion of Christian Unity*, in *IS* 36 (1978/I) 8.

to be at work"[32]. Willebrands recognized the basic roots of the World
Council of Churches in three ecumenical impulses: the missionary movement of the Edinburgh Conference of 1910, the Life and Work movement
to promote justice and peace beginning at Stockholm in 1925, and the
Faith and Order movement to seek doctrinal and ecclesial unity initiated
at Lausanne in 1927. Each of these three constitutes a basis for collaboration between the Catholic Church and the World Council. Regarding
mission, Willebrands writes:

> It is often said that unity is not in itself the object of the ecumenical move-
> ment, but that it is at the service of the mission of the Church. [...] Howe-
> ver, there is an indissoluble relationship between mission and unity. The
> church's mission is to make known the Father through the knowledge of
> Christ, to establish in faith and love the communion of man with God,
> through Christ, and thus to unite among themselves men who share in the
> Love that unites the Father and Son. This unity of Christians in faith and
> love becomes for the world the sign *par excellence* of the authenticity of
> the mission of Jesus and of his Gospel. The mission leads to unity, and unity
> is the sign of the authenticity of the mission. One can well see how the
> missionary drive, or rather the conviction of the Catholic Church that she
> is missionary by nature, as also the concern for justice and peace in the
> world, commit her to the ecumenical movement and create a basis for
> collaboration with the World Council of churches[33].

Regarding collaboration in the area of the promotion of justice and
peace, he noted on the occasion of the 50th anniversary of the Life and
Work movement:

> Christian unity is considered as a unity in life and proclamation. Unity does
> not exist for its own sake. It must be transformed into Christian action in
> the various domains of human life (cfr. *A History of the Ecumenical Move-
> ment*, edited by Ruth Rouse and Stephen Charles Neill, London, 1967,
> p. 527). [...] it was not liberalism or indifferentism which [Nathan Söder-
> blom and the other founders of the "Life and Work" movement] sought and
> promoted, but the realization of the Kingdom of God through the unity of
> all Christians in the Church of Christ, one in soul and body[34].

Finally, the plenary meeting of the Secretariat for Promoting Christian
Unity of 1983, the first after the publication of what was to become one
of the most important ecumenical documents yet produced, Faith and
Order's text on *Baptism, Eucharist and Ministry*, gave Willebrands the

---

32. WILLEBRANDS, *40 Years of the World Council of Churches* (n. 3), p. 63.
33. WILLEBRANDS, *Twenty-five Years of the World Council of Churches, 1948-1973*
(n. 27), p. 27.
34. J. WILLEBRANDS, *Christian Life and Work 50 Years after Stockholm 1925*, in *IS* 28
(1975/III) 8-9.

occasion to underline how important was Catholic involvement in the theological work of the WCC. After sketching out the long process of maturation that produced *BEM*, he added:

> This historic summary seemed to me necessary not to make us complacent about the ground covered but to acknowledge the work of the Holy Spirit and give thanks for it. It was useful too to realize the complexity of the task and the need for the Catholic Church through her theologians to take a full part in this common search for unity. [...] This Secretariat, and I think I can say the Catholic Church, observes with closest attention and not without anxieties recently, what importance is given to Faith and Order in the World Council of Churches, and what is the role played by that commission. On this importance and this role will depend largely, I think, the success of the Council in achieving its aim which is to call the Churches to unity (Constitution, art. 3). In saying this I have no wish to belittle the need for the Council's other activities. ... but we regard them as primarily directed towards the unity we seek, while at the same time they witness to an already existing unity. Orthodoxy and orthopraxis are inseparable and they interact. [...] The function of Faith and Order is more than ever relevant and decisive in this regard[35].

Willebrands was keenly aware that the ongoing relationship of the Catholic Church to the World Council of Churches in the areas of mission, social advocacy and theological dialogue unfolds within the context of personal relationships which are informed by the "spiritual ecumenism" of prayer and conversion. The joint work for the celebration of the octave of prayer for unity is an eloquent symbol of this. Willebrands insisted that the relationship between the Catholic Church and the World Council was not merely a matter of collaboration. Instead, the expression "fraternal solidarity", which Paul VI used in his message to the WCC General Assembly at Nairobi, would do more justice to the nature of this relation[36]. According to Willebrands, that expression carries the positive connotation of shared reflection and prayer inspired by Jesus' desire that "all may be one". "Fraternal solidarity" suggests the common vocation to full communion in faith and love and connotes a profound, spiritual relation "in the hope that it may lead us to a common understanding of the Church as 'a lasting and sure seed of unity, hope and salvation for the whole human race, (...) the sacrament of this saving unity' (LG 9)"[37].

---

35. J. WILLEBRANDS, *The Role of Faith and Order: Excerpt from the Cardinal President's Opening Address at the Plenary Meeting of the Secretariat*, in *IS* 101 (1999/II-III) 129; originally printed in *IS* 51 (1983/I-II) 15.

36. Cf. T. STRANSKY, *The History of the RCC/WCC Joint Working Group*, p. 79; cf. Paul VI, *Message to the Nairobi Assembly of the WCC, Nov. 20, 1975*, in *IS* 30 (1976/I) 1.

37. WILLEBRANDS, *Letter on the Fifth JWG Report* (n. 2), pp. 119-120.

Of course there were special challenges woven into this relationship between Rome and the WCC and Willebrands was not one to gloss over such difficulties[38]. Sometimes common initiatives had to be abandoned, as in the case of SODEPAX[39]. Even Catholic membership in the World Council found no easy solution, as Willebrands wrote: "The question of the Catholic Church's eventual membership in the World Council of Churches was initially studied some years ago, but an affirmative solution was not reached, not only because of differences in structure and in ways of working, but also because of problems of a pastoral nature. However, this decision has helped to clarify the extent and style of mutual relations in the immediate future"[40]. In fact, Willebrands later pointed out that, according to the General Secretary of the WCC himself, its relationship with the Catholic Church was more substantial than it was with many of its member churches[41]. The overcoming of the major difficulty that had surfaced in the Rhodes incident (1959), when some World Council leaders perceived Catholic bilateral dialogues as a potential threat to the multilateral work of the WCC, seems to be an important, if largely unrecognized, achievement of Catholic relations to the WCC. The bilateral forums conducted periodically under the auspices of the Faith and Order Commission witness to what is now the widely shared conviction of the compatibility of bilateral and multilateral ecumenical relations[42]. In addition, the extension of multilateral ecumenism below the international level of the World Council of Churches to regional,

38. Cf. WILLEBRANDS, *Twenty-five Years of the World Council of Churches, 1948-1973* (n. 27), p. 27; and *Letter on the Fourth JWG Report* (n. 24), p. 25.

39. Cf. T. STRANSKY, *Sodepax*, in N. LOSSKY, *et al.* (eds.), *Dictionary of the Ecumenical Movement*, Geneva, WCC Publications, ²2002, 1055-1056; and *Sodepax 4 Sept 1980*, in *IS* 44 (1980/III-IV) 135-137.

40. WILLEBRANDS, *The Activity of Secretariat for the Promotion of Christian Unity* (n. 31), p. 8. He addressed the question of the membership of the Catholic Church in the World Council of Churches on several occasions. Cf. paragraph 7 of J. WILLEBRANDS, *Opening Address of his Eminence Cardinal John Willebrands*, in *IS* 9 (1970/I) 7; his *Letter on the Fourth JWG Report* (n. 24), p. 25; and his *Letter on the Fifth JWG Report* (n. 2), p. 119. In his address on the 40th anniversary of the WCC (1988), Willebrands noted that Catholic membership in the WCC would not have much practical importance, since there are already good channels for working together, but that in principle whatever decision taken about membership needs to avoid any suggestion of isolating the Catholic Church from the overall ecumenical movement; WILLEBRANDS, *40 Years of the World Council of Churches* (n. 3), p. 64.

41. Cf. WILLEBRANDS' *Letter on the Fifth JWG Report* (n. 2), p. 119, where he writes: "... the relations of the Roman Catholic Church with the World Council of Churches have, in your own words, 'been far more intense than with many member churches' (Central Committee 1976 in *Ecumenical Review*, XXVIII n. 4, p. 401)". Willebrands is here referring to a report by Philip Potter.

42. Cf. *ibid.*, p. 119.

national and local settings has also been the object of reflection by the Joint Working Group in its studies on councils of churches[43].

At the end of the day, when Johannes Willebrands thought about the World Council of Churches and about the relation of the Catholic Church to it, he thought about ecclesiology. In my opinion, some of the happiest pages of the recently published diary of Willebrands are those which recall the concentrated course he offered at the World Council's ecumenical institute at Bossey, October 27-November 11, 1958, on the topic of Christ and the Church[44]. He was the first Catholic to teach at Bossey (for years now a Catholic has been part of the staff at that institution). The diary shows that he worked intensely in preparing his lectures, even having had the luxury of spending a whole day with Yves Congar, to review the principal points of Catholic ecclesiology[45]! Willebrands' course was very well received; some thought his lectures about the Church were beautiful but not very typical for a Catholic[46]. His joy at getting to know Nikos Nissiotis and other World Council figures at that time shines through his journal entries. A couple of years later, in a talk for the occasion of a special award by the Atonement friars and sisters to Charles Boyer in 1961, Willebrands revealed his sentiments about the importance of ecclesiology in the whole project of the World Council of Churches, when he wrote: "[...] I think it is not quite accurate to say that the World Council of Churches is ecclesiologically neutral. Without any doubt the World Council of Churches is not indifferent whether the cause of unity of all Christians, and in the first place of their own members, progresses or not; and it has developed definite ideas on the means and the methods by which it promotes the work of unity"[47]. Decades later, when he was nearly 80 years old and close to retiring as president of the Pontifical Council for Promoting Christian Unity he would write words

43. The first two joint consultations on Catholic participation in councils of churches by the JWG took place in 1982 and 1986, when Willebrands was still President of the SPCU; cf. the report for the 40th Anniversary of the JWG held in 2005 and published in *IS* 120 (2005/IV) 165-179, with reference to these consultations on p. 175. One of the most recent JWG studies is entitled *"Inspired by the same vision": Roman Catholic Participation in National and Regional Councils of Churches*, in *IS* 117 (2004/IV) 214-230.

44. Cf. SALEMINK, *Introduction* (n. 15), p. 7. The very first page of Willebrands' diary mentions the course he would give at Bossey and subsequent entries show that he prepared very assiduously for his lectures throughout September and October of 1958.

45. Cf. *The Diary* (n. 14), p. 36, at its entry for October 19, 1958, which refers to this session with Congar.

46. Cf. *The Diary* (n. 14), p. 40, at its entry for November 5, 1958, where Willebrands reports responding to the comment: "c'est très beau, mais ce n'est pas typique".

47. J. WILLEBRANDS, *Catholic Ecumenism*, in *Problems before Unity*, Baltimore, MD – Dublin, Helicon, 1962, p. 2.

that re-echoed his first insights about the importance of ecclesiology for the WCC: "In my opinion the World Council of Churches [needs] to study once again the nature and meaning of what the Church is, the meaning of the 'communio' (*koinonia*) between the Churches, both in the communion of faith and sacraments and in the institution as it has evolved in the theological discussion. What criteria must be met in order to be called Church of Christ? [...] For the World Council of Churches it is of great importance to come to a common understanding of what it means to be Church, and what the one Church should be"[48]. Recently, in October, 2009, the Faith and Order Commission of the World Council of Churches, with substantial participation by Catholics, held its plenary meeting at the Orthodox Academy of Crete, considering the three major studies being pursued at the present time by the commission: "The Nature and Mission of the Church", "Sources of Authority in the Church, with special reference to the patristic literature" and "Moral Discernment in the Church". Over 80% of the members of the Plenary Commission were new to it, and they expressed much enthusiasm in their contributions to advance the work on these three issues. I cannot help feeling that Johannes Willebrands looked down on that event with joy and hope.

CONCLUSION

In his opening address to the first plenary meeting of the Secretariat for Promoting Christian Unity during which he presided as president, Cardinal Willebrands paid homage to his predecessor Cardinal Bea. "The evening before his death", he recalled, "all the members of the staff met at the Church of Santa Susanna and celebrated the Eucharist according to his intentions. The last words he said to me were: 'Ich bin unendlich dankbar' (I am infinitely grateful)". With characteristic modesty, Willebrands added: "By means of these words he opened his whole soul to God for what he had been able to give and receive as President of the Secretariat"[49]. While that no doubt is true, perhaps I can be forgiven for suggesting an additional meaning to this final message of the dying Cardinal Bea. He was after all saying goodbye to a friend who had been his closest collaborator in the cause of Christian unity for many years and who had spent himself tirelessly in that effort. I think that Bea was also

48. WILLEBRANDS, *40 Years of the World Council of Churches* (n. 3), pp. 64-65.
49. WILLEBRANDS, *Opening Address of his Eminence Cardinal John Willebrands* (n. 40), p. 5.

saying that he was infinitely grateful to Willebrands himself, for all that he had done and was doing for Christian unity. When we realize how crucial was his role in establishing, evaluating, guiding and sustaining the relationship between the Catholic Church and the World Council of Churches we too might make Cardinal Bea's words to Willebrands our own: "Wir sind unendlich dankbar".

Collegio San Lorenzo   William HENN
C.P. 18382
Circonvallazione Occidentale 6850
I-00163 Roma
Italy

THE SIGNIFICANCE OF CARDINAL WILLEBRANDS' ECUMENICAL WORK FOR THE PROTESTANT CHURCHES

I. PREFACE: MY RELATIONS TO CATHOLIC ECUMENISM

My personal contacts and experiences with the new Roman Catholic ecumenical involvement after 1960 were very much connected with the person and work of Msgr. and later Johannes Cardinal Willebrands. These personal contacts and experiences included my work as assistant to Professor Edmund Schlink, one of the leading observers at the Second Vatican Council; my time at the Institute for Ecumenical Research in Strasbourg in the 1970s, an institution especially founded by the Lutheran World Federation (LWF) with the purpose to study the ecumenical developments of the Catholic Church; the long period serving as a World Council of Churches (WCC) observer on the Anglican-Roman Catholic International Commission from 1972 to 1995; my main professional commitment from 1984 until 1995 as Director of the WCC's Commission on Faith and Order with its official membership of Roman Catholic theologians and my many contacts with the Secretariat for Promoting Christian Unity (SPCU); I also was during that time a member of the Joint Working Group (JWG) between the Catholic Church and the WCC; furthermore I represented during these years the WCC on the Conference of Secretaries of Christian World Communion (CWCs).

All this provided me with many occasions to be in regular and intensive contact and cooperation with the Secretariat and since 1988 the Pontifical Council for Promoting Christian Unity (PCPCU). On several occasions I encountered Cardinal Willebrands and was impressed by his warm, reflective personality, but also by his realistic and down-to-earth attitudes when, for example, he explained to me a wooden board on the wall of his office that was holding a half dozen or more tobacco pipes for the important purpose, as he said, to let them cool down after use. The theme of my paper, thus, is closely related to my own memories.

After surveying the immense material connected with Willebrands' work, it will only be possible to present some selected glimpses on his significance for the Protestant churches. Naturally this is described in the broader context of his ecumenical involvement and with a certain emphasis on relations with my own Lutheran tribe.

II. WILLEBRANDS' SIGNIFICANCE FOR PROTESTANTISM

Msgr. Johannes Willebrands entered officially the wider ecumenical scene in 1960 at a highly fortunate moment. It was the time and atmosphere marked by the preparation of the ecumenical breakthrough of the Catholic Church enabled and signified by Vatican II. And on the personal level, one of his most important ecumenical partners was a Dutch fellow-countryman: Dr. Willem Visser 't Hooft. Willebrands and Visser 't Hooft could not only converse in their mother tongue, they were also both marked by the lively Dutch Catholic-Protestant ecclesiastical and ecumenical landscape, and the Dutch heritage of mutual tolerance. United by their love of cigars and pipes, they considered forms of future ecumenical relationships.

1. *A Main Architect of Catholic Ecumenism*

A few years later, in the context of the Second Vatican Council, Willebrands became one of the main architects (as Cardinal Kasper said at Willebrands' funeral) and artisans of the Catholic entry into the ecumenical movement and of official Catholic ecumenical engagement. Together with Cardinal Bea and later Pope John Paul II he symbolized the emerging new open ecumenical spirit of his Church. In a way he became a kind of "ecumenical face" of the Catholic Church. Representing this historical breakthrough and graced by his warm personality, radiating trust and confidence, he helped to overcome Protestant suspicions of Catholic "tricks and policies" to lure Protestants back to Rome – a suspicion, that especially in Germany is still partly alive and that explains in part the resistance to the 1999 signing of the *Joint Declaration on the Doctrine of Justification*.

2. *Elements of Willebrands' Thinking That Were Appealing to Protestants*

There were several emphases in Willebrands' thinking and activities that were especially appealing to Protestant theological concerns. Among them were, first, his basic and thoroughgoing reliance on biblical references and arguments. In a letter to the World Catholic Federation for the Biblical Apostolate (1989) Willebrands affirmed: "The Bible which constitutes the core of the apostolic activity occupies the central place in the renewal of the ecclesial life, in the mission, in catechesis, in ministerial services, and the celebration of the liturgy"[1]. Here were clear

---

1. The PONTIFICAL COUNCIL FOR PROMOTING CHRISTIAN UNITY, *Information Service* [= *IS*] 70 (1989) 69.

foundations and continuous points of reference of his reflection, reports, and statements. His concern for biblical grounding of theological as well as ecumenical reasoning was also manifested by his close relations to the United Bible Societies[2]. Protestants, naturally, liked this. Second, another emphasis was directed to the place and role of the laity in the Church. In a long presentation at the 1987 Synod of Bishops, Willebrands underlined, with many biblical references, the high calling and the dignity of the laity. "We will only give the laity the place that is truly theirs if we put aside a juridical perspective which is based too one-sidedly on the difference between clergy and laity, and discover that we are dealing with 'Christus in membris suis'"[3]. He was obviously modifying the frequent perspective of the essential distinction between the two groups.

A third element in Willebrands' theological and ecumenical reflection that was appealing especially to the Reformation tradition was his thoroughgoing accentuation of the importance and seriousness of theological reasoning in ecumenical encounters. Accordingly, he stated in "40 Years of the World Council of Churches" (1988): "Theology has an irreplaceable service to render to the ecumenical movement"[4]. In his *Prolusio* to the plenary meeting of the Secretariat in 1981 Willebrands stressed that the "insistence on doctrine denotes a clearer perception of the primal need for agreement in faith, of a common understanding of the apostolic faith so that we can bear witness together in the world of today..."[5]. Theological convergences had to be celebrated, but differences also had to be clearly stated and discussed. Not long after Willebrands had retired as President Emeritus of the PCPCU he presented a forceful plea for "The Place of Theology in the Ecumenical Movement" in 1990 in Toronto[6].

However, the social-ethical tasks were not neglected by Willebrands, who underlined in his reflection on "40 Years of the World Council of Churches" (1988): "But the theological contribution is not the only

2. Cf. e.g. his address on the occasion of the publication of the revised "Guidelines for Interconfessional Cooperation in Translating the Bible" of 1987, in *IS* 101 (1999) 129-130.
3. *IS* 65 (1987) 109-111.
4. *IS* 70 (1989) 65.
5. *IS* 47 (1981) 115.
6. Here he also criticised in an ironical way "theological syncretism" in the form of "a little Palamism plus a little Thomism plus a little Hooker plus a little Calvin plus a little Bonhoeffer does not make up theological truth. (...) What we have to do is discover whether another tradition's understanding of the Truth which our own community should try to translate into its way of thinking. ... It is clear then that ecumenism not only needs theology but cannot find its way without a foundation in theology". *IS* 101 (1999) 153.

one. Christians must work together. The basis for such cooperation was
set out by Nathan Söderblom and his work in 'Life and Work'"[7]. And
in his presentation in Stockholm, September 1975, on the occasion of
the fiftieth anniversary of the Conference on Life and Work (Stockholm, 1925) he asked: "The global challenge should bring us together
in approaching the problems and sufferings of the world. (...) Do we
respond to the global challenge which the world puts to all Christians
and their churches?"[8]. Connected with the theological emphasis in his
thinking was, fourth, his stress on ecumenical formation which "is a
challenge for all who have a specific ecumenical responsibility. We
have tended to take too much for granted that there is a sound knowledge of the ecumenical movement, of its history and of the principles
which were at stake. It is necessary that the topic of ecumenical formation be approached in terms of theological content as well as of peda-
gogical process and method"[9]. Mutual cooperation is good, but it must
be accompanied by a teaching on and understanding of the different
church traditions and their fundamental theological and spiritual convictions. Only on the basis of a solid mutual knowledge will an interconfessional dialogue lead to new steps and perspectives of *aggiornamento*[10]. Fifth, for Protestant ecumenical hopes it was important and
encouraging that Willebrands referred in a letter to Philip Potter of
1975 to "one of the important insights of the ecumenical movement
that there is an "already existing communion among Christians" that
"is as yet incomplete"[11], or when he referred at the World Synod of
Bishops of 1983 to other Christians and their communities that "are in
ecclesial communion with us, a communion that is real even though
imperfect"[12] and expressing such partial communion with similar
formulations[13].

---

7. *IS* 70 (1989) 65.
8. *IS* 28 (1975) 3.
9. *IS* 53 (1983) 121: Letter to Philip Potter, 1983.
10. *IS* 58 (1985/II) 38-39: Prolusio at the meeting of Delegates of National Ecumenical Commissions, 1985; and cf. also his paper on "Catechesis and Ecumenism" at the
Synod of Bishops of 1977, *IS* 36 (1978) 1-2.
11. *IS* 30 (1976) 24.
12. *IS* 54 (1984) 15.
13. Slightly enlarging the "ur-formulation" in *UR* 3 of "some, though imperfect, communion with the Catholic Church", then taken up by John Paul II in *Ut Unum Sint* as "the
real but imperfect communion existing between us" (no. 96) or in no. 45 as "real although
not yet full communion".

3. *Rehabilitating Martin Luther*

In July 1970, Cardinal Willebrands spoke at the Fifth Assembly of the Lutheran World Federation in Evian, France. Somehow hidden within his presentation on the main theme of the Assembly, "Sent into the World", was a short section on Martin Luther. A new tone was sounded for the first time on this subject by a prominent representative of the Vatican. The person and theology of Martin Luther have not always been correctly presented by the Catholic side in the course of the centuries, the Cardinal said. And "this has served neither truth nor love, and therefore it has not served the unity that we are endeavouring to establish between yourselves and the Catholic Church. On the other hand, we may note with pleasure that the last few decades have seen the growth of a scientifically more correct understanding of the Reformation among Catholic scholars and, consequently, also of the figure of Martin Luther and his theology"[14]. This was a kind of official legitimation or reception of the new Catholic Luther research. Willebrands explained that Luther had "retained a considerable part of the old Catholic faith" and praised his emphasis on the Bible, his concept of faith, justification and other aspects of his theology[15]. Lutherans at that time regarded this as an important ecumenical theo-political statement and a step in the direction of declaring officially (still before us) that Luther's excommunication of 1521 no longer applies today.

Thirteen years later (1983) Willebrands spoke in Leipzig's Church of St. Thomas on St. Martin's Day, Luther's name day, in much more detail about the reformer. He mentions also Luther's excommunication in 1521, and in a very frank way, typical for Willebrands, enumerates a series of Luther's doctrinal positions that contradicted the commonly held tradition of the Catholic Church. He finds again positive words on Luther's theology of the cross and underlines that it was "the central questions of life that Martin Luther, professor of theology, man of prayer, preacher and pastor, posed to himself. He pursued them with such passion and coherence that, in this respect one is in a certain sense justified in describing him as the standard bearer of the majesty, the honour and the judgeship of God and, at the same time, as the spokesman of man, who (...) can rely on nothing other than God's mercy"[16].

---

14. *Sent into the World: The Proceedings of the Fifth Assembly of the Lutheran World Federation, Evian, France, July 1970*, Minneapolis, MN, Augsburg, 1971, p. 63.
    15. *Ibid*, pp. 63-64.
    16. *IS* 101 (1999) 113-115; also in Johannes Kardinal WILLEBRANDS, *Mandatum Unitatis: Beiträge zur Ökumene*, Paderborn, Bonifatius, 1989, pp. 257-261.

In a lecture in the university of Bari in January 1984, Willebrands refers in "Martin Luther and the Reformation in Present-Day Perspective" to the "highly intensive and successful official dialogue" with the LWF and to the numerous new insights of the scholarly efforts towards a more adequate, complete and differentiated picture of the time of the Reformation and of the person and multifaceted theological opus of Martin Luther.

Luther's significance is interpreted by Catholic theologians, says Willebrands, either in the sense of Luther's remaining in the Catholic tradition (what Willebrands seems to agree with) or in the sense of Luther's constructive new approach in his understanding of revelation and salvation. Willebrands lists the insights resulting from these processes by referring to the acknowledgement of a shared responsibility for the divisions of the Church, to Luther's aim of renewing the Church and in no way of founding a new church, to a "limited consensus" that the doctrine of justification is no longer divisive, to the recognition of the integrity of Luther's existential motivation in his quest of eternal salvation[17] and, finally, to the depth of his religious personality.

Willebrands concludes by pointing to elements of a theological and spiritual convergence in both Lutheranism and Catholicism and says that Catholic efforts towards "a more faithful and just picture of Martin Luther, formed by truth and love", can be seen as an important building block on the long road of reconciliation among Christians[18]. With these and other statements Willebrands has done much to officially confirm the new Catholic view on Martin Luther. Related to this was his strong interest in Catholic-Lutheran relations as can be seen in other reflections, presentations and his frequent participation in Lutheran conferences[19].

III. WILLEBRANDS CONTRIBUTION TO CATHOLIC AND GENERAL ECUMENICAL INITIATIVES

Cardinal Willebrands has significantly contributed to a number of Catholic ecumenical initiatives that were part of the Catholic ecumenical awakening and were of importance for the Protestant churches.

---

17. Here referring to an impressive letter on Luther by John Paul II to Willebrands on October 31, 1983, cf. http://www.vatican.va/holy_father/john_paul_ii/letters/1983/documents/hf_jp-ii_let_19831031_card-willebrands_ge.html. [1]

18. *Ibid.*, pp. 262-268.

19. Cf. texts in *Mandatum Unitatis* (n. 16), e.g. his paper on "Der evangelisch-katholische Dialog: Tatsächliches und Grundsätzliches", pp. 133-154. That was dedicated to the 70th birthday of the Lutheran theologian Edmund Schlink.

1. *Preparation of Council Documents*

Willebrands' special contribution began with his involvement in the Secretariat's preparation (drafting) of the Council documents on ecumenism, non-Christian religions, religious freedom and, together with the doctrinal commission, on divine revelation[20]. Pre-eminently *Unitatis Redintegratio, Nostra Aetate, Dignitatis Humanae* and *Dei Verbum* met with much attention in Protestant churches. Basic presuppositions and orientations of Catholic ecumenism were thus laid out. This was complemented on the structural side by securing an adequate place and voice for the Secretariat/Pontifical Council for Promoting Christian Unity within the Roman Curia. As a newcomer and initially slightly marginalized, the Secretariat, thanks to the energetic advocacy of Johannes Willebrands, fought for and gained its place in the Roman system. This allowed the Secretariat to become a strong partner in inter-dicasterial discussions and enabled the full and strong presence of the ecumenical agenda in the network of the Vatican and its outreach to its constituency.

2. *Observers at Vatican II*

Furthermore, Willebrands was actively involved in making possible the invitation of non-Catholic observers to be present at the Second Vatican Council. In April 1962 he met with the Conference of Secretaries of Christian World Communions and explained to them the possible participation of observers. This step, when implemented shortly afterwards, was regarded by the other churches and communions as a major sign of the new Catholic ecumenical openness and trust. In his report to the Synod of Bishops of 1983 Willebrands considered this invitation as "based on a clear awareness of the depth of Christian brotherhood that results from the same baptism that makes us members of the Body of Christ. ... The presence at the Council of delegated observers from different Churches and ecclesial communities permitted a deep mutual experience of this brotherhood"[21].

3. *Relations with the WCC*

In 1955 Msgr. Willebrands visited Dr. Visser 't Hooft in Geneva, and in October and November of 1958 he lectured at the Ecumenical Institute

---

20. Cf. his Prolusio at the Meeting of Delegates of National Ecumenical Commissions 1985, *IS* 58 (1985) 38.
21. *IS* 54 (1984) 16.

of the WCC in Bossey. After these early contacts, Willebrands, invited by Visser 't Hooft, participated in August 1959 in the meeting of the Central Committee of the WCC on Rhodes representing the Catholic Conference for Ecumenical Questions. On this and similar earlier meetings he wrote later: "We appeared under various labels, mostly as journalists"[22]. At the meeting on Rhodes the diplomatically not yet so experienced Willebrands created quite some fuss by organising together with his colleague C.J. Dumont a special meeting of Catholic and Orthodox theologians and church leaders. Visser 't Hooft reacted furiously: "I thought I had invited the most sensible Catholics, but I got the two dumbest ones"[23]. But reconciliation followed. One year later, in 1960, Willebrands informed Visser 't Hooft confidently that a Secretariat for Promoting Christian Unity (SPCU) was to be established in Rome. A centre for relations also with the WCC was thus created. In September 1960 Willebrands arranged for and participated in a first (secret) meeting between Cardinal Bea and Visser 't Hooft in Milan[24]. Again one year later his good contacts with the WCC led to the participation of five official Catholic observers at the WCC Assembly in New Delhi, 1961[25].

This was the beginning of a first phase of relationships between the Catholic Church and the World Council of Churches that was actively fostered and nurtured by the two Dutchmen until Visser 't Hooft's retirement one year (1966) after the conclusion of the Vatican Council. By now Willebrands had become the main mediator of relations between Rome and Geneva, which in his report to the Synod of Bishops in 1977 he described as "One of the Catholic Church's most important ecumenical undertakings"[26]. He helped to establish the Joint Working Group (see below) and arranged the membership of twelve Catholic theologians in the Commission on Faith and Order and made possible that a Catholic religious sister worked since 1985 as a full time consultant in the area of mission in the WCC. Since then a great number of mutual visits, joint staff meetings and participation in each other's conferences have continued the heritage initiated by Willebrands.

---

22. *IS* 47 (1981) 142-143: Opening Address at the Cardinal Bea Symposium 1981.

23. T. SALEMINK (ed.), *"You Will Be Called Repairer of the Breach" : The Diary of J.G.M. Willebrands 1958-1961*, Leuven, Peeters, 2009, p. 9, and the notes by Willebrands himself, pp. 127-129, cf. also his notes on this event in his Opening Address to the Cardinal Bea Symposium, 1981, *IS* 47 (1981) 143-144.

24. Willebrands: "this is a historical meeting", SALEMINK (ed.), *"You Will Be Called Repairer of the Breach"* (n. 23), p. 12.

25. Cf. also p. 258.

26. *IS* 36 (1978) 8.

4. *The Joint Working Group*

Willebrands' special interest and favour were dedicated to the Joint Working Group (JWG) between the Catholic Church and the WCC. In his paper on "Twenty-Five Years of the World Council of Churches, 1948-1973", he said in 1973: "In order to appreciate to what extent the formation of the World Council of Churches was a turning point in the history of the Church, one could point (…) to the constitution, in 1965, of the Joint Working Group of the Catholic Church and the World Council"[27]. A small meeting in 1964 between staff members of the SPCU and the WCC discussed the proposal to establish a joint working group between the two bodies, and in 1965 during his visit to Geneva, Cardinal Bea, together with Willebrands, announced the positive decision of the Holy See to accept the WCC's proposal to start a joint working group[28]. Its first meeting, co-chaired by Visser 't Hooft and Willebrands, took place in May 1965.

In a letter in 1975 to WCC General Secretary Philip Potter, Willebrands affirms: "We see the Joint Working Group as a point of coordination and reflection. It is to be an instrument by which the two separate bodies may coordinate both studies and activities, (…) It is a highly useful means of assessing what can be done in terms of resources and in terms of our respective theological understandings"[29]. For him the JWG was a kind of substitute for membership of the Catholic Church in the WCC. Because the Catholic Church was not "in the near future seeking membership in the Council the role of the Joint Working Group becomes crucial"[30]. Willebrands has carefully followed the work of the JWG, especially when it undertook its own studies on *Common Witness*, *The Church-Local and Universal*, *The Notion of Hierarchy of Truths* in the 1970s and 1980s and on *Ecumenical Formation* since 1985, a theme especially dear to Willebrands. With these studies the JWG was very much in line with Willebrands' emphasis on theology. He has in these and other ways opened vistas and helped building bridges that in a fundamental manner have changed the relationships and mutual perceptions of the churches.

---

27. *IS* 101 (1999) 127.
28. *IS* 70 (1989) 63: "40 Years of the World Council of Churches. A Catholic Reflection".
29. *IS* 30 (1976) 25.
30. *IS* 39 (1976) 25: Letter to Philip Potter 1975.

5. *Faith and Order*

For Willebrands and his Church in general the most important element in the structure of the WCC became more and more the Commission on Faith and Order. This corresponded fully to his emphasis on serious theological work *in ecumenicis* and was reinforced by the full membership of twelve Catholic theologians in the Faith and Order Commission after 1968. This emphasis was clearly expressed in his report to the plenary of the SPCU in 1981, where he underlined that "fundamental theological research gives coherence and Christian significance to such various activities, which should always be inspired and directed by a theological outlook. The 'Faith and Order' element which was one of the great forces which gave birth to the World Council of Churches is more real and necessary than ever"[31]. In his reports and papers, Willebrands regularly refers to Faith and Order, its significant and encouraging results in documents such as *Giving Account of the Hope Together* (1978) and especially *Baptism, Eucharist and Ministry* (1982), and the importance of the Catholic participation in this work.

6. *Bilateral Dialogues*

When a whole series of bilateral dialogues of the Catholic Church with other world communions was initiated at the end and after the Second Vatican Council, this new ecumenical methodology was close to the heart and intentions of Willebrands. First, bilaterals corresponded to the ecumenical strategy and involvement of the Catholic Church as a world-wide communion in dialogue with other worldwide bodies. And second, these dialogues were instruments of serious, thorough theological exchange and quest for convergence and consensus. Accordingly, Willebrands, always supported by Cardinal Bea until Bea's death in 1969, was the main partner of Christian World Communions (CWCs) in planning and inaugurating official bilateral theological dialogues, beginning with Lutherans through the Lutheran World Federation in a preparatory working group in which he participated in 1965 and 1966; and then with Anglicans, Methodists, Reformed, Pentecostals and after 1980 also with Orthodox. In his opening address to the plenary session of the Secretariat in 1975 he reflected in a very differentiated way on the nature, methodology and form, as well as on the various types of dialogues and their goals

31. *IS* 47 (1981) 115.

according to the different communions-in-dialogue[32]. Naturally Wille-brands followed and considered the documents coming from the dia-logues with great interest.

On several occasions he also reflected on the methodological problems of dealing with and evaluating these bilateral texts, for example in his Prolusio to the plenary meeting of the Secretariat: "I think it is the first time in history that the Catholic Church has been faced with documents of this sort"[33]. He proposed rather broad processes of discussing and evaluat-ing results and reports, including the participation of the faithful (*sensus fidei*), and warned: "The restoration of unity cannot be the work of a few, either theologians or bishops. The history of the Church reminds us of failures coming from methods of that kind"[34]. Accordingly, he presented to the Convention of the Lutheran Church in America in 1984 a remarkably detailed analysis of processes of "reception" of ecumenical dialogues and their results[35]. This included underlining the complementarity of bilateral and multilateral dialogues, not least exemplified by the Catholic presence in both the multilateral Faith and Order studies and the increasing number of its bilateral dialogues. And he adds firmly in a letter to Philip Potter (because of a tendency in the WCC to be critical of bilateral dialogues): "It is important for the well-being of the Roman Catholic/World Council of Churches relationship that this fact [i.e. of the complementarity of bilateral and multilateral dialogues] be kept clearly in mind"[36].

In this perspective Willebrands also welcomed the plan for a Forum on Bilateral Dialogues (which was established in 1978) in order to follow trends in bilateral conversations and to consider the interrelationship of bilateral and multilateral dialogues[37]. His high esteem of bilateral dia-logues was underscored when in his report to the Synod of Bishops of 1983 he considered them a form of common witness. "When we enter into dialogue we are saying together that we have a will for reconcilia-tion, that we have a hope of reconciliation"[38].

Logical implications of this involvement were the regular contacts Willebrands had with Christian World Communions. He remarked that these Communions "have increased in importance, not only in the organ-isational aspect, but also at the level of Church. This could be illustrated

---

32. *IS* 27 (1975) 4-5; *IS* 36 (1978) 6-7.
33. *IS* 47 (1981) 115, cf. also *IS* 27 (1975) 4-5; *IS* 36 (1978) 6-7; *IS* 44 (1980) 119-120.
34. *IS* 27 (1975) 4-5: Opening Address at the Plenary Session of the Secretariat, 1975.
35. *IS* 101 (1988) 140-143.
36. *IS* 53 (1983) 118.
37. *IS* 30 (1976) 24: Letter to Philip Potter, 1975.
38. *IS* 54 (1984) 18.

by the development of the Lutheran World Federation". Here "the notion of communion was discussed (Addis Ababa, 1988) as a primary way of expressing the bond of unity between member Churches"[39]. A few examples of his contacts with CWCs were his presentations at LWF assemblies in Evian in 1970 and in Budapest in 1984, his participation in the Lambeth Conference of 1968, in the World Methodist Conference in Denver in 1971, and in the Synod of the Russian Orthodox Church in Zagorsk in 1988.

IV. WILLEBRANDS AS SPOKESMAN ON DIFFICULT ECUMENICAL ISSUES

It was part and expression of Willebrands' realistic, open and direct personal manner that he acted, so to speak, as Vatican spokesman on difficult ecumenical issues. Their clarification and resolution were and are even more so today desiderata of many Protestants.

1. *Intercommunion*

There is, first of all, the question of intercommunion, an old and continuing concern in the ecumenical movement.

The long ecumenical discussion on intercommunion as the eminent expression of unity achieved or as a means facilitating the movement toward that goal had produced differentiated concepts and forms of eucharistic communion. New hopes for such communion, at least in the form of eucharistic hospitality for mixed marriages and ecumenical groups and gatherings were awakened in post-conciliar Catholic-Protestant exchanges and for some time officially granted (1972) by Bishop Elchinger of Strasbourg and in some other places. A widespread unofficial practice of some form of occasional eucharistic sharing referring often to the already existing real though imperfect communion continuous until today. In his report of the Secretariat at the World Synod of Bishops in 1983 Willebrands sets the context by mentioning that before the Council the question of a common sharing of the Eucharist was not raised. "But once there is renewed awareness of the baptismal bonds that unite us, there is a much more painful perception of the scandal of our division at the Table of the Lord to which the whole dynamism of our baptismal life leads us". He concludes that an effort has to be made to

---

39. *IS* 70 (1989) 64: Paper on "40 Years of the World Council of Churches. A Catholic Reflection".

educate the Catholic faithful to an understanding of the ecclesial dimension of the Eucharist. He also calls for "an intensified effort to hasten the day when such a common celebration will be possible"[40].

In his *Prolusio* to the plenary meeting of the Secretariat in 1986 Willebrands used the revision of the Ecumenical Directory to explain the Catholic position by clearly spelling out the ecclesial dimension of the Eucharist mentioned before: "However, participation in eucharistic communion is a celebration of full communion". Appreciating the changes in relations among Christians brought about by the ecumenical movement and the convergences in the understanding of the Eucharist, Willebrands nevertheless feels that he has to remind others of the reality that "the Catholic faith has a different conception of the mystery of the Church: it means the sacramental, hierarchical Church, as we have received it from Christ through the apostles. In the eucharistic celebration we express that faith in the one, holy, catholic and apostolic Church, whose shepherds are the successors of the apostles under the leadership of the Church of Rome and its Bishop"[41]. Admitting realistically that often it is difficult to communicate the Catholic position, the Cardinal reproaches leaders of other churches "who are exhorting their people" to receive communion in Catholic celebrations (probably here overstating the case – I know of statements where Lutheran faithful are officially given the liberty to partake communion in Catholic services where possible). In any case, the Cardinal is strict: "Whatever may be their personal conviction, we must ask leaders and theologians in other churches to respect the doctrine and the discipline of the Catholic Church"[42]. Willebrands does not reflect on ways towards a solution, at least in terms of provisional steps. Obviously this was not considered a task of a Vatican official.

2. *Ordination of Women*

A second debated issue on which Cardinal Willebrands had to present the Catholic position was the ordination of women to the priesthood.

Interestingly this question did not burden the Catholic bilateral dialogues with Lutherans, Presbyterians and Methodists because the ordination of women was already a fact in many member churches of these communions when the dialogues began. This was very much different in the Anglican-Catholic dialogue. Anglicans did not ordain women when

---

40. *IS* 54 (1984) 17.
41. *IS* 61 (1986) 117.
42. *Ibid.*, 118.

the international dialogue began in 1970. The dialogue reached significant results in the ensuing years that aroused strong hopes (I still remember vividly the excited atmosphere in ARCIC), that a recognition of Anglican Orders – after *"Apostolicae Curae* of 1896 had declared Anglican ordinations as "absolutely null and utterly void" – was now possible and the way open towards eucharistic sharing.

Great was the disappointment on both sides when later in the 1970s Anglican churches began ordaining women to the priesthood (and later to the episcopate). After an exchange of letters between Pope John Paul II and Archbishop Robert Runcie in 1984-1985, it was Cardinal Willebrands who responded in a letter to Archbishop Runcie in June 1986, in a rather detailed way to the reasons brought forward in favour of the ordination of women. He repeated and explained the two main arguments against the ordination of women. First, the one from tradition by stressing that the "ordination only of men for the presbyterate and episcopate is the unbroken Tradition of the Catholic and Orthodox Churches. Neither Church understands itself to be competent to alter this tradition. (...) The constant tradition of the Catholic and Orthodox Churches has considered the practice of Christ and the Apostles as a norm from which she could not deviate"[43]. The second argument is that of representing Christ: "His male identity is an inherent feature of the economy of salvation, revealed in the Scriptures and pondered in the Church. The ordination only of men to the priesthood has to be understood in terms of the intimate relationship between Christ the Redeemer and those who, in a unique way, cooperate in Christ's redemptive work. The priest represents Christ in His saving relationship with His Body the Church"[44].

All of this is explained in Willebrands' letter to Runcie in quite some detail and connected with rather forthright conclusions that are typical of the straightforward manner of Willebrands: "In saying this I wish simply to make the point that the arguments you (i.e. Runcie) relay cannot count as reason for the radical innovation of ordaining women to the priesthood, the arguments do not negotiate the manifold theological issues which this matter raises"[45]. Thus speaks the theology professor turned church official! And in another place: "Our greater unity must be a fundamental concern, and it has to be stated frankly that a development like the ordination of women does nothing to deepen the communion between us and weakens the communion that currently exists. The ecclesiological consequences are serious"[46]. Here speaks disappointed love, and, indeed,

---

43. *Ibid.*, 110.
44. *Ibid.*, 111.
45. *Ibid.*, 111.
46. *Ibid.*, 110.

there followed a clear cooling down of Anglican-Catholic relations that is reinforced by other Anglican decisions in recent years.

3. *Membership in the WCC*

Willebrands was also the spokesman for the Vatican on a third issue that was raised again and again by Protestants and their churches: the hope for membership of the Catholic Church in the World Council of Churches. Slightly naively, Protestants advocated such a membership unaware of the reality that a worldwide church body would hardly fit into an ecclesial "zoo" (the words of my doctor-father Edmund Schlink in a letter to me), an organisation of several hundred smaller and larger national churches. Accordingly, Willebrands explained in a letter of 1983 to WCC General Secretary Philip Potter: "(…) on the one hand there is a Church with all that implies of a precise doctrinal position and of pastoral responsibility and on the other (hand) a Council of Churches of which the Roman Catholic Church is not a member and which as such does not present its own doctrinal position, apart from its Basis, and which does not have direct pastoral responsibility. … Inevitably the very different nature of the two bodies affects the relationship"[47]. Then in 1988 in a speech on "40 Years of the World Council of Churches" Willebrands referred to the nature of the Church as, among others, a sacrament of salvation and unity, served by the successor of Peter and his universal juridical position. This and other theological and canonical elements make the Catholic Church basically different from the national independence and other positions of the Protestant churches and the different canonical structures of the Orthodox churches. And in one sentence: "That question [i.e. of membership] is not really of great practical importance"[48]. For Willebrands, however, there exists an important *Ersatz*, a substitute for this membership: the Joint Working Group between the Catholic Church and the WCC.

V. Concluding Remarks

Several trajectories of the ecumenical activity and the personal ecumenical involvement and emphasis of Johannes Willebrands are of importance for the Protestant churches. These churches had behind them and were marked by a history of bitter and divisive theological, social

47. *IS* 53 (1983) 120.
48. *IS* 70 (1989) 64.

and political conflicts with Roman Catholicism since the time of the
Reformation until the middle of the twentieth century. It was, therefore,
no easy task for the Catholic Church and its Second Vatican Council to
reverse this history and its theological and psychological impact. Nor was
it an easy task for Protestants to change their perspectives on Catholicism
and begin, together with ecumenically minded Catholics a process of
"healing of memories" and creating new mutual understandings and relationships. Conscious of this history and the new ecumenical challenges,
Willebrands has spoken repeatedly on the need of repentance for the past
and the will for reconciliation[49]. On the basis of such "spiritual ecumenism" and grounding his thoughts and words on the Bible, documents of
Vatican II, and papal statements, he has untiringly interpreted to Protestants basic convictions of Catholic faith and ecumenical orientation.

Willebrands has exercised his ministry as a loyal representative of the
faith and tradition of his Church without trying to extend the limits of its
official positions. At the same time he was a loyal representative of the
common ecumenical quest for the visible unity of Christians and their
churches. He has helped, not without initial struggles within the Roman
Curia, to develop ecumenical concepts and to build ecumenical relations
that were appreciated by Protestants and contributed to mutual understanding and trust. Willebrands served the establishment of contacts and
forms of communion with Protestant churches and their worldwide communities, especially through enabling and supporting bilateral dialogues
and by his personal presence in these churches. He was the major artisan
for constructing closer connections between the Catholic Church and the
WCC, the privileged ecumenical instrument of all the traditional
Protestant and most Orthodox churches. In this context his special interest was directed to the Joint Working Group and Faith and Order. His
theological competence, spiritual sensibility, and his open-hearted as well
as straightforward and frank personal attitude has won him respect among
Protestant ecumenists and has considerably facilitated the exercise of his
ecumenical responsibilities. For Protestants, Cardinal Willebrands has,
indeed, been a major ecumenical bridge-builder in the 20th century, a
bridge-builder whom they should remember with gratitude.

Marienstrasse 4a   Günther GASSMANN
D-82327 Tutzing
Germany

---

49. E.g. *IS* 54 (1984) 15-16, 17: Intervention at the 1983 Synod of Bishops; *Mandatum
Unitatis* (n. 16), pp. 172-173: Presentation at the LWF Assembly in Budapest, 1984.

IV. WILLEBRANDS AND JUDAISM

MSGR. WILLEBRANDS AND *NOSTRA AETATE* 4

DIPLOMACY AND PRAGMATISM

Introduction

In this paper we would like to concentrate on the role of Msgr. Wille-brands in the negotiations with the patriarchs of the Middle East during the final stage of the approval of the document on non-Christian religions, *Nostra Aetate*, of the Second Vatican Council. Indeed, these patriarchs had many difficulties with this document, especially with the text about the Jews. As is known, the literature on Vatican II and the Jews is abundant[1]. John XXIII's efforts to put the issue of the Jews on the agenda of Vatican II are well known[2]. The same can be said of Augustine Cardinal Bea (1881-1968)[3]. He became, as president of the newly established Secretariat for Promoting Christian Unity (Secretariatus ad christianorum unitatem fovendam, henceforth SCUF), John XXIII's most trusted representative in matters related to ecumenism, a topic the pope wanted to be discussed at the council[4]. Bea, who knew Johannes Willebrands' interest in and merits for ecumenism very well, suggested his name to the pope as first secretary of the SCUF, a suggestion followed by John XXIII who appointed Willebrands on June 28, 1960.

---

1. The literature on Vatican II and the Jews is abundant; see, for example, A. GILBERT, *The Vatican Council and the Jews*, Cleveland, OH – New York, 1969. With respect to the Catholic teaching on non-Christian religions during the Council see, for example,

M. RUOKANEN, *The Catholic Doctrine of Non-Christian Religions according to the Second Vatican Council* (Studies in Christian Mission, 7), Leiden – New York – Cologne, 1992.

2. With regard to John's actions in favor of the Jews during the Second World War, see A. MELLONI, *Fra Istanbul, Atene e la Guerra: La missione di A.G. Roncalli (1935-1944)*, Genova, 1992, pp. 258-279. In 1959, he in person scrapped the term *perfidi* from the prayer for the Jews during the intercessions on Good Friday; see Cf. GIOVANNI XXIII-ANGELO RONCALLI, *Lettere ai familiari 1901-1962*. A cura di L.F. CAPOVILLA, Rome, 1968, vol. II, p. 484.

3. For Bea see the biography written by his personal secretary, S. SCHMIDT, *Augustin Bea, Der Kardinal der Einheit*, Graz, 1989.

4. See in this regard G. ALBERIGO, *The Announcement of the Council: From the Security of the Fortress to the Lure of the Quest*, in G. ALBERIGO – J.A. KOMONCHAK (eds.), *History of Vatican II. Vol. I: Announcing and Preparing Vatican Council II. Toward a New Era in Catholicism*, Maryknoll, NY – Leuven, 1995, 1-54, pp. 28-30.

From the very beginning, the SCUF was of the opinion that the Council should deal with the topic of the Jews[5], for it considered relations with Jews together with the relationship between the two Testaments as one of its primary tasks[6]. Although the SCUF had gradually started to compose its own texts with a view to the forthcoming Council, before its official recognition as a conciliar commission on October 19, 1962, it could not really influence the council's activities[7], partly an explanation why there was no text on the Jews among the schemata to be discussed at the Council[8].

I. TOWARDS A TEXT ON THE JEWS: A BRIEF HISTORY

During the first session and intersession, the topic of the Jews was not a central issue, although bishops in Europe (especially in Germany – needless to remind that Bea, one of the main promoters of a text on the Jews, was a German) and the US were very much in favour of a declaration on the Jews. The idea to integrate a text about the Jews into the forthcoming schema *De Oecumenismo* caused some problems and this for good theological reasons: the inclusion of the Jews in the same schema as that dealing with non-Catholic Christian denominations might give the impression that everything non-Catholic had been lumped together under one and the same category[9]. On the other hand, Protestant circles experienced the explicit reference to the bond with Jews as an

---

5. G. MICCOLI, *Two Sensitive Issues: Religious Freedom and the Jews*, in G. ALBERIGO – J.A. KOMONCHAK (eds.), *History of Vatican II*. Vol. IV: *Church as Communion. Third Period and Intersession. September 1964-September 1965*, Maryknoll, NY – Leuven, 2004, p. 137.

6. Cf. J.A. KOMONCHAK, *The Struggle for the Council during the Preparation of Vatican II (1960-1962)*, in ALBERIGO – KOMONCHAK (eds.), *History of Vatican II*. Vol. I (n. 4), 227-296, p. 265; cf. also T. SALEMINK, *"You Will Be Called Repairer of the Breach" : The Diary of J.G.M. Willebrands 1958-1961*, Leuven, 2009, p. 206 (September 8, 1960): "Visit Mgr Oesterreicher. He is coming to talk about the question of Israel. Everything appears that this question will be entrusted to our Secretariat".

7. From the very beginning of its existence, the SCUF and its president wanted to be more than an information-office, but only now this ambition became reality; cf. KOMONCHAK, *The Struggle for the Council* (n. 6), pp. 265-266 (with further bibliographical references).

8. *ADP* II,4, pp. 22-23. Cf. also KOMONCHAK, *The Struggle for the Council* (n. 6), p. 271 (with additional literature).

9. Cf. J. FAMERÉE, *Bishops and Dioceses and the Communications Media (November 5-25, 1963)*, in G. ALBERIGO – J.A. KOMONCHAK (eds.), *History of Vatican II*. Vol. III: *The Mature Council. Second Period and Intersession (September 1963-September 1964)*, Maryknoll, NY – Leuven, 2000, 117-188, p. 164.

important element for ecumenism[10]. A seriously complicating factor, and this from the preparatory period, was the situation in the Middle East: both Arab nations and the churches in the Middle East considered a text on the Jews inappropriate. The presence of a Catholic minority within the population of Palestine, expelled by the newly created Jewish state, made it difficult for the Holy See to recognize the State of Israel. Christians lived in both the Jewish and Arab regions. Every theological statement about the Jews could be interpreted either in favor of the Jews or of the Arabs[11]. At the same time, Jewish circles in Europe and the US were looking forward with interest to a text about the Jews[12]. It ought to be noted at this juncture that, from the Roman Catholic perspective, a text on the Jews was a somewhat delicate matter, especially given the perceived attitude of Pius XII to the Jews during World War II. Pius XII's silence with respect to the Jews during the war gave rise to significant criticism from elsewhere[13]. In sum, a text on the Jews was a delicate affair. In any case, the text on the Jews ended up as part of the schema *De Oecumenismo* (chapter 4 of the Schema) and was entitled: *De catholicorum habitudine ad non christianos et maxime ad Iudaeos*[14].

Although the text was not discussed during the second session, the Middle East protested yet again. Therefore, A.G. Cardinal Cicognani, Secretary of State and president of the Commission for the Eastern Churches, stressed that the text only had a religious aim, a position explicitly repeated by Cardinal Bea in his presentation of the fourth chapter of the schema on November 19th, 1963[15]. Such statements were not of great help since opposition to the text remained. Especially bishops of the Middle East considered such a text inappropriate, given the complicated

---

10. FAMERÉE, *Bishops and Dioceses* (n. 9), p. 164.

11. *ADP* II,4, pp. 22-23. Cf. also KOMONCHAK, *The Struggle for the Council* (n. 6), p. 271 (with additional literature).

12. See, e.g., the telegram addressed to Cardinal Suenens on October 24th 1963 by P. Philippson, president of the Central Israelite Consistory of Belgium in which the latter expressed his hope that the Council would establish its position on the relationship between Catholics and Jews in such a way that the discrimination suffered by Jews in the past would thus be brought to an end; cf. L. DECLERCK – E. LOUCHEZ, *Inventaire des Papiers conciliaires du cardinal L.-J. Suenens* (Cahiers de la Revue théologique de Louvain, 31), Louvain-la-Neuve, 1998, nr. 1618.

13. Reference can be made in this regard to the play *Der Stellvertreter* by Rolf Hochhuth, which struck an enormously negative note – especially in Italy – on account of its biting condemnation of the Vatican's attitude towards the Jews during World War II. See also MICCOLI, *Two Sensitive Issues: Religious Freedom and the Jews* (n. 5), p. 140.

14. For the text see *AS* II,5, pp. 431-432.

15. Cf. his detailed report in *AS* II,5, pp. 481-485.

political situation in that region[16]. Others were of the opinion that if anything was to be said about the Jews, then it should be said in relation to the other world religions[17], the schema on the Church or the schema on the Church in the Modern World in which a reference could be made in the context of the condemnation of every form of discrimination[18].

In any case, at the end of the second session, the status of the text on the Jews and its future remained unclear. During the intersession and the third session, the text on the Jews had become a sort of appendix (*Declaratio altera*) to the schema on ecumenism[19], but the objections to the text remained[20], although it would be presented during the third session as part of a declaration on the non-Christian religions, a suggestion made by Cicognani[21].

Still, during the second intersession, the patriarchs of the Middle East were opposed to a text on the Jews[22]. The influential Maximos IV Saigh, Patriarch of the Melkites, wrote a letter in the name of the Melkite bishops who had been gathered in assembly from August 17th to 22nd, in which he asked that the text on the Jews be removed from the agenda[23]. The Catholic Coptic Patriarch Sidarouss likewise wrote a letter in which he pointed out that the text concerning the Jews had already been abused for political and religious reasons and that the text itself was a disaster when it came to relations with other Christians (namely the Greek

16. See in this regard the interventions of Cardinal Tappouni, Patriarch Sidarouss, and Patriarch Maximos IV Saigh (*AS* II,5, pp. 527-528; 541-542; 542-544).

17. Thus, for example, Cardinal Ruffini (Palermo); Msgr. Gori (Latin Patriarch of Jerusalem); Msgr. Jelmini (Apostolic Administrator of Lugano), speaking on behalf of the bishops of Switzerland (*AS* II,5, p. 528-530; 557; 600-602); cf. also Y. CONGAR, *Mon Journal du Concile*, Paris, 2002, I, p. 544.

18. MICCOLI, *Two Sensitive Issues: Religious Freedom and the Jews* (n. 5), p. 141; cf. also CONGAR, *Mon Journal du Concile* (n. 17), II, p. 25.

19. This procedure had already been suggested by Bea and had been proposed during the plenary meeting of the SCUF (24th February-7th March); cf. *AS* V,2, p. 168. The final decision was supported by an overwhelming majority of the members of the SCUF (19 to 1); cf. *AS* V,2, p. 152. The SCUF exhibited a degree of caution with respect to Islam, arguing that the theme in question was beyond its competence.

20. Rumours abounded at the time that the Arabic world was threatening to sever diplomatic relations with the Vatican if the text on the Jews was allowed to remain in the schema on ecumenism; see CONGAR, *Mon Journal du Concile* (n. 17), II, pp. 59-60.

21. *AS* V,2, p. 285ff. Cicognani was not only chair of the Coordinating Commission but also Secretary of State and as such he was highly sensitive towards potentially negative reactions from within the diplomatic world.

22. For the details, see M. LAMBERIGTS – L. DECLERCK, *Nostra Aetate 4. Vatican II on the Jews: Vatican II on the Jews. An Historical Survey*, in M. MOYAERT – D. POLLEFEYT (eds.), *40 Years Nostra Aetate. Past, Present and Future* (Louvain Theological & Pastoral Monographs), Leuven, Peeters, 2010, 13-56.

23. *AS* VI,3, p. 400 (letter from Maximos to Paul VI, dated September 3rd 1964).

Orthodox) and with Islam. He concluded by noting that his own small community was already being confronted with considerable problems[24].

When the new text[25], now having the status of a declaration, was discussed in the third session (September 28-30)[26], it received the support of the German bishops[27], and also of the significant majority of other speakers who were positively inclined towards the text on the Jews and continued to support its presence on the conciliar agenda[28]. However, the Eastern patriarchs remained opposed to the text, questioning the opportunity of the text (especially Cardinal Tappouni, Patriarch of the Syriac Church of Antioch), given that it might occasion political problems for Christians in the Middle East[29]. Other speakers objected that too much attention had been paid to Jews and Muslims to the detriment of other world religions and animism[30].

24. *AS* VI,3, p. 401 (letter from Sidarouss to Paul VI, dated September 22nd 1964); for other reactions see *AS* VI,3, pp. 437; 460-461; 470-471; 475. The reactions in question stem from Vatican diplomats, including those in Egypt, Jordan and Lebanon. Indeed, they were confronted with protests of mostly Islamic people.

25. See *AS* III,2, pp. 327-329.

26. The idea that the Council planned to speak in a positive manner with respect to the Jews caused a degree of consternation and resistance in certain circles, as is evident from the pamphlet that was distributed among the conciliar fathers entitled *L'Action Judéo-Maçonnique dans le Concile. Lecture exclusivement réservée à Leurs Révérendissimes Pères Conciliaires.* For the text itself see Centre Lumen Gentium (UCL), Prignon Papers, nr. 986. The pamphlet contained the following statement: "Ce sont, Seigneur, les Juifs faussement convertis, qui, une fois de plus, essaient de détruire ton œuvre divine!". The text – or better *the diatribe* – was primarily aimed at converts such as Oesterreicher and Baum (cf. p. 4). Cardinal Bea himself was not spared: "Ces thèses, élaborées certainement par quelque grand rabbin, furent présentées officiellement au Concile par le Cardinal Bea qui les reçut directement de l'Ordre B'nai B'rith, maçonnerie exclusive de Juifs, et ceci au mois de juin 1962".

27. As a matter of fact, Bea did not forget to emphasise the fact that a positive attitude towards the Jews was also a component part of the *aggiornamento* intended by John XXIII; cf. *AS* III,2, p. 564.

28. For a survey see MICCOLI, *Two Sensitive Issues: Religious Freedom and the Jews* (n. 5), pp. 159 and ff.

29. Cf. *AS* III,2, p. 582. After the conclusion of discussions in the aula, the bishops from the Middle East continued to evolve a strategy aimed at having the text on the Jews removed from the conciliar agenda; cf. N. EDELBY, *Il Vaticano II nel diario di un vescovo arabo*, ed. R.R. CANNELLI, Cinisello Balsamo, 1996, pp. 246-250. Indeed, a text on the Jews not only complicated their position with respect to Islam, it also caused problems for their relations with the Orthodox churches; for further details see MICCOLI, *Two Sensitive Issues: Religious Freedom and the Jews* (n. 5), pp. 175-176.

30. See in this regard the intervention of the bishop of Butare (Rwanda), speaking on behalf of roughly 80 colleagues, who insisted that the adherents of animism were sometimes more open to Christianity than Jews and Muslims; see *AS* III,2, p. 142. For an explanation of this intervention and the list of its signatories see MICCOLI, *Two Sensitive Issues: Religious Freedom and the Jews* (n. 5), pp. 163-164.

During the last week of the third session (on November 20th, 1964) a vote was finally taken on the attitude of the Church towards non-Christian religions[31], the section on the Jews being included in a broader context: *Declaratio De Ecclesiae habitudine ad religiones non-christianas* 4[32]. The ballot on numbers 4 and 5 – both were taken together – was a success: 1,969 fathers took part, 1,770 voted in favour of the text, 185 against and 14 votes were invalid. During the vote on the document as a whole, 1,651 votes (out of 1,996) were positive, 242 fathers abstained, 99 fathers voted against, and 4 votes were invalid. In other words, the text was overwhelmingly approved by the Council participants.

But the critique, especially from Arabic nations, remained[33], even though people like Bea insisted on the political neutrality of the text: the text on the Jews had been integrated in a text addressing all world religions[34]. Sources from the Middle East continued to insinuate that the Catholic Church supported international Zionism and was against the

---

31. For a discussion of the plans to give the text on the Jews a place in the schema on the Church see, for example, CONGAR, *Mon Journal du Concile* (n. 17), II, pp. 190; 195; 212-213. Cf. also *AS* V,2, pp. 754-757 (discussion in the Coordinating Commission); see also MICCOLI, *Two Sensitive Issues: Religious Freedom and the Jews* (n. 5), pp. 166-193, which offers a detailed survey of events surrounding our text and that on religious freedom. The proposal to integrate the text on the Jews into the schema on the Church was ultimately abandoned. On November 12th, 1964, the text as it stood was given the green light by the theological commission: it was thus considered to contain nothing contrary to faith and morals. See in this regard CONGAR, *Mon Journal du Concile* (n. 17), II, pp. 261-262 (with an interesting review of the various antitheses within the theological commission on the said topic).

32. For the text itself see *AS* III,8, pp. 637-643. The SCUF had already submitted a text on the Jews and the Muslims on October 21st to a small commission consisting of Congar, Stransky (U.S.A.), Neuner (India), Pfister (Japan) and the Belgian Moeller; cf. CONGAR, *Mon Journal du Concile* (n. 17), II, pp. 215-216.

33. With regard to other critiques of the text, see, R. BURIGANA – G. TURBANTI, *The Intersession: Preparing the Conclusion of the Council*, in ALBERIGO – KOMONCHAK (eds.), *History of Vatican II*. Vol. IV (n. 5), 546-559. Among the conservatives, especially the *Coetus Internationalis Patrum* should be mentioned; cf. the incident between Msgr. Carli of this *Coetus* and Cardinal Bea; see G. COTTIER, *L'historique de la déclaration*, in A.-M. HENRY (ed.), *Les relations de l'Église avec les religions non chrétiennes*, Paris, Cerf, 1966, 37-78, p. 71; BURIGANA – TURBANTI, *The Intersession: Preparing the Conclusion of the Council*, pp. 548-551.

34. See COTTIER, *L'historique de la déclaration* (n. 33), pp. 65-67. Cottier also makes reference to the important interventions of Maximos IV Saigh and Heenan in the press. He refers, in addition, to the role of Paul VI in helping to restore a sense of calm to the situation. Felici was to react with some bitterness to Bea's article (cf. *L'Osservatore Romano*, Nov. 30th – Dec. 1st. 1964), arguing in a letter to Macchi, private secretary to Paul VI, that no matter how positive the results of the ballot may have been, nothing had in fact been decided; cf. *AS* VI,3, p. 572. It is evident to the present authors that such a reaction bears witness to an apparent lack of respect for the said results.

claims of the Palestinians. The Arabic world was in conflict with Israel, and in such a conflict people did not (sufficiently) distinguish between politics and religion. Protest against the conciliar document even found its way onto the streets[35]. The press campaign conducted by the Arabic papers was likewise considered dangerous for Christians living in this region. It should be said that a number of Jews endeavoured to give the schema a political and Zionist spin. In an Arabic broadcast, for example, Israeli radio made reference to a conciliar acquittal of the Jews on the accusation of deicide. Such actions quite evidently influenced the atmosphere in a negative sense. A rumour also circulated at the time that the Arabic Catholic communities might join the Orthodox Churches, which were well known in those days for their comparatively anti-Semitic opinions. In any case, people were concerned that the positive reactions of the Orthodox with respect to the Decree on Ecumenism might be endangered by the proposed declaration on the Jews. Moreover, not only the Jews, but also other nations had suffered persecution. The Secretariat of State was far from pleased with the commotion that resulted[36]. It continued to fear that a positive declaration concerning the Jews would necessarily have political implications with respect to the Church's relations with Arab nations[37]. For that reason, the SCUF decided to take into account several of the proposed emendations (*modi*). Msgr. Willebrands would visit the bishops in the Middle East.

II. A MISSION IMPOSSIBLE?

Willebrands' first visit to the Middle East took place from March 18 to 23, 1965[38], i.e., shortly after the SCUF had finished its revision of the schema in the meetings of the sub-commission (from 24th to 28th February, 1965) and the plenary commission (from 1st to 6th March, 1965)[39], endeavouring to account for the 90 proposed emendations

---

35. *AS* VI,4, pp. 70-72 (letter of Batanian to Paul VI, dated January 18th, 1965); for additional examples see *AS* VI,4, pp. 73-74.

36. See in this regard, the letter addressed by Cicognani to Felici, dated December 7th, 1964 (*AS* V,3, pp. 96-97). Cf. also *AS* V,3, pp. 104-105; *AS* VI,3, pp. 628-629; *AS* VI,4, p. 37; p. 69; *AS* VI,4, p. 118.

37. The repudiate attitude of the orthodox also gave rise to a degree of unrest; cf. *AS* VI,4, pp. 83-85 (letter from Cicognani to Felici, dated February 7th, 1965; letter from Felici to Cicognani, dated February 8th, 1965).

38. With regard to the report of this travel, see ASV Conc. Vat. II 1458.

39. Cf. *AS* VI,4, p. 68. *De Ecclesiae Habitudine* was discussed on March 3-4; cf. Report of Willebrands, ASV Conc.Vat. II, 1458.

submitted by the Council fathers[40]. He visited Eastern patriarchs in Lebanon and Syria. During his visit, Willebrands had first a meeting on March 18 with Cardinal Tappouni, Patriarch of Antioch of the Syrians, who could accept the promulgation of the declaration in so far as it had a theological perspective, but was of the opinion that for political reasons it was not the right moment to do so. He referred to the threat of war between Arabs and Jews. He also mentioned that Christians in the Middle East were not prepared for such a declaration. Indeed, many of their liturgical texts, going back to the 6th century, were characterised by anti-Semitism. The message of Cardinal Meouchi, the Maronite Patriarch of Antioch, on March 19, followed the same line. Moreover, he complained about the praise addressed to Muslims: throughout the centuries his people were persecuted by Muslims. The Muslims' moral behaviour was compared to the behaviour of animals. Meouchi could only accept a rather general statement, without details, and he even suggested putting that statement either in the text on religious freedom or in schema XIII. Patriarch Batanian of Cilicia of the Armenians, for his part, expressed his fear with regard to the consequences of the text for the Christians in the Arab countries. He suggested retiring the declaration from the Council's programme and to give it to the pope. If this was no longer possible, it might be better to promulgate a rather mitigated declaration. The next day, Willebrands, now with Duprey[41] and Corbon[42], went again to Bishop Sarkissian of the Orthodox Armenian Church, an observer at the council[43]. This bishop said that he had made tremendous efforts in order to explain the declaration to his folk, but added that the Armenians are surprised that people speak about the persecution of the Jews but not of persecuted and martyred Christians such as those in Armenia[44]. The most important visit of Willebrands was probably the one to Patriarch Maximos IV Saigh, the Melkite Patriarch of the Syrians (Antioch). Willebrands, Duprey and Corbon visited the patriarch twice, the 21st in

---

40. *AS* IV,4, p. 107.

41. P. Duprey (1922-2007), a French White Father, was professor of dogmatic theology at the Séminaire de Sainte Anne in Jerusalem from 1956 to 1963. He became subsecretary of the oriental section of the SCUF in 1963. From 1983 to 1999 he was secretary of the *Pontificium Consilium ad Unitatem Christianorum fovendam*.

42. J. Corbon (1924-2001), a French Dominican, was an ecumenist and member of the international theological commission.

43. Willebrands had already visited the Armenian Katholikos Khoren and Bishop Sarkissian in the afternoon of the 20th of March.

44. In his report, Willebrands also states that the information about the Council is very poor in the Middle East: "Chez le peuple on rencontre souvent l'opinion que le Concile n'a parlé que des Juifs!" ASV Conc. Vat. II, p. 8.

the afternoon and the 22nd. At this stage Maximos was opposed to the declaration on the Jews for he considered it as inopportune. If a declaration might be needed, let it be very general without any details. The first visit ended with a meeting with the Syrian-Orthodox Patriarch Ignatius Iacoub, someone who had reacted vehemently against the declaration, but now complained about the fact that Catholic bishops no longer wanted to meet him, although he in no way wanted to be an enemy of the Catholics.

How did Willebrands answer these critiques on and objections to the declaration[45]? First, it should be said that Willebrands emphasized in the several meetings he had that many of the proposals of the fathers had been integrated in the text as corrected by the sub-commission and the plenary commission in February-March, and that even now the text was not yet definite and modifications still could be made[46]. He also mentioned that his trip was not only meant to inform the patriarchs but also to make him better aware of the situation in the Middle East.

In his discussion with Maximos Willebrands first of all emphasized that it would be unfair to put all the problems in the hands of the pope, a concern that will regularly return in Willebrands' notes. In case the text should be withdrawn from the Council, it would be better, Willebrands suggested, to hand over the matter to both the SCUF and the newly created Secretariat for relations with non-Christian religions. In any case one should not give the impression that the pressure of Arab politics and the current circumstances are the reason for giving up the project. Instead, it would be wiser to explain that the relations between church and synagogue, Christian and non-Christian religions still needed further theological reflection and that, therefore, a conciliar declaration might be premature. He also opined that a general condemnation of racism and anti-Semitism could be included in another document or in Schema XIII. Although such a solution clearly pleased Maximos, Willebrands was aware and explicitly mentioned that it would be hard to take away the declaration from the council. In this regard, he referred to both public opinion and the position of the episcopacies of both the US and a good number of European countries.

Willebrands' first report reveals that the positions of the patriarchs are quite unanimous: no to the promulgation because of political and ecumenical arguments. It also reveals Willebrands' willingness to listen to

---

45. In his report, Willebrands combines information with interpretation, explaining why patriarchs took this or that position.
46. ASV Conc. Vat. II 1458, p. 1 (visit to Tappouni).

the concerns of the patriarchs. Willebrands personally suggests means by which the impasse could be overcome, but is aware of the difficulties one is confronted with at this stage of the conciliar developments.

III. AN INCIDENT

However, Willebrands' first travel to the Middle East seemed to be "controlled" by the Secretariat of State. On March 19 the Secretariat of State had asked the nuncios of both Lebanon and Syria to write a report on Willebrands' travel. These reports arrived in Rome at the end of March, and on April 13 were sent by Secretary of State Cicognani to Bea[47]. The report by the nuncio of Lebanon makes clear that Willebrands' own report was objective, fair and honest[48]. It confirms Willebrands' awareness of the difficult situation and his willingness to look for adequate solutions: "Monsignor Willebrands gli proponeva un altro testo più attenuato, che il Cardinale, però, respingeva completamente. Questo mi diceva, inoltre, di aver avuto la impressione che il suo interlocutore si fosse convinto dalle ragioni addotte" (Meouchi to the Nuncio Alibrandi). It also offers additional information. In the meeting with Batanian, Willebrands explicitly referred to the wish of John XXIII and that of many fathers outside the Middle East. It also becomes clear that the observer Sarkissian, present at the meeting with the Katholikos, made great efforts to explain the need for a text on the Jews in the Middle East, the rationale for why he was called the "Avvocato del Vaticano". Finally, the report mentions that according to Willebrands this matter was not yet sufficiently studied by theologians and that further discussion was still needed. At the same time, Willebrands made clear that a declaration about the Jews was strongly wished for by the Germans and the Americans.

The report of the nuncio of Syria (March 27) is very similar and confirms the objectivity of Willebrands' report. The report makes clear that the nuncio was not aware that Willebrands was secretary of the SCUF, for he called him the Secretary of the Commission of non-Christians. In his report the nuncio mentions that the Eastern bishops will protest against a document that acquits the Jews of the accusation that they are the murders of Christ by leaving the Council and the nuncio himself wondering whether he can continue to do his work in Syria "essendo non solo Internunzio Apostolico ma anche Capo della Comunità siriana

---

47. ASV Conc. Vat. II, 1458.
48. For this report of March 27, 1965, see ASV Conc. Vat. II, 1458.

Latina." The report is also interesting because the nuncio himself explicitly argues against a text in favour of the Jews!

These reports were sent by the Secretary of State to Bea who let them be read by Willebrands. Bea and Willebrands were shocked by the Secretariat of State's distrust and in a letter of April 20, 1965 Willebrands even wondered whether it was worth to continue his efforts in the Middle East[49].

IV. THE SECOND VISIT

In any case people were of the opinion it was worth continuing the efforts, since from April 23 to April 30 Willebrands visited yet again the Middle East, this time meeting people in Jerusalem, Cairo, and Addis Ababa. During his visit to Jerusalem he not only met the patriarch of the Latin Church, Gori, but also representatives of other Christian denominations, such as Greek Orthodox Metropolitan Basilius, Archimandrite Germanos, Armenian Orthodox Derderian and Anglican Archbishop McInnes. Several of these non-Catholic churches had disapproved of the idea of a declaration on the Jews, and thus Willebrands wanted to personally inform them about the reasons why such a declaration might be useful. In a detailed report about this trip[50] Willebrands described the tense situation because of the creation of the Israeli state and the loss of property for the Palestinians. For Gori this was a sufficient reason to reject any declaration on the Jews. Even proposals to change the text with regard to *deicidium* or to the condemnation of anti-Semitism could not change his view. A significant number of Orthodox Christians, among them those of the Coptic Orthodox Church, were opposed to the declaration and supported the Catholics in this regard. It was said that Maximos had threatened to leave the council in case the declaration should be approved[51]. Also, the Arabic political world was hostile to the declaration: this could lead to a rupture of diplomatic relations and cause much trouble for Arab Christians[52]; Finally, Willebrands proposed in his report

---

49. ASV Conc. Vat. II 1458 and L. DECLERCK (ed.), *Les Agendas conciliaires de Mgr J. Willebrands, secrétaire du Secrétariat pour l'Unité des Chrétiens*, Leuven, 2009 (April 15, 1965), p. 171. It might be an interesting exercise to compare in detail the reports of the nuncio's with that of Willebrands.

50. See *AS* V,3, 314-320.

51. Cf. the report of internuncio Punzolo to Cicognani (March 27, 1965), ASV Conc. Vat. II 1458.

52. See Report Willebrands, 318.

either to change parts of the text or not to promulgate the declaration and consider the text as a guideline for the activities of the SCUF and the Secretariat for the non-Christian religions[53].

It should be mentioned that Cardinal Bea was not really pleased with the second proposal of Willebrands, a proposal not only suggested during the meeting with Maximos (March 21) but also during the meeting with Bishop Samuil (April 26). He requested that Willebrands should present this proposal as his personal opinion[54]. Indeed, Bea, a German and specialist of the Old Testament, really wanted to have a declaration on the Jews promulgated, while Willebrands, who already went before the council, was hesitant about the inclusion of the dialogue with the Jews into the ecumenical activities[55].

It goes without saying that, given the clear opposition of the patriarchs, the May 9-15 meeting of the SCUF would become a challenging, if not difficult, one[56]. Especially the fact that the pope informed Bea on April 25, 1965 that Maximos was vehemently opposed to the "deicidium" and that in such a context the pope could not promulgate the declaration if that might result in Maximos leaving the *aula*, complicated things[57]. In an important intervention on May 12, the Bishop of Bruges, Msgr. De Smedt insisted on the proclamation of the declaration in the council. He stressed the need to repeat again that the declaration had no political intention – if this might facilitate things, he suggested to leave out "deicidium" - but asked that the declaration should clearly state that the whole Jewish people could not be considered responsible for the death of Christ[58]. The meeting was also very much affected by the intervention of the German bishop J. Stangl (Bishop of Würzburg) who explicitly referred to the genocide[59]. The SCUF was very much aware of the difficult situation and finally opted for a compromise text – better a compromise text than no text –, for, as Congar stated: "Vingt ans après Auschwitz, il est impossible que le concile ne dise rien"[60].

53. Cf. BURIGANA – TURBANTI, *The Intersession: Preparing the Conclusion of the Council* (n. 33), p. 552. Willebrands already suggested this during his visit to Egypt; Report Willebrands, 317.

54. Cf. Agenda Willebrands, 3, 6, 8, 9 May, 1965.

55. Cf. SALEMINK, *"You Will Be Called Repairer of the Breach"* (n. 6), pp. 19-21.

56. Father Long s.j. made a substantial report of the meetings of May 12, 13, and 14. See ASV Conc.Vat. II 1458.

57. Cf. *AS* V, 3, 211.

58. Cf. F. De Smedt 1477 (Centrum voor Conciliestudie Vaticanum II, Maurits Sabbe Bibliotheek, Faculteit Godgeleerdheid, K.U Leuven) and Report Long, 5-7.

59. Report Long, 9-10; cf. also BURIGANA – TURBANTI, *The Intersession: Preparing the Conclusion of the Council* (n. 33), pp. 566-567.

60. Cf. CONGAR, *Mon Journal du concile* (n. 17), II, p. 366.

V. The Third Visit: The Wind is Changing

Meanwhile, attempts should be made to explain more properly the (yet again) corrected text to the Oriental bishops and in the Arabic world. This was the immediate cause of a new visit by Willebrands, De Smedt and Duprey to the Near East (July 18-24)[61]. The visit was requested of and approved by Paul VI. It was clearly an official visit: to every patriarch a letter, written by Cicognani, was offered[62]. The report reveals a good collaboration and interaction between Willebrands and De Smedt. It also explicitly mentions that Willebrands' earlier proposals, results of his previous visits (not to promulgate the text but to transfer it to both the SCUF and the Secretary for the non-Christians religions), were not accepted by the bishops in the SCUF. These bishops considered such a proposal too radical, for endangering the Church's authority and diminishing the Council's credibility. The report stresses the care the SCUF had taken in order to meet the requests as formulated in the *modi*, while respecting the results of the vote of 1964. Willebrands also reported about his contacts with Visser 't Hooft in Geneva, Metropolitan Chrysostom of Myra and the secretary of the Holy Synod of Constantinople in Constantinople. Visser 't Hooft insisted on the promulgation of the text, while the metropolitan and the secretary explicitly stated that the Patriarch of Constantinople agreed with the schema of the declaration. In other words, the representatives of both denominations supported the Catholic projects about the Jews. Mention was also made of the efforts that would be undertaken to ameliorate the information on the Council in the Arabic language in order to inform the Islamic world as much as possible. Both the given information and the reading of the corrected text convinced the Maronite Patriarch Meouchi (met on July 19-20), Maximos IV Saigh (during the meeting with him on July 19, a considerable time was spent on the question how to inform the Arabic world)[63], Patriarch Batanian (of the Catholic Armenians; met on July 19 in the evening), Tappouni (Patriarch of the Syriac Church; met on July 20) and, with some

61. For a substantial report of this travel, see ASV Conc.Vat. II 1459. Cf. also *Les Agendas conciliaires de Mgr. J. Willebrands*, July 18-24, 1965.
62. See ASV Conc.Vat. II 1459.
63. The report also explicitly mentions that during the meeting neither the Patriarch nor the other representatives of the Melkite Church spoke about the leaving of the Council in case of acceptance of the declaration. 3 of the 4 changes, requested by Maximos IV, will find (not without difficulty) their way into the declaration; For the emendations proposed, see De Smedt Papers, no. 1475, and the letter of Maximos to Bea, July 26, 1965 (ASV Conc. Vat. II 1459).

hesitation[64], Sidarouss (Patriarch of the Copts; met on July 23 in Cairo)[65]. The visit thus seemed to have been a success[66]. In fact, there was only one exception, Latin Patriarch, Gori, although some of his remarks were taken into account[67]. Gori continued to raise ecumenical and political objections while his colleagues finally approved the text and were prepared to defend it in the event of further difficulties.

With this visit Willebrands, De Smedt and Duprey thus finally convinced most of the patriarchs in the Middle East to support the declaration on the non-Christian religions.

By Way of Conclusion

The three reports reveal that Willebrands first and foremost acted as a diplomat, a secretary at the service of the SCUF, a man seeking an adequate solution in a very difficult and complicated dossier. Although the proposals he made during his first two visits to the East were not accepted by both Bea and the plenary council of the SCUF in May 1965, this did not result in bitterness or disappointment. Willingness to opt for compromises if this might help the case and obedience to decisions of the SCUF did not exclude each other. Like De Smedt, his good friend, Willebrands had no theological pretentions. As became clear in his letter of protest to Bea, he wanted to be a man at the service of the Church. It might be true that from a theological standpoint some of the emendations during the course of the process appeared to undermine the strength of

---

64. The report reveals that the Patriarch's auxiliary, Msgr. Youhanna Kabes, is clearly against the declaration and this because of political, ecumenical and dogmatic reasons; Sidarouss seems to be more moderate and wants to see how things will develop during the Council. The latter will sent a letter to Cicognani (July 26), expressing his fear for reactions in the Arabic world but also his willingness to obey to the Church's doctrine (ASV Conc. Vat II, 1447).

65. Cf. L. DECLERCK – A. HAQUIN (eds.), *Mgr. Albert Prignon, Recteur du Pontificio Collegio Belga. Journal conciliaire de la 4ᵉ Session*. Préface de Mgr A. JOUSTEN. Introduction par Cl. TROISFONTAINES (Cahiers de la Revue théologique de Louvain, 35), Louvain-la-Neuve, 2003, p. 269.

66. CONGAR, *Mon Journal du Concile* (n. 17), II, p. 392.

67. See his letter to Cicognani, dated August 10th, 1965 (*AS* VI,4, p. 405-407). Gori appears to have been someone who stubbornly held on to his own convictions. This is apparent, among other things, from the fact that he continued to raise problems after the declaration had been approved in October, 1965, with respect to the use of Rom 11,28 in the text, for example. When it appeared that Bea was refusing to make any changes to the text on account of the ballot results, Gori had the audacity to say: "Je ne puis vraiment m'empêcher de penser qu'un tel procédé est peu digne d'un texte conciliaire et je m'en étonne d'un exégète de la classe de Votre Éminence" (*AS* V,3, p. 513).

the *Textus approbatus*, but one has to wonder whether another solution was possible. A conciliar text has to take into account the well being of the Church as a whole. 2,312 fathers took part in the final votes of October 28th. 2,221 voted *placet*, 88 *non placet*, 2 *placet juxta modum* and 1 vote was invalid. This result made clear that an overwhelming majority of bishops approved this compromise text[68]. *Nostra Aetate* was a fact, a result, partly, of Willebrands' travels to the East.

Faculteit of Theology
and Religious Studies
KU Leuven
Sint-Michielsstraat 4/3101
B-3000 Leuven

Mathijs LAMBERIGTS

Begijnhof 7
B-8000 Brugge

Leo DECLERCK

---

68. That critiques and objections continued to exist throughout the fourth session is made clear in LAMBERIGTS – DECLERCK, *Nostra Aetate 4* (n. 22).

JOHANNES WILLEBRANDS AS A THEOLOGIAN OF THE JEWISH-CHRISTIAN DIALOGUE

I. BIOGRAPHICAL NOTES

Johannes Willebrands played an important role in the dialogue between the Catholic Church and the Jewish people. Some biographical data may shed somewhat more light on his involvement with Judaism. In his extended family there was a pioneer who was fascinated by the 'mystery of Israel'. The monk Jacob Willebrands who spent 40 years of his life in Israel contemplating and solidarizing himself with both Jews and Palestinians, was a grand-nephew of the cardinal. The story of this monk testifies to an important development within Jewish-Catholic relations, that started even before Willebrands was involved in it. Jacob Willebrands' uncle was the Franciscan friar Laetus Himmelreich, who was one of the founders of the *Amici Israel* in 1926. This movement consisted of 3,000 priests and several hundred bishops. It strove to combat anti-Semitism in the Catholic Church and wished to foster understanding for Judaism and even for Zionism. After the *Amici Israel* questioned the prayer for the Jews on Good Friday: *Pro perfidis Iudaeis*, the Vatican removed this prayer from the Good Friday service in 1928. After the Second World War, Himmelreich gave a 'retraite' in the convent of the Trappists in Zundert, where his young nephew Jacob Willebrands lived, and told about his lifelong desire to go to the Holy Land. His handicap, due to Nazi experiments in Dachau, prevented that. Jacob Willebrands then decided to go to live in Israel in contemplation and solidarity, in order to fulfill the lifelong desire of his uncle[1].

Johannes Willebrands was less of a charismatic pioneer and more of a diplomat. Still, personal experiences seem to have played a certain role in his later involvement with Judaism. In his own pastoral work as a chaplain at the Beguinage (Begijnhof) in Amsterdam during the difficult years of 1937-1940, Willebrands entertained good relations with some Jewish families there. He was even invited to religious festivities[2]. The

---

1. See M. POORTHUIS – T. SALEMINK (eds.), *Op zoek naar de blauwe ruiter: Het leven van Sophie / Francisca van Leer*, Nijmegen, Valkhof, 2000.
2. Willebrands relates how two Jewish men brought him Torah scrolls during the war. When he was professor at the seminary of Warmond, someone from the Jewish community came to fetch the scrolls. See J. WILLEBRANDS, *Het hedendaagse jodendom als vraag*

scant information suggests that after some hesitance he eventually
baptized a Jewish woman from Austria, who wished to become Catholic
out of inner conviction[3].

After the war Willebrands became acquainted with Ottilie Schwarz
(1922-1986) from Vienna, who had a Jewish father. Initially, Ottilie
belonged to the Protestant church that even paid for her theological studies. Gradually, she became convinced that, in spite of the high appreciation of Bible and Judaism in those circles, Protestant ecclesiology did not
do full justice to the 'mystery of the Church'. Under the influence of
another 'founding father' of the *Amici Israel*, the charismatic Crutched
Friar Anton van Asseldonk, she decided to become Catholic. On July
25th, 1951, she was baptized in the Willibrord Church in Utrecht. The
same year Willebrands employed her as a secretary on behalf of his work
for the *Conférence pour les Questions Oecumeniques*. Remarkably,
Willebrands took care that her theological studies continued to be paid
by the *Willibrord Vereniging voor Oecumene*, even after she had left the
Netherlands for Vienna. Eventually, Ottilie would become the first Dutch
Catholic woman to write a theological dissertation. The dissertation,
completed in 1965, dealt with one of the Qumran scrolls, the document
of the Covenant of Damascus. During the 1950s Ottilie Schwarz was
a member of the Catholic Council for Israel, affiliated with the Sint
Willibrord Vereniging voor Oecumene[4].

In 1957 the book *Het mysterie van Israel* [The Mystery of Israel]
appeared, with its title strongly referring to Jacques Maritain (whose wife
Raïssa was Jewish but had converted to Catholicism) and to Charles
Peguy and even to Leon Bloy. Ottilie Schwartz was the editor of the
book, containing two contributions by herself and prefaced by Willebrands. In that preface Willebrands emphasized that the ultimate goal for
Jews is "to recognize that Jesus is the Christ"[5].

It is no coincidence that all the encounters with Judaism so far took
place in an atmosphere of conversion. Not only were the Catholic Jews

aan het zelfverstaan van de katholieke kerk, in M. POORTHUIS (ed.), *Tot leren uitgedaagd:
Werkboek over de betekenis van het hedendaagse jodendom voor de katholieke kerk*,
's Hertogenbosch, Sint-Willibrordvereniging, 1993, 111-123, p. 111.

   3. *Ibid.*, pp. 111-112.

   4. See T. SALEMINK (ed.), *"You Will Be Called Repairer of the Breach" : The Diary
of J.G.M. Willebrands 1958-1961*, Leuven, Peeters, 2009, pp. 19-21. A more elaborate
biography of Ottilie Schwartz in M. POORTHUIS – T. SALEMINK, *Ottilie Schwartz, assumpta
a Cruce*, in M. DERKS – P. NISSEN – J. DE RAAT, *et al.* (eds.), *Het licht gezien: Bekeringen
tot het katholicisme in de twintigste eeuw*, Hilversum, Verloren, 2000, 93-117.

   5. J. COOLS – O. SCHWARTZ (eds.), *Het mysterie van Israël*, Utrecht – Antwerpen,
Spectrum, 1957, p. 8.

pioneers in the fostering of better understanding of Judaism within the Catholic Church, but Catholics themselves had hardly any knowledge of Judaism or encounters with Jews. Combating anti-Semitism had been a new phenomenon within the Catholic Church, roughly starting with the *Amici Israel* in 1926. However, this newly discovered divine love for Israel was always connected to the ultimate conversion of Judaism. At the end of the fifties, however, this changed, both in the Netherlands and abroad. Jewish thinkers and writers continued to influence Catholic theologians. The impact of the Shoah was – with a delay of some fifteen years – debated in the society at large, thanks to Jewish historians such as Lou de Jong and later on Jacques Presser. The Eichmann trial in 1961 also shocked the world. The play *Der Stellvertreter* in 1963, a quite unhistorical complaint against the alleged silence of Pius XII during the war, did even more than historical accounts to put the Jewish-Christian dialogue on the agenda of the Church. Still, the first traces of a new theology in which God "did not deplore his vocation of the Jews", based upon a covenant "that had never been revoked", could be heard already in the fifties. In the Netherlands, the chairman of the *Katholieke Raad voor Israel* (Catholic Council for Israel), Msgr. Antoon Ramselaar, brought together pioneers such as the Lutheran theologian Karl Thieme, Gertrud Luckner who was a survivor from Ravensbrück, the priest from Jewish descent John Oesterreicher (1904-1993), who would become a 'peritus' at the Second Vatican Council, and the priest Paul Démann (1912-2005), editor of the *Cahiers Sioniens* and likewise from Jewish descent. In 1960 this conference sent a text with eleven recommendations about the relationship between the Church and Judaism to the Secretariat of Christian Unity in Rome, where Cardinal Bea and Msgr. Willebrands worked, the so-called 'Apeldoorn' document[6]. Traces of this new theology would later on materialize in *Nostra Aetate*, the declaration of the Second Vatican Council on non-Christian religions.

During the preparations for *Nostra Aetate*, Willebrands had to travel to Arab countries to face the objections by the bishops there to the declaration, in which they observed a political and pro-Zionist stand, although neither the Holocaust nor the state of Israel are mentioned in it[7].

To conclude this little biographical overview, I like to point to a Dutch connection in order to assess Willebrands' involvement with the dialogue

---

6. See M. POORTHUIS – T. SALEMINK, *Een donkere spiegel: Nederlandse katholieken over joden 1870-2005*, Nijmegen, Valkhof, 2005, pp. 590-591. In the city of Apeldoorn Ramselaar was president of the seminary.

7. L. DECLERCK (ed.), *Les agendas conciliaires de Mgr. Willebrands*, Leuven, Peeters, 2009, pp. xxvii-xxviii.

with Judaism, be it at a distance. Willebrands was fascinated by a small convent for women near Egmond, the Lioba foundation with its artistic and idiosyncratic abbess Hildegard Michaelis. Willebrands helped the sisters – some 60 around 1960 – to get approval from Rome. Willebrands' colleague at the seminary of Warmond, Father Cornelis Rijk (1921-1979), served as a chaplain to the sisters. After a journey in the land of Israel, which he documented in a sympathetic account, Cornelis Rijk became a member of the board of the *Catholic Council for Israel* in the Netherlands[8]. Rijk was more versed in Bible and Hebrew than Willebrands, who had specialized in Cardinal Newman, incidentally a convert too[9]. Rijk conducted conferences about the New Testament and introduced to the convent Chaim Storosum, the *chazan* (cantor) of the Liberal Jewish Synagogue of The Hague. Storosum taught Hebrew and demonstrated to the sisters how to chant the psalms in Hebrew. At the initiative of Willebrands, Father Rijk started to work at the Secretariat for Promoting Christian Unity in Rome in 1966. However, Rijk left the Secretariat in 1972 to become the director of the SIDIC (*Service International de Documentation Judéo-Chrétienne*). A certain personal animosity between the two men seemed to have cropped up. However, different views on the necessity for the Vatican to recognize the state of Israel, strongly advocated by Rijk, may have played a more important role in an ensuing estrangement between the two from that time on.

These scant biographical notes demonstrate two things. First, for Willebrands, interest in Judaism was as it were a by-product of his interest in ecumenism, rather than a lifelong passion. Second, the atmosphere of conversion was for him paramount in the early years of Jewish-Catholic dialogue.

II. THEOLOGY OR DIPLOMACY?

The International Catholic–Jewish Liaison Committee was founded in 1971 and had as its task to enable yearly encounters between the Vatican Commission for Religious Relations with the Jews (a commission operating

---

8. C. RIJK, *Bezinning op bijbelse grond: Een reis door het land van Gods keuze*, Haarlem, De Toorts, 1959.

9. Rijk also participated in the Phoenix Bible pockets project, the largest cooperation between Jewish and Christian scholars in the Netherlands. The first volumes of the series were published in 1962. See POORTHUIS – SALEMINK, *Een donkere spiegel* (n. 6), pp. 596-597.

under the Secretariat for Promoting Christian Unity) and the International Jewish Committee on Interreligious Consultations.

The documents produced both from Jewish and from Christian sides show a lively interest in a variety of topics: religion and land in Jewish and Christian traditions, mission and witness of the Church, the image of Judaism in Christian education and vice versa, religious freedom, secularism as a challenge, sanctity of human life, youth and faith[10]. Only one lecture is from the hand of Willebrands, on the occasion of the twentieth anniversary of *Nostra Aetate*. Moreover, the procedure at these conferences is not a free theological exchange, as I had the occasion to note when being present myself in 1985. The papers are delivered by invited experts, but their reflections do not oblige either side, Catholic or Jewish. There is no discussion at the table; exchange takes place on an individual level after the official sessions. Understandable as this procedure may be, we wonder whether we might expect from Johannes Willebrands a genuine theology of the Jewish-Christian dialogue. Theological reflection should necessarily enjoy greater freedom and possibilities to explore hardly trodden paths than the magisterial teaching of the Church. Still, in an ideal situation there should be a lively interaction between both, respecting each specific and irreducible responsibility. In a sense, theological reflection could even be considered part of the magisterial teaching of the Church itself[11].

In the case of Willebrands, his reflections upon the Jewish-Christian dialogue are strongly influenced by his position as a Church leader. That does not necessarily detract from their theological relevance, but should be kept in mind. On closer scrutiny it works as follows: invited experts bring forward new ideas to offer the opportunity to official religious leaders to break new ground in the years to come[12]. The official declarations are as it were 'fed' by these conferences and the papers produced there. In what follows, we will have the opportunity to signal such influence

---

10. INTERNATIONAL CATHOLIC-JEWISH LIAISON COMMITTEE (ed.), *Fifteen Years of Catholic-Jewish Dialogue 1970-1985*, selected papers, with a preface by cardinal Willebrands and Gerhart Riegner, Vatican, Libreria Editrice Vaticana, 1988.

11. See A. DULLES S.J., *The Survival of Dogma*, New York, Doubleday, 1971. A more cautious approach in ID., *Magisterium: Teacher and Guardian of the Faith*, Naples, Florida, Sapientia, 2007, p. 27.

12. Similarly, declarations on Judaism by national conferences of bishops considered authoritative, such as the French or the American, serve as a test case for declarations by the Vatican. The French bishops first mentioned the land of Israel (April 16, 1973), to be followed by a statement of pope John Paul II during his encounter with the Jewish community of Mainz, November 17, 1980) and by the Vatican Committee for Religious relations with Judaism (June 24, 1985).

several times. Besides, Johannes Willebrands has delivered quite a few lectures on Judaism in which he expounds his ideas both as a Church leader and as a theologian. It is to that material that we now turn.

III. WILLEBRANDS AS A THEOLOGIAN OF JEWISH-CHRISTIAN DIALOGUE

We will survey Willebrands' thought on Judaism by focusing on three major questions:

1. Is Judaism the / a people of God, and is the Church the / a people of God?
2. In what way does the relationship with Judaism affect the Christian reading of the Bible?
3. Can there be a Christian mission to the Jews?

1. *Is Judaism the / a People of God and Is the Church the / a People of God?*

It seems that for Willebrands, the Church as people of God constitutes his point of departure. Ecclesiologies that seek to replace the notion of 'people' for the Church by other notions out of fear for ethnic associations that might be applicable to Judaism only, have not influenced Willebrands[13]. In line with *Lumen Gentium* section 2, for him the Church is the (new) people of God. Quite often, ecclesiologies use the term 'people of God' for the Church in a rather naïve way, as if this self-designation has no repercussions for the position of other faiths, notably for Judaism. In this light, *Lumen Gentium* is surprising. It seems that this constitution of the Church realizes that the relation with the Jewish people is not wholly extrinsic to the concept of the Church, as §16 proves:

> Finally, those who have not yet received the Gospel are related in various ways to the people of God. In the first place we must recall the people to whom the testament and the promises were given and from whom Christ

13. See about this debate: M. POORTHUIS – J. SCHWARTZ, *A Holy People: Jewish and Christian Perspectives*, Leiden, Brill, 2006, especially the contributions by H. Rikhof on *Lumen Gentium*, by E. Borgman on the 'people of God' in the theology of Schillebeeckx and by Simon Schoon on Protestant views such as Paul van Buuren's who rejects the notion of 'people of God' for the Church. The study of I. DE LA POTTERIE – B. DUPUY, *People, Nation, Land: The Christian View* (1973), in INTERNATIONAL CATHOLIC-JEWISH LIAISON COMMITTEE, *Fifteen Years of Catholic-Jewish Dialogue 1970-1985* (n. 10), 8-14, has been influential on Vatican statements afterwards.

was born according to the flesh. On account of their fathers this people remains most dear to God, for God does not repent of the gifts He makes nor of the calls He issues.

Lumen Gentium does not solve the theological question of how the Church as a people of God relates to Judaism as people of God. This issue is intrinsically related to the question of the covenant: is there one covenant of God with humankind, first contracted with Israel, and then replaced, or after *Nostra Aetate*, broadened, to include the Church? Or are there two or even more covenants such as with Noah (to include humankind), Abraham (to include the children of Abraham: Islam, Judaism and Christianity an idea more or less underlying *Nostra Aetate*)[14]? Willebrands seems to opt for one and the same covenant that was first given to Israel and fulfilled in Christ. Still he does not endorse the traditional idea that God has cancelled His covenant with Judaism[15].

The relationship between the Old Covenant and the New Covenant (which, as is known, is not a New Testament invention but was coined by Jeremiah 31 and quoted by Hebrews 8), is no longer that of contrast and rupture but of continuity. The words 'old' and 'new' receive a much more positive and mutually enriching connotation. No longer is 'old' an indication of 'anachronistic' or 'obsolete', but rather of 'venerated' and 'dear to God'. 'New' does not replace 'old', but receives the connotation of 'renewed'. It is surprising how frankly Willebrands admits that the Second Vatican Council does not claim to have solved all the theological problems concerning people and God and Covenant[16]. Still, his own preliminary conclusion, under reference to the same passage from *Lumen Gentium* quoted earlier, comes down to the following: there is a central people of God and the point to be made is how other 'peoples' are connected to it. The constitution "affirms the ongoing reality of Israel as a people, mysteriously chosen by God, and as such related to the church. Or shall we put it the other way round: the church related to Israel, Israel being what it is? Both perspectives are complementary. If *Lumen*

14. As is well-known, Massignon's thought has influenced the notion of Abrahamic religion in *Nostra Aetate*.

15. With the notable exception of the early Christian *Epistle of Barnabas*, which maintains that the covenant was already broken by the sin of the Golden Calf even before it was contracted.

16. J. WILLEBRANDS, *Faithful Minister of the Wisdom of God* (Cardinal Bea lecture 1985), in ID., *Church and Jewish People: New Considerations*, New York, Paulist, 1992, 39-56, esp. p. 43. A Dutch version of this lecture appears in M. POORTHUIS (ed.), *Vaticaan en jodendom in periode 1965-1985*, Twintig jaar in 14 documenten, 1-2-1-special, juni, Utrecht, R.K. Kerkgenootschap in Nederland, 1985.

Gentium has chosen the former, *Nostra Aetate* has chosen the latter. But both should be kept in mind"[17].

It is clear that, even if Willebrands as a theologian has not yet developed a completely coherent theology of Judaism, he clearly emphasizes the importance of a new relationship with Judaism. While stressing the latter, he admits that much work remains to be done on the former. His free admittance that his theological thought is characterized by 'a work in progress', testifies to his theological courage.

2. *In What Way the Relationship with Judaism Affects the Christian Reading of the Bible?*

The relationship with Judaism affects the Christian reading on at least two levels: on the level of the New Testament, especially the passages considered to be anti-Jewish; and on the level of the Old Testament and the proper use of it.

Willebrands devotes a separate lecture to the sensitive topic whether Christian anti-Semitism may have been fostered by passages from the New Testament. "Anti-Semitism is simply anti-Christian", he states firmly[18]. This may be true as an existential statement of how Christians should behave. However, as a historical statement, this one-liner tends to gloss over the historical entanglement of Christianity with anti-Semitism. Willebrands admits that many texts from the New Testament have had a long-lasting negative effect on the Christian view of Jews and Judaism. The classical Patristic dual perspective on the Church as, on the one hand, "a bride without spot or wrinkle", and, on the other hand, a community of human, all-too-human, sinners seems to form the background of his position. However, the application is not without its problems: the Church as immaculate bride would remain beyond any criticism by definition, whereas the Church as a community of sinners would be excused for her faults from the outset. Still, Willebrands is prepared to acknowledge that even New Testament texts themselves may contain problematic utterances about Jews and hence should be used with caution. Rightly, Willebrands points to the fact that Jesus and the apostles were Jews as was the Virgin Mary. Both the beginning of the gospel of Luke with its *Magnificat* and *Benedictus* as well as Saint Paul's Letter to the Romans

---

17. *Ibid.*, p. 43.

18. J. WILLEBRANDS, *Are the New Testament and Christianity Anti-Semitic?* (lecture in 1985), in ID., *Church and Jewish People* (n. 16), 77-94. One should realize that especially in America, the term anti-Semitism is often not distinguished from anti-Judaism, in contrast to Dutch usage.

9–11 contain strongly 'pro-Jewish' statements. "The most ancient keryg-matic presentation of Jesus, Son of Man and Son of God, includes an explicit reference to his Jewishness", namely as descended from David, Willebrands states (p. 80). He even refers to the problematic statements of Jesus to his disciples not to visit pagan territory, but rather to go to the lost sheep of Israel (Mt 10,5-6; 15,24).

Having said this, he turns to those New Testament passages that dis-play a highly negative perspective on Judaism, such as 1 Thess 2,16: "The Jews who killed the Lord Jesus and the prophets and drove us out: they displease God and oppose everyone by hindering us to speaking to the gentiles, so that they may be saved. They have constantly been filling up the measure of their sins, but God's wrath has overtaken them at last". And the other even more notorious example in Matthew 27,25: "The whole people shouted: 'Let his blood be on us and on our children". Although these texts have had a long lasting negative effect on the Chris-tian view of Judaism – Willebrands admits that they even had "anti-Semitic" consequences – it cannot be said that the New Testament as such is "anti-Semitic".

Judaism as such is not condemned in the New Testament, as the Law is upheld as holy and good, and even the Temple is visited by the first Christians after the resurrection. The crucifixion is on the deepest level what we believers in Christ commit every time when we are unfaithful to him. This notion, already present in Heb 6,4-6, was taken up by the Council of Trent, Willebrands points out. Historically, the Credo men-tions Pontius Pilate but not the Jews. To Willebrands, it is clear that historically the main burden of responsibility lies with Pilate, the Jewish leaders being accomplices. It does not seem probable, Willebrands main-tains, that a Jewish mob shouted for Jesus' death. On the contrary, Jesus was arrested in secret, because otherwise the crowd would have protested (Lk 22,2; Jn 18,3; Mk 14,49; Mt 26,4-5).

In addition to these historical notions, which Willebrands sees con-firmed in the declaration *Nostra Aetate*, there is the typological notion of the blood that brings redemption according to the Letter to the Hebrews, drawing typologically on the Day of Atonement (Lv 16,3-18). The prob-lematic text of "let his blood be upon us" (Mt 27,25) might be explained in that vein. We will deal with the remarkable emphasis on typology by Willebrands later on. Suffice it to state here that, according to Wille-brands, one should interpret problematic texts in light of the general positive stand towards Judaism in the New Testament, such as Romans 11,1-2: "has God rejected His people? Of course not". As is known, the notion of Israel as a mystery, which Maritain, Bloy and the *Amici Israel* introduced as an alternative to the theology of supersession, became prevalent in the 20th century, but has been derived from the Letter to the Romans as well (11,25).

We see how Willebrands wrestles with the chasm between the historical level and the theological level: on the historical level, the responsibility for the death of Jesus should remain with the Romans and with some Jewish leaders. However, on this historical level, the significance of the crucifixion cannot be explained exhaustively: theologically, all believers are responsible. The notion of the blood bringing forgiveness for all is clearly theological, but it has been confused in the past with the question of historical responsibility for the crucifixion. Willebrands' explanation of "let his blood be upon us", referring to Mt 27,25, as unconsciously salvific, was used already by Pope Pius XI, also referring to Mt 27,25: "Turn Thine eyes of mercy towards the children of that race, once Thy chosen people. Of old, they called down upon themselves the Blood of the Savior; may it now descend upon them as a laver of redemption and of life". However, if one wishes to avoid blaming the Jews, one should make clear that this expiatory function of Jesus' blood concerns all people, not just the Jews. Here, historical responsibility and a theological notion of forgiveness should be duly distinguished, whereas the latter cannot be applied to the Jews specifically. Willebrands' thought remains here somewhat confused in this respect, echoing the likewise ambiguous statements in Vatican declarations on the universal mission of the Church.

On the level of the proper use of the Old Testament by Christians, Willebrands emphasizes repeatedly the importance of a typological reading of the Hebrew Bible. This may come as a surprise[19]. Historically, however, he stands on firm ground as the Church developed this reading of the Old Testament in light of the similarity with the life of Christ to combat the influential 'heresy' of Marcion (2nd century CE). The latter argued that the God of the Old Testament, demanding justice and revenge, could not be equated with the loving Father of Jesus Christ. Church Fathers such as Irenaeus and Tertullian go out of their way to demonstrate the continuity between the Old Testament and the New Testament by emphasizing the lasting importance of the Jewish descent of Jesus. However, Willebrands fails to notice the dual strategy of the Church

---

19. J. WILLEBRANDS, *Unity between Old and New Covenant*, in ID., *Church and Jewish People* (n. 16), 95-114, p. 105; ID., *Het hedendaagse jodendom als vraag aan het zelfverstaan van de katholieke kerk* (n. 2), pp. 119-121. Moreover, the Vatican *Notes on the Correct Way to Present the Jews and Judaism in Preaching and Catechesis in the Catholic Church* from 1985, contain as well an emphasis on typology (§9 ff.).

Fathers, for by pleading for a typological interpretation, they simultaneously combat Jewish interpretations of the Hebrew Bible which continue
to view the Bible as a book dealing with a / their concrete Jewish people
existing until the present. In a way Marcion's reading of the Bible was
more historical and closer to the Jewish reading(s) in that he too acknowledged the people of Israel as the subject of the Hebrew Bible. However,
this is precisely one of the reasons for him to argue that the book has lost
its relevance for Christians. Willebrands errs when he states that in the
typological reading there is never the least suggestion of a replacement
of the 'ancient Israel" or of diminishing the significance of the Old
Testament[20]. On the contrary, this replacement of Israel by the Church
and of the bodily existence of a people by a spiritual and ecclesiastical
connotation is the cornerstone of typological reading. Nevertheless,
Willebrands' plea for a renewed reflection upon typological exegesis
deserves serious consideration. It might well be that a typological reading
should not be wholly abolished in view of the dialogue with Judaism.
Here the notion of a pluralist reading of the Bible should be elaborated,
in which Jewish readings figure as fully legitimate next to Christian readings of the Hebrew Bible, themselves tributary to, but distinguished from,
Jewish readings.

3. *Can There Be a Christian Mission to the Jews?*

This highly sensitive question calls for some historical background[21].
From the Jewish side, Catholic attempts at proselytizing are generally
abhorred, although there are some noteworthy exceptions to that, mainly
from the Orthodox Jewish side like Henry Siegman[22] and Jacob Neusner[23]. We should realize that the appeal to the Jews to convert, which
started in the 19th century (Lehman, Ratisbonne[24]), heralded a new

20. WILLEBRANDS, *Unity between Old and New Covenant* (n. 19), p. 105.
21. Later statements by the Vatican and by Willebrands were influenced by the paper
of T. FEDERICI, *Mission and Witness of the Church* (1977), in INTERNATIONAL CATHOLIC-
JEWISH LIAISON COMMITTEE (ed.), *Fifteen Years of Catholic-Jewish Dialogue 1970-1985*
(n. 10), 46-62.
22. H. SIEGMAN, *Ten Years of Catholic-Jewish Relations*, especially the paragraph
Christian Mission, in INTERNATIONAL CATHOLIC-JEWISH LIAISON COMMITTEE (ed.), *Fifteen
Years of Catholic-Jewish Dialogue 1970-1985* (n. 10), 27-45, pp. 39-40.
23. Neusner figures prominently in the book of J. RATZINGER, *Jesus of Nazareth*.
Neusner considers the new prayer for the Jews on Good Friday, to be discussed later, as
the counterpart of the Jewish *Aleinu* prayer, which prays for the conversion of the gentiles.
24. J. WILLEBRANDS, *Mary of Nazareth, Daughter of Zion: Sermon for the Feast of the
Apparition of the Virgin Mary to Alphonse de Ratisbonne* (January 20, 1984), in ID.,
Church and Jewish People (n. 16), 186-189.

Catholic approach towards the Jews, that of love for Israel, of rejection of anti-Semitism, and sometimes even of an understanding attitude towards Zionism (*Amici Israel*)[25]. Jews who converted to Catholicism, such as the Ratisbonne brothers, Francisca van Leer (1892-1953) and later on Joseph Stiassny (1920-2007), director of the Ratisbonne monastery in Jerusalem, John Oesterreicher, consultor of the Secretariat for Promoting Christian Unity and editor of the annual *The Bridge*, Gregory Baum[26], likewise consultor, Bruno Hussar o.p. (1911-1996), founder of a meeting centre for Jews and Christians in Jerusalem, the Isaiah House, were the pioneers in exploring the new field of Jewish-Christian dialogue. The agenda of Willebrands during the preparation of the Second Vatican Council testifies to this[27]. However, as the Catholic-Jewish dialogue developed, the prominence of converts itself became problematic.

In Protestant circles active mission to the Jews was (and in some circles still is) often felt as mandatory, precisely because of the love for Israel. This has to do with a specific ecclesiology, based upon an equally specific reading of Paul's Letter to the Galatians and his Letter to the Romans: namely, of the church consisting of Jews and gentiles. The majority of Christians are called from the gentiles to join the Jews, as wild branches grafted upon the Jewish root. For Protestants, mission to the Jews was not just another task next to mission to the 'pagans', but constituted the heart of the identity of the Church, regardless of the often poor results. In this Protestant perspective the Roman Catholic Church appeared more or less as the embodiment of the denial of the Jewish root.

The renewed interest in Saint Paul's Letter to the Romans has produced daring new theologies. Some argue that Paul wishes to combat precisely that triumphalism, to which the Church has fallen prey: of proclaiming the truth towards an erring and blindfolded Israel. The 'mystery', according to Paul, consists of the following: undeniably the gospels testify to mission to the Jews. Willebrands even emphasizes that Jesus

---

25. As is known, the Jewish convert Sophie Francisca van Leer was the 'archmother' behind the founding of the *Amici Israel* in 1926, to be abolished by the Vatican in 1928. See the biography by POORTHUIS – SALEMINK, *Op zoek naar de blauwe ruiter* (n. 1). More details about the *Amici Israel* in M. POORTHUIS – T. SALEMINK, *Katholizismus und Zionismus: Das Beispiel der Niederlanden*, in C. BOSSHART-PFLUGER – J. JUNG – F. METZGER (eds.), *Nation und Nationalismus in Europa: Kulturelle Konstruktion von Identitäten*, Stuttgart – Wien, Frauenfeld, 2002, 663-697; T. SALEMINK, *Katholische Identität und das Bild der jüdischen Anderen: Die Bewegung Amici Israel und ihre Aufhebung durch das Heilige Offizium im Jahre 1928*, in *Schweizerische Zeitschrift für Religions- und Kulturgeschichte* (2006).

26. DECLERCK (ed.), *Les agendas conciliaires* (n. 7), p. 6.

27. See SALEMINK (ed.), *"You Will Be Called Repairer of the Breach"* (n. 4), pp. 174 and 206.

forbids his disciples to go to the pagans and Samaritans. However, this movement should be considered an inner-Jewish affair. Precisely by denying the truth of the gospel, Judaism would have caused the shift from Israel to the gentiles, according to Paul. Hence Israel being 'blindfold' should not be regarded as a source of Christian triumphalism, but as an exhortation to modesty and gratitude. If it were not for Israel being 'blindfold', the gentiles would not have received the gospel at all. The Church now has as her primary mission the *goyim*, the *ethnè*, the peoples of the earth (cf. Mt 28,19). Only by an ethically outstanding behaviour, the Church may hope to make Israel 'jealous'.

This renewed reading of Romans 9–11, of which we give only a rough sketch, constitutes perhaps the greatest renewal in Jewish-Christian dialogue. Notions such as the Jewish people as the elder brother in the Parable of the Prodigal Son are traditional in Patristic literature, but they receive a wholly new interpretation as well. Christianity has converted from paganism (the youngest son) and returns home as it were, whereas Judaism had remained with the Father. That is why Christianity should maintain that only through Christ people can come to the Father. Simultaneously, Christianity should acknowledge that Judaism as it were is already with the Father. This idea, developed by the Jewish philosopher Franz Rosenzweig, constitutes a dialectical re-reading of Patristics and acknowledges the fact that Christianity is called to participate in the Jewish task of bringing the Name of God to the ends of the earth, *without replacing Israel*[28]. We will see how Willebrands picks up several of these notions, but in a very careful way.

Willebrands emphasizes that Church and Israel are profoundly connected on a theological level. Doing so, he counters Jewish objections to dialogue as something wholly extrinsic to Jewish convictions. Some Orthodox Jewish viewpoints, the most outspoken being that of Rabbi Moshe Feinstein, maintain that there can be no religious dialogue at all with any other religion. Sad memories of medieval religious disputations in which the Christian truth was forced upon the Jews with the threat of additional violence play their role here.

Well-known is the authoritative stance of Rabbi Joseph Soloveitchik, who maintained in 1964 that belief is such an intimate affair that it could not be shared with outsiders[29]. In this respect Willebrands' account of his

---

28. Incidentally, the use by Pope John Paul II of the designation of Judaism as "the elder brother" likewise constitutes a wholly new interpretation.

29. RABBI SOLOVEITCHIK, *Confrontation*, in *Tradition. A Journal of Orthodox Thought* 6 (1964), in reaction to Vatican 2, in which he defends cooperation on humanitarian and social matters, while rejecting dialogue on issues of faith. See R. KIMELMAN, *Rabbis*

conversation with Soloveichik in 1971 is highly noteworthy, as the rabbi is told to have stated: "dialogue between Jewish and Christians cannot be but theological. You are a priest, I am a Rabbi, can we speak otherwise than on the level of religion?"[30]. For Orthodox Judaism, this statement (to which, incidentally, only the cardinal can serve as a witness) is extremely important.

On a more reflective level, Willebrands argues that the Church should fulfil the obligation to preach Jesus Christ to the world. Here the words 'mission' and 'witness' are used in distinction from 'proselytizing', which refers to an active attempt to convert people to Christianity. Here it remains somewhat vague whether the preaching of Jesus Christ to 'the world' means the '*ethnè*', the peoples, Israel excepted or the peoples including Israel. Still, a specific mission to the Jews is rejected. 'Undue proselytizing' is the somewhat ambiguous expression, ambiguous because it is not clear whether this means rejection of proselytizing, which is undue anyway, or rejection of undue proselytizing only. Here Willebrands remains as vague as the Vatican declarations which reject 'undue proselytizing' while emphasizing the Church's mission to preach Christ to all humankind. "No one is excluded from the redeeming embrace of Christ, who on the cross, offered his life for the sins of everyone"[31]. As a caution, these declarations state that mission should be performed with the strictest respect for religious freedom. However, while this holds good for all people, it cannot be a fully adequate expression of the unique relationship between the Church and Judaism.

An incident in the Netherlands demonstrates this same ambiguous attitude of the cardinal. In 1988, the bishop of Haarlem, Hennie Bomers, expressed in an interview that it would be a blessing for the Jews if they would accept Christianity. The upheaval in Jewish circles reached Rome. Willebrands wrote that dialogue between Judaism and the Church should be distinguished from conversion. Quite pragmatically, he added that if dialogue were not distinguished from conversion, there would be no

---

Joseph B. Soloveitchik and Abraham Joshua Heschel on Jewish–Christian Relations, in *Modern Judaism* 24 (2004) 251-271.

30. WILLEBRANDS, *Het hedendaagse jodendom als vraag aan het zelfverstaan van de katholieke kerk* (n. 2), p. 118; J. WILLEBRANDS, *Nostra Aetate: The Fundamental Starting Point* (1985), in INTERNATIONAL CATHOLIC-JEWISH LIAISON COMMITTEE (ed.), *Fifteen Years of Catholic-Jewish Dialogue 1970-1985* (n. 10), 270-275, p. 273.

31. J. WILLEBRANDS, *Relations between the Church and Judaism* (1988), in ID., *Church and Jewish People* (n. 16), 115-122, p. 120. The continuation: "no longer can the historical responsibility of Christ's passion be blamed on all those Jews then living nor to the Jews of our own day", is a rather awkward attempt to connect salvation to the historical issue of responsibility of the death of Jesus.

dialogue at all, as far as Judaism is concerned. However, when the Dutch ecclesiastical journal headed these remarks with: "Cardinal says 'no' to mission to the Jews", Willebrands was quite upset about it[32].

Quite often, Vatican declarations bring up the universal obligation of the Church to preach Christ to the world quite abruptly, sometimes even with a polemical undertone. This had fuelled the idea of an interpolation into a text that itself would foster the dialogue and even give rise to the hypothesis of different factions within the Vatican working on the same document[33]. This may be true, but Willebrands' theological expositions display the same ambiguity here and there. It was Walter Cardinal Kasper, when president of the Pontifical Commission for the Religious Relations with the Jews, who, after similar negative reactions from Jewish side to the declaration *Dominus Jesus*, made a bold statement about conversion. He stated that conversion in the sense of liberating people from idolatry to bring them to belief in the one true God, cannot as such be applied to Judaism[34].

As is known, the recently introduced prayer for the Jews on Good Friday, which in celebrations of the Tridentine Mass should replace the old prayer *Pro perfidis Iudaeis*, expresses the wish that the Jews "should acknowledge Jesus Christ as the Savior of all men". This has raised renewed debates[35]. Has Cardinal Kasper backtracked from his earlier opinion, or does he maintain a point of view that was wrongly understood on the Jewish side? It becomes nearly impossible to distinguish the semantic intricacies of witness, mission and conversion. The argument that the Church endorses the strictest right of religious freedom holds good for all people, not only for the Jews and hence does not sufficiently clarify the unique bond between the Church and Judaism. Moreover, what alternative can there be for a Church that does not wish to use

32. See POORTHUIS – SALEMINK, *Een donkere spiegel* (n. 6), p. 720.

33. Clearest in the *Notes* of 1985, where §6 and §8 are interrupted by §7, which emphasizes that "Judaism and Christianity cannot be seen as two parallel ways of salvation", buttressed by a plethora of quotations.

34. "The term mission, in its proper sense, refers to conversion from false gods and idols to the true and one God, who revealed himself in the salvation history with His elected people. Thus mission, in this strict sense, cannot be used with regard to Jews, who believe in the true and one God. Therefore, and this is characteristic, there exists dialogue but there does not exist any Catholic missionary organization for Jews". See W. KASPER, *'Dominus Iesus': Address delivered at the 17th meeting of the International Catholic-Jewish Liaison Committee*, New York, May 1, 2001. Still, the formula leaves open that mission *in another sense of the word* is still applicable to the relation to the Jews.

35. Curiously, the other Tridentine prayers on Good Friday: 'pro paganis', and 'pro haereticis et schismaticis', likewise testify of an extremely un-dialogical and pre-Vatican 2 attitude, but were hardly debated.

outright force? Hence the appeal to religious freedom does not solve the problem. Kasper argued that the new prayer does not mandate active conversion, but only calls for Christian witness, leaving the matter as such to the Almighty[36]. Here we are invited to recognize again Saint Paul's eschatological perspective of Israel's salvation, only after all the gentiles have been reached.

Both Cardinal Willebrands and Cardinal Kasper frankly admitted that much theology still needs to be done, especially when it comes to the question of the lasting fidelity of God to the covenant with the Jews, which was never revoked. A theology of the Church having taken the place of Judaism has become obsolete after Vatican II, but has dominated history for almost nineteen centuries. To this theology of supersession *Nostra Aetate* has put an end. A new Catholic theology of Judaism is needed.

It is clear from the sometimes distorted explanations that Willebrands grappled here with one of the most sensitive issues of the Jewish-Christian relations. Pope John Paul II managed to overcome this ambiguity by concrete gestures of friendship and of dialogue from the perspective of a Church leader toward his 'elder brother', the Jewish representatives. This too was developed under the aegis of Cardinal Willebrands.

CONCLUSION

With Cardinal Willebrands we have met a theologian and a Church leader who was firmly committed to the dialogue with Judaism and displayed a high sensitivity in encounters with Jews. His ability to convey to his dialogue partners a deep sense of recognition and of respect contributed highly to the authoritative force of his reflections. His way to proceed was careful and step by step, sometimes even hesitant. Faced with new challenges, he did not always succeed to avoid contradictory statements. As such, his theology should be supplemented by Catholic theologians who have studied Jewish literature and history in depth and in correlation with the history of Christianity. They should be prepared to courageously tackle the problems and inconsistencies of Catholic theology towards Judaism. By doing so they will foster the relationship between the Church and Judaism that remains so vital for the inner life

---

36. *God Decides the When and the How*, letter from Cardinal Walter Kasper in the *Frankfurter Allgemeine Zeitung*, 21 March 2008. Although the prayer is obviously referring to Romans 11, the thrust does not seem to be the same to me.

of the Church itself. No doubt, both thorough historical reflections and free speculative imagination will open up hardly trodden paths and new windows. Still, Willebrands' reflections remain of value, not only as documents from history, but also for the present life of the Church. His careful approach is fruitful in periods of time such as ours, when fundamentalist currents seem to sweep away the gains of decades of interreligious dialogue. Above all, his thought testifies to the ardent desire to do justice to the wholly new reality of the dialogue with Judaism.

Tilburg School of Catholic Theology   Marcel POORTHUIS
Tilburg University
Heidelberglaan 2
NL 3508 TC Utrecht
The Netherlands

JOHANNES CARDINAL WILLEBRANDS AND JUDAISM

THE ARCHITECTURE OF THE JEWISH-CHRISTIAN DIALOGUE[1]

The major lines of Johannes Willebrands' thought and action regarding Jewish-Christian relations could be summarised, it seems to me, with a few particularly fruitful and apt Hebrew terms used to express his fundamental contribution in this field to the substance of religious thought in the twentieth century. These terms are *Emuna, Shoah, Torah, Tzedeq – Tzedaqah, Tiqqun olam, Teshuvah, Qehillah* and *Darke ha-Mashiah*. Above all, the sense of responsibility for and of the urgency of a knowledgeable and passionate action towards the re-establishment of fraternal relations between Christians and Jews can be found in the massive contents of the *Mishnah* and in the *Talmud*, which, in synthesis, pose the questions, "If not me, who else? And if not now, when"?

I. A Special Anniversary

On November 19th, 1962, Augustin Cardinal Bea – from whom Johannes Cardinal Willebrands would receive and develop his spiritual inheritance – presented to the Second Vatican Council the working text on ecumenism, which at that time, in its first version, still included the themes of Judaism and religious freedom[2]. In that initial text the wide-ranging themes of Christian unity, of Judaism and anti-Semitism, of religious freedom and of human rights, compared in a solidly interrelated manner and according to a criterion that guided the Council, made Willebrands capable of speaking to contemporary humanity with a message of meticulous efficacy, dialoguing with every culture, ethnicity, religion or philosophical and civic conviction. Today – after almost a half-century and a century since Willebrands' birth – we will briefly examine some aspects of the activity of the "Cardinal of dialogue", in

---

1. Rome, Presentation to the Colloquium held at the Pontifical Gregorian University on November 19th, 2009: *Il Cardinale Johannes Willebrands e l'Ebraismo: L'architettura del dialogo ebraico-cristiano.* English translation by Fr. Robert Mosher SSC.
2. S. SCHMIDT, *Agostino Bea il cardinale dell'unità*, Roma, Città Nuova, 1987, pp. 571-572.

particular that of an "architect and prophet of Jewish-Christian dialogue".

At the beginning of this proposal, two texts can efficaciously guide us which, I believe, were often present in the mind and heart of the cardinal. In the first text Paul creatively applies to a fundamental criterion of architecture to the proclamation of the Gospel: "According to the grace of God given to me, like a wise master builder I laid a foundation, and another is building upon it. But each one must be careful how he builds upon it, for no one can lay a foundation other than the one that is there, namely, Jesus Christ" (1 Cor 3,10-11).

The second text marvelously sums up the urgency that appeals to action according to the spirit of Judaism:

> Rabbi Tarfon said: The day is short and the task is great and the labourers are idle and the wage is abundant and the master of the house is urgent. He used to say: It is not thy part to finish the task, yet thou art not free to desist from it. If thou hast studied much in the Law much reward will be given thee, and faithful is thy taskmaster who shall pay thee the reward of thy labour. And know that the recompense of the reward of the righteous is for the time to come (*Avoth* 2, 15-16)[3].

It has been a precious gift for me to have been able to collaborate directly with "the Cardinal of Jewish-Christian dialogue" while serving first as Secretary of the Commission for Religious Relations with Judaism and later as consultor. The years 1986-1993 were particularly intense and of unique importance. They followed the historic visit of Pope John Paul II on April 13 1986, to the central synagogue of Rome. Then in 1989 was the succession in the presidency of the Pontifical Council for Promoting Christian Unity of Edward Cardinal Cassidy, assuming the post of Willebrands, who continued, as president emeritus, working daily with dedicated effort in the office set aside for him in the *palazzo* of the Congregation for the Eastern Churches overlooking the *Via della Conciliazione*. One could still breathe in the original atmosphere of the Council within the corridors and the small workroom, and the voice of Cardinal Bea still seemed almost to revive and reverberate, engrossed in exposing before the Council Fathers the basic themes of Jewish-Christian relations, themes that Willebrands would interpret and apply masterfully in the following decades.

---

3. *The Mishnah*, ed. and trans. H. DANBY, Oxford, Oxford University Press, [12]1977, p. 447.

II. EMUNÀ: LIFE, FAITH, ACTION

However, what could be the roots of this epochal turning-point in Jewish-Christian relations that Willebrands gathered from the hands of Bea? In order to understand it, and thereby to understand how this formed the basis of Willebrands' choices, we cannot ignore his formation within the ecumenical movement during the first half of the twentieth century, a movement widely studied by historians. There were the principal protagonists – John R. Mott, Nathan Söderblom, Patriarch Athenagoras, Yves Congar, W.A. Visser 't Hooft, Bea – in whose wakes he entered, sharing their passion for Christian unity, as he himself often recalled many times:

> We could consider the ecumenical movement of our times a very special gift, full of promise and of responsibility. That encouraged us to share the passion of Christ and the apostles [...] I would like to remember just two of these persons that I have been able to know personally and to admire, Doctor W. A. Visser 't Hooft and Augustin Cardinal Bea[4].

Equally, Willebrands also remembered with gratitude the example, the friendship and the collaboration of many Jews, among them Gerhart M. Riegner, Marc Tanenbaum, Joseph Lichten, Leon Klenicki, Abraham Heschel, Mordecai Waxman, Zachariah Schuster.

III. SHOAH

Characteristic of this pioneering movement was the determination to meld together faith, life and public action, in a personal and ecclesial interweaving in which solidarity and resistance to evil in its crudest form were built during the terrible trial of the Second World War. Just as the bellicose contest offered impetus to the ecumenical movement, so in an analogous manner the growing consciousness of the abyss of evil of the *Shoah* – the *mysterium iniquitatis* (John Paul II) – committed against the People of the Covenant – produced an ecclesial turning point of solidarity and collaboration with the Jews. Cardinal Bea had already lucidly recognized this – and after him, Willebrands, with the pontiffs and the Magisterium – when he presented to the Council the project of the declaration *Nostra Aetate*, on the relations between the Catholic Church and the other religions of the world:

---

4. J. WILLEBRANDS, *Una sfida ecumenica, la nuova Europa (Discorsi)*, Verucchio, Pazzini, 1995, p. 52.

The two-thousand-year-old problem of the relations of the Church with the Jewish people, as old as Christianity itself, has been rendered more acute, and is therefore brought to the attention of the Second Ecumenical Vatican Council, above all because of the excruciating extermination of millions of Jews on the part of the Nazi regime in Germany[5].

IV. Torah: Bible, Justice, Charity

Johannes Willebrands' participation in the Council as secretary of the new Secretariat for Promoting Christian Unity, starting in 1960, deeply symbolized as well a maturation in regard to attitudes towards the Jews. The conciliar accent on the importance of the ecumenical movement and on biblical renewal, the foundation of a renewed ecumenical theology as well as theological reflections on Judaism found in Bea its principal promotor, creating a movement that was supported and developed by exegetes, theologians and pastors such as Pietro Rossano, Franz Mussner, Clemens Thoma, Carlo Maria Martini. This was the life blood that nurtured, as well, the opening and the building up of fraternal relations with Judaism. It was this same conciliar perspective that had allowed Willebrands to work in deep harmony with the three papal protagonists of the historic turning point in the rediscovery of spiritual brotherhood between Israel and the Church: John XXIII, Paul VI and John Paul II.

This conciliar doctrine also included, among other robust biblical and theological foundations exposed in the dogmatic constitutions *Dei Verbum* (14-16) and *Lumen Gentium* (16), the great manifesto of the ecclesial and social struggle for justice and charity, expressed above all in the pastoral constitution *Gaudium et Spes*, and reflected in other conciliar texts, such as the declaration *Dignitatis Humanae*.

V. Tzedeq and Tzedaqah: *Nostra Aetate*

The synthesis of conciliar teaching on the relations between the Church and Judaism is found masterfully condensed in Section 4 of *Nostra Aetate* (October 28 1965), after due consideration of the important development of Jewish-Christian relations from the beginning of the Council on. The substance of this doctrine, in the elaboration of which

---

5. A. Bea, *La Chiesa e il popolo ebraico*, Brescia, Morcelliana, 1966, p. 7.

Willebrands lent the best of his own resources and energy, included five principal points:

(1) The Jewish people continue to be beloved of God, by strength of a Covenant never revoked.

(2) The Church, which in the people of Israel finds its own roots, continues to partake of this spiritual patrimony, beginning with the revealed Sacred Scriptures that the Hebrew Bible constitutes and up to this present time.

(3) The thesis of "deicide" and of the collective responsibility of the Jewish people for the legal process and the death of Jesus cannot be held.

(4) The Church abhors, deplores and condemns antisemitism in all its forms (and thereby, as well, in its various characteristic expressions, be they religious, cultural, political, etc.).

(5) The Church abstains from affirming the need for mission among the Jews as a people: in regard to this proposition, referring to – I believe – his colloquium with Rabbi Joseph Soloveitchik on March 8 1971 in New York, Willebrands informed me of a detail following up one of his questions about an eventual Jewish reaction[6].

Willebrands had requested of his authoritative interlocutor what would have been his own reaction if the Council had expressed an encouragement for the mission of the Church towards the Jews, focused on their conversion to Christianity. Soloveitchik firmly replied: For the Jewish people, this would have been worse than the *Shoah*.

The whole of the authoritative conciliar teaching inspired and supported Jewish-Christian dialogue, and the consequent common social efforts of Jews and Christians, as became evident in Latin America, especially in Brazil and Argentina, were described in a joint document of the International Catholic-Jewish Liaison Committee on the theme of justice and charity[7].

---

6. Willebrands made reference to this encounter with Rav Joseph Soloveitchik at other times. It was decisive for guaranteeing solid bases at the beginning of the official dialogue between the Catholic Church and the Jewish people. As a matter of fact, it is to be remembered that the first meeting of the International Liaison Committee (ILC) was held in Paris in December of 1971, cf. THE INTERNATIONAL CATHOLIC-JEWISH LIAISON COMMITTEE, *Fifteen Years of Dialogue, 1970-1985. Selected Papers*, Vatican City, Libreria Editrice Vaticana; Rome, Pontifical Lateran University, 1988, p. 273.

7. The document *Tzedeq and Tzedaqà* – Justice and Charity, Buenos Aires, 2004.

VI. Tikkun olam

An overall evaluation to sum up this course and its direction for the future is found in the program that the cardinal sketched out in 1989, on the occasion of an award – given jointly to him and Doctor Gerhart M. Riegner of the World Jewish Congress – of international recognition in São Paulo, Brazil. Speaking of the roots "of our common responsibility to promote human dignity, peace and freedom according to the high ethical standard God has given to us [Christians and Jews]", he wondered:

> In what ways can we Christians and Jews cooperate in this responsibility to work for the 'mending of the world' (the *tikkun olam*), to make this world a better place while serving the kingdom of Heaven? In his recent encyclical *Sollicitudo Rei Socialis* (December 30, 1987), John Paul II suggested that all people 'by their activity, by contributing to economic and political decisions and by personal commitment to national and international undertakings' implement 'the measures inspired by solidarity and love of preference for the poor.' Then the Pope addressed an appeal 'to the Jewish people, who share with us the inheritance of Abraham, *our father in faith* (*Rm* 4: 11), as well as to the Muslims who, like us, believe in the just and merciful God' (SRS II, 47)[8].

This programmatic line would be taken up again both by Edward Cardinal Cassidy and by Walter Cardinal Kasper, during their years at the Pontifical Council for Promoting Christian Unity, and would find mature formulation in the Buenos Aires document *Tzedeq and Tzedaqah* (Justice and Charity) mentioned above. The social encyclical *Caritas in veritate* by Pope Benedict XVI contains an ulterior in-depth examination of the motifs and of the areas of cooperation in which Jews as well as Christians could bring together all people of good will, particularly Muslims, who are also "children of Abram". As a sign of this continuity we value all that was rich and fertile in the intuition of Willebrands. In this common effort we seek to understand how to bring together in a genuine and prophetic way the two demands – only apparently opposed but, in reality, complementary – of service to humanity and of service to the messianic mission among Christians and their especially esteemed Jewish brothers, in a harmonic convergence that reveals them united, *diversi sed non adversi*, in a symphony of love and truth.

---

8. J. WILLEBRANDS, *Witness to the Living God*, address on the occasion of the presentations to Johannes Willebrands and to G. Riegner of the Awards "Patriarch Abraham Prize", São Paulo, June 11, 1989 (*Information Service* 70 [1989/ II] 75).

VII. TESHUVAH: STRUCTURES AND DOCUMENTS

Willebrands' actions turned out to be particularly effective upon instituting, in collaboration with Jewish institutions and organizations, common organisms and forms of action. Experts, secretaries and consultors joined them, people who knew how to discern and make decisions with determination and attention. Here we recall among them: Father Cornelius Rijk, first in charge of Jewish-Christian relations, Dominican Father De Contenson, Father Jorge Mejía (afterwards made a cardinal), Roger Cardinal Etchegaray, Bishop Pierre Duprey. Up to 1970 they were instituted together with the principal Jewish world organizations – the International Catholic-Jewish Liaison Committee – which on the Catholic side included five members nominated by the pontiff. This mixed international committee continues to be the principal instrument of dialogue between the Catholic Church and Judaism, and has produced over a period of forty years a series of declarations and joint documents[9]. A few years later, in 1974, Willebrands was the inspiration for the institution, by Paul VI, of the Holy See's Commission on Religious Relations with Judaism (*Commissio pro religiosis necessitudinibus cum Hebraeismo fovendis*), an organ of fundamental importance for the promotion of dialogue and collaboration, carrying out the conciliar declaration *Nostra Aetate*.

Of the three documents published up to now by this commission of the Holy See – *Guidelines*, 1974; *Notes*, 1985; *We Remember*, 1998 – the first two bear Willebrands' signature. The third owes to the cardinal its programmatic intuition, formulated and decided upon by him in August of 1987 – after Gerhart Riegner's inspiration – and reflects his many strong convictions. Great consequential results are derived from these documents: the renewal of catechesis and of the pastoral activity of the Church in its relations with the Jews, more mature convictions[10] regarding the Jewishness of Jesus, greater attention to the Jewish people who live in the State of Israel, consciousness of the historical sin of anti-Judaism and of anti-Semitism, and of the consequent ecclesial process of

---

9. Cf., THE INTERNATIONAL CATHOLIC-JEWISH LIAISON COMMITTEE, *Fifteen Years of Dialogue* (n. 6); AA. VV., *Chiesa ed Ebraismo oggi: Percorsi fatti, questioni aperte*, ed. N.J. HOFMANN – J. SIEVERS – M. MOTTOLESE, Rome, Editrice Pontificia Università Gregoriana, 2005; English translation: *The Catholic Church and the Jewish People: Recent Reflections from Rome*, ed. P.A. CUNNINGHAM – N.J. HOFMANN – J. SIEVERS, New York, Fordham University Press, 2007.

10. Cf. P.F. FUMAGALLI, *Roma e Gerusalemme: La Chiesa cattolica e il Popolo di Israele*, Milano, Mondadori, 2007, pp. 222-223, 272.

repentance, or *teshuvah*, of which Pope John Paul II made himself spokesman during the Holy Year of 2000. The institution in 2001 of a second mixed international Commission between the Holy See and the Chief Rabbinate of the State of Israel for Catholic-Jewish dialogue in Israel following the Fundamental Agreement of 1993 and the visit of Pope John Paul II to Israel and Jerusalem during the Holy Year 2000 represent as many steps forward, long hoped for and made possible thanks to the solid theoretical and institutional installation put into effect by Willebrands over some thirty years of untiring activity[11].

The same continuity can be seen today, in the "new bullet points for Jewish-Christian dialogue" in the pontificate of Pope Benedict XVI, as illustrated by Walter Cardinal Kasper[12], points that constitute other maturing, forward steps in the direction already indicated by Willebrands.

VIII. QEHILLAH: EUROPEAN AND GLOBAL PERSPECTIVES

In the final years of his activity Cardinal Willebrands wanted to highlight in a more explicit way some values, dimensions and aspects of Jewish-Christian dialogue that make it particularly relevant today. The fact that such a dialogue developed in the course of fifty years principally in Europe confirms its primarily European dimension, but this does not limit it. Rather, this drives it towards assuming wider responsibilities. The cardinal writes:

> When we refer to Europe as a 'common home' and speak of 'new evangelization', it is not possible to omit the theme of the relationship with the Jewish people, be this relationship historical, cultural or religious. Theological and historical motives, while definitively converging, move us to treat the subject: the *spiritual affinity* that unite us and the two thousand years during which the long event of our relationship has not always been easy. All these reasons make it urgent for Christians and for Jews to share the responsibilities, challenges and needs of the contemporary world[13].

Gathering together this challenge, in the program of the present pontificate, Pope Benedict XVI invites all humankind, of whatever religion and culture, to collaborate in 'charity in truth', looking for "a new

---

11. For a comprehensive evaluation of the themes and principal initiatives see J. WILLEBRANDS, *Church and Jewish People: New Considerations*, New York – Mahwah, NJ, Paulist Press, 1992.

12. W. KASPER, *Quando i cristiani vanno incontro agli ebrei nella Terra di Santità: Alla scoperta dell'eredità comune*, Vatican City, Libreria Editrice Vaticana, 2009.

13. WILLEBRANDS, *Una sfida ecumenica, la nuova Europa* (n. 4), p. 193.

humanistic synthesis" (*Caritas in veritate*, 21). In this perspective too, the efforts of Willebrands for a new ecumenical synthesis take on a greater sense and continuity for the future of interreligious dialogue, employing ecumenism as a key of interpretation or prophecy for globalization.

IX. To Come Out from the Night

I would like to conclude with a thought about night, prelude to messianic redemption. Thinking about the dark night of the *Shoah* – defined as "a wound that still bleeds" – the cardinal often remembered, among those who inspired his meditation, Etty Hillesum, the Dutch Jewish woman who lived for a long time in the Westerbork camp before becoming a victim, along with her entire family, of extermination in Auschwitz. The intellectual and spiritual lucidity, and the suffered charity with which Etty lived, in particular the last, tremendous test of the concentration camp, and then of the journey without return, bring her close to other, similar experiences like those of Edith Stein or Janusz Korczak. The dark night was not lived in desperation, however, but in the light of love and of compassion illumined by hope. During this night a tenuous, but tenacious, flickering flame was visible, like the pleasant memory that today unites us while we reflect on the faith that sustained Johannes Cardinal Willebrands in his loving engagement with the "favored brothers" of the people of Israel, the people faithful to the divine Covenant revealed at Sinai – after the night and the dark waters – to Moses. Together with them, side-by-side with all men and women of good will, we feel that we are on our way in the paths of the Messiah – *Darke ha-Mashiah- darke ha-Shalom.*

Biblioteca Ambrosiana   Pier Francesco FUMAGALLI
Piazza Pio XI 2
I-20123 Milano
Italy

JOHANNES WILLEBRANDS: A JEWISH VIEW

Thomas Stransky has noted in his brilliant preface to the Willebrands diaries: "it is impossible to understand modern Catholicism, indeed modern Protestantism and Eastern Orthodoxy, without taking into account Vatican II". [I would add that it is also not possible to understand the contemporary Jewish community and the broad field of Jewish-Christian relations without taking into account the changes wrought by Vatican II.] But, he goes on to note:

> it is also true that this 'convulsive alteration of the whole religious land-scape' (Garry Wills) took place before most of today's Catholics and others have been born (…) Vatican II promulgated SPCU documents on ecumen-ism, on religious freedom, on the relation of the Church to Non Christian Religions (…) But for most who are interested, these (…) stand by them-selves, without a history. The end product is stripped of unpredictable and threatened journeys, of surprises, setbacks and blessings along the way. And alas, falling back into darker shadows are the actors (…)[1].

The actors who brought about the momentous changes in ecumenical and Jewish-Christian relations that we shall review here are heroes with-out doubt. But there are heroes and heroes. Some are daring and confron-tational; they leap fearlessly, perhaps even obsessively, into the struggle for justice as they see it. Resistance and hostility only sharpen their resolve and intensify their efforts. Like our biblical prophets, they are not the most patient people in the world; they have little concern about alien-ating people; they may make enemies along the way, and some of them pay a heavy price for their passionate commitment.

Then, there are other heroes, who put patience and fortitude to the service of progress, who are endowed with exceptional diplomatic skills, who use restraint combined with persistence to advance their goal, who understand the need to compromise without compromising away the desired end. They may not upset the apple cart, but they stay the course. They are not as confrontational, but they are steadfast.

Profound changes that shake the foundations of long-established atti-tudes and prejudices require both kinds of heroes, but it is clear that Johannes Willebrands was the second kind. What emerges from his diaries and from his historic role in the ecumenical movement is a man

---

1. The texts outlive the contexts [emphasis added].

of friendly, open disposition and extraordinary patience, but with a strong backbone. One senses through his journals that he was nobody's fool: he was frequently annoyed and occasionally outraged by the negative attitudes and obstructionist tactics of members of the curia and others who, during the Second Vatican Council, were vehemently opposed to renewal in the Church and determined to prevent it at all costs. Yet he never lost his cool. He remained civil and respectful, even to the enemies of his goals and aspirations. I suspect he never made a personal enemy.

How deeply human he was! He loved companionship and conversation, he enjoyed good meals, movies, theater and concerts, he was very close to his family, devoted to his parents and siblings. He made lifelong friends and cherished his friendships, and – rare at the time – he had women friends and professional associates, and respected their opinions. He had a lively intellectual curiosity that was unthreatened by new ideas, although he was very solidly rooted in his spiritual tradition and sincere in his piety. He was an avid reader and actually enjoyed studying. Perhaps most remarkable, he was indefatigable, often working from daybreak until late at night. Just to read a few of his daily schedules is exhausting! In the detailed diaries and more succinct agendas covering some five years of daily work, I discovered only two days on which he counted himself "malade". His capacity for work and his good health proved to be a blessing to those of us who benefited from his achievements.

He was earlier involved – and, I believe, more interested and more innovative – in ecumenical than in Jewish-Christian relations. He had contacts and connections in the Protestant and Orthodox churches long before the Secretariat for Promoting Christian Unity was created[2]. His primary interests were for building relationships with Protestant and Orthodox Christian churches. Yet, when the SPCU was given the "Jewish portfolio" in 1961, he extended his concern and commitment to the passage of what emerged from the Council, promulgated by Paul VI as *Nostra Aetate*, and he used his considerable diplomatic skills to negotiate with the document's enemies and to manoeuvre its passage through the thickets of theological and political opposition.

His theology of Jews and Judaism was, understandably, pre-Vatican Council II. He believed that Judaism found its fulfilment in Christianity, and I believe he hoped that Jews would find their way into the Church. He might have been surprised – pleasantly, I would hope – by more recent affirmations of Catholic theologians and scholars that Judaism

---

2. Indeed, these connections and the good will he had developed may explain why he received his appointment to the secretariat when it was created.

provides a saving faith for Jews, and disclaimers of missionary intent to the Jewish community. Whatever his hopes regarding ultimate Jewish conversion to Christianity, he was staunchly opposed to anti-Semitism in both its religious and political dimensions, and he had an empathetic understanding of the suffering and persecution of Jews during the Shoah. Fr. Stransky notes that Willebrands' friend and mentor, Frans Thijssen, introduced him to Catholics and Protestants who were aiding helpless refugees from the Nazis, Jews in particular, in the late 1930s. This may have been the source of his identification with Jewish experience on a human, rather than a theological level.

Because of this identification, he was quick to acknowledge and promote Church documents that corrected the negative images of Jews and Judaism still found in Catholic tradition. On 18 October, 1977, during a discussion in the synod on religious education, he made a written intervention on the image of Judaism in Catholic teaching. Drawing on official Church documents, he emphasized that it was theologically and practically impossible to set forth Christianity without reference to Judaism, and that the image of Judaism used to illustrate Christianity "is rarely exact, faithful to or respectful of the theological and historical reality of Judaism". Quoting directly from Church documents, he underscored the continuity of the two testaments, the voluntary passion and death of Christ, for which the Jewish people should not be blamed, or depicted as rejected and cursed by God, and emphasized that the history of Judaism did not end with the destruction of Jerusalem, but continued to develop a tradition rich with religious values. Cardinal Willebrands did not invent these phrases, but he put the weight of his authority behind them. And he certainly brought his diplomatic skills to use in defending what was then called *De Iudaeis*, as well as the declaration on religious liberty, against powerful forces bitterly opposed to renewal during the course of the Council. He was extremely cautious in his attitudes toward Israel, and may have had a falling out with his former secretary, Fr. Cornelius Rijk, over Fr. Rijk's activities on behalf of Church recognition of Israel.

A word about myself. Like Fr. Stransky, I am a child of the Second Vatican Council – he on the Catholic side, I on the Jewish side. That is, I cut my teeth in the field of Jewish-Christian relations as part of a relatively small group of Jewish activists who mounted an initiative on behalf of an authoritative statement on Jews and Judaism to be adopted at the Council – a statement that would condemn anti-Semitism, repudiate the deicide charge against the Jewish people, correct teachings of contempt about Jews and Judaism, acknowledge that Judaism did not end with the emergence of Christianity but continued to develop as a living faith, and inaugurate an ongoing dialogue between the Church and the Jewish community. We further hoped these policies would be implemented through the establishment of some permanent structure within the Church.

I worked under the leadership of Rabbi Marc H. Tanenbaum, who, together with Zachariah Shuster, director of the European office of the American Jewish Committee, led this initiative. Tanenbaum also enlisted Rabbi Abraham Joshua Heschel in the effort, and set up meetings between Cardinal Bea, Heschel and other Jewish religious and community leaders during Bea's trip to the United States in 1963.

Like Fr. Stransky, I look around at the actors in that drama – and, believe me, it was a drama – what they call in movies a "cliffhanger". From the Catholic side, he notes that almost all are gone[3]. From the Jewish side, those active in some sustained fashion on behalf of the so-called "Jewish decree" and the declaration on religious liberty during the Council: Tanenbaum, Heschel, Dr. Eric Werner of Hebrew Union College[4], Dr. Joseph Lichten of the Anti-Defamation League, Dr. Gerhardt Riegner of the World Jewish Congress, all have passed on. I and Rabbi Tanenbaum's former secretary remain somewhat battered veterans of that 50 year old struggle. In Fr. Stransky's poignant words, "Fifty years later we remember, mis-remember and forget".

What struck me most going through the Willebrands' papers – both the diary and the conciliar agendas – is how thin a slice of his time is taken up with the question that absorbed my time almost entirely. Much more of his schedule is devoted to inter-Christian relationships and the goal of Christian unity.

When John XXIII was elected to the papacy in 1958, and shortly thereafter surprised everyone by announcing the summoning of an ecumenical council, we were approached by a French Catholic author and scholar, Mme. Claire Huchet Bishop, an ardent devotee of the work of Jules Isaac[5]. She urged the American Jewish Committee to become involved, insofar as possible, in the forthcoming council, to engage in a vigorous initiative for the repudiation "at the highest level of the Church" of that anti-Jewish and anti-Semitic tradition of teaching and preaching whereby Jews had been segregated, degraded, charged with wicked crimes, and

---

3. Of the 2500 bishops who attended the Council, 30 were still alive as of January, 2008. Of the staff of the SPCU, all of the bishops are gone; of the consultors, two remain alive; of the staff, himself and two secretaries.

4. Who drafted the memorandum on anti-Jewish elements in Catholic liturgy.

5. It was she who was largely responsible for the publication of his books in the United States, and thus, indirectly, for familiarity with the expression, "the teaching of contempt" on the North American continent.

valued only as potential converts. Ecumenical councils are few and far between, she said, and this is a historic opportunity. "Seize it".

Another historic event added urgency to that goal. At the same time that the preparatory commissions for the Council were going about their work, the nightmarish details of the Nazi genocide against the Jews were being vividly recalled by the trial of Adolf Eichmann in Jerusalem. The moral questions posed by the Eichmann trial were not lost on religious spokesmen, some of whom pointed to the need to root out the sources of hatred and contempt for Jews and Judaism for once and for all.

It soon became apparent that the key figure with regard to a "Jewish decree" at Vatican II was Augustin Cardinal Bea, and that he and his secretariat had been entrusted by Pope John to draft a statement and to seek representative Jewish viewpoints. The way was open for communication and dialogue. We at the American Jewish Committee (AJC) vigorously engaged in both.

On July 31, 1961, over a year before the opening of the Council's first session, the American Jewish Committee submitted to Cardinal Bea, by prior agreement, the first of several comprehensive memoranda. Entitled, *The Image of the Jew in Catholic Teaching*, the 32-page document identified and illustrated slanderous interpretations, oversimplifications, unjust or inaccurate comparisons, invidious use of language and significant omissions in American Catholic textbooks, and it cited existing Catholic sources that could serve as corrections. I authored that document, based on the findings of a self-study of Catholic textbooks undertaken at St. Louis University by Sr. Rose Thering, O.P.[6].

On November 17, 1961, a second memorandum, *Anti-Jewish Elements in Catholic Liturgy,* was submitted to Bea. While acknowledging the recent deletion of problematic passages in the liturgy, the document noted that the concept of Jews as deicides still figured in some liturgical passages, in popular and scholarly commentaries on the liturgy, and in homiletic literature.

In December, 1961, Professor Abraham Joshua Heschel met with Cardinal Bea in Rome[7]. One of the outcomes of that meeting was an invitation for Heschel to submit suggestions for positive Council action

---

6. Transformed by the implications of her own research, Sr. Thering became an important educator in the field, serving with Msgr. John Oesterreicher at the Center for Judaeo-Christian Studies at Seton Hall University. She was also a lively activist on behalf of Israel, and led over fifty study tours to the Jewish state.

7. Since there are no Willebrands diaries for that period – or, at least, none have been found – we do not know whether Willebrands was present at the meeting.

to improve Catholic-Jewish relations. In May, 1962, he followed up with a memorandum, prepared in cooperation with the American Jewish Committee, recommending a number of specific actions: forthright rejection of the deicide charge against the Jewish people, recognition of Jews as Jews (rather than as potential converts), promotion of scholarly and civic cooperation, and the creation of church agencies to help overcome religious prejudice[8].

Like Fr. Stransky, I find Willebrands' entries frequently rich in daily details (appointments, lunches, conversations with specific personalities) and yet lacking in theme and substance. What were the conversations about? Who said what to whom? What is ignored or overlooked? Stransky notes that Willebrands mentions routine luncheons with staff colleagues at a local restaurant, but fails to note the date of a working audience with Pope Paul VI; a long, revealing conversation about the difficulties of drafting *De Iudaeis* is narrated by Yves Congar in his own writings, yet the Willebrands agenda lists nothing for the same day. It is somewhat frustrating to find these lacunae, but some of them may have been due to his sense of discretion about very inflammatory issues.

In similar fashion, Cardinal Willebrands notes his three trips to the Middle East in 1965: the first, March 18-23, accompanied by Fr. Duprey, to Beirut, where he met with Catholic, Armenian, Syrian and Greek Orthodox patriarchs and other clergy, and with the papal nuncios to Lebanon and Syria; the second, April 22-30, accompanied again by Fr. Duprey, to Beirut, Jerusalem, Cairo and Addis-Abeba, where he met with Catholic, Orthodox, Anglican church leaders and ambassadors; and the third, apparently at the request of the pope, July 19-24 – after the text of the Jewish declaration had already been modified to eliminate the word "deicide" and the expression "condemn" referring to anti-Semitism – to Beirut, Jerusalem and Cairo, accompanied by Fr. Duprey and this time, also by Msgr. De Smedt. Again, they met with a variety of Catholic, Orthodox and Anglican church leadership.

Although Willebrands' journals do not specify the purpose of these visits, we know for a fact that it was to try to overcome Arab hostility and objections to the statement on the Jews. In the third trip, he was partly successful.

The vehemence and vitriol of the Arab hostility still astonish me. From an almost fifty year post-Vatican II perspective, reading the objections

---

8. None of these documents are mentioned in the Willebrands diaries or agendas, but as Bea's close assistant, it is likely he read them.

raised by Arab government and religious leadership to any effort by the
Church to lift an accusation "of infamy and execration", in the words of
Bishop Stephen Leven of San Antonio, Texas, which "was invented by
Christians and used to blame and persecute the Jews (...) for many
centuries, and even in our own (...)" still sets my teeth on edge. As I
wrote in an article in the American Jewish Year Book, 1966[9]: "The interest of the Arab world in the charge of deicide against Jews cannot be
attributed to religious concern: the question is of little or no consequence
to Islam. The Arab opposition to any statement expressing esteem or
affection for Jews, suggesting a special relationship between Christianity
and the Jewish people, deploring specific acts of persecution against
Jews, and removing a theological basis of anti-Semitism is politically
motivated, and this opposition has been carried out on the highest political and diplomatic levels". Indeed, the campaign included threats
of reprisals against Christian minorities in Arab lands. These never mate-
rialized.

If we did not know the specifics of this vitriolic campaign from other
sources, we would not have derived them from Cardinal Willebrands
journals of his visits to the Arab world. But at one point, he was so
discouraged by the intensity of Arab objections to the document that he
was willing to suggest removing it from the Council's agenda. Fortunately for us, Cardinal Bea and other members of the commission insisted
on the necessity of a statement on the Jews.

In addition to the Arab initiatives, there was a sustained campaign
against the so-called Jewish declaration on doctrinal grounds by conservative elements within the church who believed that Jews, as a people,
did indeed bear collective responsibility as deicides, and that their
suffering across the ages was proof of providential punishment for this
crime. Representatives of this position may have constituted only a small
minority within the Council, but they had access to extraordinary channels of distribution. Thus, a few days before the conclusion of the second
Council session, every prelate found in his mailbox a privately-printed
900 page volume, *Il Complotto contro la Chiesa* ["The Plot Against the
Church"] filled with the most primitive anti-Semitism. Described by
Msgr. George Higgins, a columnist for the National Catholic Welfare
Conference's press service as "a sickening diatribe against the Jews", it
charged that there was a Jewish fifth column among the Catholic clergy,
plotting against the Church, and it even justified Hitler's acts against

---

9. J. HERSHCOPF, *The Church and the Jews: The Struggle at Vatican II*, in *American Jewish Year Book* 66 (1965) 99-136 and 67 (1966) 45-77.

the Jews. The "fifth column" accusation was undoubtedly directed at converts from Judaism who were associated with Bea's secretariat and who played some role in the drafting of the declaration, such as Fr. Gregory Baum and Msgr. John Oesterreicher, both of whom had written widely on issues of Jewish-Christian relations[10]. Revisiting the paranoia of the ultra-right and the fierce opposition of the Arab world, we must admire Willebrands for having steered a cautious but determined course between them. Yet, these anti-Semitic eruptions are not mentioned in his agendas, although those of us in the Jewish community who followed the tortured path of the statement on the Jews were very much aware of them.

In March, 1963, Cardinal Bea, accompanied by Willebrands and Fr. Schmidt, visited the United States to lecture at Harvard University. Subsequently, he was honored at an interfaith agape in New York City devoted to the theme, "Civic Unity Under God". He used that occasion – attended and addressed by such personalities as U Thant, Zafrulla Khan, N.Y. State Governor Nelson Rockefeller, New York City Mayor Robert F. Wagner, Henry Luce, Dr. Henry Pitney Van Dusen, Richard Cardinal Cushing, Greek Orthodox Archbishop Iakovos and Rabbi Heschel – to issue an affirmative statement in support of freedom of conscience. The question of religious liberty being another "hot potato" at the Council, his comments were viewed as explicit support for a forthcoming declaration.

But Bea's visit was also the occasion of an unpublicized and unprecedented meeting with a group of Jewish religious leaders – representing Orthodox, Conservative and Reform branches of Judaism – held at the AJC's headquarters on March 31. Responding to prepared questions regarding the prospects for Council action on Jewish concerns, Bea declared that the events of the Passion could not be charged against Jewry as a whole; that it was necessary to clarify the true sense intended by the writers of the New Testament; that there was a need for interreligious communication and cooperation, and that his views were endorsed by Pope John.

This meeting, whose candor and substance were considered deeply important – and encouraging – for those in the Jewish community

---

10. During the third session of the Council, America's most famous home-grown anti-semite, the Protestant Gerald L.K. Smith, wrote to all American bishops offering to supply them, free of charge, with an English translation of the very same book. His four-page letter claimed that the American bishops had been taken in "by a fraternity of deceivers too close to the centers of authority in the affairs of the church".

engaged in the Vatican Council initiative, is referenced by Willebrands only as "Conversation au Jewish Committee"[11].

Fortunately, Willebrands has provided us with a fuller and richer recollection of that event in his Introduction to Marc Tanenbaum's biography:

> I met Rabbi Marc Tanenbaum for the first time in New York on a Sunday afternoon, March 31, 1963, on the occasion of a meeting of Jewish scholars with Cardinal Bea. [He] was Director of the Department of Interreligious Affairs of the American Jewish Committee and convened the meeting that was chaired by Rabbi Abraham Joshua Heschel. I shall never forget that meeting, not only the setting and the historical happening, but especially the atmosphere, characterized by Cardinal Bea as 'excellent and fraternal'. The Jews present were fairly representative of the various existing religious currents within Jewish life. Rabbi Tanenbaum told Fr. Schmidt, Cardinal Bea's private secretary: 'It is a miracle, not that these people met with the cardinal, but that they met with each other'. Nevertheless it was the person of Bea and the hope that the Vatican Council would lead the Catholic Church to a new insight and attitude regarding the relations between the church and the Jewish people that brought the Jewish dignitaries together. I felt a sense of awe for the presence of God among us. To me it was clear that we had broken new ground, that a new era had begun in the relations between the church and the Jewish people[12].

Another recollection of Cardinal Willebrands seems most apt to conclude this paper. It took place in Rome, probably at the time when the Jewish statement was under attack by theological and political opponents and its outcome uncertain. In his own words:

> One of the most significant and moving events of my life occurred on a Saturday evening when I had already made my prayers for the preparation of the Sunday. The bell rang. I was not expecting any visit, and was very surprised to see Rabbi Tanenbaum. He had come right from the celebration of the Sabbath in the synagogue. In my study he embraced me, opened an embroidered cover from which he took out his tallith and put it over my head and shoulders. I could not say a word. By this gesture he wished to share with me and to involve me in his prayers. For a moment I remained silent and embraced him. Our relationship was not only one of common study and interest, but it included our relation to God. We wanted together to stay before God and to invoke His blessing. His grace.

---

11. On the following day, he notes a discussion with Heschel at the Jewish Theological Seminary.

12. J. HERSHCOPF BANKI – E.J. FISHER (eds.), *A Prophet for Our Time: A Selected Anthology of the Writings of Rabbi Marc H. Tanenbaum*, New York, Fordham University Press, 2002, p. xiv.

I leave you with that picture: Cardinal Willebrands draped head and shoulders in Marc Tanenbaum's tallith, the two of them asking God's blessing on their sacred mission.

In our tradition we say: *zeher zadik l'vracha*, the memory of the righteous is a blessing. May the memory of Johannes Willebrands, a righteous man, bless the work we still have to do together.

Tanenbaum Center for
Interreligious Understanding
254 West 31st Street, 7th floor
New York, NY 10001
USA

Judith HERSHCOPF BANKI

V. FINAL LECTURE – TESTIMONIES – BIBLIOGRAPHY

THE LEGACY OF JOHANNES CARDINAL WILLEBRANDS
AND THE FUTURE OF ECUMENISM

It is a great joy for me to speak about Johannes Cardinal Willebrands. Cardinal Willebrands was one of the important figures in the history of the church in the last century. He was one of those giants on whose shoulders we stand as far as ecumenism as well as religious relations with the Jews are concerned. On the occasion of the 100th anniversary of his birth we remember him with profound gratitude, as a loving man and a distinguished theologian.

My reflection will cover three aspects. First of all, I wish to recall Cardinal Willebrands' important contribution during his ecumenical career. Second, I will focus on the changed situation after Cardinal Willebrands' retirement. And third, I will conclude with a glance at the future, asking the following question: How can we make the most of Cardinal Willebrands' rich legacy and inspiration in our current situation?

I. CARDINAL WILLEBRANDS' LIFE AND WORK

Johannes Willebrands embarked on his ecumenical commitment during and (especially) after the Second World War. Europe was dispirited both from a material and a moral point of view. The era of Euro-centrism was over. The totalitarian ideologies and utopias of the nineteenth and the first half of the twentieth centuries failed and left the world as a field of ruins with millions of dead people. The need for a new direction was strongly felt. The foundations for this new direction were laid in the inter-war period by the liturgical movement, the biblical movement, the new role that lay people had started playing in the Church, the beginning of the ecumenical movement, as well as the new interest in patristic sources. After the war, it was clear that no way forward was possible on the basis of confessional separation and conflict. As well, after the atrocities of the Shoah, commitment to dialogue and new relations with Jews became imperative. Christians had to speak with one voice in the process of the reconstruction of a new Europe and in the building of a new worldwide order of peace. Thus they rediscovered the importance of Jesus' will on the eve of his death: "that they all may be one" (John 17,21).

Johannes Willebrands was not the only person – or the first one – to promote the unity and reconciliation of Christians well before the Second Vatican Council, in a time when ecumenism was still a difficult and thorny question in the Catholic Church. Before him and together with him many shared the same concern in France, Germany, Belgium, the Netherlands and the United States. Already in 1949 Pope Pius XII referred to the ecumenical movement as an impulse of the Holy Spirit – a concept that was later deepened and developed by the Second Vatican Council, which spoke of the "inspiring grace of the Holy Spirit" (*UR* 1; 4).

However, through the Catholic Conference for Ecumenical Questions it was Johannes Willebrands who, together with Frans Thijssen, built contacts and networks, travelled throughout Europe, gathering distinguished names in the theological field. He had contacts with the then Fr. Augustine Bea and the first General Secretary of the World Council of Churches (WCC), Willem A. Visser 't Hooft, with whom a true friendship soon developed. Founded a decade before the opening of Vatican II, the Catholic Conference for Ecumenical Questions actively participated in the work of the WCC. According to Visser 't Hooft, this contribution had far-reaching consequences for the ecumenical movement.

Thus Willebrands managed to create a network that proved very useful when in 1960 Pope John XXIII established the Secretariat for Promoting Christian Unity, following the suggestion of Archbishop Lorenz Jäger of Paderborn. John XXIII was indeed able to recognise the signs of the time – one can even say, the signs of the Holy Spirit in that time. It was he who decided that the theme of the Council announced on 25th January 1959 should be the unity of all Christians. It was he who gave an institutional channel to the ecumenical movement in the Catholic Church at the level of the universal Church.

As its first secretary, Willebrands helped shape the newly founded Secretariat which was presided initially by Augustin Cardinal Bea and then by Willebrands himself from 1969 until his retirement in 1989. He had the gift of finding and inspiring the right co-workers. To mention just a few, I recall here Jerome Hamer, Charles Moeller and Pierre Duprey, who worked for the Secretariat (later Pontifical Council) for Promoting Christian Unity for thirty-six years, from 1963 till 1999. Co-workers in a wider sense were Yves Congar, Gustave Thils, Balthasar Fischer, Karl Rahner, Johannes Feiner, Jean Corbon, Emmanuel Lanne, Raymond Brown and others. Willebrands could also count on the collaboration of Corinna de Martini and Josette Kersters. We are deeply grateful to all the men and women who were there in those early years.

During the council regular discussions with the ecumenical observers took place at the Foyer Unitas near Piazza Navona under the presidency of the then Bishop Willebrands. These observers played an active role which proved extremely fruitful for the Council itself and for its achievements. The scope and amount of work that was accomplished is amazing. It includes not only the Decree on Ecumenism, but also the Dogmatic Constitution on Divine Revelation, the Declaration on the Church's Relations to Non-Christian Religions and the Declaration on Religious Freedom. These three documents elicited rather heated debates and, due to bitter opposition, received approval only during the last session of the Council. In such contexts, Willebrands was always capable of finding the right balance between his own ecumenical vision and what was needed in order to achieve a wider consensus within the Council. He had both cardinal virtues: prudence and fortitude.

In what follows I will focus on the Decree on Ecumenism, *Unitatis Redintegratio*. Its approval on 21 November 1964 by an overwhelming majority with only 11 opposing votes was the result of the decisive role played by Cardinal Bea as well as the work accomplished by Bishop Johannes Willebrands.

After the negative approach of Pope Pius XI's Encyclical Letter *Mortalium animos* (1928) and the 1948 *Monitum* of the then Holy Office, the Decree on Ecumenism provided a new direction and represented a true breakthrough for the Church, which is sometimes much too easily taken for granted today. The Decree speaks of other Christians not in terms of anathema, but in terms of dialogue. Dialogue was not – and is not – intended to be an attempt to reach a diluted diplomatic compromise. *Unitatis Redintegratio* rightly points out that dialogue presupposes conversion, renewal and reform. Dialogue is always dialogue in truth and in love. Dialogue is therefore a deep process both on a spiritual and an ecclesial level.

Understood in this spirit, the Decree on Ecumenism represents the end of the Counter-Reformation and the beginning of a new era in the relations with the divided churches and church communions, an era that has already brought many positive fruits but requires an ongoing renewal, even now, almost fifty years after the proclamation of *Unitatis Redintegratio*. However, it was not meant as a break with the wider Tradition of the Church. On the contrary, it was based – as Cardinal Bea especially emphasised – on the recognition of the one common baptism (*unum baptisma*) binding all Christians in a deep – though imperfect – communion with Jesus Christ and the Church.

The theological foundations of the Decree on Ecumenism are to be found in the Dogmatic Constitution on the Church *Lumen Gentium* – in particular paragraphs 8 and 15 – which was approved on the same day, 21 November 1964. Thus *Unitatis Redintegratio* is based on, develops and applies the content of *Lumen Gentium*. When he solemnly proclaimed the Decree on Ecumenism, Pope Paul VI explained that it clarified and complemented the Dogmatic Constitution. These words should be remembered by all those who question the binding character of the theological affirmations of *Unitatis Redintegratio*.

When today we reflect on the discussions and debates of that time, we sense the momentum and the magic of a new beginning. It was a charismatic breakthrough, accompanied by a great hope. One senses the amazement of the secular world and other Christians in the face of what the Holy Spirit had accomplished before their eyes, when a church, considered to be unyielding in many of its positions, all of a sudden proved fresh and lively. And one senses the joy felt by the Catholics who had rediscovered other Christians as their brothers and sisters.

It is obvious that this breakthrough did not occur overnight. Its way was paved by the prayer movement which emerged independently on different continents and in different churches during the eighteenth century and gave birth to the World Day of Prayer for Christian Unity, already at the time of Pope Leo XIII (1878-1903). This breakthrough had also been prepared by leading theologians such as Johann Adam Möhler and John Henry Newman, who are now seen as true ecumenical pioneers. Extremely significant for the Second Vatican Council were also the events that had occurred outside the Catholic world after the World Missionary Conference held in 1910 in Edinburgh and the formation of the World Council of Churches in Amsterdam in 1948. This impetus of the Holy Spirit through the prayer of many faithful and the reflection of theologians became finally clear and took concrete shape in the Catholic Church. People such as Johannes Willebrands were receptive and sufficiently long sighted to hear the call of the Spirit and to courageously become its instruments.

One of the first fruits of Willebrands' efforts was his opportunity to publicly present the Common Declaration of Pope Paul VI and Ecumenical Patriarch Athenagoras on the eve of the official conclusion of the Council on 7 December 1965. The reading received a long ovation. In this declaration the pope and the patriarch state that they "regret and remove both from the memory and from the midst of the Church the sentences of excommunication" of 1054, and pledge to promote "full communion" between the two churches.

After the Council, Willebrands' task was to translate the Council's thought into reality. Again, we can only marvel how much would be accomplished in only a few decades. The Joint Working Group between the Roman Catholic Church and the World Council of Churches had already been created during the Council. A series of bilateral dialogues with the Christian World Communions was subsequently undertaken: with Lutherans and Methodists in 1967; with the Anglicans and Reformed in 1970; with classical Pentecostals in 1972; with Evangelicals and Disciples of Christ in 1977; and with Baptists in 1984. In particular, we call to mind the moving meeting between Pope Paul VI and the Archbishop of Canterbury, Michael Ramsey, in 1966 in Rome, when the pope as an unexpected sign put his own bishop's ring on the primate's finger.

Contacts with the Orthodox churches developed initially through a series of visits to Constantinople, Greece, Romania and Russia leading to the start of the official dialogue on Patmos and Rhodes in 1980, with Willebrands as co-president on the Catholic side. Important contacts were also established with the Eastern Orthodox churches: with the Patriarch/Pope Shenouda III of the Coptic Church, with Catholicos Karekin II of the Armenian Church and with Patriarch Ignatius Zakka I of the Syrian Orthodox Church. Also thanks to the work of Pro-Oriente, the institution founded in Vienna by Franz Cardinal König, these contacts led to the christological declarations which resolved a 1,500 year-old problem underlying church division. Finally, it is worth mentioning the Catholic participation in the Faith and Order Commission whose most important document remains the Lima text, *Baptism, Eucharist and Ministry* (1982).

Johannes Willebrands was not only the organiser and moderator of these initiatives; he gave his personal imprint to all of them. I will mention only briefly two thoughts.

My first reflection. God is at work through people also in the ecumenical field. Johannes Willebrands' personality was crucial especially in that initial phase. He had many qualities: sensitivity and discernment in judging people and situations; great capacity to communicate; the gift of nurturing true friendships. All this is fundamental for ecumenical dialogue since ecumenism means overcoming suspicion and building trust; it also means creating friendships. I have already mentioned Johannes Willebrands' capacity for both prudence and courage, namely the gift to sensitively evaluate a situation. In Willebrands we also find the right balance between loyalty and flexibility, between passionate eagerness for unity and patience, which does not try to force things but lets them grow and mature. Not least, Johannes Willebrands had an exceptionally fine sense of humour. Humour is often the only way of facing small-minded and sheepish attitudes. Humour is a form of sovereignty that is ultimately founded on prayer. To the end, the question is not "my" church, "my" ecumenism, but the Church of Christ and the ecumenism that is desired by God, who sometimes is probably smiling with irony at our small human dealings.

My second reflection. Cardinal Willebrands based his ecumenical work also on theological reflection, which was shaped by John Henry Newman's concrete analysis of faith. In April 1990, a few months after leaving the Pontifical Council for Promoting Christian Unity, he gave an address in Toronto entitled "The Place of Theology in the Ecumenical Movement: Its Contribution and its Limits". He said: "most of the great architects of ecumenism have been theologians". Willebrands' fundamental themes include: the interesting theses of the different *typoi* of the Church, communion as the main and central idea of the ecumenical movement, the importance of reception for the Church and for ecumenism, the correct interpretation of the expression *subsistit in* which contains *in nuce* the whole ecumenical problem, and the fundamental importance of spiritual ecumenism. All these issues still have a deep impact on our work today and will mark it also in the future.

Thus Cardinal Willebrands has left us a great legacy; he has also set tasks for us that need to be carried out with renewed energy. We thank God for having given us, in a decisive time of the history of our church, the theologian, bishop and cardinal, Johannes Willebrands, with all his personal and spiritual gifts. We will be always deeply grateful.

II. THE CHANGES OF THE LAST TWENTY YEARS

It suffices to mention the atmosphere and the achievements of the work accomplished in those golden years of the Secretariat for Promoting Christian Unity to realize immediately how much the world as well as the situation in the Church and ecumenism have deeply changed since the day – in 1989 – when the 80 year-old Cardinal Willebrands went into a much deserved retirement from the presidency of the Pontifical Council for Promoting Christian Unity.

1989 is the year of the fall of the Berlin Wall and the end of the division of the world into two cold war blocs. Ecumenism was experiencing a new situation too: it was in expectation of a great new hope, a hope that unfortunately has not yet been fulfilled. 1989 marks the year of freedom for the churches in Eastern Europe after a long period (40 or even 70 years) of severe repression and persecution. One would assume that this would have made dialogue easier. But things did not go that way. The freshly regained freedom in the East meant freedom also for the Catholic Eastern churches. They had suffered much under communist rule and could now resurface from illegality to public life. However, on the Orthodox side this led to the reappearance of the old deep-rooted fears and prejudices concerning proselytism and uniatism.

During the first session of the Joint International Commission for Theological Dialogue Between the Catholic Church and the Orthodox Church after the fall of the Berlin Wall, that took place in Freising in June 1990, the new president of the Pontifical Council for Promoting Christian Unity, Edward I. Cardinal Cassidy, had a difficult "baptism of fire". In 1993 in Balamand it was possible to find a practical solution to the problem of so-called uniatism. However, there was no unanimous agreement among the Orthodox. When in 2000 in Baltimore the Commission tried to deal with this thorny issue again, this led to a fiasco and a *de facto* failure of the dialogue. Thus the Jubilee Year of 2000 which, according to the aspirations of Pope John Paul II, should have brought decisive positive developments especially with the Eastern churches, was marked on the contrary by crisis and division in ecumenical relations.

A new start was possible only after many patient discussions, with the meetings of Belgrade in 2006 and Ravenna in 2007, thanks to the strong support of the Ecumenical Patriarch. On the Orthodox side, Metropolitan John Zizioulas played a crucial role. It is interesting to note that already Cardinal Willebrands had stressed the importance of the famous canon 34 of the Apostolic Constitution, the same canon that became fundamental for the discussions in Ravenna. This canon proved to be the best instrument for making progress on the question of the close relation between synodality and primacy also on the universal level. However the discussions during the last meeting during the session held in Cyprus in October 2009 – this time again with the participation of the delegation from the Russian Orthodox Church – showed that further progress in this crucial matter no doubt is possible but only in small and patient steps.

Similarly, it was possible to resume the dialogue with the Eastern Orthodox churches in 2003. This dialogue had come to a standstill after its encouraging initial phase in the 1980s and 1990s. As far as ecclesiology is concerned, it was for me personally almost a miracle that in a common document of 2008 we were able to state that we have been able to preserve the common apostolic structure despite 1,500 years of division.

However, despite this gratifying progress, the current situation is clearly very different from the initial phase of dialogue, for which Cardinal Willebrands was responsible. The initial enthusiasm has disappeared; the atmosphere has become more sober. Even if we do not doubt the power of the Holy Spirit, it is realistic to expect that the way ahead remains long. It will take some time in the Eastern churches to overcome more intractable prejudices and fears, and to achieve a wider reception of the ecumenical idea and its results. But efforts should be made not only by the Orthodox churches. Conversion, renewal and reform are needed on all sides. Concerning the question of primacy and synodality, the Catholic Church should reflect further and define in more concrete terms the shape of full communion with the Petrine ministry, in such a way that it does not entail mutual absorption or fusion (Enc. *Slavorum apostoli*, 1985, 27).

The dialogues with the churches of the Reformed tradition were also influenced by the changes that occurred after 1989. In 1999 we experienced an unprecedented success in our bilateral dialogues with the signing of the Joint Declaration on the Doctrine of Justification with the Lutheran World Federation. This was a true milestone. In the meantime, in 2006 in Seoul the World Methodist Council produced a Statement of Association with the Joint Declaration on the Doctrine of Justification, which declares "that the common understanding of justification as it is outlined in the Joint Declaration on the Doctrine of Justification (JDDJ 15-17) corresponds to Methodist doctrine". In 2009 we celebrated in Augsburg the 10th anniversary of this important achievement, which is also part of the cardinal's legacy.

However, the Jubilee Year of 2000 marked paradoxically a difficult time also for the relations with the churches of the Reformed tradition. In that year, the Congregation for the Doctrine of Faith published texts, among which the well-known declaration *Dominus Iesus* which provided an interpretation of the *subsistit in* present in *Lumen Gentium* 8 and *Unitatis Redintegratio* 4. Already the main author of *Lumen Gentium*, the Belgian theologian Gérard Philips, had reflected that this *subsistit in* contained *in nuce* the whole ecumenical problem and that much ink would flow about it in the future.

Undoubtedly, the declaration *Dominus Iesus* correctly explains Catholic doctrine and ecclesiology because, as a matter of fact, the different sides do not mean exactly the same thing when they speak of Church. But unfortunately from an ecumenical perspective the correct content of *Dominus Iesus* was expressed in a less sensitive form. This caused tensions that are still present today and that have made our relations much colder. Many question whether the bilateral dialogues are facing now a crisis or even a dead end.

There have been developments also on the Protestant side that have not made dialogues easier. The post-modern mentality, which spread quickly after 1989 especially in Western Europe and is often characterised by phenomena such as relativism and pluralism, has had a clear impact also on ecumenism. The fundamental problem within the post-modern context became the loss of a common goal of the ecumenical movement. The idea of visible unity faded, and people became sceptical towards the so-called "ecumenism of consensus". Some want to declare its end; some blame it for blurring identities. The search for unity and communion in truth was often substituted by preservation of one's own confessional and cultural identity, and its mutual recognition. So Protestants often revert to an "ecumenism of profile" or an "ecumenism of difference". Others consider theological ecumenism irrelevant, since it focuses on questions that seem to be uninteresting to the average believer.

Within the new context, where we are confronted with a loss of the idea of unity in truth, the churches in the tradition of the Reformation themselves have become more pluralistic in many cases. This tendency concerns Church doctrine and ministry, as well as – increasingly – ethical questions. As we sadly see in the Anglican Communion and, more recently, in some Lutheran churches, this can easily lead to an inner pluralism and even divisions. This is why we are facing today, on the one hand, some philo-catholic groups within these churches and, on the other, more and more splinter groups and confessional alliances, so-called united churches, in which the confessional identity of each member church is no longer clear, so that we often deal with dialogue partners whose confessional identity is not easily recognisable.

At the same time Evangelicals have grown worldwide, as have members of the charismatic and Pentecostal movements, and independent churches. This is often called the third wave in the history of Christianity, after the churches of the first millennium and the church communions born of the Reformation of the sixteenth century. This third wave does not yet have clear contours, and its lack of clear self-definition represents a new difficult ecumenical challenge.

So the great enthusiastic common vision of the past has now vanished; this is a lack under which the World Council of Churches suffers as well. Public opinion referred to a stagnation in ecumenism or an ecumenical winter. Cardinal Willebrands was long-sighted enough to predict some disenchantment after the initial enthusiasm. He warned against believing that Christian unity was achievable in only a few years. Such expectations would inevitably lead to disappointment.

In this difficult situation the Catholic Church cannot simply stop and wait. It has a special responsibility. Its unique ecumenical responsibility comes paradoxically from the Petrine ministry, which is often seen as the main obstacle for unity but which understands itself as ministry of unity. It is precisely in this situation particularly the Church of Rome has to take responsibility as the "See which presides in love" (Ignatius of Antioch). Let us focus then on these questions: What is our vision for the future of ecumenism? What is our task in this new century and new millennium? How can we make the most of the legacy of the Second Vatican Council and of Cardinal Willebrands today and tomorrow?

III. The Future of Ecumenism

I am not a prophet and cannot play such a role when I try to identify the way forward for ecumenism. The Holy Spirit has its own plans and will always surprise us. But one thing is certain: the Holy Spirit is loyal. It has given the impulse, and we can be sure that it will fulfil what it has begun. Therefore pondering about the future of ecumenism in our current situation, which is much changed since the past and keeps changing very quickly, does not mean reshaping ecumenism completely anew. Ecumenism is founded on the task that was entrusted to us by Jesus himself. It is rooted in the mandate of the Second Vatican Council that considered the unity of all Christians as one of its priorities. As Pope John Paul II rightly stated and Pope Benedict XVI repeated with different words, ecumenism is an irreversible process. Ecumenism has a future, not because we want it, but because Jesus Christ wants it and because his Spirit helps us in our commitment.

Ecumenism in truth and love is not just an option that the Church can take or leave; it is our sacred duty. Nor is ecumenism an appendix to our common pastoral tasks or a 'luxury article' of our pastoral activity: it is 'the' perspective of the entire life of the Church. The Catholic principles of ecumenism, as they were expressed by the Council in the decree *Unitatis Redintegratio*, i.e., ecumenism in truth and love, are valid also for the future. This decree remains the magna charta in our ecumenical journey ahead. Cardinal Willebrands' legacy will be for us a good guide on this way.

This is also true regarding the recent developments where individual persons or groups of persons from other churches, especially from the Anglican Communion, by the grace of God and by reasons of their conscience, want to become members of the Catholic Church while preserving the legitimate elements of their liturgical and spiritual tradition. If this comes to a good end, it will not at all be a new ecumenism, which has been suggested by ill-informed news sources. On the contrary, this has happened exactly in conformity with the Decree on Ecumenism (*UR* 4), which clearly distinguishes between conversion of individual persons or groups of persons on the one hand and, on the other, ecumenism as dialogue with the other churches with the goal of full communion. While we cannot close our doors when others knock at them, this does not exonerate us from the mandate of our Lord to open in love our hearts to all our brothers and sisters in Christ.

I repeat: There is no new ecumenism and not the end of the old. On the contrary, there is *one* fruit of ecumenical dialogues in the last decades, and it is the strong impulse to go on in our ecumenical commitment, also in the dialogue with the Anglican Communion that has been so fruitful to date. Together, conversion (individual and corporate) and ecumenical dialogue should be undertaken with the greatest possible transparency, tactfulness and mutual esteem in order not to entail meaningless tensions with our ecumenical partners.

So nothing essentially has changed with regard to the fundamental orientation of *Unitatis Redintegratio*. Nevertheless, there are also new aspects. First, I want to mention a basic theological aspect. In his first encyclical letter, *Deus caritas est* (2005), Pope Benedict XVI focused on the theological foundations of ecumenism in a deeper way and within a wider theological context. The letter does not speak explicitly of ecumenism. However, in his message at the end of the Week of Prayer for Christian Unity in January 2006, the pope underlined that this encyclical is important also from an ecumenical perspective. He added that love is the true driving force of ecumenism. Love is founded on the self-revelation and self-communication of God in Jesus Christ through the power of the Holy Spirit. The fundamental task of the Church is to convey and to communicate this love to the world.

This applies both for ecumenism and for mission. Ecumenism is the twin of mission. Since the World Missionary Conference in Edinburgh in 1910, the 100th anniversary of which we celebrated in 2010, we know that the divisions among Christians are the greatest obstacle to ecclesial mission in the world. Thus ecumenism has a particular urgency also from the point of view of mission and of new evangelization, so much needed in overly secularised Europe and in other parts of the western world.

As an expression of self-giving love, ecumenical dialogue is a type of witness. Those who witness act and speak not only with their mouths, but with their whole existence. But unlike proselytism, ecumenism does not force anyone into something. Love respects the freedom of the other and respects one's otherness. So as an expression of self-giving love, ecumenism is closely bound to mutual respect and esteem, friendship and fraternity, encounter and cooperation. But finally, love desires unity. This is why the final objective of ecumenism can only be the full communion of faith, sacraments, apostolic ministry and mission. In this sense, ecumenism will be an ecumenism of consensus also in the future. At the same time, love makes room for the legitimate differences and for the charisma of the other churches. In this context, Cardinal Willebrands' idea of different *typoi* of church within the one Church is still contemporary.

Stressing that ecumenism is based on love clearly shows that ecumenism is not a political programme which tends to an enlargement of the Church's empire, as some ridiculously think. Neither is it a diplomatic compromise of the Church based on the least common denominator. Love is selfless and yearns to communicate its own richness to the other. Ecumenical dialogue in truth is therefore, as Pope John Paul II reminded us, an exchange not simply of ideas but of gifts (*Ut unum sint* 28). Ecumenical dialogue does not deprive each other from our respective richness, but wants to share the richness. Through ecumenical dialogue we can learn from the other and be guided by the Spirit in the whole truth (John 16,13) so that we can share more and more in the fullness of Christ (Eph 4,13).

After this more fundamental reflection let us now ask more poignantly: How can we make some concrete progress on this deepened theological basis? One thing is clear from the very beginning. Even when we are and have to be fully committed in our ecumenical work, we know that we cannot 'make' or organise the unity of the Church. The unity which we seek will not come about by theological debates in an ecumenical commission, as helpful and necessary this approach may be. Unity is a gift of the Holy Spirit. Therefore spiritual ecumenism is the very heart of ecumenism (*UR* 8) and has become much more relevant in the last decade. It is in train to be discovered more and more in all parts of the ecumenical world. It presupposes a renewal of mentalities, an inner conversion and the willingness to reform. The prayer for Christian unity is the heart of this spiritual ecumenism. In this sense, we have rediscovered the teaching of Abbé Paul Couturier (†1953). According to him, ecumenism means bearing witness to Jesus' prayer, to join him in his prayer, to make his prayer our own with him and in him. Paul Couturier spoke of an invisible cloister, namely a community spread throughout the world in which all individuals nevertheless are bound together by Jesus' prayer that all may be one.

In our day this invisible community is growing and becoming more visible in different places. Religious communities and spiritual movements belonging to different churches around the world meet regularly, engage in spiritual exchanges and pray for one another. Immediately after the signing of the Joint Declaration on the Doctrine of Justification in 1999 they met in Ottmaring near Augsburg and decided to embark together in its reception. Under the title "Together for Europe", they gathered in Stuttgart twice for two important international congresses. Their work now goes on at the level of regional and national associations. What belongs together grows together. This represents for me the greatest ecumenical hope.

It is still to be seen whether this phenomenon will result – in the foreseeable or distant future – in the creation of a differentiated unity, namely a unity preserving legitimate confessional diversity, with such churches and ecclesial communities that are close to us. This model of unity would not be the model envisaged in the first phase after the Council, when we hoped for a corporate union with one or another church. But we all are left in the hands of Providence and must trust in the guidance of the Holy Spirit, who will decide when, where and how he will fulfil this or another form of unity.

If we further consider the results accomplished so far, we become aware that there is no reason for resignation. Our ecumenism of consensus, that has often been wrongly criticized, has achieved much more in the last decades than we could have ever imagined 40 years ago. I am referring here to the goodwill, cooperation, common witness and friendship that we have shared. There has been a reception of our churches' spirituality, hymns, liturgical forms and symbols. We have learned much from one another also in terms of biblical exegesis, in which today the lines no longer run along confessional borders but cross them. Thanks to God, a new situation has been given to us.

The theological achievements are also much greater than many think. In 2009 the Pontifical Council for Promoting Christian Unity summarised the 'Harvest Project', the results of 40 years of bilateral dialogues with the churches belonging to the classical Reformation tradition (Anglicans, Lutherans, Reformed and Methodists). We summarised all under four headlines: Jesus Christ and Trinity, justification and sanctification, Church and both the major sacraments Baptism and Eucharist. In every part of *Harvesting the Fruits* much more has been achieved than I personally could have imagined in my most optimistic expectations.

Of course we were not blind to the remaining open questions. We have also clearly presented the issues. There are fundamental questions of hermeneutics, of anthropology, of ecclesiology, and of sacramental theology that still need to be resolved. However, a problem that has been clearly identified already represents half of the solution.

We started this project with two precise intentions. First, we are of the opinion that the time had come to facilitate the reception of the results of our dialogues. So we wanted to start a reception process in our churches in order that the fruits of forty years would not get dusty on some book-shelves but become a living reality in the body of our churches. Second, a new generation of ecumenists is growing up with new and fresh ideas, but which is not aware of all that has been achieved so far and of what open question we hand on to them. With this book we 'oldies' pass the torch on to a new generation. We hope and trust that it will offer them inspiring encouragement to make further progress in the ecumenical journey that has been so fruitful so far.

This is why we should take the steps that are possible to take here and now with the same trust and the same balance of courage and realism, of patience and impatience that Cardinal Willebrands successfully achieved in the first phase of the ecumenical dialogue. We can take these steps trusting in the Holy Spirit and in the prayer of so many Christians of all the churches all over the world. These are the true players in the ecumenical movement and our most important co-workers. We have been assured that when we pray in Jesus' name our prayers will be fulfilled (John 14,13). And which prayer in Jesus' name can be better heard than the prayer of Jesus himself 'that all may be one' (John 17,21)?

The prayer of many and the promise of Jesus himself gives us courage and trust in the accomplishment of our work undertaken as his instruments. One thing is sure: ecumenism will be one of the construction sites for the future of the Church. Cardinal Willebrands has shown us import of commitment to Christian unity. His legacy calls us to renew this commitment.

Pontifical Council for   Walter Cardinal KASPER
Promoting Christian Unity   President emeritus
VA-00120 Città del Vaticano

MEMORIES OF J. WILLEBRANDS AT VATICAN II

AN INSIDER'S STORY

The historian Annette Wieviorka calls our times "The Era of the Witness". The personal testimonies of direct witnesses are *the* way to convey historical truth. Thus the importance of oral and written recordings of such witnesses while they are still alive and whose fading memories are not displaced by fantasies which others then create into myths. "History is not in the truth but in the telling" (Robert Penn Warren).

I apply this generalization to the Second Vatican Council (1962-1965), to the infant years of the Secretariat for Promoting Christian Unity (SPCU) and to Johannes Willebrands. Ruthless time is dispossessing us of "insider's stories" from participants who in their tellings could still *re-present* the events and their personalities. At last count (January 2008), of those 2,500 bishops from 134 countries who experienced Vatican II, less than 30 are still breathing. Of the bishops and consultors and staff of the SPCU, every bishop has passed away; the last, Donal Lamont of Rhodesia (2003), age 92. Of the consultors only Gregory Baum (Montreal) is still active. Of the fulltime original and expanded staff, with the deaths of Cardinal Willebrands (August 2006) and of Bishop Pierre Duprey (May 2007), only I still wake up in the mornings, as does one secretary, Josette Kersters of The Grail. Fifty years later, we remember, misremember and forget.

True, it is impossible to understand modern Catholicism, indeed modern Protestantism and Eastern Orthodoxy, without taking into account Vatican II. But it is also true that this "convulsive alteration of the whole religious landscape" (Garry Wills) took place before most of today's Catholics and others were born. For these, the gravity of history is not the past and our narratives, but the future and their predictions. Vatican II promulgated SPCU documents on ecumenism, on religious freedom, on the relation of the Church to Non Christian Religions and on Divine Revelation, this last co-drafted with the Theological Commission. But for most who are interested, these four and the twelve others stand by themselves, without a history. The texts outlive the contexts. The end product is stripped of unpredictable and threatened journeys of surprises, setbacks and blessings along the way. And alas, falling back into darker shadows are the actors, such as Johannes Willebrands. Fading faster than what he *did* is what he *was* – his persona and personality, his Dutchness in ecumenical diplomacy, his style of leadership, his ostensible enjoyment of friends and ease with co-workers, his moods.

I am a SPCU witness with an insider's story. I flaunt my own credentials. In early June 1958 I left the USA on a ship to Rotterdam, on my way to Münster, Germany. Its eminent university professor of missiology, Thomas Ohm, OSB, had agreed to tutor me in the histories and theologies of Catholic and Protestant foreign missions, and the missionary beginnings of the modern ecumenical movement. Ohm had strongly urged me not to confine myself to libraries, but also to interview mission and ecumenical leaders in the Netherlands and Belgium, in Germany and France, and in Geneva (World Council of Churches, WCC).

I lodged the first days at the international headquarters of The Grail, in Tiltenberg. Its president Dé Groothuizen contacted Father Willebrands in nearby Warmond. We had a long lunch. He described the history, work and participants of the Catholic Conference for Ecumenical Questions (CCEQ) which he and Frans Thijssen had co-founded in 1951. Six weeks after this interview the Dutch hierarchy appointed Willebrands its representative for ecumenical affairs – the first such national post, anywhere. With this responsibility begins the first page of three notebooks or cahiers from 1 August 1958 to 6 March 1961; the journal has now been translated into English and annotated by Theo Salemink.

In January 1959 Fr. Willebrands came to Münster to engage Prof. Ohm in addressing the next CCEQ in Paderborn, late August. The major theme was mission-in-unity, in anticipation of the integration of the International Missionary Council into the WCC at the New Delhi assembly, December 1961. Ohm recommended me to the Paderborn conference. Willebrands invited me. We had met once more at Tiltenberg before he arrived in Rome in July 1960. He invited me to come aboard the new Bea/Willebrands boat to prepare the council as one of two SPCU crewmen (the other was Jean-François Arrighi, a CCEQ participant at Paderborn, a private secretary to Eugène Cardinal Tisserant and a consultor to the Congregation for the Eastern Churches).

Indeed a surprise! I asked, how long are council preparations? How long the council itself? The reply: "Not even the pope knows". And in my first conversation with Bea: "No one can tell us what was done last year". The SPCU boat had no map. Yet this impatient American with understandable jitters intuited serious commitment, calm not nervous guides. I answered with an enthusiastic yes. Then the required curial clearances before the public announcement, 3 September 1960, which happened to be my birthday, age 30.

Before we could move into Vatican quarters then occupied by a family and needing paint and repairs, in mid-September Willebrands and I were in Gazzada near Milano for the CCEQ meeting on ecumenical hopes, wishes and desires for the council. To our surprise there arrived on the last day Cardinals Montini (Milano), Alfrink (Utrecht, on holidays in the Italian Alps), and Bea. Bea talked at length with those ten who already had been papally appointed SPCU consultors. This was "although limited to those who happened to be present, the first meeting, unofficial, of the SPCU" (Willebrands, 1981). We were wandering into a great historical event, unpredictable its outcome.

I cannot compare the above prelude with the day-to-day experiences with Johannes Willebrands, the council preparations, the council itself, the interims, the immediate post-Vatican II activities, the annual plenary of the SPCU, and meetings of the RCC/WCC Joint Working Group; in June 1982 a vacation with him and Thijssen in my native rural environment; two weeks of pilgrimage in the Holy Land with him and his only living seminary classmate, Piet Schoonebeek (1993), and the last time together, old friends, during his declining years with caring nuns at Denekamp. In this personal context, I place *The Agenda, 19 February 1963 to 8 December 1965*, translated from the Dutch and superbly annotated by Leo Declerck.

The trickiness of perusing this Agenda depends on what one is looking for and expecting. Willebrands shorthanded selective episodes for his own purposes, however puzzling they may seem to a curious detective. He did not envisage a future historian and publisher looking over his shoulder, as did Yves Congar and his *Journal du Concile* – two volumes, 1,191 pages! *The Agenda* is not a customary journal à la Congar of personal feelings and moods, ups-and-downs in physical health, and blunt descriptions and judgements of others. Nevertheless, *The Agenda* presents an embarrassing question: may the publication be an intrusive entrance into a private world?

I cannot detect a consistent pattern in the selective items, and why Willebrands ignores far more memorable ones. Why the fact of a few of several routine luncheons with staff members at Roberto's, a modest restaurant near to the offices, yet he does not note even the date of a working audience with Pope Paul VI? Why only the dates of his studied preparation of a conference, and nothing on the theme and the listeners? Congar narrates a long, revealing conversation with Willebrands on the snags in drafting *De Judaeis,* yet *The Agenda* lists nothing for the same day.

I easily give flesh-and-blood to the flattened skeletons of several names, and I clearly or hazily recall an episode. Even the weeks of blanks

create a vacuum which I rush in to fill, or I simply allow to rest because
of no recollection. "Where is the truth of unremembered things?" asks
C. Milosz. What *The Agenda* leaves out often creates in me more arrest-
ing reality than the recorded, for left out is his direct participation and
influence in events which were turning points for the SPCU and Vatican
II, and which illustrate Willebrands' leadership skills and style.

For example, among the names, Willebrands mentions Frans Thijssen
fifty-six times without comment – evening dinners at Willebrands'
residence on Monte Mario; getaway weekends at a convent on Lake
Bracciano. They were the closest friends, mutually consulting *entre nous*.
One cannot understand Willebrands without also knowing Thijssen.

In 1937 Willebrands had returned from Rome with a doctorate in philosophy, and the young priest became a resident chaplain at the Beguinage
in central Amsterdam. The older Thijssen introduced him to Catholics
and Protestants who were aiding helpless refugees from the Nazis, Jews
in particular. Thijssen was later called "the prophet of Holland" because
of his bold actions in the underground movement during the Nazi occupa-
tion, when the dignity of the Netherlands and the integrity of the Church
were at stake. After the war he was vocal in promoting positive relations
in common witness among the churches, more so since the 1948 first
assembly of the WCC in Amsterdam. In J. Grootaers's description,
Thijssen was "the *vox clamans* of the ecumenical movement in its
prophetic years". A year before the WCC assembly, the Dutch bishops
appointed Willebrands president of Sint Willibrordvereniging, then a
staunch and aggressive organization which defended the Catholic Church
vis-à-vis the Dutch Protestants, and boasted its unembashed aim of their
"conversion". Thijssen helped his friend to soften the approach, develop
positive relations with the other churches and seek like-minded Catholics
beyond the national borders.

Thijssen's doctoral studies at the Gregorianum in Rome and his
residency at the Germanicum-Hungaricum on the Via S. Nicolò da
Tolentino gained him lasting friends in Germany, Austria, Hungary, Slo-
venia and Croatia. He recruited several of them to become members of
the CCEQ. In naming the two co-founders of the CCEQ, Willebrands is
always the first. In fact, initially peripatetic Frans Thijssen was the more
visible and active, and he recognized in the rector of the Philosophicum
in Warmond calmer leadership and organizational skills. The demeanor
was contrasting. The expansive Thijssen could not speak with stranger
or friend without moving hands and grand body gestures – Dutch
panache. He had a brilliant theological mind, yet not always easy to
understand – the wry judgment of Henry Davis (Birmingham), a member

of the CCEQ executive committee: "Thijssen speaks Dutch and French, German, Italian and English, all in the same sentence!".

After each CCEQ conference, Willebrands submitted the executive committee report to the Holy Office, and with Thijssen he went to Rome, there to discuss it with Pius XII's unofficial consultor on ecumenical affairs – Father Augustin Bea at the Biblicum. Prudent in church diplomacy the Dutch pair did not want only the complainers to inform the Holy Office.

When Willebrands had been appointed SPCU secretary, Cardinals Alfrink and Bea readily approved his recommendation that Frans Thijssen represent the Netherlands as a SPCU consultor.

What was the relationship of Cardinal Bea with Willebrands, the original staff (Arrighi and Stransky) and its expansion (Eric Salzmann, Pierre Duprey and John Long)? In August 1960, after Bea and Willebrands had put together the first list of members and consultors, the cardinal made his annual retreat in Germany. In this week of prayerful reflection on his new responsibilities, Bea resolved: "with subordinates, always friendly, patient, kind and not familiar, firm and clear" (private retreat notes). And another retreat entry after two years of working with the given staff: "Towards all who work with me, show confidence for them, prove my love of them whenever I can, be patient with them – making allowances for the character of each individual – and make sure that it is a joy to work with me. Pay tribute to the work they do". We all experienced Bea's fidelity to his private resolution. He treated us as he treated Willebrands, who in 1981 recounted that, when he became the SPCU secretary in June 1960, "The cardinal advised: I shall not mind if you sometimes make mistakes, but I shall mind if you do not do something practical". Bea wanted to start a *new* tradition in *practical ecumenism.*

Cardinal Bea also followed his resolution, "not to be familiar" with his staff. I admired his dove-like simplicity *and* serpentine wisdom. He never seemed to lose his calmness or to dull his extraordinary sense of timing: when to push whom for what, when to lie 'back and wait (this quality I appreciated after the fact). I never questioned his loving trust in affirming what I was doing right and in correcting my awkward mistakes. I was a loyal collaborator with the paterfamilias, but without familiarity. Willebrands was so different. In our small family he was an easy friend, he preferred in English to be called "John". He enjoyed being just that, a friend.

The arrangements and working routine conditioned these relationships with the cardinal and his secretary. During the council preparations the Vatican administration designated our office space on the first floor (*primo piano*) of an old and large palazzo on the Via dei Corridori, two blocks east of the Piazza San Pietro. The quarters were very small – a midget entrance parlour, four rooms. Seventy-nine year old Bea followed a strict discipline of study and prayer and work, and he adhered to careful abstemious diet. He seldom came to his SPCU office, except to preside over a "congresso" every month. He preferred to remain at his simple quarters at the Collegio Brasiliano on the Via Aurelia. There he did his business with Willebrands and occasionally with a summoned staff member. Also at his residence he received all visitors, and kept most of the names to himself. He was protecting his privacy. He relied on his private secretary, fellow Jesuit and former secretary of the Biblicum, Stjepan Schmidt, a Croatian. Daily a driver exchanged the post and memoranda.

This arrangement meant that Willebrands, not Bea, directed the staff at the Via dei Corridori. Work and informality mixed. We were at the office at 08:00, if not before. From 08:30 to 09:00 Willebrands presided over a "congressetto" with staff and secretaries in sharing and discussing the new correspondence or recent travels, assigning responsibilities of answers, either directly or drafts for him, and offering suggestions for improving or initiating projects and contacts. This nuclear unity was of an extended family. The first plenary, November 1960, was held in a stuffy, ill-lit room in the Vatican, adjacent to a junk room of sculptured fragments called the Hall of Broken Heads. With Bea's strong support, for future plenaries we will go outside the city. Willebrands, Arrighi and I found an isolated retreat institute at Ariccia on Lago di Nemi, far enough from Rome to prevent bishops skipping out during meetings for Vatican business or for visits with city friends. Ariccia provided an atmosphere which quickly bonded members, consultors and staff into a democratic community of intense work, shared liturgy and recreation. Of the five pre-council plenaries all were at Ariccia but one, away from the Italian August heat, in Bühl, Germany, near Bea's birthplace at Riedböhringen.

By symbiosis the SPCU adjusted to a *modus vivendi*: accept the unpredictable, settle for immediate resolution, with no pretense of long-range visions and strategies. The staff enlarged, beginning with Eric Salzmann who joined us four weeks before the second plenary, February 1961. A diocesan priest from Brig (Switzerland) and Bea's former student, he was an adept Latinist and competent archivist. He had an eagle eye on the ordinary order, or occasional disorder, of the office. With Arrighi he organized the complicated logistics for the lodging of the delegated Observers. He was self-effacing, and zealous in his own way away from the office as chaplain to the de la Salle Christian Brothers' generalate. Archbishop Felici, secretary of the council preparatory commission, refused to accept Salzmann as a SPCU employee: "You are the smallest of the preparatory organs, not even a proper commission, and you need an extra on the staff?" Bea and Willebrands would have Salzmann in their own way. For the next two years his salary came from the cardinal's private pocket. *The Agenda* lists Salzmann twenty-five times.

Two more staff members are Pierre Duprey and John Long. In establishing the SPCU, *Superno Dei Nutu* (5 June 1960) did not separate the two major groups of other Christians: those of the Orthodox churches of the Byzantine (Greek and Slavic) and of the Oriental Orthodox (Syrian, Armenian, Coptic and Ethiopian), and those of the Anglican and Protestant Communions. Would the SPCU be responsible for contacts with both or leave the Orthodox and the Oriental to the Preparatory Commission for the Eastern Churches (Amleto Cardinal Cicognani)? Prior to the appointment of Willebrands, the cardinal preferred the division. He told the pope that he considered himself little qualified to handle the problems of the Eastern Churches. The pope would have it otherwise but conceded. Willebrands questioned the practicality of a structured division of ecumenical relations. The WCC, as prime example, had both Protestant and Orthodox under the same roof. So did the CCEQ, among whose regulars were Olivier Rousseau, Pierre Dumont and Emmanuel Lanne from Chevetogne; Christophe Dumont from the Istina Centre in Paris; and from the Middle East, Pierre Duprey, Jean Corbon, and Robert Clément.

The original list of SPCU members and consultors had not even an Eastern Catholic bishop-member. The first plenary heard many objections, especially from Christophe Dumont: the Orthodox will shun any initiative from the Congregation for the Eastern Church, pejoratively called "Uniates" and their very existence judged to be "proselytic". The Vatican Congregation was not noted for ecumenical initiatives. Bea admitted his initial mistake and reported to Pope John who happily replied: "All right, Your Eminence, by all means take the Orthodox" (Bea, 1967).

Willebrands soon proved to be very acceptable to the Orthodox hierarchs. They welcomed his frank diplomatic ways and genuine faith in the unity of the one Church of Christ. Not by letter but in person, he travelled eastwards in February and May 1962. He asked if the heads and synods would delegate Observers. Twice he visited Ecumenical Patriarch Athenagoras. These contacts *in situ* convinced him that the SPCU needed full-time staff experts who were knowledgeable in the theologies and historical contexts of each Eastern church, and who in particular knew the strengths and weaknesses of living leaders.

For the first council session Willebrands had selected Pierre Duprey to serve as theologian/interpreter/translator (Greek, Arabic and French) for the delegated observers of the Middle East churches. Since 1956 Duprey was the rector of the Melchite seminary of St Anne in the Old City of Jerusalem, and editor of *Proche-Orient Chrétien*. He became familiar with the region ever since he had studied in Tunisia in 1940 and ordained as a White Father in Carthage in 1950. After the first session Willebrands facilitated the enlistment of Duprey and, mainly at Duprey's request, the American Jesuit John Long. Duprey had a quick intuitive intellect, impatience with bureaucratic delays, and impulsive outbursts among friends. "Stupide" and "bêtise" and Arab words felicitously never translated were no strangers to his lips. The more reserved Long had studied at the University of Athens, and, like Duprey, at the Jesuit Oriental Institute in Rome. He was fluent in Russian and familiar with the Russian and Slavic churches "behind the Iron Curtain". Both Duprey and Long warmly accepted Willebrands's direction of the SPCU office and its milieu – the combination of serious, intense work and constant consultation, informality and humour. They joined myself who was resistant to walking down the trodden path of *romanità*, the *stylus Curiae*.

I presume a missing cahier from March 1961 to December 1962. The first entry in *The Agenda* here is February 1963. The context was different. After the first session and before the death of Pope John, we were experiencing a qualitative shift in the SPCU's perception of itself because of the council Patres' perception of the SPCU. On October 22 they received the pope's clarification that the SPCU, like the commissions, had the right to present its own schemata and to cooperate in joint-commissions. In the discussion and voting on the preparatory *De Fontibus Revelationis* as a basis for future discussion, the pope intervened; he called for a new schema to be drafted by members from the newly composed theological commission and from the SPCU. Then on December 1, the bishops voted, 2,068 to 36, for one schema on church unity which would harmonize the three drafts of the preparatory theological commission, the commission for the Eastern churches and the SPCU. Bishops were trusting the SPCU's competence to evaluate the "ecumenical dimension" of schemata without ever seeing SPCU's own; they were not yet printed! The most single important disclosure of the first session was the strength shown by advocates of renewal and reform. Unintentionally the SPCU was mirroring this majority tendency, and the opposing minority began to mobilize. Bea became an icon. Wits who read public advertising for British European Airlines or BEA were exclaiming: "Fly with

BEA". Monsignor Willebrands was still unknown to most bishops; he was the SPCU secretary who sat in the Observers' tribunal.

He had his own coup, but *The Agenda* leaves it out in the January 1963 negotiations for the release of Archbishop J. Slipyj (L'viv, Ukraine) from a seventeen-year confinement in a Siberian prison town. To avoid direct political relations between the Kremlin and Cicognani's Secretariat of State, Pope John empowered Bea and Willebrands with the negotiations. The pope had been impressed with the positive outcome of Willebrands' receiving approval in the Moscow Patriarchate (and Kremlin) for Russian Orthodox Observers at the first session. On 24 January Bea and Willebrands received news that the Soviet Premier Nikita Kruschev was permitting Slipyj to leave Russia for Rome, but no publicity before or during the exit. Willebrands flew to Moscow, accompanied the ex-prisoner to Vienna, then by train to Grottaferrata, the Eastern church monastery north of Rome (February 10). For the first time in seventeen years the robed Archbishop fully celebrated the high Slavic rite. Willebrands, Arrighi and I witnessed the tears. The dramatic release and the Romeward journey with Willebrands reached the press the next day, Monday, giving the Vaticanologists fresh stuff for speculation.

Willebrands, I know, regarded this episode as one of his most gratifying. Archbishop Slipyj and his freedom were a fact and prophetic symbol, a small positive voice from "the Church of Silence". He was personally wounded and saddened when Slipyj had pleaded in his first intervention in aula (11 October 1963) for raising the prestige of the metropolitan see of Kiev to patriarchal rank. Paul VI and the SPCU had opposed the request for "ecumenical reasons", and the decision was bitterly resented by Slipyj and the church in Ukraine and by the emigrant Ukrainians, such as Archbishop M. Hermaniuk (Winnipeg, Canada), later a member of the SPCU.

The Agenda leaves out Willebrands' and Duprey's essential role in the encounter and embrace of Pope Paul and Ecumenical Patriarch Athenagoras, on the Mount of Olives, 6 January 1964: "Two pilgrims, their eyes fixed on Christ" – the words of their joint communiqué. Thirty years later, October 1993, I accompanied the cardinal to that same room, and there greeting him were the incumbent Patriarch of Jerusalem, his entourage, and, yes, his visiting sister and brother-in-law. Driving back to Tantur, he remarked about the 1964 gesture: "one of the most privileged events in my long life".

I am often surprised at the lack of an entry on some of those temporary but critical unexpected worries, almost panics. For example, on 24 April 1964, the prosaic note: "Lunch with Long and Stransky". The simple fact triggers my memory of a sudden challenge to crisis-management.

During the second session the Observers were more publicly commenting on council issues in press interviews and publicized conferences in Rome. Some comments were not nuanced, too much of 'we' versus 'they' to designate the council-minority – the "ecumenical opposition". The conservative Coetus Internationalis Patrum directly went to Pope Paul with their troubling rhetorical question: Were the Observers becoming too influential on the council processes? Perhaps confirming his own worries, the pope wrote to Bea in mid-April 1964, to consider if the presence of the "separated brethren" and of their *mentalità* were "excessively dominating the Council thus diminishing its psychological freedom". "It seems", he concludes, "that far more important than pleasing the Observers is protecting the coherence of the teaching of the Catholic Church". Years later the insider at the time of the letter, Cardinal Villot, commented that Paul VI was considering "dis-inviting" the Observers delegated by other communions.

Willebrands had just returned from Athens and Istanbul, and the cardinal showed him the pope's letter. At lunch with Long and me he expressed his irritation and sought our counsel about possible responses: "We did not invite the Observers to particular sessions but to the Council". I do not know how Bea answered the papal letter. Nothing ensued. The crisis never travelled beyond us four.

In 2004 a cross-section of Willebrands' friends and colleagues fittingly celebrated at Denekamp his anniversaries: 95 since birth; priest, 70; bishop, 40; and cardinal, 35. From Tantur I telephoned my congratulations. He commented: "The most important gift to me is my priesthood". Until 1964 he bore the honorific (non biblical) title of prelate, "Monsignor". But "Father" fit him better.

During the first two council sessions he was not a bishop, not of the Vatican II Patres as were the SPCU members. The status gives him no right to speak or vote in aula, but he had a certain freedom. During the days of a *congregatio generalis*, he could remain in his office on Via dei Corridori, or he could join the SPCU staff, the translators/interpreters, the delegated Observers and SPCU Guests ad personam. The designated tribunal was near the high altar and across from the cardinals' seats. Located under Bernini's Saint Longinus, the Observers called themselves "The Separated Brethren of St. Longinus". Willebrands enjoyed the two council coffee bars, quickly named Bar-Jona and Bar-Abbas, highlighted by Oscar Cullmann for their "ecumenical role". In this relaxed milieu he could more easily read the council pulse. The Observers were of his extended family. His Agenda notes only a few of many luncheons at the Pensione Sant'Angelo, where most of the Protestant and all of the

Orthodox Observers lodged; they invited to table *periti*, visiting clergy and spouses, lay friends, and Patres. On most free Thursdays he joined the Observers on one-day bus trips outside Rome. We lunched too sumptuously with generous local hosts, such as the monasteries of Subiaco, Monte Cassino, Casamari, Assisi and Grottaferrata, or in the towns of Viterbo, Orvieto, Napoli and the Castelli Romani.

On 4 June 1964, Pope Paul nominated Father (monsignor) Willebrands a titular bishop. He was in France; 1-9 June – a flurry of diverse activities in Geneva, Lyons, Ars and at Taizé. *The Agenda* highlights his conversations with lay leaders of la Petite Église. His *Agenda* skips the ordination itself by the Pope in St. Peter' s Basilica, June 28; and it omits the joyful celebration at the Collegio Olandese, in fact the first family reunion since the funeral of his mother – his father, brothers and sisters and their children, and his brother a Redemptorist for years a missionary in Dutch Guiana (Surinam).

Now Bishop Willebrands had the right to *interventiones* in aula, to submit written *animadversiones* and to vote. But in order of seniority of episcopal consecration his new council seat was in the very back of the long aula: "I am not able to see the Observers!". Whereas Cardinal Bea delivered eighteen *interventiones* and wrote even more *animadversiones*, Willebrands never spoke in council. He added his name to a few written *animadversiones* of groups. The only one with his sole signature was his ecumenical concern for deeper, more balanced Marian doctrine in *De Ecclesia* which could challenge Protestant doctrine, attitudes and pieties about Mary. Most of them were ignorant of the Scriptures and the ancient tradition of the undivided Church, and even the teachings of Luther and Calvin. He was against the title of Mary as Mediator (Mediatrix). The word itself should not be in *De Ecclesia*; it seemed to juxtapose Christ, the sole Mediator. The additional Marian title would create even more problems with the Protestants.

The sole public appearance of Bishop Willebrands in aula was at the last solemn assembly, 7 December 1965. In the presence of Pope Paul and at his side on the high altar, Greek Orthodox Metropolitan Meliton of Constantinople, Bishop Willebrands read in French the Common Declaration of Pope Paul VI and Ecumenical Patriarch Athenagoras, which decided to "remove from memory and from the midst of the Church", the sentences of mutual excommunications of 1054. Pierre Duprey, indispensable in the drafting and negotiations, described the Declaration as "a major step towards the healing of schism". *The Agenda* states only the fact of the Declaration and on the same day the promulgation of another ecumenical triumph of Willebrands's patience – *On Religious Freedom.*

If some judged Willebrands shy, it was a deceptive shyness which seemed not to obstruct his initiatives in meeting people eye-to-eye. His unsought popularity came from his quiet honesty, his speaking the truth in unfeigned charity, his conveying realistic hopes without being preachy. He told me, as I presume he told a few others, what Pope Paul expected from him in audience or memoranda, in the pope's words: "Help me by being completely honest and frank". Even with His Holiness he could be himself. His irritation was duplicity or vagueness in speech which hides true intent and thought. He disdained mediocre incompetence in those who wield ecclesiastical power over others. He described one such cardinal: "Sub-Zero". Already in the 1950s, when he and Frans Thijssen reported in Rome, they spoke not only always with Father Bea but also often with Cardinal Ottaviani, secretary of the Holy Office. In the council years Ottaviani vigorously opposed the SPCU in some critical areas, such as religious freedom and church-state relations. Willebrands respected him and his competence: "He always clearly says what he clearly thinks necessary to defend the faith".

I have recorded here but a few of my personal recollections which may complement Leo Declerck's penetrating analysis of the 1963-1965 *Agenda*. Sometimes, as old people are wont to do, I savour my most enjoyable times with John Willebrands. Coming to mind are those occasions when together we made the Rome-Geneva-Rome trip. He was trusting me to be the staff member who would help him strengthen the SPCU bonds with WCC personnel and WCC programmes. The WCC officers were cramped into a former home on the route de Malagnou (at present a museum of Swiss clocks). Visser 't Hooft always greeted Willebrands as a colleague who shared the same ecumenical commitment. We lodged nearby, in an old Swiss-style hotel with a long outside porch; after a tiring day we would sit in rocking chairs, and chat, and he smoked his cigar and I my pipe.

I conclude with another personal memorable. On the occasion of Cardinal Willebrands' funeral in Utrecht (August 2006), his friends Louis and Maria ter Steeg asked me to summarize the cardinal's *persona*. To my surprise the expected pious eulogizing formalities vanished. I answered, briefly: "He was a Dutch gentleman".

St. Paul's College   Thomas STRANSKY
3015 4th Street, NE
Washington, DC 20017-1102
USA

JOHANNES WILLEBRANDS,
"AN AUTHENTIC PROTAGONIST OF CHRISTIAN UNITY"
(JOHN PAUL II)

EXPERIENCES AND INSIGHTS

If we are to pursue the legacy left by Johannes Willebrands, we will repeatedly be led to Paderborn. Long before the Second Vatican Council and then time and again afterward he came to this North Rhine-Westphalia city. What motivated him to do so?

First of all, Willebrands was looking for allies on the path to Christian unity. Among the first allies found were Archbishop Lorenz Jaeger; the two other one's were Josef Höfer and Eduard Stakemeier. Willebrands and Jaeger became close ecumenical companions. In 1948, when Professor Willebrands became president of the Sint Willibrordvereniging, the so-called Jaeger-Stählin Kreis, named after its two founders, initiated a dialogue between Roman Catholic and Lutheran theologians in Germany, Willebrands strongly appreciated this initiative. On one occasion he confessed, "Here real pioneering work is being done which is of great impact on the Lutheran-Catholic relations"[1]. From 1947-1957 the Catholic theologian and professor Josef Höfer was the academic director of this body. As a counselor of the German embassy to the Holy See and given his ecumenical contacts, he has been one of the most important collaborators of the Secretariat for Promoting Christian Unity in its initial phase.

When in 1952 the international Catholic Conference on Ecumenical Questions was founded and Willebrands became its secretary, this motivated him even more to deepen the contacts with Archbishop Jaeger and Professor Höfer. When Willebrands was appointed a permanent delegate of the Dutch bishops for ecumenical questions and relations in 1958, Archbishop Jaeger was the president of the ecumenical commission of the German Bishops' conference and thus *ex officio* became his closest colleague.

Willebrands' connection with Paderborn reached a new level in 1957 when the Johann-Adam-Möhler Institute was founded. From the beginning Willebrands felt himself closely related to the institute. Its objective,

---

1. Johannes Cardinal WILLEBRANDS, *Mandatum Unitatis: Beiträge zur Ökumene*, Paderborn, Johann-Adam-Möhler-Institut, 1989, p. 89.

originally stated as "for denominational and diaspora studies" ("für Konfessions-und Diasporakunde"), was changed in 1966 into "for ecumenics" ("für Ökumenik"). This reflected a similar development that took place in the Netherlands where, after the 'palace revolution' of 1948, the apologetical Vereniging St. Petrus Canisius lead into the ecumenically oriented Sint Willibrord Vereniging. The new institute in Paderborn and its first director, Eduard Stakemeier, became useful companions on the ecumenical path. Professor Willebrands attended the meetings of the institute's academic advisory board. This offered the occasion to meet leading ecumenical theologians, to exchange experiences and to discuss matters of common interest. Johannes Willebrands continued his participation in these meetings even after the establishment of the Secretariat for Promoting Christian Unity and notwithstanding the many tasks the "flying Dutchman" then had to fulfil on the global level. His reports and reflections became an integral part of the board's programme. Still in the year of his retirement, 1989, Cardinal Willebrands provided an extensive report about the activities of the Pontifical Council for Promoting Christian Unity[2].

Since 1964 when I was a section head and from 1971 on as successor to director Stakemeier, who died unexpectedly in 1970, I came to know and appreciate first the secretary and then the president of the Pontifical Council during these board meetings.

From the beginning I witnessed Willebrands' friendship with Franz Thijssen. They always arrived together, spent the pauses together and together stood up to plead matters that seemed appropriate to them. Yet, they were different characters. While Willebrands operated in a calm and yet determined way, Thijssen was agile, spirited and sometimes also vociferous. For good reasons, he was called 'the caller in the desert'. I had met him already at the Council. During its third session, which I reported about as a journalist, I noticed how much he took care of the non-Catholic observers and hosts. For many of them he became a permanent and available Catholic interlocutor who was important for them because of his knowledge, his contacts as well as his spontaneous and cordial demeanour. In this way, he set the ambience in which the texts his friends worked on could bear fruit.

The spirit of friendship also inspired what Willebrands reported on in the advisory board. In a trustful openness he informed the board about the activities of the Secretariat and later of the Pontifical Council. Thereby, he passed over the difficulties within the curia that his private

2. Published in *Catholica* 44 (1990) 73-90.

diary reveals. He never presented himself as a victor over confrontation. Moreover, his personal vocation to "suffer into unity"[3] was not visible. Likewise, he never complained that he "spent the last years in that holy agony of seemingly unending commission meetings and planning committees"[4]. Instead, he always pointed to the positive. Every possible occasion for a new ecumenical opening was discerned as an advance. In addition to providing objective information he also addressed basic ecumenical questions. He was able to listen. With all his dialogue partners he endeavoured to "come to a common understanding and to a common expression of the truth"[5]. In a presentation to the advisory board in 1975 Willebrands revealed his vision of dialogue in the following way: "The ecumenical dialogue calls upon the whole human person; it cannot be something secondary, something additional such as the make-up on the face; it must be an expression of life. The meanest allegation one can address to dialogue is to call it a new political maneuver, a new strategy, or a concession to fashion. Rather, it is a norm originating from the Gospel"[6]. Willebrands understood dialogue as a spiritual way of life. He repeatedly declared: part of our ecumenical dialogue is "repentance, forgiving, conversion of heart, reconciliation"[7]. Let us add: "and hope!".

Willebrands committed himself to ward off hopelessness. He was convinced that this could only work if our small hopes are "surrounded and carried by a total and universal hope, the one of an encompassing and ultimate meaning"[8]. As many others, I have known Willebrands as a really hopeful person. Among the many things we owe him, his testimony of hope is the most important for today. His living and striving tell us: "You may hope the best! You have to do the best!".

Domerschulstr. 19   Bishop Paul Werner SCHEELE
DE-97070 Würzburg
Germany

---

3. *Mandatum Unitatis* (n. 1), p. 334.
4. *Ibid.*
5. *Ibid.*, p. 182.
6. *Ibid.*, p. 185.
7. *Ibid.*, p. 191.
8. *Ibid.*, p. 269.

BIBLIOGRAPHY JOHANNES CARDINAL WILLEBRANDS[1]

1929

1. *Recensie* [F. Strotman, Jahwe Shaphat], in *Cassicianum* 4 (1929-1930), nr. 6, 235-239.

1930

2. *Ascensio mentis ad Deum. Het godsbewijs van St. Augustinus*, in *Cassicianum* 5 (1930-1931), nr. 5, 129-137.
3. *Het godsidee bij Aristoteles II*, in *Cassicianum* 5 (1930-1931), nr. 6, 166-173.
4. *De godskennis bij Aristoteles*, in *Cassicianum* 5 (1930-1931), nr. 2, 44-50.

1932

5. *Bernard Bolzano en de moderne wijsbegeerte. Zijn tijd – zijn werk – zijn invloed*, in *Cassicianum* 5 (1932-1933), nr. 3, 90-104.

1937

6. *John Henry Cardinal Newman: Zijn denkleer en haar Toepassing op de Kennis van God door het Geweten*. Dissertatio Philosophico-Historica quam ad gradum Doctoris Philosophiae apud Institutum Pontificium Angelicum assequendam exaravit Joannes Willebrands, Presbyter Diocesis Harlemensis. Romae 1937, 157 pp.
7. *Kardinaal Newman*. Pars dissertationis ad obtinendam lauream in philosophia apud Pontificium Institutum Angelicum de Urbe, Roma, 1937, 36 pp.
   → 8 + 9.

1941

8. *Het christelijk platonisme van kardinaal Newman*, in *Studia Catholica* 17 (1941) 373-388.
   → 7, 1-16.
9. *Kardinaal Newman: De persoonlijke aard van het denken*, in *Studia Catholica* 17 (1941) 425-444.
   → 7, 17-36.

1. This is a first version of Cardinal Willebrands' bibliography; additions and corrections are most welcome. We are indebted to Prof. Dr. A. Denaux, Prof. Dr. P. De Mey, Dr. Karim Schelkens, Prof. Dr. Jared Wicks, Mrs. R. Corstjens and Mrs. Josette Kersters for their help in composing this bibliography. Abbr: DC = *Documentation Catholique*; IS/SI = *PCPCU, Information Service*, English and French; OR = *Osservatore Romano* (Italian, French, English and German version).

1944

10. *De natuurlijke Godskennis als probleem bij Newman*, in *Theologische opstellen aangeboden aan Mgr. Dr. G.C. van Noort*, Utrecht, Het Spectrum, 1944, 257-274.

1946

11. *Newman, een licht voor onzen tijd*, in *Streven* 14 (1946) 193-209.
12. *De ontwikkeling der idee volgens Newman vergeleken met Hegel*, in *Bijdragen* 7 (1946) 60-79.

1948

13. *Een nieuw begin. Het Schild des geloofs (Ef. 6,16)*, in *Het Schild* 26 (1948-1949) 97-98.
14. *Seminarie-opvoeding en humanisme* (Priesterstudiedagen te Stein, augustus 1948), in: *Priesterschap en humanisme*.

1949

15. *John Henry Newman*, in H. VAN OYEN (ed.), *Philosophia*. Deel II, Utrecht, W. de Haan, 1949, 69-74.
16. *De wijsbegeerte der Scholastiek na de Middeleeuwen*, in H. VAN OYEN (ed.), *Philosophia*. Deel II, Utrecht, W. de Haan, 1949, 28-68.

1950

17. *Studiedagen over het oecumenisch vraagstuk*, in *Het Schild* 28 (1950-1951) 3-8.

1952

18. *Derde Wereldconferentie voor Geloof en Kerkorde* (Lund, 15-28.8.1952), in *Het Schild* 29 (1951-1952) 280-284.
19. *Die Glaubensverkündiging für Nichtkatholiken in den Niederlanden*, in *Ite missa est* (Wiedervereinigung im Glauben, Paderborn) 13 (1952) 11-28.

1954

20. *Einige Gedanken zur Einführung in das Diasporaproblem*, in *Sociaal kompas* 2 (1954/3) 85-87.
21. *Voorwoord*, in *Bethanië-Bloemendaal. Het ware licht. Handleiding voor de praktijk van het geloofsonderricht*, Den Haag, Pax, 1954, 7-9.

1957

22. *Katholiciteit*, in *Het Schild* 34 (1957) 125-134.
23. *Voorwoord*, in J. COOLS, *et al.*, *Het Mysterie van Israël*, Utrecht – Antwerpen, Het Spectrum, 1957, 7-8.

1958

24. *Kerk-in-diaspora als gestalte en opgave* (Drachten, 4.10.1958), in *Nederlandse Katholieke Stemmen* 55 (1959) 207-221.

25. *Liturgie en oecumenische beweging*, in *Het Schild* 35 (1957-1958) 128-132.

1959

26. *Het algemeen concilie en de Reformatie*, in *Nederlandse Katholieke Stemmen* 55 (1959) 169-178.
27. *12ᵈᵉ Bijeenkomst van het Centraal Comité van de Wereldraad van Kerken (W.C.C.), gehouden te Rhodos 19-28.8.1959*, in *Het Schild* 36 (1959) 157-173.
28. *Naspel van Rhodos: Het gesprek van Orthodoxen en Katholieken*, in *De Tijd/Maasbode*, 8.10.1959.
    Zu den Vorgängen auf Rhodos, in *Informationsblatt für die Gemeinden in den Niederdeutschen Lutherischen Landeskirchen* 9 (1960) 24-26.
    Ökumenische Rundschau 9 (1960) 20-25.
    Vers l'Unité Chrétienne 23 (1960/1-2) 1-4.
29. *Onze oecumenische verantwoordelijkheid: Huidige situatie en perspectieven* (Sint Adelbert-Vereniging, 10-11.10.1959), in *Sint Adelbert* 59, nr. 9, 145-151.
30. *De plaats van het concilie*, in *Het Schild* 36 (1959) 113-122.

1960

31. *Il movimento ecumenico: Sviluppi e speranze* (Conferences sponsored by Unitas-groups in Milano [6.2.1960], Bergamo and Brescia), in *Humanitas* 15 (1960) 263-277.

1961

32. *La théologie de l'Église et le problème de l'unité*, in *DC* 43 (1961) 453-454.

1962

33. *Catholic Ecumenism*, in Graymoor Foundation (ed.), *Problems before Unity* (Graymoor Symposium), Baltimore, MD – Dublin, Helicon, 1962, 1-14.
34. *Concilie en christelijke eenheid* (Interview), in *De Gelderlander*, 6.10.1962.
35. *Gesprek op de Kahlenberg* (Interview), in *Deventer Dagblad*, 2.7.1962.
36. *Mgr. Willebrands en zijn taak in Secretariaat van eenheid* (Interview), in *Het Vaderland. Weekjournaal*, 16.6.1962.

1964

37. *Aspetti ecumenici del pelegrinaggio di Paolo VI*, in *Rocca*, 1.1.1964, 15-16.
38. *Die katholische Kirche und die getrennten Christen*, Süddeutsche Rundfunk, 15.7.1964.
39. *Il movimento ecumenico*, in *Osservatore della Domenica* 19.4.1964.

1965

40. *Cattolicesimo aperto ed ecumenismo*, in *L'Unità dei Cristiani* (Ecclesiam Suam, 1), Napoli, Edizioni domenicane italiane, 1965, 23-30.
41. *Inhalt, Ziel und Aufgabenbereich möglicher Kontakte und Zusammenarbeit zwischen Römisch-katholischer Kirche und Lutherischem Weltbund – Rückblick und Hoffnung* (Strasbourg, 25.8.1965) → 426, 15-28.

42. *Le mouvement œcuménique à l'heure du Concile* (Lyon, 14.1.1965, Saint-Étienne, 15.1.1965, Clermont-Ferrand, 16.1.1965), in *Vers l'Unité Chrétienne* 18 (1965) 17-23.

1966

43. *Chiesa Cattolica e Consiglio Mondiale delle Chiese*, in *OR* 24.2.1966.
   OR (French) 25.2.1966.
44. *Chiesa Cattolica e Federazione mondiale Luterana*, in *OR* 23.7.1966.
   IS 1 (1966) 6 (extracts).
   OR (French) 29.7.1966.
   DC 48 (1966) 1691-1693.
45. *Zur Einführung*, in Augustin Kardinal BEA – Willem VISSER 'T HOOFT (eds.), *Friede zwischen Christen*, Freiburg – Basel – Wien, Herder, 1966, 9-25.
46. *Meeting the Others* (Address Eucharistic Congress, Bombay), in *The Examiner*, Bombay, 17.12.1966.
47. *Oecumenische aspecten en perspectieven van Vaticanum II* (Brussel, 21.1.1966), in *De Maand* 9 (1966) 202-214.
   Ecumenical Aspects and Perspectives of the Second Vatican Council (Oslo, 25.1.1966), in *Mid-Stream* 5 (1966) 1-15.
   Lumen (Danmark) 9 (1966) 1-13.
   E. SCHILLEBEECKX – J. WILLEBRANDS – W. VISSER 'T HOOFT (eds.), *Christendom en wereld*, Roermond, Romen, 1966, 62-81.
   E. SCHILLEBEECKX – J. WILLEBRANDS – W. VISSER 'T HOOFT (eds.), *Christentum im Spannungsfeld von Konfessionen, Gesellschaft und Staaten*, Freiburg – Basel – Wien, Herder, 1968, 37-58.
   → 426, 98-111.
   → 77, 15-31.
48. *The Present Orientation of the Ecumenical Movement* (Lecture at an exposition of French religious books, Rome, 5.12.1966), in *Unitas* 19 (1967) 83-89.
49. *La responsabilité œcuménique en matière d'information* [1966]. → 77, 147-155.

1967

50. *De betrekkingen tussen de katholieke kerk en de orthodoxe kerken na het Tweede Vaticaans Concilie*, in *Apostolaat voor de Hereniging*, 25.11.1967.
   L'Église catholique et les églises orthodoxes après Vatican II → 77, 33-49.
51. *The Bible and the Ecumenical Movement* (conferences Uppsala 1.11.1967 and Helsinki 6.11.1967).
   Teologinen Aikakauskirja 73 (1968) 57-71.
   La fede, la Bibbia e il movimento ecumenico, in *Fede e mondo moderno*, Rome, Gregoriana, 1969, 9-30.
   → 77, 51-68.
52. *The Ecumenical Significance of the Visit of the Archbishop of Canterbury to the Holy Father*, in *Unitas* 19 (1967) 8-17.
53. *Ecumenismo: Occasione di pace per gli uomini*, in *Il Mulino* 16 (1967) 287-295.
   → 77, 157-167.

54. *Einführung in das Ökumenische Direktorium*, in *Ökumenisches Direktorium I* (Konfessionskundliche Schriften des Johann-Adam-Möhler-Instituts, 8/1967, 9/1970), Paderborn, Bonifatius, 1967, 9-12.

55. *De Eucharistie, sacrament der eenheid* (Jaarvergadering Gezelschap van de Stille Omgang, Amsterdam, 15.1.1967), s.l., s.d., 19 pp.
→ 77, 131-145.

56. *Die katholische Kirche und die ökumenische Bewegung*, in K. VON BISMARCK – W. DIRKS (eds.), *Neue Grenzen: Ökumenisches Christentum morgen* (vol. 2), Stuttgart – Berlin u. Olten – Freiburg i. Br., Kreuz-Verlag, 1967, 201-206.
→ 426, 48-53.
→ 77, 7-13.
Nuove frontiere II, Studi e opinioni, Milano, Ed. I.P.L. 1968, 245-251.

57. *Letter to the General Secretary of the WCC about the Joint Working Group*, in *IS* 3 (1967) 3.
DC 49 (1967) 1561-1563.

58. *La liberté religieuse et l'œcuménisme*, in J. HAMER – Y. CONGAR (eds.), *La liberté religieuse: Déclaration 'Dignitatis humanae personae'* (Latin, French translation) (Unam Sanctam, 60), Paris, Cerf, 1967, 237-251.
J. HAMER – Y. CONGAR (eds.), *Die Konzilserklärung über die Religionsfreiheit*, Paderborn, Bonifatius, 1967, 261-274.
→ 426, 54-69.
De godsdienstvrijheid en het oecumenisme, in *Godsdienstvrijheid*, Tielt – Den Haag, Lannoo, 1967, 341-362.

59. *Le mouvement œcuménique et la sécularisation du monde* (Symposium à l'occasion du centenaire de l'université américaine, Beyrouth, 10-15.4.1967), in *Proche-Orient Chrétien* 17 (1967) 113-125.
Seminarium 20 (1968) 333-347.
→ 77, 69-89.
C. MALIK (ed.), *God and Man in Contemporary Christian Thought* (Proceedings of the Philosophy Symposium, Beirut, 1967), Beirut, American University of Beirut, 1970, 25-37.

60. *Préface*, in W. VAN DE POL, *La communion anglicane et l'œcuménisme d'après les documents officiels* (Unam Sanctam, 63), Paris, Cerf, 1967, 9-12.

61. *Presentation of the Ecumenical Directory* (26.5.1967), in *IS* 2 (1967) 13-15.

62. *Reform and Reformation Today* (University of Lund, 31.10.1967, 450th anniversary of the beginning of the Reformation, 1517).
Lumen (Danmark) 11 (1968) 1-20.
→ 426, 29-47.
DC 50 (1968) 443-460.
→ 77, 91-111.
Svensk Teologisk Kvartalskrift 44 (1968) 16-33.

1968

63. *Address to the United Bible Societies Executive Committee* (10.1.1968), in *IS* 4 (1968) 7-8.

64. *Le Cardinal Bea, apôtre de l'unité*, in *DC* 50 (1968) 2159-2162.

65. *Bericht über die ökumenische Gesamtsituation vom Standpunkt des Ein-heitssekretariates* (Tagung des Wissenschaftlichen Beirats des Johann-Adam-Möhler-Instituts, Paderborn, 20-23.3.1968), in *Catholica* 22 (1968) 119-131.
   → 426, 70-85.

66. *Common Witness and Proselytism* (The Lauriston Lecture, Edinburgh, 21.10.1968), in *One in Christ* 6 (1970) 5-16.
   DC 51 (1969) 235-240.
   → 77, 195-208.
   → 426, 86-97.

67. *Liturgical Research and Ecumenics*, in *Worship* 42 (1968) 386-392.

68. *Partecipazione cattolica alla commissione Fede e Costituzione del Con-siglio Mondiale delle Chiese*, in *OR* 3.7.1968.
   DC 50 (1968) 1515-1518.

69. *Personal Reflections on Church Union Plans within the Context of the Wider Ecumenical Task* (Consultation on Church Union, 8th meeting, Atlanta GA, 17-20.3.1968), in *Midstream* 8 (1968) 139-147.

70. *Report to the Plenary of SPCU* (10.1.1968), in *IS* 4 (1968) 7-8.

71. *Theology in the City of Man* (Sesquicentennial Symposium of St. Louis University, 15-17.10.1968), in *Cross Currents* 20 (1969) 522-534.
   → 77, 169-194.

72. *Wort des Gedenkens für Kardinal Bea* (Begräbnisgottesdienst Riedböhrin-gen, 21.11.1968), in *Augustin Kardinal Bea, Wegbereiter der Einheit*, Augsburg, Verlag Winfried Werk, 1972, 310-314.
   IS 6 (1969) 1-3.

1969

73. *Address* (Consultation on Church Union, Atlanta, 18,3,1969), in *Consulta-tion on Church Union*, Princeton, NJ, 1969, Vol. VIII.

74. *Christus, als Ursprung und Zeichen der Einheit in einer geteilten Welt*, in *Christus, Zeichen und Ursprung der Einheit in einer geteilten Welt* (Refe-rate von J. Willebrands und H. Ott, 7.12.1969, Peterskirche, Zürich) (Ein-heit in Christus, 5), Einsiedeln, Benziger; Zürich, Zwingli, 1970, 12-38.

75. *Diversité dans l'unité.* → 77, 115-129.

76. *Intervention* (Bishops' Synod, 15.10.1969), in *Deux interventions impor-tantes au IIe synode des évêques*, in *Irénikon* 42 (1969) 533-539.
   DC 52 (1970) 83-84.

77. *Œcuménisme et problèmes actuels* (Bibliothèque œcuménique, 1), Paris, Cerf, 1969, 208 pp. → 47, 49, 50, 51, 53, 55, 56, 59, 62, 66, 71, 75.

78. *Opening Address of the SPCU Plenary Meeting* (18.11.1969), in *IS* 9 (1970) 5-8.
   SI 9 (1970) 5-8.

79. *La problématique œcuménique actuelle* (Conference at the opening of the Centro Pro Unione, Rome, 4.3.1969), in *Bulletin Centro Pro Unione* 1 (1969) 13-20. English: 20-27.
   DC 52 (1970) 74-79.
   Unitas 28 (1970) 1-12.

80. *Réponse au Patriarche œcuménique* (Istanbul, 29.11-3.12.1969), in *SI* 9 (1970) 15-16.
   IS 9 (1970) 15-16.

81. *Il Segretario per l'Unione dei Cristiani fa il punto sulla situazione ecumenica* (Interview), in *Nuovi Tempi* 3 (1969) 8.

1970

82. *Address to Catholicos Vasken I* (Rome, 8.5.1970), in *IS* 11 (1970) 3.
    SI 11 (1970) 3.
    → 477, 97-98.
83. *Address to Catholicos Vasken I* (Rome, 9.5.1970), in *IS* 11 (1970) 6-7.
    SI 11 (1970) 6-7.
84. *Cardinal Willebrands' Letter to Meeting of Ecumenical Training*, in *OR* (English) 13.08.1970.
85. *Cinquant'anni di Fede e Costituzione*, in *OR* 2.8.1970.
    OR (English) 20.8.1970.
    Unidad Cristiana 20 (1970) 373-376.
86. *Gesandt in die Welt* (Fifth Assembly Lutheran World Federation, Evian-les-Bains, 15.7.1970), in *Lutherische Rundschau* 20 (1970) 447-460.
    Die Zeichen der Zeit 24 (1970) 451-455.
    → 426,112-125.
    Lutheran World 17 (1970) 341-352.
    L. GROSC (ed.), *Sent into the World* (Proceedings), Minneapolis, MN, Augsburg, 1971, 54-65.
    → 477, 107-113.
    DC 52 (1970) 761-767.
87. *Interview*, in *Avvenire* 5.6.1970.
    DC 52 (1970) 775-778.
88. *The Notion of 'Typos' within the One Church* (Homily, Great St. Mary's Church, Cambridge, 18.1.1970), in *IS* 11 (1970) 11-14.
    The Unity of the Church, in H. MONTEFIORE (ed.), *More Sermons from Great St. Mary's*, London-Sydney-Auckland-Toronto, Hodder and Stoughton, 1971, 177-186.
    → 477, 130-134.
    SI 11 (1970) 11-15.
    DC 52 (1970) 265-269.
89. *Ökumenischer Situationsbericht 1969-1970 aus der Sicht des Einheitssekretariates* (Johann-Adam-Möhler-Institut, Paderborn, 11.3.1970), in *Catholica* 24 (1970) 224-239.
    DC 52 (1970) 883-891.
90. *Official Visit of the Cardinal President to the Ecumenical Patriarchate*, in *IS* 9 (1970) 14-16.
    → 477, 84-86.
    E. STORMON SJ (ed.), *Towards the Healing of Schism: The Sees of Rome and Constantinople* (Ecumenical Documents III), New York, Paulist, 1987, 223-227.
    Tomos Agapis: Vatican-Phanar (1958-1970) (Editions in French and Greek), Vatican City, Vatican Polyglot Press, 1971, Doc. 275, 590-599.
    Le livre de la charité, Paris, Cerf, 1984, 148-152.
    Tomos Agapis: Dokumentation zum Dialog der Liebe zwischen dem Hl. Stuhl und dem Ökumenischen Patriarchat (Pro Oriente, Reihe 3), Innsbruck, Tyrolia, 1978, 169-172.

Al encuentro de la unidad, Madrid, Biblioteca de Autores Cristianos, 1973, 245-247.

91. *Opening Address of the SPCU Plenary Meeting* (4.11.1970), in *IS* 13 (1971) 4-9.
    SI 13 (1971) 4-8.

92. *The Position of the Catholic Church concerning a Common Eucharist between Christians of Different Confessions,* in *IS* 9 (1970) 21-23.

93. *Preface* (to the document Reflections and Suggestions Concerning Ecumenical Dialogue, 15.8.1970), in *IS* 12 (1970) 3-4.
    → 477, 80-82.
    SI 12 (1970) 3-4.

94. *Presentation of the Second Part of the Ecumenical Directory* (15.5.1970), in *IS* 10 (1970) 11-13.
    SI 10 (1970) 12-15.
    → 477, 78-80.

95. *Sermon* (summary, Anglican Cathedral, Liverpool, 21.1.1970), in *IS* 11 (1970) 15.
    SI 11 (1970) 15-16.
    DC 52 (1970) 269-270.
    La Rivista del Clero Italiano 51 (1970) 315-331.
    Unidad Cristiana 20 (1970) 348-358.

96. *Le Service International de documentation judéo-chrétienne.* (Inauguration du Sidic, 21.5.1970), in *DC* 52 (1970) 613.

97. *Les tendances actuelles du mouvement œcuménique et le rôle du monachisme* (International Congress of the Benedictine Confederation, S. Anselmo, Rome, 26.9.1970), in *DC* 53 (1971) 621-625.
    OR (French) 15.1.1971.
    D. HUERRE (ed.), *L'expérience de Dieu dans la vie monastique*, St. Léger, Presses monastiques, 1973, 222-233.
    The Present Tendencies of the Ecumenical Movement and the Role of Monasticism, in *Pax, The Review of the Benedictines of Prinknash* 61 (1971) 1-11.
    Cistercian Studies 6 (1971) 109-118.
    Heutige Tendenzen der Ökumenischen Bewegung und die Rolle des Mönchtums, in *Erbe und Auftrag* 47 (1971) 449-458.
    Le tendenze attuali del movimento ecumenico e il ruolo del monachesimo, in *Dio vivo o morto?*, Subiaco, Tipografia S. Scolastica, 1971, 195-203.
    Actuele tendenzen in de oecumenische beweging en de taak van de monniken, in *De Godservaring in het Monastieke Leven*, s.l., s.d., 239-250.

98. *Le travail du Secrétariat pour l'Unité des Chrétiens*, in *DC* 52 (1970) 775-778.
    Avvenire 5.6.1970.

99. *L'Unité des Églises catholique et orthodoxe* (Interview, 30.11.1970), in *Elefthèros Cosmos* (Agence Typos), 20.12.1970.
    Proche-Orient Chrétien 21 (1971) 1-5.
    SI 13 (1971) 16-18.
    DC 53 (1971) 67-69.
    IS 13 (1971) 16-18.
    Diaspora (1971) 19-23.

1971

100. *Address to H.H. Amba Shenouda III, Coptic Orthodox Patriarch* (Enthronement, Cairo, 14.11.1971), in *IS* 16 (1972) 12.
→ 477, 96-97.

101. *Allocution à l'Académie orthodoxe de Gonia* (Crète), in *SI* 15 (1971) 17-18.
IS 15 (1971) 17.

102. *Allocution à l'église St. Tite d'Héraklion* (20.5.1971), in *SI* 17 (1972) 16-17.
IS 17 (1972) 15-16.

103. *Allocution au clergé et aux théologiens* (Héraklion, 20.5.1971), in *SI* 17 (1972) 17-18.
IS 17 (1972) 16-17.
→ 477, 88-89.

104. *Allocution du cardinal Jean Willebrands au Concile de Moscou* (30.5.1971), in *ЛОГОС* (Paris-Bruxelles) 5 (1972) 53-54.
SI 15 (1971) 7-8.
IS 15 (1971) 6-7.

105. *El alma del movimiento ecumenico*, in *Unidad Cristiana* 21 (1971) 323-328.
SI 16 (1972) 12.

106. *Augustin Bea, der Kardinal der Einheit. Eine Würdigung*, in *Humanum* (Lugano), 1971, 3-19.

107 *Augustinus Bea*, in *De Bijbel*, band 1, nr 13, Haarlem, De Spaarnestad, 1971.

108. *La collaboration avec les non-catholiques* (Bishops' Synod 1971), in *DC* 53 (1971) 1035-1036.

109. *Un commentaire du Chap. 12 de la Ire Épître aux Corinthiens*, in *OR* (French) 12.2.1971.

110. *Commentary on the Letter of the Ecumenical Patriarch* (21.3.1971), in *IS* 15 (1971) 5-6.
SI 15 (1971) 5-6.
DC 53 (1971) 708-709.

111. *Dialogo tra il papa e Athenagoras I*, in *OR* 10.7.1971.
OR (French) 23.07.1971.

112. *Discours au Patriarche œcuménique Athénagoras Ier* (7.12.1971), in *SI* 16 (1972) 6.
IS 16 (1972) 6.

113. *Discours de félicitations à S.S. Pimen* (3.6.1971), in *SI* 15 (1971) 8.
IS 15 (1971) 7.

114. *La diversité des charismes et la communion du St. Esprit* (Homily, Marseille, 18.1.1971), in *DC* 53 (1971) 266-269.
OR (French) 12.2.1971.

115. *Der Geist der Einheit wirkt in der Kirche: Ist das Werk der Einheit sichtbarer geworden?* (Radio Vaticana, German), in *KNA-Konzil-Kirche-Welt* (1971/4) 4-7.
Lebendiges Zeugnis 26 (1971) 79-85.
→ 426, 126-132.
OR (English) 27.1.1972.

116. *Interview: The Relations with the Russian Orthodox Church*, in *IS* 15 (1971) 7-10.

SI 15 (1971) 8-10.
DC 53 (1971) 713-715.

117. *Letter to the General Secretary of the WCC* (10.1.1971), in *IS* 14 (1971) 3.
SI 14 (1971) 3.

118. *La levée de l'excommunication de Martin Luther* (Lettre à M. R. Knecht, président de la Commission décanale catholique de Worms, 14.7.1971), in *DC* 54 (1972) 32-33.

119. *Le mouvement œcuménique: Unité des chrétiens ou unité humaine* (Marseille, 19.1.1971), in *OR* (French) 05.02.1971.
DC 53 (1971) 259-266.
OR (English) 18.02.1971.
Rivista del Clero italiano 51 (1971) 311-324.

120. *Ökumenischer Situationsbericht 1970 aus der Sicht des Einheitssekretariates* (Johann-Adam-Möhler-Institut, Paderborn, 25-26.3.1971), in *OR* (Deutsch) 9.7.1971.
Catholica 25 (1971) 304-324.
DC 53 (1971) 612-620.
La Rivista del Clero Italiano 1972/2.
Unidad Cristiana 21 (1971) 388-400.

121. *Parola di Dio ed ecumenismo* (Lettera indirizzata alla Prof. M. Vingiani in occasione della IX sessione di Formazione Ecumenica, Napoli, 30.7-7.8.1971), in *Rassegna di teologia* (suppl.) 12 (1971) 65-67.
Lettera inaugurale, in M. VINGIANI (ed.), *La Parola di Dio e l'ecumenismo*, Rome, Editrice AVE, 1972, 11-14.

122. *La première communauté chrétienne et notre travail œcuménique* (Homily, Las Palmas, 22.1.1971), in *DC* 53 (1971) 269-272.

123. *Les problèmes du sacerdoce dans la perspective œcuménique* (Bishops' Synod 1971), in *DC* 54 (1972) 38-40.

124. *Réponse à l'Archevêque d'Athènes* (18.5.1971), in *SI* 15 (1971) 14-15.
OR (French) 6.6.1971.
DC 53 (1971) 710-712.
IS 15 (1971) 13-14.
→ 477, 86-88.

125. *Réponse à l'archevêque Evghenios de Crète* (23.5.1971), in *SI* 15 (1971) 17-18.
IS 15 (1971) 16-18.

126. *'Where the Spirit of the Lord is, There is Freedom'* – *2 Cor 3,17* (World Methodist Council, Denver, 23.8.1971), in L. TUTTLE (ed.), *World Methodist Conference, 12ᵗʰ, 1971, Denver, Proceedings*, Nashville, TN, Abingdon, 1971, 266-276.
IS 16 (1972) 16-22.
→ 477, 117-122.
SI 16 (1972) 16-22.
DC 54 (1972) 24-30.

1972

127. *Allocution* (WCC, Utrecht, 21.8.1972), in *DC* 54 (1972) 884.

128. *Das Einheitssekretariat 1965-1968*, in *Augustin Kardinal Bea, Wegbereiter der Einheit*, Augsburg, Verlag Winfried Werk, 1972, 125-131.

129. *Franklin Clark Fry, a Commemoration*, in *Franklin Clark Fry: A Palette for a Portrait*. Suppl. Number of the *Lutheran Quarterly* 24 (1972) 329-331.
130. *Guided by the Spirit, let us seek God's Will concerning Unity*, in *OR* (English) 30.11.1972.
    Unidad Cristiana 22 (1972) 325-330.
131. *Da Lui tutto il corpo... si va edificando nella carità*. Vatican Radio 17.1.1972.
    Consacrazione e Servizio 21 (1972) 14-18.
    Bayerische Rundfunk 17.1.1972.
    KNA Informationsdienst 9.2.1972.
132. *Ökumenischer Situationsbericht 1971 aus der Sicht des Einheitssekretariates* (Johann-Adam-Möhler-Institut, Paderborn, 16.3.1972), in *Catholica* 26 (1972) 325-344.
    DC 54 (1972) 516-526.
    La Rivista del Clero Italiano 1972/7-8.
    Unidad Cristiana 22 (1972) 235-252.
133. *Panorama of the Ecumenical Scene to 1971*, in *OR* (English) 16.11.1972.
    OR (German) 19.5.1972.
    OR (French) 27.7.1973.
134. *Preface to the Documents of the Meeting of Ecumenical Commission Representatives* (Rome, 15-22.11.1972), in *IS* 20 (1973) 3.
    SI 20 (1973) 3.
135. *Prospects for Anglican-Roman Catholic Relations* (Lambeth Palace, 4.10.1972), in *The Tablet* 226 (1972) 963-966.
    One in Christ 9 (1973) 11-23.
    → 477, 100-105.
    DC 54 (1972) 1061-1066.
136. *Réponse à la délégation roumaine* (Rome, 18.3.1972), in *SI* 17 (1972) 15-16.
    IS 17 (1972) 14-15.
137. *Ricordando il Patriarca scomparso* (Hommage au patriarche Athénagoras, décédé le 7.7.1972), in *OR* 9.7.1972.
    OR (French) 14.7.1972.
    SI 19 (1973) 4-6.
    DC 54 (1972) 721-723.
    Paneurope-Hellénisme (1973/15) 3-4.
    OR (English) 20.07.1972.
    IS 19 (1973) 4-6.
138. *Le sens de la primauté confiée à Pierre et à ses successeurs* (Rome, 25.9.1972), in *DC* 54 (1972) 1067-1069.
139. *Télégramme au nouveau Patriarche œcuménique* (17.7.1972), in *SI* 19 (1973) 6.
    IS 19 (1973) 6.
140. *L'unité des Chrétiens: Œcuménisme 1971*, in *OR* (French) 10.11.1972.
141. *Les visites du Cardinal Willebrands en Orient* (Interview), in *OR* (French) 28.7.1972.
    OR (English) 3.8.1972.
    OR (German) 11.8.1972.
    Unidad Cristiana 22 (1972) 368-371.

142. *Cardinal Willebrands on Church Unity* (Vatican Radio), in *OR* (English) 27.01.1972.
143. *Cardinal Willebrands Interviewed* (by Fr. John COVENTRY, London, BBC, October 1972), in *One in Christ* 9 (1973) 4-10.

1973

144. *Allocution au Patriarche Œcuménique Dimitrios* (Visite au Phanar, Istanbul, 29-30.11.1973), in *Episkepsis* (Chambésy, Genève) 11.12.1973.
     DC 56 (1974) 65-66.
145. *Le Commissioni Miste e i loro primi risultati*, in *OR* 13.12.1973.
     OR (French) 28.12.1973.
     DC 56 (1974) 63-64.
     OR (English) 10.1.1974.
     OR (German) 24.5.1974.
146. *El ecumenismo ha de progresar en la fe, en el amor y en la paciencia*, in *Unidad Cristiana* 23 (1973) 289-292.
147. *The Eucharist and Unity* (Monash University, 13-16.2.1973), in *Eucharist, Ecumenism, Community*, Melbourne, Victorian Council of Churches, October 1973, 57-63.
148. *Der Evangelisch-katholische Dialog: Tatsächliches und Grundsätzliches* (Edmund Schlink zum 70. Geburtstag), in *Ökumenische Rundschau* 22 (1973) 182-202.
     → 426, 133-154.
149. *L'impegno ecumenico di Paolo VI*, in *Osservatore della Domenica* 1.7.1973.
     OR (German) 10.8.1973.
     KNA Informationsdienst 27.6.1973.
150. *Joint letter with the General Secretary of the WCC* on the project of 'An Ecumenical Initiative to Promote Peace in Ireland' (Holy Thursday 1973), in *IS* 22 (1973) 28-29.
     The Ecumenical Review 25 (1973) 364-365.
     SI 22 (1973) 30-31.
151. *Letter to Dr. Philip Potter, General Secretary of the WCC* (18.7.1973), in *IS* 22 (1973) 20-21.
     SI 22 (1973) 22-23.
152. *Lord, Teach Us to Pray* (Week of Prayer, 1973), in *OR* (English) 25.01.1973.
     OR (German) 19.1.1973.
     Bayerischer Rundfunk 21.1.1973.
     KNA Informationsdienst 24.1.1973.
153. *A Note about Certain Interpretations of the Instructions concerning Particular Cases when Other Christians May be Admitted to Eucharistic Communion in the Catholic Church* (17.10.1973, signed by J. Willebrands and C. Moeller), in *IS* 23 (1974) 25-26.
     SI 23 (1974) 25-26.
154. *Ökumenischer Situationsbericht 1972 aus der Sicht des Einheitssekretariats* (Johann-Adam-Möhler-Institut, Paderborn), in *OR* (German) 22.6.1973.
     KNA Dokumentation 18.7.1973.
     Catholica 28 (1974) 57-70.
     OR (French) 27.7.1973.

DC 55 (1973) 764-771.
OR (English) 26.7.1973.
La Rivista del Clero Italiano 54 (1973) 722-732.
Unidad Cristiana 23 (1973) 201-214.

155. *Œcuménisme à Melbourne* (Interview, Vatican Radio, 21.3.1973), in *OR* (French) 6.4.1973.
DC 55 (1973) 387-388.
SI 21 (1973) 12-14.
OR (English) 5.4.1973.
IS 21 (1973) 11-13.
OR (German) 23.3.1973.
OR 24.3.1973.

156. *Opening Address of the SPCU Plenary* Meeting (6.11.1973), in *IS* 23 (1974) 2-6.
SI 23 (1974) 2-6.

157. *I venticinque anni del Consiglio Ecumenico delle Chiese, 1948-1973*, in *OR* 5.8.1973.
OR (French) 10.8.1973.
SI 22 (1973) 28-30.
DC 55 (1973) 773-774.
OR (English) 26.9.1973.
IS 22 (1973) 26-27.
→ 477, 127-128.
Unidad Cristiana 23 (1973) 326-328.

1974

158. *Why Is Anglican/Roman Catholic Dialogue Possible Today?*, in A. CLARCK – C. DAVEY (eds.), *Anglican/Roman Catholic Dialogue: The Work of the Preparatory Commission*, London – New York – Toronto, Oxford University Press, 1974, 26-36.

159. *The Ecumenical Movement: Its Problems and Driving Force* (Princeton Theological Seminary, Princeton, NJ, 25.11.1974), in *One in Christ* 11 (1975) 210-223.
Die ökumenische Bewegung: Ihre Probleme und Antriebskraft → 426, 165-178.

160. *Ecumenismo oggi: Problemi e fatti* (Facoltà Teologica dell'Italia Meridionale, sez. Capodimonte, 18.1.1974), in *Asprenas* 21 (1974) 80-101.

161. *Einheit als Fernziel: Ein Gespräch mit Kardinal Jan Willebrands in Rom*, in *Lutherische Monatshefte* 13 (1974) 183-187.
OR (German) 26.7.1974.
→ 426, 155-164.
DC 56 (1974) 579-583.

162. *To What Extent Can or Should There Be Diversity in a United Church*, in A. CLARCK – C. DAVEY (eds.), *Anglican/Roman Catholic Dialogue: The Work of the Preparatory Commission*, London – New York – Toronto, Oxford University Press, 1974, 60-73.

163. *Gesù Cristo è il Signore*, in *OR* 19.1.1974.
OR (French) 25.1.1974.

OR (English) 31.1.1974.
OR (German) 18.1.1974.
KANN Informationsdienst 6.2.1974.
Erbe und Auftrag (1974) 132-137.

164. *Homélie* (7ᵉ Centenaire du Concile de Lyon, Cathédrale de Saint-Jean, Lyon, 20.10.1974), in *SI* 25 (1974) 11-13.
DC 57 (1975) 65-67.
Istina 20 (1975) 302-306.
Vers l'Unité Chrétienne 37 (1975) 20-24.
IS 25 (1975) 10-12.
OR 25.10.1974.

165. *Ökumenischer Situationsbericht 1973 aus der Sicht des Einheitssekretariates*, in *OR* (German) 8.11.1974.
KNA Informationsdienst 27.11.1974.
Ökumenische Rundschau 24 (1974) 101-108.
Catholica 29 (1975) 61-81.
DC 57 (1975) 67-68.
La Rivista del Clero Italiano 56 (1975/1).
Unidad Cristiana 24 (1974) 31-36.

166. *Response to Dr. Philip Potter, General Secretary of the WCC in the Presence of the Fathers of the Synod* (10.10.1974), in *IS* 25 (1974) 6-7.
OR (French) 12.12.1974.
SI 25 (1974) 7-8.
DC 56 (1974) 928-929.
OR 14-15.10.1974.

167. *Ein Schatz in irdenen Gefässen: Rückfragen an Kardinal Jan Willebrands*, in *Lutherische Monatshefte* 13 (1974) 250-252.

168. *Statement on Retirement of Archbishop Michael Ramsey* (15.11.1974), in *IS* 25 (1974) 22.
SI 25 (1974) 23.

169. *The Paul Wattson Lecture* (Washington DC, 19.11.1974), in *Conversations* (Graymoor Ecumenical Institute) 12 (1975) 1-12.

1975

170. *Address for the Anniversary Celebrations of the Romanian Orthodox Church* (Bucarest 1.11.1975), in *IS* 28 (1975) 12.
SI 28 (1975) 12-13.

171. *Addresses for the Celebration of the Fiftieth Anniversary of the Stockholm Conference on Life and Work* (Stockholm, 5-7.9.1975): *A Global Challenge; Jesus Christ Frees and Unites; Christian Life and Work 50 Years after Stockholm 1925*, in *IS* 28 (1975) 1-3; 4-7; 8-9.
SI 28 (1975) 1-9.
50 År efter Stockholm 1925: Anförande i storkyrkan (Stockholm, 7.9.1975), in *Svensk Teologisk Kvartalskrift* 63 (1975) 201-204.

172. *L'avenir de l'œcuménisme* (10th Anniversary of Pro Oriente, Vienna, 3.2.1975), in *Proche-Orient Chrétien* 25 (1975) 3-15.
One in Christ 11 (1975) 310-323.
→ 477, 134-140.

173. *Cammino difficile ma costante verso la comunione*, in *Avvenire* 7.12.1975.
174. *Déclaration du Cardinal Willebrands à Radio Vatican à l'occasion de la Semaine de Prière pour l'Unité*, in *OR* (French) 31.1.1975.
    OR (English) 6.2.1975.
    OR (German) 17.1.1975.
175. *Dieci anni di Nostra Aetate* (Rome, 12.11.1975), in *Sidic* 8 (1975) 33-35.
    IS 28 (1975) 17-19.
    Ten Years in the New Spirit of the Vatican Council. → 455, 7-13.
176. *Gottes Heilswille: Alles in Christus vereinen (Eph. 1,6)*, *Vatican Radio/ Bayerischer Rundfunk*, 20.1.1975.
    DC 57 (1975) 267-268.
177. *Guidelines and Suggestions for Implementing the Conciliar Declaration Nostra Aetate (n.4)* (signed by J. Willebrands and P.-M. de Contenson OP, 1.12.1974), in *IS* 26 (1975) 1-7.
    Istina 20 (1975) 340-346.
178. *The Holy Spirit and the Church* (International Meeting Charismatic Renewal, Rome, 16-19.5.1975).
    OR (French) 27.6.1975.
    DC 57 (1975) 565-568.
    OR (German) 27.6.1971.
179. *Introduction* (22.2.1975, signed by J. Willebrands and C. Moeller) to the document Ecumenical Collaboration at the Regional, National and Local Levels, in *IS* 26 (1975) 8-9.
    SI 26 (1975) 10-11.
180. *Letter to Dr. Philip Potter, General Secretary WCC* (21.11.1975), in *OR* (English) 4.12.1975.
    IS 30 (1976) 1.
    SI 30 (1976) 1-2.
181. *Un maître: Le père Charles Boyer s.j.*, in *Unité Chrétienne* 38 (1975) 5-8.
182. *Message à l'occasion de la célébration de la Pâque orientale* (4.5.1975), in *SI* 27 (1975) 40.
    Episkepsis (Chambésy, Genève) 13.5.1975.
    DC 57 (1975) 598.
    IS 27 (1975) 39.
    OR (English) 3.7.1975.
183. *Message à la 5ᵉ Assemblée du COE* (Nairobi, 23.11-10.12.1975), in *DC* 58 (1976) 156-157.
184. *Opening Address of the SPCU Plenary Meeting* (17.2.1975), in *IS* 27 (1975) 1-5.
    SI 27 (1975) 1-4.
185. *Preghiera per l'unità dei cristiani*, in *OR* 19.1.1975.
186. *A proposito della risoluzione dell'ONU sul sionismo. Una dichiarazione del Card. Willebrands,* in *OR* 16.11.1975.
    Statement about UN Resolution on Zionism, in *IS* 28 (1975) 35.
    OR (English) 27.11.1975.
    → 455, 183.
    Sidic 8 (1975) 19.
    OR (French) 21.11.1975.
    DC 57 (1975) 1041.

187. *Überlegungen zum ökumenischen Dialog* (Sitzung des Wissenschaftlichen Beirats des Johann-Adam-Möhler-Instituts, Paderborn, 13.3.1975), in *Catholica* 29 (1975) 341-359.
→ 426, 179-197.

188. *Die Zukunft der ökumenischen Bewegung* (Gesamthochschule Eichstatt, 30.6.1975), in A. BAUCH – A. GLÄSSER – M. SEYBOLD (eds.), *Zehn Jahre Vaticanum II*, Regensburg, Pustet, 1976, 76-94.
→ 426, 198-215.

1976

189. *L'activité œcuménique de Fernand Portal* (Conférence au cinquantenaire de sa mort, Paris, 19.6.1976), in *DC* 59 (1977) 18-25.

190. *De betekenis van de kerkmuziek voor de liturgie* (KRO symposium over kerkmuziek, 12.6.1976), in *Analecta Aartsbisdom Utrecht* 49 (1976) 403-410.
Dokumenten van de Nederlandse Kerkprovincie, Utrecht, 1976.

191. *Eerste pastorale brief* (21-22.2.1976), in *Archief van de kerken*, 16.3.1976.

192. *The Eucharist and the Hungers of the World* (Conference, 41ˢᵗ Internatonal Eucharistic Congress, Philadelphia, 1-8.8.1976), in J.B. DeMAYO – J.J. CASINO (eds.), *The Forty-First International Eucharistic Congress (Philadelphia), 1-8.8.1976: A History*, Pennsauken, NJ, DeVlieger Associates, 1978. *DC* 59 (1977) 85-90.
Archief van de Kerken 1976, 904-915.

193. *Growing Hope in Ecumenical Work, General Intention*, in *Apostleship of Prayer*, January 1976 (+ French and Spanish translations).

194. *De identiteit van het katholiek onderwijs* (Nederlandse Katholieke Oudervereniging, 11.12.1976), in *Analecta Aartsbisdom Utrecht* 50 (1977) 61-74.

195. *The International Roman Catholic/Lutheran Dialogue: An Appraisal* (St. Olaf's College, North MN, July 1976), in *One in Christ* 13 (1977) 98-107.
→ 426, 216-226.

196. *Interview on the Relations with the Orthodox Church. Bayerischer Rundfunk*, 18.2.1976.

197. *Katechese, openbaring en ervaring* (Opening R.K. Scholengemeenschap Presikhaaf te Arnhem, 13.10.1976), in *Analecta Aartsbisdom Utrecht* 49 (1976) 482-488.

198. *De Moeder Gods Maria: Het Tweede Vatikaans Concilie over Maria in het mysterie van Christus en de kerk* (Onze Lieve Vrouwe Broederschap 's Hertogenbosch, 22.5.1976), in *Analecta Aartsbisdom Utrecht* 49 (1976) 311-320.

199. *Orientations et suggestions pour l'application de la déclaration conciliaire Nostra Aetate*, in *Foi et Vie* 75 (1976) 63-72.
Oikoumenikon 18 (1978) 105-111.

200. *Persoonlijk lijden en medische techniek* (Homily, 25th Anniversary Faculty of Medicine, Katholieke Universiteit Nijmegen, 31.10.1976), in *Analecta Aartsbisdom Utrecht* 49 (1976) 479-481.

201. *Het primaatschap van Petrus en zijn heilsbetekenis* (Homily, 13th Anniversary Election Pope Paul VI, 11.7.1976), in *Analecta Aartsbisdom Utrecht* 49 (1976) 335-339.

202. *Progress and Limits of Christian Unity* (Homily, Ecumenical Service, 5.8.1976), in J.B. DEMAYO – J.J. CASINO (eds.), *The Forty-First International Eucharistic Congress (Philadelphia), 1-8.8.1976: A History*, Pennsauken, NJ, DeVlieger Associates, 1978, 489-492.
DSP Pamphlets, Boston, MA, Daughters of St. Paul, 1978.
OR (French) 12.11.1976.
Analecta Aartsbisdom Utrecht 49 (1976) 455-459.

203. *The Role of the Theologian in the Search for Unity in the Eucharist* (Ecumenical Theological Symposium on the Eucharist, 3.8.1976), in J.B. DEMAYO – J.J. CASINO (eds.), *The Forty-First International Eucharistic Congress (Philadelphia) 1-8.8.1976: A History*, Pennsauken, NJ, DeVlieger Associates, 1978, 391-401.
DC 59 (1977) 85-90.

204. *Roman-Catholic/Lutheran Dialogue in the USA: Papal Primacy: An Appraisal* (St. Olaf's College, North MN, July 1976), in *One in Christ* 13 (1977) 207-219.
Der Primat des Papstes: Römisch-katholischer/lutherischer Dialog in den Vereinigten Staaten. Eine Würdigung → 426, 227-240.

205. *Verantwoordelijkheid in christelijk perspectief* (Algemene Ledenvergadering Nederlandse Christelijke Werkgeversorganisatie NCW, afdeling West, 8.12.1976), in *Analecta Aartsbisdom Utrecht* 50 (1977) 1-18.

206. *Verklaring* (on Intercommunion, Sint Pancratiusparochie, Tubbergen), Utrecht, Secretariaat Nederlandse Kerkprovincie, 1.11.1976.
Il Card. Willebrands sul caso 'Tubbergen', in *OR* 14.11.1976.
OR (English) 25.11.1976.
OR (French) 3.12.1976.
DC 58 (1976) 1041-1042.

1977

207. *L'activité du SPUC* (Synode des Évêques, Rome, octobre 1977), in *SI* 36 (1978) 49.
IS 36 (1978) 4-8.
Gen's (Generazione Nuova Sacerdotale) 8 (1978) 1.4-7.

208 *Address on the Occasion of the Enthronement of His Beatitude Patriarch Justin of Romania* (Bucharest, 19.6.1977), in *IS* 35 (1977) 4-5.
→ 477, 89-90.
SI 35 (1977) 5.

209. *Allocution à la fin de la liturgie eucharistique de la fête de St. André* (Phanar, 30.11.1977), in *SI* 37 (1978) 1-2.
Istina 23 (1978) 384-385.
DC 60 (1978) 79-80.
IS 37 (1978) 1-2.

210. *Allocution à Paul VI* (Visit Ad Limina, Rome, 17.11.1977), in *DC* 59 (1977) 1007.

211. *Catéchèse et Judaïsme* (Bishops' Synod, 18.10.1977), in *DC* 59 (1977) 1022-1023.
IS 36 (1978) 3-4.
→ 455, 73-76.

Sidic 11 (1978) 21-22.

R. RENDTORFF – H. HENRIX (eds.), *Die Kirchen und das Judentum: Dokumente von 1945 bis 1985*, Paderborn – München, Bonifatius – Kaiser, 1988, 170-173.

Oikoumenikon 18 (1978) 57-60.

212. *Catéchèse et œcuménisme* (Bishops' Synod, 18.10.1977), in *SI* 36 (1978) 1-2.

DC 59 (1977) 924-926.

IS 36 (1978) 1-2.

AFER 20 (1978) 50-53.

Oikoumenikon 18 (1978) 50-54.

213. *Letter in the Name of Paul VI on Common Date of Easter* (15.3.1977), in *IS* 35 (1977) 17.

SI 35 (1977) 17-18.

OR (English) 12.05.1977.

OR (French) 10.05.1977.

214. *Lettre à Son Excellence Amba Samuel* (28.1.1977), in *SI* 76 (1991) 23-25.

IS 76 (1991) 22-23.

215. *Mechitar e l'unione dei cristiani* (3d Centenary Mekitar di Sebaste, Venezia, 22.10.1977), Venezia, S. Lazzaro, 1978, 22 pp.

Bazmavep (1977) 417-436.

Proche-Orient Chrétien 28 (1978) 3-17.

Communio (Dutch) 3 (1978) 144-160.

216. *Le nouveau style de vie* (Bishops' Synod, 17.10.1977), in *DC* 59 (1977) 1023.

217. *Die Ökumene und die Einheit der Menschheit*, in W. LEISNER (ed.), *Staatsethik*, Köln, Hanstein Verlag, 1977, 243-247.

218. *Paulus VI en de vrede* (Homily, 14th Anniversary Election Pope Paul VI, 26.6.1977), in *Analecta Aartsbisdom Utrecht* 50 (1977) 270-273.

219. *Paus Paulus tachtig jaar*, in *Analecta Aartsbisdom Utrecht* 50 (1977) 349-350.

220. *Tritt die Ökumene auf der Stelle?* (Interview), in *Tag des Herrn* 27 (1977/2).

221. *Vastenbrief*, special *Analecta Aartsbisdom Utrecht*, 1977.

222. *Vorwort*, in H. MEYER – H. SCHÜTTE – H.J. MUND (eds.), *Katholische Anerkennung des Augsburgischen Bekenntnisses: Ein Vorstoss zur Einheit zwischen katholischer und lutherischer Kirche* (Ökumenische Perspektiven, 9), Frankfurt, Lembeck/Knecht, 1977, 7. → 260.

1978

223. *Ten bate van het leven der wereld* (Lent 1978), in *Analecta Aartsbisdom Utrecht* 51 (1978) 77-79.

224. *Condolences* (Funeral Service for Metropolitan Nikodim, Cathedral of the Holy Trinity, Leningrad, 10.9.1978), in *In Memoriam His Eminence Nikodim (1929-1978), The Journal of the Moscow Patriarchate*, 1979/4, 32-33.

IS 39 (1979) 18-20.

SI 39 (1979) 19-21.

DC 60 (1978) 942-943.

225. *Douze années de dialogue œcuménique* (Prolusio Plenaria SPCU, 13.11.1978), in *DC* 61 (1979) 36-39.

Communio (Dutch) 4 (1979) 128-134.

226. *Ten geleide*, in J. WILLEBRANDS – L. SUENENS, *Zijn toespraken tijdens 33 dagen pontificaat – Johannes-Paulus I*, Boxtel, Katholieke Bijbelstichting, 1978, 5.

227. *In memoriam Paus Johannes Paulus*, in *Analecta Aartsbisdom Utrecht* 51 (1978) 365.

228. *De naam Paulus was als een program* (Commemoration Pope Paul VI), in *Gazet van Antwerpen*, 8.8.1978.

229. *Een nieuwe paus, een nieuw program* (Pastoral Letter), in *Analecta Aartsbisdom Utrecht* 51 (1978) 329-330.

230. *Een nieuwe paus* (Pastoral Letter), in *Analecta Aartsbisdom Utrecht* 51 (1978) 406.

231. *Paulus VI overleden* (Pastoral Letter), in *Analecta Aartsbisdom Utrecht* 51 (1978) 309-311.

232. *Een paus met een program: Na het overlijden van paus Paulus VI*, in *Analecta Aartsbisdom Utrecht* 51 (1978) 312-315.

233. *Preek* (Homily, Requiem Pope John Paul I, Utrecht Cathedral, 1.10.1978), in *Analecta Aartsbisdom Utrecht* 51 (1978) 366-368.

234. *Het primaat van de Bisschop van Rome* (Anniversary Election Pope Paul VI, 25.6.1978), in *Analecta Aartsbisdom Utrecht* 51 (1978) 249-251.

235. *Progressi nel dialogo tra cattolici e ortodossi*, in *Oikoumenikon* 18 (1978) 61-69.

236. *Voorwoord*, in B. MEULENBROEK (ed.), *Zuid-Afrika en de katholieke kerk*, Amersfoort, De Horstink, 1978, 1.

1979

237. *Aanbeveling*, in *Genodigd aan de maaltijd des Heren: Inleiding tot de Eucharistie volgens het Romeins Missaal*, Haarlem, Gottmer, 1979, 7.

238. *Anglican-Roman Catholic Dialogue* (Toronto, 8.6.1979), in *One in Christ* 15 (1979) 290-304.
   Irénikon 52 (1979) 323-343 and 423 (English summary).

239. *Brief an Mgr Georg Moser über Hans Küng* (24.12.1979), in *Katholisches Sonntagsblatt*, 13.1.1980.
   DC 62 (1980) 283.

240. *Discours à la fin de la liturgie à la cathédrale de Sioni (Georgia)* (11.3.1979), in *SI* 40 (1979) 13-14.
   IS 40 (1979) 12-14.
   → 477, 90-91.

241. *Bij de encycliek Redemptor Hominis van paus Johannes-Paulus II*, in *Analecta Aartsbisdom Utrecht* 52 (1979) 133-135.

242. *Interventions du Cardinal Willebrands au Synode des Évêques*, in *Istina* 24 (1979) 81-86.

243. *Het Latijn en de eenheid van de Katholieke Kerk* (Vereniging voor Latijnse liturgie, 12.5.1979), Geschriften van de Vereniging voor Latijnse liturgie, 6, Utrecht, 1979, 23 pp.
   Latinity and Catholic Unity, in M. BURSON (ed.), *Worship Points the Way: Celebration of the Life and Work of Massey H. Shepherd Jr.*, New York, Seabury, 1981, 181-199.

244. *Oprichten wat zwak is* (Robert Hollmann Stichting, Cannero-Riviera, 21.7.1979), in *Analecta Aartsbisdom Utrecht* 52 (1979) 263-264.

245. *Un passo nuovo nei rapporti con la Chiesa bizantina* (Declaration *Vatican Radio*), in *OR* 30.11.1979.

246. *Persverklaring* (Rome, 21.1.1979), Utrecht, Persdienst Nederlandse Kerk-provincie, 5.2.1979.
    DC 61 (1979) 240.
247. *Réponse* (à la lettre de S. Ém. Juvenaly, 22.9.1979). in *DC* 61 (1979) 974-975.
248. *Un seul Dieu, une seule espérance* (Homily, commemoration of Prof. C. Rijk, 15.10.1979), in *Sidic* 13 (1980) 35.
    → 455, 184-185.
249. *Trouw* (Vastenbrief), special *Analecta Aartsbisdom Utrecht* 51 (1979).
250. *Vorwort*, in Pro Oriente (ed.), *Ökumene, Konzil, Unfehlbarkeit,* Innsbruck – München – Wien, Tyrolia-Verlag, 1979, 7-8.

1980

251. *Address to the Plenary of SPCU* (4.2.1980), in *IS* 43 (1980) 39-40.
    SI 43 (1980) 45-47.
    DC 62 (1980) 704-706.
252. *S. Agostino e l'unità della chiesa*, in *OR* 17.1.1980.
253. *Allocution à la fin de la liturgie en l'église St. Georges au Phanar* (30.11.1980), in *IS* 45 (1981) 24-26.
    IS 45 (1981) 23-24.
    OR (French) 6.01.1981.
254. *Allocution durant la doxologie d'ouverture de la réunion de la commission internationale catholique-orthodoxe pour le dialogue théologique* (Patmos, 29.5.1980), in *SI* 44 (1980) 116-118.
    IS 44 (1980) 106-108.
    → 477, 91-93.
255. *Emmanuel D'Alzon and John Henry Newman: The Road to Christian Unity* (Honorary Degree at Assumption College, Worcester MA, 17.8.1980), Worcester, Assumption College, 1980, 12 pp.
256. *Fifteenth Anniversary of Nostra Aetate* (Rome, 25.10.1980), in *Sidic* 14 (1981) 28-30 (French and English).
    → 455, 14-20.
257. *Some Aspects of the Activity of the SPCU, 1977-1980*, in *IS* 44 (1980) 118-120.
    SI 44 (1980) 129-131.
258. *Après l'attentat de la rue Copernic, M. Jacob Kaplan, grand rabbin de France* (Telegram), in *DC* 62 (1980) 1127.
259. *Dialogo tra i Cristiani e matrimoni misti* (Bishops' Synod, 1980, summary), in *OR* 4.10.1980.
    Mixed Marriages and Their Families, in *IS* 44 (1980) 116-118.
    Origins 10 (1980) 289-292.
    One in Christ 17 (1981) 78-81.
    SI 44 (1980) 127-128.
    OR (English) 13.10.1980.
    OR (French) 14.10.1980.
    DC 62 (1980) 1001-1002.
    AFER 23 (1981) 84-88.
260. *Foreword*, in J.A. BURGESS, *et al., The Role of the Augsburg Confession,* Philadelphia, PA, Fortress, 1980, vii. → 222.

261. *L'indirizzo del Cardinale Willebrands*, in *OR* 1.2.1980.
  OR (English) 11.2.1980.
  OR (French) 5.2.1980.
262. *L'Héritage* (Prof. C. Rijk), in *Sidic* 8 (1980) 35.
263. *Préface*, in J.-É. DESSEAUX, *Nouveau vocabulaire œcuménique*, Paris, Cerf, 1980, 3-4.
  Lessico ecumenico (Universale Teologica, 17), Brescia, Queriniana, 1986, 5.
264. *La prière pour l'unité des chrétiens dans sa simultanéité visible et convergente avec la prière commune*, in *Unité Chrétienne* 60 (1980) 36-40.
  OR 14.1.1981.
265. *Rapport* (Synod Dutch Bishops, Rome, 14.1.1980), in *DC* 62 (1980) 172-173.
266. *Reflections on Twenty Years of the Secretariat for Promoting Christian Unity* (D'Alzon Memorial Convocation, Assumption College, Worcester MA, 18.8.1980), 16 pp.
  The Catholic Free Press, Worcester, MA, 22 August 1980.
  Irénikon 54 (1981) 5-24.
  Analecta Aartsbisdom Utrecht 54 (1981) 2-17.
267. *Symbol des kirchlichen Gewissens*, in *KNA* 22.5.1980.
  OR (German) 6.6.1980.
268. *À l'occasion du Synode des Evêques des Pays-Bas* (Address), in *OR* (French) 22.1.1980.
269. *Venga il Tuo Regno* (Week of Prayer 1980), in *Nuovo Servizio Informazioni Settimanali (SIS)* 31, 160-161.
270. *Wort bei der Schlussversammlung* (450th Anniversary Confessio Augustana, Augsburg, 29.6.1980), in R. KOLB (ed.), *Confessio Augustana, den Glauben bekennen: Berichte, Referate, Aussprachen*, Gütersloh, Mohn, 1980, 140-141.
  Una Sancta 35 (1980) 198-199.
  → 426, 241-242.
  Message of Greeting, in H. MEYER (ed.), *Lutheran/Roman Catholic Discussion on the Augsburg Confession: Documents – 1977-1981*, LWB-Report 1982, nr. 10, 53-55.

1981

271. *Attitudes and Initiatives towards Christian Unity in Eastern Africa* (Foreword), in *Ecumenical Initiatives in Eastern Africa*, October 1981.
272. *De band met de bisschop* (Statement on the 'Vereniging van Pastoraal Werkenden'), in *Analecta Aartsbisdom Utrecht* 54 (1981) 245-246.
273. *Augustin Bea: Vorkämpfer für die Einheit der Christen, für die Religionsfreiheit und ein neues Verhältnis zum jüdischen Volk* (Katholische Akademie, Freiburg i. Br., 9.5.1981), in D. BADER (ed.), *Die Hinwendung der Kirche zur Bibelwissenschaft und Ökumene* (Schriftenreihe der katholischen Akademie der Erzdiözese Freiburg), München – Zürich, Schnell und Steiner, 1981, 33-55.
  Christian-Jewish Relations 14 (1981) 3-17.
274. *Card. Bea's Attitude to Relations with the Jews – Unpublished Details*, in *Atti del Simposio Card. Agostino Bea* [6-19 dicembre 1981], Communio

N.S. 14, Lateranense, Rome, Libreria editrice, 1983, 79-83.
→ 455, 57-61.
→ 477, 166-168.

275. *Le Concile de Constantinople de 381, IIe œcuménique: Son importance et son actualité* (Chambésy, Genève, 24.5.1981), in *Irénikon* 54 (1981) 163-191.

276. *La contribution du Cardinal Bea au mouvement œcuménique, à la liberté religieuse et à l'instauration de relations nouvelles avec le peuple juif* (Conference Symposium Cardinal Augustin Bea, Rome, 16-19.12.1981), in *SI* 47 (1981) 148-159.
DC 64 (1982) 199-207.
IS 47 (1981) 142-152.
→ 477, 70-77.
Atti del Simposio Card. Agostino Bea, Communio N.S. 14, Lateranense, Rome, Libreria editrice, 1983, 1-23.

277. *Discours au Patriarche Dimitrios I* (Istanbul, 30.11.1981), in *DC* 63 (1981) 74-76.
OR (French) 19.12.1981.

278. *Discours au St. Père* (Plenary SPCU, 13.1.1981), in *DC* 63 (1981) 1052.

279. *Het eeuwig leven* (Pastoral Letter, Easter), in *Analecta Aartsbisdom Utrecht* 54 (1981) 1-3.

280. *Eucharistie et unité de l'Église* (Eucharistic Congress, Lourdes, 20.7.1981), in *Eucharistie vers un monde nouveau* (Proceedings), Paris, Centurion, 1981, 249-266.
DC 63 (1981) 755-760.
Jezus Christus, brood gebroken voor een nieuwe wereld, Teksten uit de R.K. Kerk, 2, Amersfoort, De Horstink, 1981, 23 pp.
J. VAN KEMSEKE (ed.), *Internationaal Eucharistisch Congres: Enkele belangrijke toespraken*, Gent, I.E.C. 81, 97-110.
Kristen Enhet (Sweden) 16 (1981) 13-20.

281. *Geloof en levensvervulling: De jeugd en de tijdgeest en de rol van het geloof hierin*, in *Analecta Aartsbisdom Utrecht* 54 (1981) 209-218.

282. *Een jaar later: De Particuliere Synode van de Nederlandse bisschoppen* (Pastoral Letter), in *Analecta Aartsbisdom Utrecht* 54 (1981) 125-130.
DC 63 (1981) 708-711.

283. *Kardinal Bea zum 100. Geburtstag* (Mainz, 24.7.1981).
Unité des Chrétiens 43 (1981) 27-28.
Città Nuova 25 (1981/12).

284. *Open staan voor het geloof* (Landelijk Pastoraal Overleg, 30.10.1981), in *Analecta Aartsbisdom Utrecht* 54 (1981) 282-286.

285. *Papa Giovanni XXIII e l'ecumenismo* (Prolusio, Simposium Papa Giovanni XXIII, Università Lateranense, 10.11.1981), in *Lateranum* 47 (1981) 333-342.
OR 25.11.1981.
La vita in Cristo e nella Chiesa 31 (1982) 11-16.
OR (English) 14.12.1984.
OR (German) 14.1.1983.

286. *Prolusio to the Plenary of SPCU* (9.11.1981), in *IS* 47 (1981) 113-116.
SI 47 (1981) 117-120.

287. *Le Saint-Père reçoit les participants à la plénière du Secrétariat pour l'Unité des Chrétiens: Adresse du Cardinal Willebrands*, in *OR* (French) 17.11.1981.

288. *Secretariat for Christian Unity*, and *The Holy Father and Ecumenism* (Interviews, Crossroads Radio Program, West Springfield MA, January 1981), in *Crossroads* 66 (1981/9).

1982

289. *Arbeidsongeschikt*, special *Analecta Aartsbisdom Utrecht*, May 1982, 12 pp.

290. *Attitudes and Initiatives towards Christian Unity in Eastern Africa* (Foreword), in Brian HEARNE (ed.), *Ecumenical Initiatives in Eastern Africa (Final Report of the Joint Research Project of the AACC and ANECEA 1967-1981)*, Nairobi, AACC/ANECEA, 1982.

291. *Die Bedeutung der Einheit der Christen für Europa* (Michaelsempfang, Bonn, 29.9.1982), in *Europa – Krise und Hoffnung*, Bonn, Kommissariat der Deutschen Bischöfe, 1983, 21-29.
→ 474, 101-110.
Analecta Aartsbisdom Utrecht 55 (1982) 245-253.

292. *Christen – Botschafter neuer Horizonte* (Verleihung St.-Liborius-Medaille für Einheit und Frieden, 24.10.1982), in *Für die Einheit der Kirche und der Welt*, Paderborn, Bonifatius Verlag, 1983, 40-46.

293. *Dienaar in Gods gemeente: Het priesterlijk ambt in de Katholieke Kerk.* Bisschoppelijke Brieven, Secretariaat van de Nederlandse Kerkprovincie, 1982, nr. 15.
Serviteur dans la communauté de Dieu, in *DC* 64 (1982) 923-927.

294. *Discours prononcé à la fin de la célébration liturgique au Phanar* (30.11.1982), in *SI* 50 (1982) 133-135.
OR (French) 12.1.1982.
IS 50 (1982) 125-127.

295. *Erinnerungen an Kardinal Bea*, in *Almanach* 82, Heimatjahrbuch Schwarzwald-Baar-Kreis, 1982, 14-16.

296. *Letter for the Fiftieth Issue of the Information Service*, in *IS* 50 (1982) 115.
SI 50 (1982) 1.

297. *Preface*, in T. STRANSKY – J. SHEERIN (ed.), *Doing the Truth in Charity: Statements of Pope Paul VI, Popes John Paul I, John Paul II and the Secretariat for Promoting Christian Unity 1964-1980* (Ecumenical Documents, 1), New York, Paulist, 1982, xiii-xiv.

298. *Priesterroepingen* (Vastenbrief 1982), special *Analecta Aartsbisdom Utrecht*, 1982, 4 pp.

299. *The Significance of the Roman Catholic – Disciples of Christ International Dialogue* (Patron of Christian Unity Award, Indianapolis, 18.10.1982), in *Mid-Stream* 22 (1983) 114-119.
→ 477, 123-125.

300. *Testimonium*, in *Testimonia oecumenica in honorem Oscar Cullmann Octogenarii 25.11.1982*, Princeton Theological Seminary, Princeton, NJ, 1982.

301. *Called to Unity and Wholeness* (Peter Ainslie Inaugural Lecture, Baltimore MD, 20.10.1982), in *Ecumenical Trends* 12 (1983) 54-59.
Mid-Stream 22 (1983) 1-9.
Communio (English) 10 (1983) 117-127.
Communio (Dutch) 8 (1983) 66-74.

302. *Der einzige Weg zur Einheit ist die Liebe* (Homily, St.- Liborius Medaille für Einheit und Frieden, Paderborn, 24.10.1982), in *Für die Einheit der*

Kirche und der Welt, Paderborn, Bonifatius Verlag, 1983, 9-15.
Lebendiges Zeugnis 38 (1983) 64-67.

1983

303. *Activité du SPUC* (Intervention, Bishops' Synod, 1983), in *SI* 54 (1984) 18-21.
   IS 54 (1984) 16-19.
304. *Discours prononcé à la fin de la célébration liturgique au Phanar* (30.11.1983), in *SI* 53 (1983) 112-113.
   OR (English) 12.01.1984.
   DC 65 (1983) 91-92.
   IS 52 (1983) 100-101.
305. *Letter* (to the WCC General Secretary Dr. Philip Potter (4.7.1983), accompanying the Fifth Report of the Joint Working Group), in *IS* 53 (1983) 119-121.
   SI 53 (1983) 133-136.
   DC 66 (1984) 102-105.
   Istina 29 (1984) 90-96.
   Una Sancta 38 (1983) 341-345.
   Studi Ecumenici 2 (1984) 119-125.
306. *Luther – Gegenwärtig in der Ökumene: Ein gemeinsames Zeugnis geben* (500th Anniversary Martin Luther, St.-Thomas-Kirche, Leipzig, 11.11.1983), in *Materialdienst Konfessionskundliches Institut 'Bensheim'* 34 (1983) 117.
   OR (German) 9.12.1983.
   → 426, 257-261.
   IS 52 (1983) 92-94.
   OR (English) 14.11.1983.
   → 477, 113-115.
   SI 52 (1983) 103-106.
   Istina 29 (1984) 408-413.
307. *Pénitence et réconciliation* (Intervention Bishops' Synod, 4.10.1983), in *DC* 65 (1983) 994-996.
   SI 54 (1984) 17-18.
   IS 54 (1984) 15-16.
   Reconciliatio et paenitentia, in *La Reconciliatio et Paenitentia commentata* (Pastorale, 24), Vatican City, Libreria Editrice Vaticana, 67-72.
   Analecta Aartsbisdom Utrecht 56 (1983) 246-250.
308. *Prolusio to the Plenary of SPCU* (31.1.1983), in *IS* 51 (1983) 12-16.
   Proche-Orient Chrétien 32 (1983) 312-319.
   SI 51 (1983) 13-17.
   Vivere In 12 (1984/4).
   Excerpts → 477, 105-106 and 128-129.
309. *Toespraak Ad Limina bezoek Nederlandse bisschoppen* (Rome, 22.1.1983), in *Analecta Aartsbisdom Utrecht* 56 (1983) 32-33.
310. *Werkloos* (Pastoral Letter), special *Analecta Aartsbisdom Utrecht*, 1983, 8 pp.

1984

311. *Address to the Convention of the Lutheran Church in America* (Toronto, 3.7.1984), in *Proceedings*, Dept. for Ecumenical Relations Lutheran Church in America, New York, 1984, 5-14.

Ecumenical Trends 14 (1985) 38-47.
→ 477, 140-143.

312. *In Christus – Solidaritätsgemeinschaft in Hoffnung und Leid*, in *Una Sancta* 39 (1984) 329-335.

313. *Discours prononcé à la fin de la célébration liturgique au Phanar* (30.11.1984), in *SI* 56 (1984) 103-106.
OR (French) 12.1.1984.
DC 66 (1984) 76-77.
IS 56 (1984) 92-93.

314. *L'engagement œcuménique: Perspective catholique romaine*, in *Positions Luthériennes* 32 (1984) 341-352.

315. *Lutero, un ritratto, non una caricatura* (Università di Bari, 24.1.1984), in *Rocca* 5 (1984) 47-50.

316. *Mary of Nazareth, Daughter of Zion* (Homily, Feast of the Apparition of the Virgin Mary to Alphonse de Ratisbonne, 20.1.1984) → 455, 186-189.

317. *A Meditation on St. Paul's Letter to the Colossians 1,15-26* (Canterbury, British Church Leaders' Meeting, 6-9.4.1984), in *One in Prayer* (BCC/CTS, London), 1984, 39-46.
One in Christ 20 (1984) 388-394.

318. *Ökumenische Verpflichtung: Eine römisch-katholische Sicht* (7. Vollversammlung des Lutherischen Weltbundes, Budapest, August 1984), in *LWB-Report* 19/20 (1985) 135-143.
→ 426, 269-278.
Actualidad Pastoral (Buenos Aires, Argentina) 17 (1984) numero extraord., pp. 187-193.

319. *Prolusio to the Plenary of SPCU* (12.11.1984), in *IS* 56 (1984) 94-97.
SI 56 (1984) 103-106.

320. *La ricerca dell'unità dei cristiani nell'attuale momento ecumenico* (Pavia, 27.2.1984), in *Studi Ecumenici* (*A 20 anni dal decreto Unitatis Redintegratio*) 2 (1984) 441-460.

321. *Saluto al Santo Padre* (Bari, 26.2.1984), in *OR* 27-28.2.1984.
DC 66 (1984) 416-417.

322. *Le Secrétariat pour l'Unité des Chrétiens*, in Mgr. P. POUPARD (ed.), *Dictionnaire des religions*, Paris, PUF, 1984, 1558-1560.

323. *Una svolta profonda* (20th Anniversary of *Unitatis Redintegratio*), in *OR*, Speciale, 29.12.1984.
OR (German) 18.1.1985.

324. *Visit of the Pope to the WCC* (Addresses and Statement, Geneva, 12.6.1984), in *Ecumenical Review* 36 (1984) 438-447.
Joint Statement by the Roman Catholic Church and the World Council of Churches (Card. J. Willebrands and Ph. Potter, on the occasion of the visit of Pope John Paul II to the WCC, 12.6.1984), in *Diakonia* 9 (1985) 225-228.
One World 97 (1984) 11.
Materialdienst Konfessionskundliches Institut Bensheim 35 (1984) 78.
Una Sancta 39 (1984) 3.
Evangelische Kommentare 17 (1984) 393.

325. *Wie kann eine Ortskirche zur Annäherung zwischen der katholischen und orthodoxen Kirche beitragen?* (20th Anniversary Pro Oriente, Vienna, 8.11.1984), in A. STIRNEMANN (ed.), *Am Beginn des theologischen Dialogs: Dokumentation des römischen, des Wiener und des Salzburger Ökumenismus. Zehn Pro Oriente-Symposien 1982 bis 1985. Festschrift Theodor Piffl-Percevic. Pro Oriente* 10, Innsbruck, Tyrolia, 1987, 46-54.

1985

326. *I 25 anni del Segretariato per l'Unione dei Cristiani*, in *OR* 5.6.1985.
     OR (French) 30.7.1985.
327. *Battuta d'arresto per l'ecumenismo?* (Interview, 20th Anniversary *Unitatis Redintegratio*), in *Bollettino Salesiano* 109 (1985) 22-24.
328. *Come la Chiesa è entrata a pieno titolo nel movimento ecumenico* (Interview), in *Il Tempo*, 2.11.1985, 18.
329. *Is Christianity Antisemitic?* (Oxford Union Society, Oxford University, 13.3.1985), in *Christian-Jewish Relations* 18 (1985) 8-20.
330. *The Decree on Ecumenism: Twenty Years Later* (Interview), in *National Catholic Register*, May-June 1985.
331. *Dialogo ecumenico e riconciliazione*, in *OR* 8.1.1985.
332. *Il dialogo ecumenico ad un ventennio dal Concilio Vaticano II* (Congress 20th Anniversary of Second Vatican Council, Pontifical Urban University, Rome, 20.2.1985), in *Portare Cristo all'Uomo*, vol. 2, Testimonianze, Studia Urbaniana, 1985, 9-28.
     Catholica 39 (1985) 241-254.
     → 426, 243-256.
333. *Discours prononcé à la célébration liturgique au Phanar* (30.11.1985), in *DC* 67 (1985) 174-175.
334. *Ecumenical Commitment: A Roman Catholic Perspective*, in *Budapest 1984: In Christ – Hope for the World*, Proceedings, 7th Assembly, Lutheran World Federation, *LWF-Report* 19-20 (1985) 128-136.
335. *Ecumenical Dialogue and Its Reception* (Centro Pro Unione, Rome, 27.3.1985), in *Centro Pro Unione Bulletin* 27 (1985) 3-8.
     Origins 14 (1985) 720-724.
     DC 68 (1986) 117-121.
     (as a Lecture in Toronto, Canada, 27.3.1985), in *One in Christ* 21 (1985) 217-225.
     Diakonia 9 (1984-85) 118-128.
     → 426, 279-290.
336. *Églises particulières et Église universelle* (Catholic University of Lublin, 8.6.1985, Doctorate h.c.), in *Proche-Orient Chrétien* 35 (1985) 3-14.
     Studia i Dokumenty Ekumeniczne (Warsaw) 1 (1985) 24-31.
337. *Faithful Minister of the Wisdom of God* (Cardinal Bea Memorial Lecture, Westminster Cathedral Conference Centre, London, 10.3.1985).
     Christians and Jews: A New Vision (adapted), in A. STACPOOLE (ed.), *Vatican II: by Those Who Were There*, London, Chapman, 1986, 220-236.
     → 455, 39-56.
     → 477, 168-175.
     Sens 1985/10-11.
338. *Hadrian VI und die katholische Reform. Hypothesen über die Vergangenheit, Überlegungen zur Gegenwart* (Trento, 27.5.1985) → 426, 291-301.
339. *Interview*, in *Vrij Nederland* 9.3.1985, 5-6.
340. *Juden und Judentum in Katechese und Predigt: Hinweise der Vatikanischen Kommission für die Beziehungen zum Judentum*, in *Herder Korrespondenz* 39 (1985) 467-471.
     Istina 31 (1986) 207-219.

Informatiebulletin van het Secretariaat van het R.K. Kerkgenootschap in Nederland (special) 13 (1985) 58-66.

341. *Nostra Aetate: A Catholic Retrospective* (Colloquium 20th Anniversary of Nostra Aetate, Rome, 17.4.1985), in *Face to Face* 12 (1985) 10-12.
→ 455, 21-28.

342. *Nostra Aetate: The Fundamental Starting Point for Jewish-Christian Relations* (Conference, 20th Anniversary of Nostra Aetate, Rome, 28.10.1985), in *Christian-Jewish Relations* 18 (1985) 16-30.
IS 59 (1985) 34-37.
Origins 15 (1985) 412-414.
Fifteen Years of Catholic-Jewish Dialogue (Teologia e Filosofia, 11), Città del Vaticano, Libreria Editrice Vaticana; Rome, Libreria Editrice Lateranense, 1988, 271-275.
→ 455, 29-36.
→ 477, 175-177.
DC 68 (1986) 122-125.

343. *Opening Address* (20th Anniversary of Nostra Aetate, Rome, 28.10.1985), in *Fifteen Years of Catholic-Jewish Dialogue* (Teologia e Filosofia, 11), Città del Vaticano, Libreria Editrice Vaticana; Rome, Libreria Editrice Lateranense, 1988, vii.

344. *Un pioniere dell'ecumenismo: La scomparsa del Dr. Visser 't Hooft*, in *OR* 15-16.7.1985.
OR (French) 30.7.1985.
OR (German) 20.9.1985.
Una Sancta 40 (1985) 178-179.

345. *Preface*, in Mgr. J. OESTERREICHER, *The New Encounter between Christians and Jews*, New York, Philosophical Library, 1985, 12-13.

346. *Prolusio at the Meeting of Delegates of National Ecumenical Commissions* (Rome, 22.4.1985), in *IS* 58 (1985) 38-39.
→ 477, 82-83.
SI 58 (1985) 43-44.

347. *La question de la validité des ordinations anglicanes* (Letter to ARCIC II, 13.7.1985), in *DC* 68 (1986) 354-355.

348. *Dalle sofferenze uno slancio ecumenico* (at the occasion of the beatification of Titus Brandsma o.carm), in *OR* 1.11.1985.

349. *La vocazione ecumenica della Chiesa di Bari*, in *Quaderni di o Odigos*, Bari, 1 (1985/2) 41-49.

1986

350. *Adresse prononcée à la fin de la célébration liturgique au Phanar* (30.11.1986), in *SI* 63 (1987) 9-10.
IS 63 (1987) 9-10.

351. *Anglicans and Roman Catholics: Progress towards Closer Unity*, in *One in Christ* 22 (1986) 199-204.

352. *Circular Letter to Bishops on Certain Aspects of Ecumenical Teaching in Catholic Theological Institutions* (15.12.1986), in *IS* 62 (1986) 196-198.
SI 62 (1986) 213-325.
DC 70 (1988) 17-19.

353. *Il dialogo cattolico-ortodosso: L'imminente incontro di Bari. Molti progressi qualche problema,* in *30 Giorni,* 1986/5, 7.

354. *L'ineludibile dovere dell'unità nel rispetto della volontà del Padre,* in *OR* 25.1.1986.

355. *Introductory Note to Ecumenical Aspects of the Code* (19.5.1986), in *IS* 60 (1986) 53.
    SI 60 (1986) 58.

356. *Letter to Dr. Allan Boesak on the 450th anniversary of Calvin's Arrival in Geneva* (13.5.1986), in *IS* 64 (1987) 88-89.
    SI 64 (1987) 92-93.

357. *Letter to Dr. R. Runcie, Archbishop of Canterbury* (17.6.1986), in *Briefing,* 4.7.1986.
    D. WETHERELL (ed.), *Women Priests in Australia: The Anglican Crisis,* Melbourne, Spectrum, 1987, 138-142.
    → 477, 115-116.
    DC 68 (1986) 804-806.

358. *Marga Klompé, Miles Christi. Persoonlijke herinneringen,* in *Informatiebulletin van het Secretariaat van het R.K. Kerkgenootschap in Nederland* 14 (1986/20).
    M. VAN DER PLAS (ed.), *Herinneringen aan Marga Klompé,* Baarn, Arbor, 1989, 155-157.

359. *Il Nuovo Testamento è antisemita?* (Amicizia Ebraico-Christiana, Rome, 24.11.1986), in *Il Regno* (Documenti) 32 (1987) 541-546.
    Je Nový Zákon antisemitský? (Czech version), in *Studie* II-III (1987) 85-100.
    Are the New Testament and Christianity Antisemitic? → 455, 77-94. → 477, 179-185.

360. *L'ordination des femmes au sacerdoce: Nouvelle difficulté pour la réconciliation entre catholiques et anglicans,* in *OR* (French) 12.8.1986.
    OR (English) 7.7.1986.

361. *Un passo importante sulla via dell'unità. Dichiarazione del Cardinale Willebrands e del Vescovo Spiridione,* in *OR* 27-28.1.1986.

362. *Prolusio to the Plenary of SPCU* (3.2.1986), in *IS* 61 (1986) 115-120.
    SI 61 (1986) 126-131.

363. *Salvation and Redemption: Themes of a Common Faith* (Second International Catholic-Jewish Theological Colloquium, Rome, 4-6.11.1986), in *IS* 63 (1987) 15-16.
    → 455, 152-154.
    → 477, 177-179.

364. *Schritt nach vorn: Kardinal Willebrands zu den anglikanischen Weihen,* in *Herder Korrespondenz* 40 (1986) 159.

365. *Le Secrétariat pour l'Unité des Chrétiens* (Éloge funèbre de Mgr. Ch. Moeller, 7.4.1986), in J.-M. VAN CANGH (ed.), *In Memoriam Charles Moeller,* Louvain-la-Neuve, Collection Académique, 1986, 61-63.
    OR 2-3.5.1986.

366. *Unterschiede nicht vertuschen: Der gemeinsame Glaube ist Voraussetzung zur Kommunionsgemeinschaft* (Interview), in *KNA Ökumenische Information* 31, 30.7.1986, 12-16.
    Klerusblatt 66 (1986) 206-207.
    → 426, 312-317.

367. *Verschiedenheit wird es immer geben* (Interview), in *Lutherische Monats-hefte* 25 (1986) 454-457.
→ 426, 318-324.

368. *Der lange Weg zur Einheit: Die katholische Kirche und die ökumenische Bewegung* (Ökumenische Bildungsstätte Kloster Frenswegen, Nordhorn, 15.6.1986) → 426, 302-311.

1987

369. *Address on the Occasion of Signing the Revised Edition of the 'Guidelines for Interconfessional Cooperation in Translating the Bible'* (16.11.1987), in *IS* 65 (1987) 105-106.
→ 477, 129-130.
IS 65 (1987) 112-113.

370. *Allocution prononcée au début de la célébration liturgique au Phanar* (30.11.1987), in *SI* 66 (1988) 7-8.
DC 69 (1987) 72-73.
IS 66 (1988) 7-8.

371. *Anglicans, Roman-Catholics and Authority*, in St.W. SYKES (ed.), *Author-ity in the Anglican Communion: Essays presented to Bishop John Howe*, Toronto, Anglican Book Centre, 1987, 229-235.

372. *Aus der Arbeit des Einheitssekretariates*, in *Catholica* 41 (1987) 169-176.
Dacia (Johanniter) 53 (May 1987).

373. *The Catholic Church and the Ecumenical Movement* (New York Archdi-ocesan Ecumenical and Interreligious Commission's Forum, Columbia SC, Day of Dialogue, 11.9.1987)*, in A Day of Dialogue*, Dept. Ecumenical Relations Lutheran Church in America, New York, 1987, 7-24.
The NY Archdiocese Clergy Report, March 1988, 5-6; April 1988, 5-6; May 1988, 5-8.
Mid-Stream 27 (1988) 13-34.

374. *Christifideles: Laity and Clergy* (Intervention, Bishops' Synod, 1987), in *IS* 65 (1987) 110-111.
SI 65 (1987) 118-119.
OR (French) 27.10.1987.
OR 17.10.1987.

375. *Sua Santità Dimitrios I a Roma* (3-7.12.1987), in *OR* 3.12.1987.

376. *Discours de présentation de la Curie romaine à la reception par le Patri-arche Dimitrios I* (Rome, 4.12.1987), in *SI* 66 (1988) 11.
IS 66 (1988) 11.

377. *Die Einheit zwischen altem und neuem Bund* (Universität München, Doktorat h.c., 9.7.1987), in *Münchener Theologische Zeitschrift* 38 (1987) 295-310.
FIST Informazione (Federazione Interreligiosa per gli Studi Teologici, Torino) 9 (1989-1990) 69-81.
→ 455, 95-114.

378. *Il grande gesto del Concilio* (Interview), in *Popoli e Missione* (1987) 17-18.

379. *Interview* (on the Bishops' Synod on Laity, 1987), in 1-2-1, Utrecht, Secretariaat Nederlandse Kerkprovincie, 3.11.1987.

380. *Introduction of the Representatives of UBS-WCFBA-SPCU to the Holy Father*, in *IS* 65 (1987) 106-107.
SI 65 (1987) 114.

381. *Letter from Cardinal Willebrands, President of the Vatican Commission for Religious Relations with the Jews*, in *Christian-Jewish Relations* 20 (1987) 52-54.

382. *La Madre di tutti i cristiani* (Interview), in *Avvenire* 14.8.1987.
L'Enciclica Redemptoris Mater nel cammino verso l'unità di tutti i cristiani, in *Seminarium* 27 (1987) 534-540.

383. *The Passion for Unity* (National Association of Diocesan Ecumenical Officers, Atlanta GA, 5.5.1987), in *One in Christ* 23 (1987) 285-297.
→ 426, 325-340.
→ 474, 39-55.

384. *Premessa*, in *Il Documento di Bari, Atti, discorsi ufficiali e risonanze della IV sessione plenaria della commissione mista per il dialogo teologico ufficiale tra la Chiesa cattolica e le Chiese ortodosse*, Bari, 1987, 11-14.

385. *Presentazione*, in S. SCHMIDT S.J. (ed.), *Agostino Bea: Il cardinale dell'unità*, Rome, Città Nuova Editrice, 1987, 7-11.
OR 21.1.1988.
S. SCHMIDT S.J. (ed.), *Augustin Bea: Kardinal der Einheit*, Graz – Wien – Köln, Styria, 1989, 7-11.
S. SCHMIDT S.J. (ed.), *Augustin Bea: The Cardinal of Unity*, New Rochelle, NY, New City Press, 1992, 9-12.

386. *Die Tätigkeit des Sekretariates für die Einheit der Christen*, in *Dacia* (Johanniter) 53 (1987) 3-6.

387. *Vatican II's Ecclesiology of Communion – 'Subsistit in' in Lumen Gentium* (Workshop National Association of Diocesan Ecumenical Officers), Atlanta GA, 5.5.1987, and Washington DC, 8.5.1987), in *One in Christ* 23 (1987) 179-191.
Origins 17 (1987) 27-33.
→ 477, 142-149.
DC 70 (1988) 35-41.
→ 426, 341-356.
→ 474, 83-98.

388. *Vocation and Mission of the Laity* (Bishops' Synod, 6.10.1987), in *IS* 65 (1987) 109-110.
SI 65 (1987) 117-118.
DC 69 (1987) 1163-1164.

1988

389. *Address Introducing Members, Consultors and Staff of SPCU to the Holy Father* (6.2.1988), in *IS* 67 (1988) 67.
SI 67 (1988) 68-69.

390. *Aus der Arbeit des Einheitssekretariates*, in *Catholica* 42 (1988) 85-91.

391. *Il cammino della riconciliazione. Giovanni Paolo II e gli Ebrei*, in *OR* 11.11.1988.
→ 455, 65-69.
OR (German) 25.11.1988.

392. *The Church Facing Modern Antisemitism* (Malcolm Hay Memorial Lecture, Aberdeen/London, 17.10.1988), Aberdeen University, 1988, 17 pp.
Christian-Jewish Relations 22 (1989) 5-17.
→ 455, 123-135.
→ 477, 186-190.

393. *Discours prononcé lors de la célébration liturgique en l'église patriarcale du Patriarche syrien orthodoxe d'Antioche* (Damas, 13.4.1988), in *SI* 68 (1988) 148-150.
Courrier œcuménique du Moyen-Orient 2 (1988/5) 36-41.
IS 68 (1988) 127-128.
→ 477, 99-100.

394. *Discours prononcé durant la liturgie arménienne dans la cathédrale patriarcale d'Antélias* (17.4.1988), in *SI* 68 (1988) 150-151.
IS 68 (1988) 129-130.

395. *Discours de réponse à la bienvenue donnée par S.B. Ignace IV Hazim, Patriarche grec-orthodoxe d'Antioche* (19.4.1988), in *SI* 68 (1988) 154-156.
IS 68 (1988) 133-135.

396. *Discours au Synode extraordinaire de l'Église orthodoxe russe* (Millénaire du baptême de la Rus' de Kiev, Kiev, 6.6.1988), in *SI* 68 (1988) 159-162.
DC 70 (1988) 743-745.
IS 68 (1988) 138-141.
OR (English) 10.6.1988.
→ 477, 93-96.

397. *Discours prononcé à la commémoration publique à l'Opéra de Kiev* (Millénaire du baptême de la Rus' de Kiev, Kiev, 14.6.1988), in *SI* 68 (1988) 166-167.
OR (French) 28.6.1988.
DC 70 (1988) 757-759.
IS 68 (1988) 144-146.

398. *Discours prononcé à la fin de la célébration liturgique à la cathédrale de St. Vladimir de Kiev* (Millénaire du baptême de la Rus' de Kiev, Kiev, 15.6.1988), in *SI* 68 (1988) 167-169.
OR (French) 28.6.1988.
DC 70 (1988) 759-760.
IS 68 (1988) 146-147.

399. *Discours prononcé à la fin de la célébration liturgique au Phanar* (30.11.1988), in *SI* 69 (1989) 14-15.
IS 69 (1989) 14-15.

400. *Giovanni Paolo II e la ricerca della piena unità dei cristiani*, in S. MAGGIOLINI (ed.), *Giovanni Paolo II: Linee di un Magistero*, Roma, Città Nuova, 1988, 74-92.

401. *Interview*, in *Courrier œcuménique du Moyen-Orient* 2 (1988) 48-49.

402. *Intervista sul Millennio della RUS: Nessuna benedizione, tante speranze*, in *30 Giorni* (1988/6) 51-53.

403. *Message*, in A. WALKER (ed.), *Different Gospels: Christian Orthodoxy and Modern Theologies*, London, Hodder and Stoughton, 1988, 14-17.

404. *Le mouvement œcuménique aujourd'hui* (Centre d'études St. Louis de France, Rome, 4.1.1988), in *DC* 70 (1988) 663-669.

405. *Oecumene en communio*, in *Analecta bisdom Haarlem* 35 (1988) 76-90.

406. *Prayer for Christian Unity*, in *Ecumenical Trends* (*The Week of Prayer for Christian Unity: 80 Years*) 17 (1988) 1-4.
407. *Preface*, in *This Is Ecumenism*, Pinner, The Grail, 1988, 5-6.
408. *Preface*, in *Fifteen Years of Catholic-Jewish Dialogue, 1970-1985, Selected Papers*, Città del Vaticano, Libreria Editrice Vaticana; Rome, Libreria Editrice Lateranense, 1988, vii.
409. *Prolusio to the Plenary of SPCU* (1.2.1988), in *IS* 67 (1988) 64-67.
     SI 67 (1988) 65-68.
410. *Vers la publication d'un nouveau Directoire œcuménique* (Plenary SPCU, 5.2.1988), in *DC* 70 (1988) 256-258.
411. *Quindici anni di dialogo tra la Chiesa e l'Ebraismo* (Presentation of *Fifteen Years of Catholic-Jewish Dialogue, 1970-1985*, Rome, 22.3.1988), in *OR* 24.3.1988.
     IS 68 (1988) 165-168.
     → 455, 115-122.
412. *Rechercher l'unité donnée par le Christ* (Inauguration du concile local de l'Église Orthodoxe Russe à Zagorsk), in *OR* (French) 19.7.1988.
     OR (English) 11.7.1988.
413. *Réponse à la réception officielle offerte par le Catholicos Karekine II, en l'honneur du cardinal* (18.4.1988), in *SI* 68 (1988) 152-154.
     Courrier œcuménique du Moyen-Orient 2 (1988/5) 43-45 (extracts).
     IS 68 (1988) 131-133.
     → 477, 98-99.

1989

414. *Aus der Arbeit des Einheitssekretariates*, in *Catholica* 43 (1989) 233-247.
415. *A Catholic Reflection on 40 years of WCC* (Free University of Amsterdam, 20.8.1989), in *IS* 70 (1989) 61-65.
     SI 70 (1989) 64-68.
416. *Commencement Address* (Hellenic College, Holy Cross Greek Orthodox School of Theology, Brookline MA, 20.5.1989), in *Greek Orthodox Theological Review* 34 (1989) 239-248.
     Proche Orient Chrétien 38 (1988) 272-280.
417. *Déclaration sur la controverse d'Auschwitz*, in *OR* (French) 26.9.1989.
     DC 71 (1989) 884.
418. *Discours lors de la visite de la délégation du Saint-Siège au Patriarcat œcuménique* (30.11.1989), in *SI* 73 (1990) 29-30.
     IS 73 (1990) 29-30.
419. *Dynamiek van de vooruitgang is niet tegen te houden* (Interview, Religieuze persdienst België), in *Gazet van Antwerpen*, 22.12.1989.
420. *Ebrei e Cristiani ad Auschwitz: L'umile cammino della riconciliazione*, in *OR* 30.9.1989.
     OR (French) 17.10.1989.
     DC 71 (1989) 956-957.
     IS 70 (1989) 78-79.
     → 455, 172-175, 176.
     Tygodnik Poszechny 46 (1989) 1, 12 November.
421. *Ecumenism and Evangelism*, in *Origins* 18 (1989) 715-716.

422. *Ecumenism and Evangelization* (Meeting with the U.S. Bishops, Vatican, 8-11.3.1989), in *Evangelization in the Culture and Society of the United States*, Washington, DC, United States Catholic Conference, 1989, 121-132.

423. *Ecumenismo color porpora*, in *30 Giorni* 1989/4, 15-19.

424. *Letter* (20th Anniversary of WCFBA, 24.2.1989), in *IS* 70 (1989) 69.
    SI 70 (1989) 72.

425. *Lettre* (to the presidents of ARCIC II on Anglican ordinations), in *Istina* (B. DUPUY [ed.], *L'identité anglicane en question*) 34 (1989) 181-186.

426. *Mandatum Unitatis: Beiträge zur Ökumene* (Konfessionskundliche Schriften des Johann-Adam-Möhler-Instituts, 16), Paderborn, Bonifatius, 1989, 363 pp. → 41, 47, 56, 58, 62, 65, 66, 86, 115, 148, 159, 161, 187, 188, 195, 204, 270, 306, 318, 332, 335, 338, 366, 367, 368, 383, 387.

427. *Message to Cardinal Hume's Address on the Twenty-Fifth Anniversary of the Decree on Ecumenism*, in *One in Christ* 25 (1989) 381-382.

428. *Vi racconto Paolo VI* (Interview), in *Giornale del Popolo*, Lugano, 17.1.1989.

429. *La responsabilità di portare in compimento la volontà di Cristo, il Buon Pastore*, in *OR* 16.10.1989.

430. *Una significativa prospettiva ecumenica*, in *OR* 31.5.1989.

431. *The Specific Religious Dimensions of Christian-Jewish Relations* (Reception of the International Jewish Committee on Interreligious Consultations, New York, 16.5.1989), in *IS* 70 (1989) 76-78.
    → 455, 190-193.

432. *Speech Introducing the Representatives of the UBS and the WCFBA to the Holy Father* (26.10.1989), in *IS* 71 (1989) 135.
    SI 71 (1989) 135.

433. *Il viaggio del S. Padre in Scandinavia: Una tappa importante nel cammino ecumenico*, in *OR* 15.6.1989.
    OR (German) 23.6.1989.

434. *Kardinaal Willebrands tachtig jaar. Oecumenische bruggenbouwer* (Interview), in *Het Binnenhof*, 2.9.1989.

435. *Witness to the Living God* (Address on the occasion of the presentations to Johannes Willebrands and to G. Riegner of the Patriarch Abraham Award, Sao Paulo, 11.6. 1989), in *IS* 70 (1989) 75.
    → 455, 136-140.

436. *Words of Welcome Spoken at the Reception Given for Archbishop Runcie* (Casina Pio IV, 29.9.1989), in *IS* 71 (1989) 112-113.
    SI 71 (1989) 118-119.

1990

437. *Allocution à la fin de la Ste Liturgie en la cathédrale de l'Épiphanie à Moscou, pour les funérailles de S.S. le Patriarche Pimen* (6.5.1990), in *SI* 73 (1990) 27.
    IS 73 (1990) 27.

438. *Aus der Arbeit des Päpstlichen Rates für die Förderung der Einheit der Christen*, in *Catholica* 44 (1990) 73-90.

439. *Wie die Christen sich näherkommen: Von der Entwicklung der Ökumene in unserem Jahrhundert* (90. Deutschen Katholikentag, Berlin, 23-27.5.1990),

in *Wie im Himmel so auf Erden*, Dokumentation II, Zentralkomitee der Deutschen Katholiken (ed.), Paderborn, Bonifatius, 1991, 1756-1762.

440. *Il dramma della divisione* (Centro San Domenico, Bologna, 27.11.1990) → 474, 57-70.

441. *Église et mouvement œcuménique dans la nouvelle réalité européenne* (Centre Orthodoxe du Patriarchat Oecuménique, Chambésy, Genève, 4.5.1990), in *DC* 72 (1990) 750-753.
Christian Orient 11 (1990) 151-155.
Vita monastica 50 (1996) 97-102.
→ 474, 111-123 (extracts).

442. *Homily of Cardinal J. Willebrands, President emeritus, at the Closing Mass of the Week of Prayer* (Rome, 25.1.1990), in *IS* 75 (1990) 147-148.
SI 75 (1990) 148-149.

443. *Honouring Bishop Lesslie Newbigin*, in *International Review of Mission* 79 (1990) 100.

444. *The Impact of the Shoah on Catholic-Jewish Relations* (International Conference of the Interfaith Council on the Holocaust, Philadelphia, 18.11.1990) → 455, 157-171.

445. *The Place of Theology in the Ecumenical Movement: Its Contribution and Its Limits* (The President's Lecture, University of St. Michael's College, Toronto, 26.4.1990), in *Mid-Stream* 30 (1991) 101-110.
→ 477, 150-154.
Grail 7 (1991) 11-26.
P. NEUNER – H. WAGNER (eds.), *In Verantwortung für den Glauben: Beiträge zur Fundamentaltheologie und Ökumenik. Für Heinrich Fries*, Freiburg i.Br., Herder, 1992, 257-266.
→ 474, 71-82.
Théologie et œcuménisme, in *25 Anys de Servei Episcopal. Miscelània per Dr Ramon Torella i Cascante, Arquebisbat de Tarragona*, Barcelona, Editorial Claret, 1993, pp. 71-78.
Oecumenereeks 93/2, 's Hertogenbosch, St. Willibrordvereniging, 1993, 25 pp.

446. *Religious Pluralism within and beyond the Catholic Church* (12th National Workshop on Christian-Jewish Relations, Chicago, 5.11.1990), in *Catholic International* 2 (1991) 140-145.
→ 455, 141-151.

447. *Témoignage au Synode des Évêques* (25th Anniversary, 1.10.1990), in *Synodus Episcoporum, VIII Coetus Generalis Ordinarius*, Vatican City, 1990, 11 pp.
DC 72 (1990) 961-964.

1991

448. *Die Einheit Europas und die Verpflichtung zum Engagement in der Ökumene* (5e Europäische Begegnung, Mission und Evangelisation in Europa heute, CCEE-KEK, Santiago de Compostela, 16.11.1991), in *Bericht über die Fünfte Europäische Ökumenische Begegnung*, Genf/St. Gallen, 1992, 109-124.
H. STEINDL (ed), *Die Kirchen Europas: Ihr ökumenisches Engagement, Die Dokumente der Europäischen Ökumenischen Begegnungen (1978-1991)*, Köln, Bachem, 1994, 474-489.
→ 474, 141-156.

449. *La fatica dell'ecumenismo* (Interview), in D. DEL RIO – R. GIACOMELLI (eds.), *San Pietro e il Cremlino: Memoria della Ostpolitik vaticana*, Casale Monferrato, Piemme, 1991, 148-162.

450. *Foreword*, in *No Religion Is an Island: Abraham Joshua Heschel and Interreligious Dialogue*, Maryknoll, NY, Orbis Books, 1991, xi.

451. *Der jüdische Beitrag zur Europäischen Zivilisation*, in H. STEINDL (ed.), *Die Kirchen Europas: Ihr ökumenisches Engagement, Die Dokumente der Europäischen Ökumenischen Begegnungen (1978-1991)*, Köln, Bachem, 1994, 490-493.
    Istina 38 (1993) 72-74.
    → 455, 194-197.
    → 474, 191-195.
    Circular, Centro de Estudios Judeo-Cristianos, 99, December 1991.

452. *Der Päpstliche Rat für die Förderung der Einheit der Christen im Jahre 1990*, in *Catholica* 45 (1991) 163-180.

453. *Theologische Grundlagen der Arbeit für Ökumene unverzichtbar* (Mainz, 16.4.1991), in *Mainzer Bistumnachrichten*, 17.4.1991, 3-5.

454. *Tribute to Dr. Gerhart Riegner* (on his 80th birthday), in *Christian-Jewish Relations* 24 (1991) 32-34.

1992

455. *Church and Jewish People: New Considerations*, New York, Paulist, 1992, 280 pp. → 175, 186, 211, 248, 256, 274, 316, 337, 341, 342, 359, 363, 377, 391, 392, 411, 420, 431, 435, 444, 446, 451, 460.

456. *La grande speranza ecumenica* (Interview), in *Avvenire* 13.11.1992.

457. *Het hedendaagse jodendom als vraag aan het zelfverstaan van de katholieke kerk* (Conference 40th Anniversary Katholieke Raad voor Israël, 26.10.1992), in M. POORTHUIS (ed.), *Tot leren uitgedaagd. Werkboek over de betekenis van het hedendaagse jodendom voor de katholieke kerk*, 's-Hertogenbosch, KRI/SWV, 1993, 111-123.

458. *Il 'management' della Chiesa* (International Meeting CEGOS Italia), *Le nuove sfide europee: verso quale futuro?* (Bologna, 12.5.1992), in *I Martedì* 16 (1992) 6.
    → 474, 157-172.

459. *Un messaggio da cuore a cuore*, in *17 Maggio 1992, La beatificazione di Josemarìa Escrivá fondatore dell' Opus Dei*, Ares Edizioni, 1992, 104-105.

460. *The Place of Sidic as a Center for Study and Dialogue* (Inauguration Address, Rome). → 455, 179-182.

461. *Die Verantwortung der Christen beim Aufbau eines neuen Europas* (42th International Congress Kirche in Not, Königstein, 15.10.1992), in W. GRYCZ (ed.), *Europas Christen nach der 'Wende'*, Königstein, Albertus-Magnus-Kolleg, 1992, 34-50.
    → 474, 173-189.

462. *La vocazione all'unità* (Università Salesiana di Roma, 20.1.1992), in *Salesianum* 54 (1992) 429-452.
    → 474, 15-27.

1993

463. *Bea, ambasciatore dell'unità e apripista sulla via del Concilio* (Interview), in *Avvenire* 24.1.1993.

464. *Festansprache bei der Einweihung des Geburtshauses und des Museums Kardinal Bea* (Riedböhringen, 7.11.1993).
    OR 18.11.1993.
    → 474, 29-38.

465. *Let Us Give Praise and Thanks to the Lord* (8th International Seminar, Catholic Chaplains and Chaplaincy Teams of Civil Aviation, Rome, 4.5.1993), in *Proceedings*, Pontifical Council for the Pastoral Care of Migrants and Itinerant People, Vatican City, November 1993, 57-71.

466. *Samenwerken met vicaris-generaal dr. A.J. Vermeulen, 1975-1983*, in *Een lange adem: Opstellen over kerkelijk beleid in het Aartsbisdom Utrecht*, Utrecht, Aartsbisdom Utrecht, 1993, 19-29.

467. *È tornata la speranza della pace* (Interview), in *La Discussione*, Roma, 41 (1993) nr. 36.

468. *L'Unità in cima alla comprensione*, in *Avvenire* 17.1.1993.

469. *Valori culturali, spirituali e religiosi nell'esperienza umana*, in *Quale unità per l'Europa? Per un'Europa della solidarietà* (Spoleto, 14-15.9.1993), Milano, Vita e Pensiero, 1994, 67-83.
    → 474, 125-140.

470. *Vorwort*, in W. ROOD, *Rom und Moskau: Der heilige Stuhl und Russland bzw. die Sowjetunion von der Oktoberrevolution 1917 bis zum 1. Dezember 1989* (Münsteraner Theologische Abhandlungen, 23), Altenberge, Oros Verlag, 1993, 7-9.
    W. ROOD, *Rome en Moskou: Historische notities bij het thema Betrekkingen tussen de H. Stoel en Rusland c.q. de Sovjet-Unie in de periode 1917-1989*, Nijmegen, Stichting Communicantes, 1994, 7-8.
    Rim i Moskva, Lviv, Svitchado, 1995, 7-8.

1994

471. *Le cardinal Congar, fils fidèle de l'Église et homme d'unité* (handing over of the signs of cardinalate, Paris, 8.12.1994), in *DC* 77 (1995) 67.

472. *Une route ensemble, 'un caminho novo'*, in C. PERREAU, *Un chemin d'unité: Hommage au Père Jacques Elisée Desseaux (1923-1984)*, Paris, Cerf, 1994, 9-12.

1995

473. *Prefazione.* → 474, 7.

474. *Una sfida ecumenica: La nuova Europa* (Koinônia: Dialogo ecumenico e interreligioso, 1), Verucchio, Pazzini, 1995, 195 pp. → 291, 383, 387, 440, 441, 445, 448, 451, 458, 461, 462, 464, 469, 473.

1996

475. *Voorwoord*, in J. KOET – L. GALEMA – M. VAN ASSENDELFT, *Vuurhaard van eenheid: Vrouwen van Bethanië en Oecumene in Rome*, Roma, Fratelli Palombi, 1996, 9-11.

Preface, in J. KOET – L. GALEMA – M. VAN ASSENDELFT, *Heart of Unity: Ladies of Bethany in Rome*, Roma, Fratelli Palombi, 1996, 9-11.

1997

476. *La rencontre entre Rome et Moscou: Souvenirs*, in A. MELLONI (ed.), *Vatican II in Moscow*, Leuven, Peeters, 1997, 331-338.

1999

477. *A Tribute to Johannes Cardinal Willebrands on the Occasion of His Nine-tieth Birthday* (33 Addresses and Lectures), in *IS* 101 (1999/II-III), 192 pp. (French and English edition). → 82, 86, 88, 90, 93, 94, 100, 103, 124, 126, 135, 157, 172, 208, 240, 254, 274, 276, 299, 306, 308, 311, 337, 342, 346, 357, 359, 363, 369, 387, 392, 393, 396, 413, 445.
478. *Vriendschap als wapen: Johannes kardinaal Willebrands* (Interview by A. BROERS), Utrecht, Aartsbisdom Utrecht, 1999, 32 pp.

2000

479. *Commission for Religious Relations with the Jews*, in *Radici dell'anti-giudaismo in ambiente cristiano* (Atti e Documenti, 8), Città del Vaticano, Libreria Editrice Vaticana, 2000, 345-364.
480. *Foreword*, in M. WIJLENS, *Sharing the Eucharist: A Theological Evaluation of the Post Conciliar Legislation*, Washington, DC, University Press of America, 2000, xi-xiv.
481. *Préface*, in J.-M. TILLARD O.P. (ed.), *Agapè: Études en l'honneur de Mgr Pierre Duprey M. Afr.* (Analecta Chambesiana, 3) Chambésy–Genève, 2000, 13-15.
482. *Words of Cardinal Willebrands* (Excerpts from Addresses to the Assembly of the Lutheran Church in America, Toronto, 3.7.1984, and to the International Liaison Committee, Vatican City, 1985), in *Ecumenical Trends* 29 (2000) 110-112.

2003

483. *Préface*, conçue pour YVES CONGAR, *Mon Journal du Concile*, Paris, Cerf, 2002, in J.-P. JOSSUA, *Le Concile d'Yves Congar*, in *Cristianesimo nella Storia* 24 (2003) 149-153, 153.

Tilburg School of Catholic Theology   Maria TER STEEG
Heidelberglaan 2
NL 3508 TC Utrecht
The Netherlands

INDEX OF NAMES

BIBLIOTHECA EPHEMERIDUM THEOLOGICARUM LOVANIENSIUM

SERIES III

173. M.J.J. MENKEN, *Matthew's Bible: The Old Testament Text of the Evangelist*, 2004. XII-336 p. 60 €
174. J.-P. DELVILLE, *L'Europe de l'exégèse au XVIe siècle. Interprétations de la parabole des ouvriers à la vigne (Matthieu 20,1-16)*, 2004. XLII-775 p. 70 €
175. E. BRITO, *J.G. Fichte et la transformation du christianisme*, 2004. XVI-808 p. 90 €
176. J. SCHLOSSER (ed.), *The Catholic Epistles and the Tradition*, 2004. XXIV-569 p. 60 €
177. R. FAESEN (ed.), *Albert Deblaere, S.J. (1916-1994): Essays on Mystical Literature – Essais sur la littérature mystique – Saggi sulla letteratura mistica*, 2004. XX-473 p. 70 €
178. J. LUST, *Messianism and the Septuagint: Collected Essays*. Edited by K. HAUSPIE, 2004. XIV-247 p. 60 €
179. H. GIESEN, *Jesu Heilsbotschaft und die Kirche. Studien zur Eschatologie und Ekklesiologie bei den Synoptikern und im ersten Petrusbrief*, 2004. XX-578 p. 70 €
180. H. LOMBAERTS & D. POLLEFEYT (eds.), *Hermeneutics and Religious Education*, 2004. XIII-427 p. 70 €
181. D. DONNELLY, A. DENAUX & J. FAMERÉE (eds.), *The Holy Spirit, the Church, and Christian Unity. Proceedings of the Consultation Held at the Monastery of Bose, Italy (14-20 October 2002)*, 2005. XII-417 p. 70 €
182. R. BIERINGER, G. VAN BELLE & J. VERHEYDEN (eds.), *Luke and His Readers. Festschrift A. Denaux*, 2005. XXVIII-470 p. 65 €
183. D.F. PILARIO, *Back to the Rough Grounds of Praxis: Exploring Theological Method with Pierre Bourdieu*, 2005. XXXII-584 p. 80 €
184. G. VAN BELLE, J.G. VAN DER WATT & P. MARITZ (eds.), *Theology and Christology in the Fourth Gospel: Essays by the Members of the SNTS Johannine Writings Seminar*, 2005. XII-561 p. 70 €
185. D. LUCIANI, *Sainteté et pardon. Vol. 1: Structure littéraire du Lévitique. Vol. 2: Guide technique*, 2005. XIV-VII-656 p. 120 €
186. R.A. DERRENBACKER, JR., *Ancient Compositional Practices and the Synoptic Problem*, 2005. XXVIII-290 p. 80 €
187. P. VAN HECKE (ed.), *Metaphor in the Hebrew Bible*, 2005. X-308 p. 65 €
188. L. BOEVE, Y. DEMAESENEER & S. VAN DEN BOSSCHE (eds.), *Religious Experience and Contemporary Theological Epistemology*, 2005. X-335 p. 50 €
189. J.M. ROBINSON, *The Sayings Gospel Q. Collected Essays*, 2005. XVIII-888 p. 90 €
190. C.W. STRÜDER, *Paulus und die Gesinnung Christi. Identität und Entscheidungsfindung aus der Mitte von 1Kor 1-4*, 2005. LII-522 p. 80 €
191. C. FOCANT & A. WÉNIN (eds.), *Analyse narrative et Bible. Deuxième colloque international du RRENAB, Louvain-la-Neuve, avril 2004*, 2005. XVI-593 p. 75 €
192. F. GARCÍA MARTÍNEZ & M. VERVENNE (eds.), in collaboration with B. DOYLE, *Interpreting Translation: Studies on the LXX and Ezekiel in Honour of Johan Lust*, 2005. XVI-464 p. 70 €
193. F. MIES, *L'espérance de Job*, 2006. XXIV-653 p. 87 €
194. C. FOCANT, *Marc, un évangile étonnant*, 2006. XV-402 p. 60 €
195. M.A. KNIBB (ed.), *The Septuagint and Messianism*, 2006. XXXI-560 p. 60 €

218. G. VAN BELLE – J.G. VAN DER WATT – J. VERHEYDEN (eds.), *Miracles and Imagery in Luke and John. Festschrift Ulrich Busse*, 2008. XVIII-287 p.
78 €

219. L. BOEVE – M. LAMBERIGTS – M.WISSE (eds.), *Augustine and Postmodern Thought: A New Alliance against Modernity?*, 2009. XVIII-277 p. 80 €

220. T. VICTORIA, *Un livre de feu dans un siècle de fer: Les lectures de l'Apocalypse dans la littérature française de la Renaissance*, 2009. XXX-609 p.
85 €

221. A.A. DEN HOLLANDER – W. FRANÇOIS (eds.), *Infant Milk or Hardy Nourishment? The Bible for Lay People and Theologians in the Early Modern Period*, 2009. XVIII-488 p. 80 €

222. F.D. VANSINA, *Paul Ricœur. Bibliographie primaire et secondaire. Primary and Secundary Bibliography 1935-2008*, Compiled and updated in collaboration with P. VANDECASTEELE, 2008. XXX-621 p. 80 €

223. G. VAN BELLE – M. LABAHN – P. MARITZ (eds.), *Repetitions and Variations in the Fourth Gospel: Style, Text, Interpretation*, 2009. XII-712 p. 85 €

224. H. AUSLOOS – B. LEMMELIJN – M. VERVENNE (eds.), *Florilegium Lovaniense: Studies in Septuagint and Textual Criticism in Honour of Florentino García Martínez*, 2008. XVI-564 p. 80 €

225. E. BRITO, *Philosophie moderne et christianisme*, 2010. 2 vols., VIII-1514 p.
130 €

226. U. SCHNELLE (ed.), *The Letter to the Romans*, 2009. XVIII-894 p. 85 €

227. M. LAMBERIGTS – L. BOEVE – T. MERRIGAN in collaboration with D. CLAES – M. WISSE (eds.), *Orthodoxy, Process and Product*, 2009. X-416 p. 74 €

228. G. HEIDL – R. SOMOS (eds.), *Origeniana nona: Origen and the Religious Practice of His Time*, 2009. XIV-752 p. 95 €

229. D. MARGUERAT (ed.), *Reception of Paulinism in Acts – Réception du paulinisme dans les Actes des Apôtres*, 2009. VIII-340 p. 74 €

230. A. DILLEN – D. POLLEFEYT (eds.), *Children's Voices: Children's Perspectives in Ethics, Theology and Religious Education*, 2010. X-450 p. 72 €

231. P. VAN HECKE – A. LABAHN (eds.), *Metaphors in the Psalms*, 2010. XXXIV-363 p.
76 €

232. G. AULD – E. EYNIKEL (eds.), *For and Against David: Story and History in the Books of Samuel*, 2010. X-397 p.
76 €

233. C. VIALLE, *Une analyse comparée d'Esther TM et LXX: Regard sur deux récits d'une même histoire*, 2010. LVIII-406 p.
76 €

234. T. MERRIGAN – F. GLORIEUX (eds.), *"Godhead Here in Hiding": Incarnation and the History of Human Suffering*, 2012. X-327 p.
76 €

235. M. SIMON, *La vie dans le Christ dans le catéchisme de Jean-Paul II*, 2010. XX-651 p.
84 €

236. G. DE SCHRIJVER, *The Political Ethics of Jean-François Lyotard and Jacques Derrida*, 2010. XXX-422 p.
80 €

237. A. PASQUIER – D. MARGUERAT – A. WÉNIN (eds), *L'intrigue dans le récit biblique. Quatrième colloque international du RRENAB, Université Laval, Québec, 29 mai – 1er juin 2008*, 2010. XXX-479 p.
68 €

238. E. ZENGER (ed.), *The Composition of the Book of Psalms*, 2010. XII-826 p.
90 €

239. P. FOSTER – A. GREGORY – J.S. KLOPPENBORG – J. VERHEYDEN (eds.), *New Studies in the Synoptic Problem: Oxford Conference, April 2008*, 2011. XXIV-828 p.
85 €

240. J. Verheyden – T.L. Hettema – P. Vandecasteele (eds.), *Paul Ricœur: Poetics and Religion*, 2011. xx-534 p.   79 €
241. J. Leemans (ed.), *Martyrdom and Persecution in Late Ancient Christianity. Festschrift Boudewijn Dehandschutter*, 2010. xxxiv-430 p.   78 €
242. C. Clivaz – J. Zumstein (eds.), *Reading New Testament Papyri in Context – Lire les papyrus du Nouveau Testament dans leur contexte*, 2011. xiv-446 p.   80 €
243. D. Senior (ed.), *The Gospel of Matthew at the Crossroads of Early Christianity*, 2011. xxviii-781 p.   88 €
244. H. Pietras – S. Kaczmarek (eds.), *Origeniana Decima: Origen as Writer*, 2011. xviii-1039 p.   105 €
245. M. Simon, *La prière chrétienne dans le catéchisme de Jean-Paul II*, 2011.   70 €
246. H. Ausloos – B. Lemmelijn – J. Trebolle-Barrera (eds.), *After Qumran: Old and Modern Editions of the Biblical Texts – The Historical Books*, 2012. xiv-319 p.   84 €
247. G. Van Oyen – A. Wénin (eds.), *La surprise dans la Bible. Festschrift Camille Focant*, 2012. xlii-474 p.   80 €
248. C. Clivaz – C. Combet-Galland – J.-D. Macchi – C. Nihan (eds.), *Écritures et réécritures: La reprise interprétative des traditions fondatrices par la littérature biblique et extra-biblique. Cinquième colloque international du RRENAB, Universités de Genève et Lausanne, 10-12 juin 2010*, 2012. xxiv-648 p.   90 €
249. G. Van Oyen – T. Shepherd (eds.), *Resurrection of the Dead: Biblical Traditions in Dialogue*, 2012.   85 €
250. E. Noort (ed.), *The Book of Joshua*, 2012. xiv-698 p.   90 €
251. R. Faesen – L. Kenis (eds.), *The Jesuits of the Low Countries: Identity and Impact (1540-1773). Proceedings of the International Congress at the Faculty of Theology, KU Leuven (3-5 December 2009)*, 2012.   65 €
252. A. Damm, *Ancient Rhetoric and the Synoptic Problem: Clarifying Markan Priority*, 2013.   Forthcoming